Silja Graupe
The *Basho* of Economics
An Intercultural Analysis of the Process of Economics

PROCESS THOUGHT

Edited by

Nicholas Rescher • Johanna Seibt • Michel Weber

Advisory Board

Mark Bickhard • Jaime Nubiola • Roberto Poli

Volume 15

Silja Graupe

The *Basho* of Economics

An Intercultural Analysis of the Process of Economics

Translated and Introduced by Roger Gathman

ontos
verlag

Frankfurt I Paris I Ebikon I Lancaster I New Brunswick

Bibliographic information published by Deutsche Nationalbibliothek
The Deutsche Nastionalbibliothek lists this publication in the Deutsche Nationalbibliographie;
detailed bibliographic data is available in the Internet at http://dnb.ddb.de

North and South America by
Transaction Books
Rutgers University
Piscataway, NJ 08854-8042
trans@transactionpub.com

United Kingdom, Eire, Iceland, Turkey, Malta, Portugal by
Gazelle Books Services Limited
White Cross Mills
Hightown
LANCASTER, LA1 4XS
sales@gazellebooks.co.uk

Livraison pour la France et la Belgique:
Librairie Philosophique J.Vrin
6, place de la Sorbonne ; F-75005 PARIS
Tel. +33 (0)1 43 54 03 47 ; Fax +33 (0)1 43 54 48 18
www.vrin.fr

©2019 ontos verlag
This volume is text- and page-identical with the hardback published in 2007.
P.O. Box 15 41, D-63133 Heusenstamm
www.ontosverlag.com

ISBN 13: 978-3-11-065419-6
2019

No part of this book may be reproduced, stored in retrieval systems or transmitted
in any form or by any means, electronic, mechanical, photocopying, microfilming, recording or otherwise
without written permission from the Publisher, with the exception of any material supplied specifically for
the purpose of being entered and executed on a computer system, for exclusive use of the purchaser of the
work

Printed on acid-free paper
ISO-Norm 970-6
FSC-certified (Forest Stewardship Council)
This hardcover binding meets the International Library standard

Printed in Germany
by buch bücher **dd ag**

For Christof

Table of Contents

FOREWORD BY ROGER GATHMAN   xiii

ACKNOWLEDGMENTS   xxv

1   **INTRODUCTION**   1

2   **METHODOLOGICAL PRESUPPOSITIONS**   23

3   **THE IMPLICIT IMAGE OF THE PERSON IN ECONOMICS**   34

    3.1   The Actor in Objective Economic Method   36
       3.1.1   The Field of Consciousness as the Unthought Locus of Objective Methods   37
       3.1.2   The Implicit Properties of the Field of Consciousness   48
       3.1.3   A Time and Place-Independent Field of Consciousness   59
       3.1.4   Action as Unconscious Behavior   68
       3.1.5   The Logical Impossibility of Calculating Human Action   73

    3.2   Conceiving the Actor in Subjective Economic Methodologies   81
       3.2.1   The Subjective Consciousness as Reason   83
       3.2.2   The Subjective Consciousness as an Accumulation of Feelings and Desires   85
       3.2.3   The Subjective Consciousness as Will   88

    3.3   The Actor 'Beyond' the Subject-Object Split   96
       3.3.1   An 'East Asian' Theory of Habits   96
       3.3.2   Economic Activity as Habit   105
       3.3.3   Habit as the Unconscious Locus of Economic Activity   116
       3.3.4   The Creative Actor 'Beyond' all Habits   123
       3.3.5   The Freedom of the Self-Aware Will   131

4 THE IMPLICIT WORLD PICTURE OF ECONOMICS 141

4.1 The Definition of the Individual in Economic Methodology 142
4.1.1 The Private and Social Definition of the Individual 143
4.1.2 The Contradictory Determination of the Individual 145
4.1.3 Excursus: The Irreconcilability of Individual and General Equilibrium 155

4.2 The Determination of the Individual as a Context Dependent Existence (I) 158
4.2.1 The Context Dependence of Individuals 159
4.2.2 The Market as a Social Context 164
4.2.3 The Context-Dependent Properties of the Economic Actor 171

4.3 The Determination of the Economic World 175
4.3.1 The Economic World as a Field of Action 176
4.3.2 The Individual in the Economic World 181
4.3.3 The Logical Impossibility of the Determination of the Economic World 185
4.3.4 The Economic World as a Place of Nothingness 189
4.3.5 The Inconsistency of the Economic World 191

4.4 The Properties of the Economic World 192
4.4.1 The Creative, Dynamic Character of the Economic World 193
4.4.2 The Logical Impossibility of the Calculation of the Economic World 197

4.5 The Determination of the Individual as a Context Dependent Existence (II) 206
4.5.1 The Determination of Individuals in East Asian Philosophy 206
4.5.2 The Economic Actor as a Contradictory Self-Identity 210

4.6	**The Significance of Egoism for the Economic World**	**223**
4.6.1	The Egoism of the Normal Consciousness	224
4.6.2	The Economic World as the Struggle of All against All	226
4.7	**The State and Its Relationship to the Market**	**236**
4.7.1	The State as a Context Independent Universal	238
4.7.2	The Interdependence of the State and Individual Calculation	241
4.7.3	The Inherent Contradiction of the State's Coercive Authority	246
4.7.4	The Conflict of the Market and the State	252
4.7.5	Ordoliberalism: A Unity of Market and State	255
4.7.6	Excursus: The Standpoint of the Social Scientist	260
4.8	**A World 'Beyond' Egoism**	**262**
4.8.1	The Normal and the Original Consciousness	263
4.8.2	Harmonic Human Engagement	270
4.8.3	Spontaneously Mindful Actions and the Meaning of Rules	279
4.9	**The Relation of the Economic World to Other Worlds**	**287**
4.9.1	The Conflict of Many Worlds	289
4.9.2	The Idea of One Common World	292
4.9.3	The Idea of the 'Worldly World'	296
4.9.4	The Freedom of the Individual in the Worldly World	300
5	**CONCLUSION**	**303**
6	**BIBLIOGRAPHY**	**313**

Foreword

by Roger Gathman

i.

Silja Graupe's book signals the continuing viability of two recent trends in process philosophy. One is the attempt to open up the area of process-philosophical research for inquiry alongside Whiteheadian metaphysics – itself an increasingly lively field of scholarship in the philosophy of science – and to explore alternative possible constructions of processes. There are numerous examples, now, of such work, from Nicholas Rescher's recent introduction to process metaphysics including and beyond Whitehead, which draws attention to the explanatory potential of a general "processual view" in many systematic areas of metaphysics,[1] to Johanna Seibt's theory of "general processes" or "generic dynamics", which develops a new, non-Whiteheadian ontological category of process within a mereological framework and shows its application in analytic ontology.[2] As Rescher has put it: "If there indeed is a 'philosophy' of process, it must pivot not on a thinker but on a theory. What is at issue must, in the end, be a philosophical position that has a life of its own."[3] Contrasting Whitehead's thought with old and new process-metaphysical alternatives will deepen our understanding of all positions in the area.

Graupe's innovation is to import into this set of ontological styles a completely other group of assumptions taken mainly, although not exclusively from Japanese process philosophy, which, in Graupe's version, is firmly rooted in the Kyoto school, and identified closely with the writings of Nishida Kitarō. Graupe has also borrowed from the East Asian philosophical background that was drawn upon by the Kyoto school. Most notable, I think, is her borrowing on the Confucian notion of ritual, which she uses in discussing the social mediation of individual action. However, it isn't

---

[1] Rescher, Nicholas, *Process Metaphysics: An Introduction to Process Philosophy*, 89-90.
[2] See J. Seibt, "Free Process Theory: towards a typology of occurings," in *Process Theories: Cross-disciplinary Studies in Dynamic Categories*, edited by Johanna Seibt.
[3] Rescher, 49.

Graupe's intent to mount a defense of Nishida's ontology in this book per se. Instead – and this takes us to the second trend – she has used his notion of processes, and in particular the processes that shape and are shaped within the field of social interaction between agents, as a point of view from which to intervene in the philosophy of science – or, in this case, one of its subdisciplines, the philosophy of economics.

This unusual critique of economics performs a difficult pas de deux, giving us a thick description of the substantivist assumptions and models of mainstream economics, which requires some technical expertise in that field, from a point of view coming from a very different field of specialization, that was given to us by Nishida's notion of bashō, which requires specialization of a quite different kind.

Mindful of the gap between the specialized constituencies of the philosophy of economics and Japanese philosophy, this preface will outline three interrelated stories that are entangled in the critical section of Graupe's text in terms that are more familiar, perhaps, to those with more in depth knowledge of issues in the philosophy and history of economics.

Three stories – but it might be more accurate to say that there is one story in the text with three parts. That one story could be seen as a kind of explanatory fable: How did economics come to be the science that it presents itself as?

Graupe's story goes something like this: the continuity of mainstream economics is the result of its underlying metaphysical structure, which tenaciously skews to a substantivist ontology. This has a distinct impact on the kind of science economics became over the long duree, from the eighteenth century all the way up to the neo-classical resurgence in the 1980s. Since economics as a science must deal with the dynamic processes of the real economy, but does so under the consensus assumption that science is ultimately a deductive enterprise, the foundations of which are, ideally, axiomatized, economics has evolved from the 'conjectural history' of Adam Smith to the mathematical models of neo-classicists with a prominent place accorded to theory and abstract modeling and a much lesser status granted to empirical research and experiment. Unlike other sciences, in which the vital connection to empirical data – Baconian science – is conjoined, however roughly, to theory construction, positive economics tends to impose upon reality its normative models. As economist Alan Blinder once joked, an economist is "someone who sees that something works in practice and wonders if it also works in theory."

To make this conceptual reconstruction work, Graupe follows the canonical history of economic analysis of Joseph Schumpeter, agreeing with Schumpeter that the central pattern of mainstream economics is the creating and defense of equilibrium models to explain economic processes. Following Phillip Mirowski, Graupe notes how these models, many of them borrowed in the nineteenth century from the physics of that time, were adapted to economic thinking, with the adaptations revealing two things: an incongruence between the objects of physics and economics, and the systematic need, by economists, to justify the grouping of the science around static equilibria. This brings us to the third part of the story. To preserve the closed state of economics as a science, economic agents had to be denuded of their dynamic characteristics, which logically lead to the mainstream economic position with regard to agency: instead of unpredictable individual agents acting as constraints on the equilibrium of the price system, the equilibrium models operated to define agency in its own terms. Agents became those things that cleared markets, with the order of the clearing revealing the order of their preferences, and the sign of their collective rationality being the price system.

While some of the conclusions of this story are shared with other philosophers of science who have looked at mainstream economics – for instance, John Dupré has noted the dependence of rational choice theory on a naïve and impoverished methodological individualism,[4] and Nancy Cartwright has deflated the place of law in economics as well as in physics[5] – Graupe's point is fundamentally different from any variant of positivism insofar as her emphasis on the ontology underlying the problems of economics is presented as the result of applying another schema to political economics altogether. This is the "logic of basho," to use Nishida's phrase. This is a logic that posits various interrelated levels of conceptualization and actualization – the two are inextricably interwoven in his thought. The index that identifies each level is the extent to which it can reflect upon itself. The limits of each level is defined, negatively, by the inability of a

---

[4] See J. Dupré, *Human Nature and the Limits of Science*, Chapter 6.
[5] Nancy Cartwright has used both physics and economics as the exemplary sciences with relation to which she has pursued her deflationary thesis about law, and her defence of 'capacity', in a number of articles and a trilogy of books: *How the Laws of Physics Lie*, 1981; *Nature's Capacities and their Measurements*, 1994; and *The Dappled World*, 1999.

level to explicitly encompass its own presuppositions. In this way, Graupe is able both to show how economic theories have functioned with substantivist presuppositions and how their functioning defines only one possible range of economic thought. Her critique of mainstream economics starts with pointing out the antinomies that result from the inability of economics to logically order its fundamental principles: for instance, in the unresolved conflict between the individual, constructed as a sort of selfish machine in economic models, and the universal, constructed in terms of markets attracted to equilibrium. No scenario can match up these two equally necessary elements of mainstream economic thinking. Instead, Graupe proposes, following Nishida's suggestion that the individual is not centered inside herself, that the individual is thoroughly socially mediated and context dependent:

> "We exactly invert the relationship of the individual and society in our explanation in comparison to methodological individualism: society does not emerge out of the combined performance of individuals, but necessarily precedes any idea about the individual. It is the locus, in which individuals are determined, their unthought presupposition, but not a product of their aggregation. Kimura formulates this insight in this way: the between-ness of person and person represents a basho, in which all ideas about individuals are encompassed: 'The betweenness of person and person (*hito to hito to no aida*) and betweenness (*aida*) do not signify merely a relationship between two individuals. The betweenness of person and person is the locus (*basho*) functioning as the source from out of which both I and others arise.'" (159)

The "natural state" of static equilibrium that is premised by economics is displaced by a flux of states of disequilibria:

> "Finally, ... mechanical analysis proves itself as logically impossible, because a stable equilibrium does not ground the economic world. (...) [Also,] the world doesn't find itself in one disequilibriated state (which is actually logically impossible, because this state is unsteady), but is moved so to speak from one disequilibrium to another, without at any moment arriving at a resting point." (199)

For the framework of action analysis, which in neo-classical macroeconomics is built upon the 'rational expectations' of aggregates, and which decomposes into some theory of rational choice on the individual level, Graupe uses a notion of habits and habitus, and borrows from Confucian philosophy a ritual centered notion of individual action that is always embedded in the social:

"In contrast to rational preferences, the actions of the non-self [the 'I' as betweeness] are spontaneous. The latter accepts no decision space as given, but is continually reshaping it relative to situations. Such spontaneity implies – as Confucianism makes clear – no complete independence of all social habits, but rather a social creativity within specific relations. What is decisive is the meaning of rituals. Rituals describe a specific relation between different persons (father-son, wife-husband, etc.). They are in this sense habits of human practices that survive in a society over space and time. But thus they represent no fixed or irrevocable modes of actions that must blindly be followed. They are rather vague rules of thumb over the ways humans should interact." (276)

ii.

So much for the broad outline of Graupe's critique. I'd like to look at two questions that occurred to me in translating this book. One is, does this history of economic thought accurately reflect the totality of economic thought in the West? Here, one wants to know why Keynes and the institutional economists have so largely fallen out of the picture. Granted, Graupe's focus is explicitly focused on mainstream, or classical and neoclassical, economics, yet Keynesian and institutionalist economics are rooted in the same historically conditioned historical habitus, and there has been, to say the least, a dialogue between mainstream economic thought and its others. The other question is, does Graupe's notion that an ontological skew towards substantivism do as much as she wants it to? I'm thinking here of one of the important threads in her work: the meshing together of the presuppositions of the economists with the methodology of economics.

In making this case, Graupe brackets the history of economic analysis from economic history – hers is not a Marxist story of the superstructure being determined by the means of production underneath, nor even a more modified, Weberian story correlating economics with regimes of political legitimation. Graupe's singlemindedness here is clarifying, and yet one feels here the intimation of that characteristic that Matthew Arnold identifies with the puritan: a style of thinking in which everything, finally, reduces to some one principle. Porro unum est necessarium,[6] one thing is needful – in this case, the needful thing is an ontological skew towards substantivism. One problem, it seems to me, with this approach is that it does not fully ac-

---

[6] Arnold, Matthew, *Culture and Anarchy*, Chapter 5.

count for divergences in economic thought that a more pluralistic approach would notice. Notably, the Keynesian revolution seems to be underplayed, here, perhaps because Keynes rejected Say's law – the axiom of market clearing – and thus allowed for ad hoc conditions to determine market realities.[7] Keynes move had the effect of shaking mainstream economic assumptions all the way down the line – in effect, the self-organizing market became an intentionally organized one, responding to exogenous shocks that were inherently outside the reach of any fine tuning. Similarly, a tradition in economics that is foreshadowed in Schmoller's historical school and initiated by Veblen, bringing a different heuristic to economic phenomena, is also underplayed in Graupe's story.

However, this objection seems to point to the fact that the Schumpeterian paradigm doesn't capture all economic analysis, but not that the paradigm is wrong in claiming that equilibrium centered economics is the defining parameter of economics since the 18th century. Keynesian economists tried to reconnect with the mainstream by developing models that could incorporate mainstream models. The neo-classical 'counter-revolution' in macro-economics, associated with Robert Lucas and Thomas Sargent in the late seventies and early eighties, focused specifically on the failure of Keynesian economics to preserve some form of Say's law – for Lucas, the "condition of intelligibility" of economic analysis. As Alessandro Vercelli puts it:

> "By non-intelligible Lucas apparently means 'arbitrary' (ad hoc). He has in mind the adjustment mechanisms that come into play when there is an excess of supply or demand, or those that characterize the hypothesis of adaptive expectations. In such cases the practice of traditional econometrics is based on the use of 'free parameters', to be determined by purely inductive means. The good econometric fit obtained through this methodology is rightly considered by Lucas to be misleading, since the parameters involved are not determined a priori on the basis of theoretical considerations. From this substantially correct observation Lucas derives the principle that such a theoretical foundation can indeed never be possible when the situation under analysis is one of disequilibrium."[8]

The question of the broadness of the historical pattern, then, is ultimately secondary, and has less effect on Graupe's history than one might at first

---

[7] Galbraith, John Kenneth, *American Capitalism: The Concept of Countervailing Power*, 69.
[8] Vercelli, A. *Methodological Foundations of Macroeconomics: Keynes and Lucas*, 37.

think. The more interesting philosophical question is my second one: has Graupe given us an account that explains all of the features she picks out?

Here one might be inclined to give her a rougher time, insofar as the unum est necessitatum boils down to a fetishized attachment to a substantivist ontology. It isn't clear that the pattern she is speaking about is so clearly a total extension of that ontology, a sort of projection of metaphysics upon the system of production and consumption. There's a gap here to be filled – a gap that calls for a social epistemology. In fact, Graupe herself provides us with hints as to how to do this in her theme of habits and rituals.

But first, let's get a clearer picture of the problem here.

To do this, put Graupe's conceptual reconstruction in slightly different terms. Using Lakatos' notion of a negative heuristic – those explanatory principles that, according to Lakatos, are common to all sides in the debates between theories within a given normal science – what Graupe shows is how uncommonly successful – weirdly successful – the negative heuristic of economics has been. This is Lakatos's notion of how the negative heuristic works within normal science:

> "All scientific research programmes may be characterized by their *'hard core'*. The negative heuristic of the programme forbids us to direct the modus tollens at this 'hard core'. Instead, we must use our ingenuity to articulate or even invent 'auxiliary hypotheses', which form a protective belt around this core, and we must redirect the *modus tollens* to these. It is this protective belt of auxiliary hypotheses which has to bear the brunt of tests and get adjusted and re-adjusted, or even completely replaced, to defend the thus-hardend core. A research programme is successful if all this leads to a progressive problemshift; unsuccessful if it leads to a degenerating problemshift."[9]

To make her case, Graupe has to make us see that there is a problem here that should haunt the philosophy of economics: why has economics, unlike the natural sciences, never suffered the kind of ruptures, the kind of interfield asymmetries,[10] that have brought about standard reduction problems in the other sciences? While controversy reducing the objects and concepts of classical genetics to molecular biology, or the objects and concepts of mechanics to quantum mechanics, have determined research projects in the

---

[9] Lakatos, I. *Philosophical Papers*, 48.
[10] See Lindley Darden and Nancy Maull (1977), "Interfield Theories," *Philosophy of Science*, 44.

philosophy of biology and the philosophy of physics, no parallel exists in the philosophy of economics. The closest economics comes to such structural ruptures is in the question of value – with the marginalist rejection of the labor theory of value paving the way for marginal utility theory. But there is no real functional conflict here: the equilibrium theory of classical economics, formulated by Say, and the model of the self-organizing market, transfer without difficulty into the marginal utility vocabulary. For Graupe, this problematic lack of a problem has an ontological solution.

Yet readers may be uncomfortable with using ontology as the universal driver, here, especially as Graupe leaves a motivating gap in her explanation of the adoption, by economists, of the models of 19th century physics – which, following Mirowski, she shows to be a deeply flawed program. It is at this point that one wants a more concrete sense of the autonomy of epistemology.

Dugald Stewart coined the term conjectural history in his influential introduction to Adam Smith's collected works in 1799. Using it as the key to the methodological commonalities in Smith's essays on astronomy, the origin of language, and economics, Stewart writes:

> "I shall only observe farther on this head, that when different theoretical histories are proposed by different writers, of the progress of the human mind in any one line of exertion, these theories are not always to be understood as standing in opposition to each other. If the progress delineated in all of them be plausible, it is possible at least that they may all have been realized, for human affairs never exhibit, in any two instances, a perfect uniformity. But whether they have been realized or not, is often a question of little consequence. In most cases, it is of more importance to ascertain the progress that is most simple, than the progress that is most agreeable to fact; for, paradoxical as the proposition may appear, it is certainly true, that the real progress is not always the most natural. It may have been determined by particular accidents, which are not likely again to occur, and which cannot be considered as forming any part of that general provision which nature has made for the improvement of the race."[11]

This is the kind of two step process – from grasping the essence of a state of human affairs to abstracting a certain model of 'progress' – which, of course, has a rich career in economics. It foregrounds the ill wrought translation of the models of the natural sciences into economics that are examined by Graupe in the light of Mirowski's work. The evidence for the

---

[11] Stewart, D. *The Collected Works of Dugald Stewart*, 37.

weirdness of economics has even been quantified, in a way. Leontief did a survey of the American Economic Review between 1972 and 1981 which showed that 50 percent of the articles were mathematical models without any data; Morgan updated the analysis in 1988, using the American Economic Review and the Economic Journal from 1982 to 1986, and found a similar percentage of purely theoretical articles, and compared them to articles in political science, sociology, chemistry and physics, finding the comparable amounts were 18, 1, 0 and 12 percent.[12] However, all of those sciences developed in the same community of ontological biases. The substantivist skew is not unique to economics alone. We need some bridging story to get us from Graupe's conceptual reconstruction to the peculiarity of economics as a science. That story, I imagine, would come out of looking at the economics itself as a community that developed rituals of intelligibility – rituals that gave or retracted status to economists and to scientific practices. A social epistemology that took the notion of ritual seriously and applied it to economics as it evolved over time would go a ways towards clearing up the mystery of why economics systematically undervalued Baconian science. Acculturated to a discipline that valued innovative model-building over testing, economics has too often valued the elegance of apriori parameters over the messiness of ceteris paribus conditions, has too often posited agents whose actions are determined by the exigencies of the models in which they are slotted rather than by observation of real human behavior, has too often used simplifying heuristic shortcuts – such as the unmediated notion of 'choice' – rather than going out and looking for the heuristics that are really used in groups and communities. Understanding model-building as a ritual practice helps us to understand how the underconceptualization of the empirical side of economics occurred.

iii.

I hope I have suggested, here, both the richness and suggestiveness of Graupe's work for the philosophy and historiography of economics. I have neglected the intercultural dimension, which a glance at the title tells us is of equal importance. Just as Francois Jullien, by comparing strategic thinking in China and Europe, showed how this could reveal unexpected ideological structures in both domains, Graupe's use of Japanese thinkers to analyze mainstream economics reveals some unexpected structures of

---

[12] For a summary, see Clive Beed & Owen Kane, "What is the critique of the mathematization of economics?," *Kyklos* 44 (4), 1991.

Western thinking. For centuries, the direction of comparison has gone mostly one way, with the attempt to overlay European patterns of thought on non-European conceptual systems. But the notion that orientalism or the colonialist mindset is a timeless template of Western thinking is misleading – rather, it emerged in specific circumstances in the early 19th century, and formed itself partly by being critical of an earlier, and more tolerant, era. When James Mill, John Stuart Mills father, wrote about the earlier Orientalists in his History of India, he was scathing about their ecumenical stance – for James Mill, Indian civilization was a barbarism that needed to be destroyed, and rebuilt on the Western model. This was typical of a whole turn in thinking about non-European societies, a devaluation that we mistakenly project back to the beginning of the modern era. We seem, finally, to be returning to that period in early modernity where the direction of comparison went both ways – when Leibniz could be inspired by the I Ching, and Xu Guangqi could translate Euclid with the help of Mateo Ricci.[13] Intercultural thought is not only about finding similarities between cultures, but de-familiarizing cultural patterns – making us see again realities that have become so habitual to us that they have faded into the material of our everyday lives. Graupe, by using Japanese thinking as a tool to unlock one of the truly central Western patterns of thought since the beginning of modernity, opens us not only to the surprising reality of the Other, but to the process by which we have become who we are.

Bibliography

Arnold, Matthew 1883. Culture and Anarchy, New York: Macmillan.

Cartwright, Nancy 1999. The Dappled World, Oxford: Oxford University Press.

Cartwright 1981. How the Laws of Physics Lie, Oxford: Oxford University Press.

Cartwright 1994.Nature's Capacities and their Measurements

Darden, Lindley and Nancy Maull 1977. "Interfield Theories," in Philosophy of Science, 44, 1977.

Dupré, John 2003. Human Nature and the Limits of Science, Oxford: Oxford University Press.

---

[13] For a comprehensive account of Leibniz's interest in China, see Frank Perkins *Leibniz and China: A Commerce of Light*; for I Ching, 125. For Matteo Ricci's collaboration with Xu Guangqi, see Peter Mark Engelfriet, *Euclid in China: The Genesis of the First Chinese Translation of Euclid's Elements, Books I-V*.

Engelfriet, Peter Mark 1998. Euclid in China: The Genesis of the First Chinese Translation of Euclid's Elements, Books I-V, Leiden, Boston: Brill.

Galbraith, John Kenneth 1993 (1953) American Capitalism: The Concept of Countervailing Power, Piscataway, NJ: Transaction Press.

Graupe, Silja forthcoming. The Basho of Economics, Frankfurt: Ontos Verlag.

Lakatos, Imre 1978. Philosophical Papers Cambridge: Cambridge University Press.

Perkins, Frank 2004. Leibniz and China: A Commerce of Light, Cambridge: Cambridge University Press.

Rescher, Nicholas 1996. Process Metaphysics: An Introduction to Process Philosophy, New York: SUNY Press.

Seibt, Johanna 2003. "Free Process Theory: towards a typology of occurings," in Process Theories: Cross-disciplinary Studies in Dynamic Categories, edited by Johanna Seibt, Dordrect: Springer.

Stewart, D. 1858. The Collected Works of Dugald Stewart, Edinburgh: T. Constable.

Acknowledgments

My interest in Japanese culture, Buddhism and Southeast Asian schools of philosophy was awakened by my studies at Sophia University in Tokyo. I'd like to thank Thierry Roboüam, SJ, for his impressive introduction into Buddhism as well as the community of the Kōtoku-Tempel, Sakuradai/Tokyo, which accepted me warmheartedly and openly, letting me experience the living spirituality of Zen. I am also grateful to the DAAD and the Studienstiftung des deutschen Volkes which made possible my stay in Japan.

This book is based on my German doctoral thesis which was published by Ontos in 2005. I'm grateful to my doctoral 'fathers', Professor Dr. Hans H. Lechner und Professor Dr. Karl-Heinz Brodbeck for their spirit, their engagement and their time, all of which they dedicated to the difficult task of remaining true to the canons of science while engaging in an interdisciplinary and intercultural dissertation project that abandons pre-formated research paths. Scientific advice also came to me from other sides: PD Dr. Rolf Elberfeld and Professor Dr. Ryōsuke Ohashi gave me comments on my work from the Japanese standpoint as well as Professor Dr. Claudia Bickmann from the standpoint of Intercultural Philosophy. I also received valuable suggestions from Professor Lik Kuen Tong about Daoism and the concept of Field-Being. The Studienstiftung des Deutschen Volkes provided generous support in the form of a promotion stipend, both financially and academically. To all of them I wish to express my deepest thanks.

Roger Gathman not only translated with infinite care, patience and expertise the updated German manuscript into English, he also agreed to write the foreword. My deep appreciation to you for this magnificent contribution, and to PD Dr. Johanna Seibt who has, as the coeditor of the series *Process Thought*, helped manage the transition of the translation into a book.

To blaze a new path of thought is often a tiring and lonely business. That I did not entirely feel how onerous it was I owe to my friends and family. Many of you helped in untold ways, and to all of you I offer my heartfelt thanks for your caring suggestions, and for your support throughout. Most of all I thank my parents, Heide and Klaus Graupe, and my husband, Christof Knur-Graupe, who have been by my side both in times of risk and uncertainty as well as happiness and fulfillment.

1 Introduction

In today's globalized world, there is a growing consciousness of the cultural multiplicity of cognitive and behavioral styles. In this book I will attempt a theoretical initiative that exploits the critical potential of this multiplicity in order to meditate fruitfully upon economic processes, and thereby create a ludic space for economic thought. Borrowing a phrase from Francois Jullien, we may designate the opening up of such a ludic space as a kind of cognitive detour, a journey of thought.[1] This journey will travel through Japanese thought in order to interrogate economic thinking anew, from a wholly other standpoint. This standpoint, not sharing the basic assumptions of economics, enables us to gaze upon those basic assumptions from the outside and make them the explicit object of reflection. We will disembed economic thought from its usual context and bring it back to its hidden 'sources': to what isn't thought, to what is so self-evident to the economists that they cannot regard it as an object for economic theory, but let it serve entirely as the implicit presupposition of their thought. Intercultural dialogue, with its continual shifts of perspective, offers us not only the possibility of coming to terms creatively with what is un-thought, but also the possibility of finding alternatives to it.

An important insight emerging from intercultural dialogue is that a scientific tradition, in spite of its surface appearance of heterogeneity, rests upon countless collusions and unanalyzed concurrences that form a kind of "footing of thought."[2] This footing is uncommonly influential, because it consists of unreflected presuppositions of thought that are never given as objects for scientific reflection. A main thesis of this book is that mainstream economics, in spite of having developed through historically distinct phases and being divided into various schools that differ on this or that technical matter, rests on one such "footing of thought." Furthermore, an imminent part of this footing is shaped by what we may call the Substance Paradigm.[3] A number of substance theoretical presuppositions are contained within this paradigm: for instance, the assumption that objects exist independently of other entities, or the belief in the immutable, given

---

[1] F. Jullien, *Der Umweg über China: ein Ortswechsel des Denkens*, Berlin 2002.
[2] Ibid., 184.
[3] For the concept, see J. Seibt, "Individuen als Prozesse: Zur ontologischen Revision des Substanz-Paradigmas," *Logos, Zeitschrift für systematische Philosophie*, 2/4 (1995), 355.

individuality of an entity. Common to all of these presuppositions is that they are neither recognized nor characterized as premises that could be subject to argument.[4] We can discern the substance paradigm that serves as the basis of economics from the outside if we take the perspective of modern Japanese philosophy, because the latter does not participate in this paradigm. Instead, a new, unusual theoretical paradigm underlies the economy from the Japanese viewpoint: processes, not substances, are the fundamental category of explanation and description. This is the reason we characterize this viewpoint as, in essence, a process philosophical one. Modern Japanese philosophy draws its inspiration and methods of justification from many sources, not just the Far Eastern philosophical traditions associated with Buddhism, Taoism and Confucianism. Rather, this interpretation of everyday reality is deeply rooted in Japanese culture and speech. For all their theoretical differences, these sources still hold in common that processes and not substances, a subject-less net of reciprocal determinants and not an agglomeration of individual molecules serve as the actual ground of the world of human experience. Based on this other "footing of thought", Japanese philosophers (in particular, for our purposes, Nishida Kitarō[5]) provide us with a new beginning of scientific thought. Their way of thinking has already led to revisions in the normal research paradigms of some disciplines, such as the natural sciences[6],

---

[4] Ibid, 355.
[5] Nishida is credited as the founder of modern Japanese philosophy. He was born in Unoke, Japan on May 19, 1870. After studying Western philosophy at Tokyo University, teaching German and engaging in intense Zen meditation practice, Nishida received the appointment of assistant professor in Ethics at the Imperial University of Kyoto in 1910. In the same year, he published his first work, „Studie of the Good." In 1913, Nishida became a professor of the history of religion, and in 1914, of the history of philosophy, at Kyōto. He founded a scholarly tradition through his research and teaching activities that is known today as the Kyōto School. He became an emiritus in 1928, but continued to work on his philosophy until his death on June 7, 1945.
[6] See for instance the works of Japanese cognitive scientist Shimizu Hiroshi. Translated into West European languages are: S. Hiroshi, Ba-Principle: "New Logic for the Real-Time Emergence of Information," *Holonics*, 5/1 (1995), 67-69. See also, "Die ordnende Kraft des 'Ba' im traditionellen Japan," in: C. Maar et al. (ed.), *Die Technik auf dem Weg zur Seele*, Reinbek 1996.

medicine[7], or systems theory[8]. Especially, the innovation and management theories developed by Nonaka Ikujiro and his co-authors which explicitly refer to Nishida's philosophy have fundamentally changed the understanding of how the dynamics of the knowledge-creating processes is created within companies.[9] Our aim in this book is to show how fruitful an encounter with Japanese philosophy can be for economics.

As the following pages will demonstrate, the dialogue of Japanese philosophy and economics can contribute in three ways to a process philosophical critique of economics and the renewal of its foundations: firstly, we will make visible substance-theoretical presuppositions that remain unconceptualized within the limits of economic theory. Secondly, we will show how these presuppositions lead to numerous problems – most notably, contradictions and gaps in explanation – and even generate them. Thirdly, we develop new approaches that do not participate in the set of substance-theoretical presuppositions and therefore contribute to a new, comprehensive understanding of economic processes[10]. It is by this means that we will breach the discourse of goods, individuals, formal regularities, etc. and ground a new conception of the economy in dynamic processes, mutual determinations and subject-less activities.

In these three steps, our pathbreaking analysis concentrates on the direct confrontation of Japanese philosophy and mainstream economic theory; the philosophical and historical backgrounds that are the contexts of both scientific traditions will therefore be often touched upon, but – being irrelevant to our main purposes – never represented with a lot of depth. The proximity of Japanese thought to Buddhism, Daoism and Confucianism will be emphasized in some places, in order to make it easier for the West-

---

[7] For example: Y. Yuasa, *The Body, Toward an Eastern Body-Mind Theory*, translated by P. Nagatomo, T.P. Kasulis, New York 1987.
[8] T. Latka, Topisches Sozialsystem, Die Einführung der japanischen Lehre vom Ort in die Systemtheorie und deren Konsequenzen für eine Theorie sozialer Systeme, Heidelberg 2003.
[9] I. Nonaka and Takeuchi, H., *The Knowledge-Creating Company, How Japenese Companies Create the Dynamics of Innovation*, New York 1995; Nonaka, I., Toyama R. and Konno, N., "Emergence of 'Ba', A Conceptual Framework for the Continuous and Self-transcending Process of Knowledge Creation," in: Nonaka, I. and Nishiguchi, T. (ed.), *Knowledge Emergence, Social, Technical and Evolutionary Dimensions of Knowledge Creation*, New York 2001, 13-28
[10] In Western process philosophy, this corresponds to the procedure of theory revision suggested by J. Seibt. See J. Seibt, "Individuen als Prozesse," 355.

ern reader, unacquainted with these ways of thinking, to follow along. The manifold connections of Japanese philosophy to Western philosophy will be, conversely, given only surface treatment, even when the path through foreign (i.e. Western) philosophy is most characteristic of Japanese philosophy. In this way we can open up an easy to understand approach to economic questions that is unburdened by the extensive, complicated interventions and associations of the Western history of philosophy. Choosing to go at our argument in this way means that even the proximity of some patterns of thought to Western process philosophy will not always be made clear in the text. The following remarks should serve as a sufficient but provisional sketch of this nearness.

The first section of the work (chapter 3) reflects, in a step-by-step fashion, the implied assumptions in economics about human actors, using as our point of orientation Nishida's "Logic of Place" (*basho no ronri*, 1926). We will point out those presuppositions that determine a certain level of argumentation without being explicitly made into objects of reflection on this level themselves. Then we will make transitions to deeper levels of knowledge, resulting in making conscious the moment of reflection. Through such multiple "place changes of thinking," our knowledge of economic action will be deepened. Gradually, from this process emerges a comprehensive picture of economic man. In regard to our critique of the substance paradigm, it is a decisive point that this critique allows us to see through the delusive character of substance-theoretical assumptions operating on every conceptual level, and to see that those assumptions lead to both logical contradictions within the theory and to obstructing the project of creating a comprehensive picture of economic action. For example, one may query whether the economic assumption of an independent world of goods, existing objectively and independent of human consciousness, can be sustained logically, since in the formal economic principle of optimization a relation to subjective consciousness is always already presupposed, although it is not explicitly thematized. Moreover it will be shown that economic theory implicitly presupposes the substance-metaphysical principle of determinateness insofar as it constructs the agent as a static substance with given qualities in order to allow actions to be calculable. But this systematically blocks the possibility of picturing important aspects of agency, like the mutability of an agent's qualities in space and time or her conscious reflection over her own action. Thus, contrary to its own claims, economic theory narrowly limits its own explanatory power. Altogether it can be seen that humans and their environment cannot be held apart as substances, but are determined in a process of mutual formation that is itself to be grasped neither subjectively nor objectively, but just as that which underlies every subject-object division.

Over and above a critique on implicit economic assumptions, the first section makes a positive proposal for describing economic activity without presupposing an underlying substance. This is where East Asian theories of habitus processes can be fruitfully used to represent economic activity. Habits are represented as differentiating activities of the consciousness without presupposing a bearer of the activity. Instead, turning this around, this bearer is regarded, in general, as a subject firstly specified by those habits as being in opposition to an objective outer world. A habitual process is thereby revealed that implicitly precedes all subjective and objective economic methods without being itself reflected within them. This process shouldn't be seen as the alternative to the category of substance, but simply as its logical presupposition.

The second section of the work (chapter 4) uncovers the substance theoretical presuppositions of economic theory as they extend to construing 'society', in order to reveal alternatives to them. In the foreground we put the critique of the economic notion that society is to be explained by positing substantial entities as its foundation. Again, this critique borrows from Japanese philosophy – in particular, from Nishida and Nishitani – but also exploits the resources of other East Asian schemas of explanation. It is important to show that two absolutely contradictory ideas operate within economics, but are not regarded as such: firstly, methodological individualism conceives society as something agglomerated out of sheer individual atoms. But the consequence of understanding those atoms collectively is to have recourse to the assumption of an abstract universal that lawfully, and as a mechanism, coordinates them into a unity. But in doing so these individuals lose just that independence that methodological individualism postulates. The substantiality of the universal negates their individuality. In spite of this problem, mainstream economics holds uncritically to the idea of substantial individuals and a substantial universal. Our critique of economics pierces this substance metaphysics, which lies beneath both ideas, until it reaches the core of the actual problem: individuality and universality cannot be thought coherently so long as one presupposes them to be independent, self-determinate substances. This insight leads to rejecting these notions as insufficient and seeking a real alternative beyond the substance conception. Such an alternative outlines itself in the idea of the economy as a process of formation that is not supported by any substance and in which everything in mutual dependence becomes shaper and shaped. Borrowing from Nishida's "world" concept (*sekai*), we grasp the economic world as a field of activities that through economic forms of action like exchange, the division of labor, and the use of money is subjectlessly determined. This dynamic world, moving without a firm point of reference, proves itself to be not only the actual ground or place of economic action, but also the un-conceptualized presupposition within economics that seeks to divide this world into strictly separate entities. Building on this insight, new light can be cast upon some further fundamental problems of economics, like the relationship of the market and the state or the meaning of egoism, so that new, surprising perspectives on socioeconomic processes open up. Out of these different perspectives, it can be shown that the economic world cannot be systematically explained from the standpoint of the science of economics. Most importantly, calculating and predicting this world by means of formal models, which economics uncritically takes from the physical sciences, can be demonstrated to be not only a problem that has so far eluded a solution in terms of those models, but to be logically impossible to resolve.

The dialogue of economics and Japanese philosophy, however, does not merely penetrate into the deep structure of economic thought, but it shows how very much this kind of thinking is interwoven with our everyday perceptions. For Japanese philosophy, as well as other process philosophies, a central concern is to connect the place of the observer explicitly to the description of the world. Applied to economics, this means: the economist is not independent of the world he describes. He is neither a neutral observer nor a social engineer, who can shape economic processes from the outside without thereby himself being (unconsciously) pulled into the formation process. And inversely it is clear that the supposedly 'objective' goods are not independent of the way that the economist represents them. The economic world doesn't exist independently of the conditions of its references. It only appears to be an ineluctable reality, an objective mechanism or a chain of necessary states of affairs, so long as the abstract, theoretical constructs of economic theory that are continually, in our globalized world, forcing themselves upon us are misunderstood to be the everlasting facts of our everyday life.

From the Japanese point of view, theoretical constructs are no more nor less than the habits of thought, which are rooted deep in everyday human understanding about human nature and its surrounding environment while, inversely, also grounding this understanding. While the overpowering role of social norms for the image of economic man and his world are emphasized, one thing should become clear: insofar as the habitus is thematized at all in economics, it is construed to be the irreplaceable presupposition of action. It is judged to be the unconscious mode of acting that determines the economic everyday while not being subject to change itself. Therefore, the conscious, creative shaping of living together outside or beyond economic habits doesn't even appear as a prospect in the mainstream economic perspective. Against this, Japanese philosophy sees through such substantification of social habits and considers it a deception. We are not simply slavishly obedient to supposedly given habits, but can become conscious of them, shape them creatively, and so modify them.

Through the detour of thought between East and West, between economics and philosophy we ought to be able to find a way of thought in the following pages that takes into account this Japanese insight: economic habits, which are increasingly unconsciously determined, may be made gradually visible, and their border lines may be surveyed and penetrated. By means of this, I hope to give a push to economic thinking that will put it on new, creative paths that traverse disciplinary and cultural borders.

In closing, two remarks are necessary: Japanese names appear in the sequence usual in Japan (the family name first, and then the surname). Brackets in the texts will be used to enclose cross-references that refer to a section of another chapter. The bracket (3.3.2), for example, refers to the division "Economic Activity as Habit" in Chapter 3.3.2.

2 Methodological Presuppositions

Within economics, hardly any importance is accorded to reflection on the discipline's own method. This is prima facie recognizable just from the amount of space taken up by methodological considerations in economic textbooks – which is, in general, seldom more than a few pages.[1] Milton Friedman puts this disinterest in his own methodological principles in a nutshell: "I decided I'd better do methodology, as it were, instead of make methodology." Reflection on his own method seemed to him to be an enterprise of little significance.[2] In the center of economic thought stands the content of a theory, but the method that was applied to get to the knowledge of this content does not form the object of explicit reflection. In other words: the center of gravity of analysis lies on the question of the 'what', meaning the description of things and relations, and not on the question of 'how' this description came to be and what relation holds between it and the described object. Behind this is hidden the postulate of traditional theory building which says that contents can be segregated from the method used to discover them.[3] In the following pages, this postulate and its validity shall be extensively examined from the point of view of Japanese philosophy. Nishida's view that the content is dependent on the theoretical frame in which it is conceived will play an important role here; for Nishida, theoretical statements are only given a stable context-dependent value in the way the scientist thinks. Method and content can thus not be segregated. Instead, another relationship emerges: the method appears as

---

[1] Thus, Cezanne's textbook entirely waives the science-theoretical introduction (W. Cezanne, *Allgemeine Volkswirtschaftslehre*, München-Wien 2002). Siebert's textbook contains only two and a half pages devoted to the topic (see. H. Siebert, *Einführung in die Volkswirtschaftslehre*, Stuttgart et al. 2000); editions of Samuelson's textbook always give it 8 pages at maximum (see. P. A. Samuelson, *Volkswirtschaftslehre*, Vol. 1, Köln 1973). Varian consciously waives the reference to the scope and method of political economics. This theme could be very interesting, according to Varian, but „it hardly seems appropriate to begin our studies of economics with such material." H.R. Varian, *Intermediate Microeconomics*, Berkeley 2002, 1.
[2] M. Friedman in J.D. Hammond, "An Interview with Milton Friedman on Methodology," *Research in the History of Economic Thought and Methodology*, Vol. 10 (1992), 107.
[3] K.-H. Brodbeck, *Die fragwürdigen Grundlagen der Ökonomie, Eine philosophische Kritik der modernen Wirtschaftswissenschaften*, Darmstadt 2000, 5.

the presupposition of a scientific statements; a presupposition that clearly, from the standpoint of the scientist, remains constantly un-thought.

Consequently, an important condition should be elaborated that has to be satisfied in order to segregate content and method: for this, we must observe the methodical instrument that is in most cases applied in economics - abstraction. An abstract model observes only a few snippets of reality. It ignores all circumstances that the modeler considers inessential or confusing[4], and takes into its scope only a few elements and their relations to each other. It is in this manner that the neoclassical theory of demand, for instance, ignores the qualities of goods such as form, color or beauty, and concentrates solely on the relation of quantity and price of a commodity. In such abstraction the economist sees a possible key to the exact administration of economic processes; after isolating a few factors, he can specify and calculate their relationship according to the laws of economics as a relation of cause and effect. In economics, this kind of operation is seen, for the most part, as the only possible path to achieving certain knowledge of economic processes:

> It "is necessary for man with his limited power to go step by step; breaking up a complex situation, studying one bit at a time and at last combining his partial solutions into a more or less complete solution of the whole riddle. In breaking it up, he segregates those disturbing causes, whose wanderings happen to be inconvenient, for the time in a pound called Ceteris Paribus. The study of some group of tendencies is isolated by the assumption other things being equal: the existence of other tendencies is not denied, but their disturbing effect is neglected for a time. The more the issue is thus narrowed, the more exactly it can be handled: but also the less closely does it correspond to real life. Each exact and firm handling of a narrow issue, however, helps towards treating broader issues, in which that narrow issue is contained, more exactly than would otherwise be possible. With each step more things can be let out of the pound; exact discussions can be made less abstract, realistic discussions can be made less inexact than was possible at an earlier stage."[5]

This passage makes clear how the scientist agrees to a compromise through the method of abstraction: the more he achieves a desirably exact formula for calculating a social process, the more he distances himself from con-

---

[4] L. Walras writes in his equilibrium theory that „one must provisionally distance oneself from small, confusing auxilliary circumstances." See his *Mathematische Theorie der Preisbestimmung der wirthschaftlichen Güter, Vier Denkschriften* (1881), Reprint Stuttgart 1972, 7.

[5] A. Marshall, *Principles of Economics* (1920), Reprint London 1961, 366.

structing realistic processes. Yet the economist sees this problem as resolvable. All that needs to be done is a), isolate conceivably different abstract processes out of real processes; b), investigate the abstract processes in themselves, separately; and, c), in a step by step manner, consolidate the results of the investigation to form one complex picture. Thus, reality appears as an aggregation of individual, abstract regularities. It functions as though it were put together out of foundation stones and therefore can be treated in principle as exactly as calculable and manipulable as abstract processes. This representation is clearly grounded in an essential, even if mostly unconceptualized assumption: things and their functional relations to each other which are researched and described within a model, must continue to exist in the same way when they are placed in a more extensive connection. Inalterable substances must be assumed, that remain the same in different contexts, from abstract theories up to an all-including reality. Within economic theory the validity of such an assumption is presupposed to be self-evident, as the following passage makes clear:

> "The task of economic theory is to identify functional quantitative relationships as well as to explain real connections and the course of events (cause-effect relationships), and to identify causal rules and law-like regularities. Quantities whose mutual influences must be investigated include sales, yields, amounts, prices, costs, etc. Between them stand dependencies that generally can be designated as functions... *It is indisputable that there exist in reality such functions as production, cost, sales, demand, savings, output, production factors, consumption, proceeds, growth, gain, and others, which means that there exist corresponding functional connections.*"[6]

If the elements, functions and laws that make up the content of economic theory actually existed as inalterable substances, then it would be a matter of indifference with what method one chose to investigate them. A thing that is self-identical would always show itself as the thing it is, independently of the means of observation to which it was subjected by scientists. But it is just this idea of an entity remaining stable across different contexts that is revealed as an illusion upon closer examination, resting on the fundamental misunderstanding that the object of a theory can precede its theoretical conceptualization or be independent of it. This, at least, is the objection that Nishida would raise against this procedure in economics.

---

[6] D. Ohse, *Mathematik für Wirtschaftswissenschaftler*, Vol. 1, München 1993, 233, emphasis added.

Let's look at Nishida's argument a little closer. Nishida is not pursuing the goal of determining exactly what an object is in order to make it easier to predict or control, but poses a wholly other question: how is knowledge about the existence of an object or a set of relations between objects possible and how does this knowledge stand in relation to its object? He answers his question like this: a thing exists always and only within a certain context. It has a context-dependent existence, but is not an autonomous, independent substance, that is given without question:

> "In order to be able to say that an object and another object are interrelated, construct a system and preserve themselves, something must be assumed that contains this system in itself, in which this system is found and can take place. Being must be located in something (*nanika ni oite*)."[7]

But a further question presents itself. What determines the things and their relationship to each other? In a general way, Nishida names this a basho[8], a Japanese concept that literally translates as 'site', 'place', or 'position.' Such a 'locus' – as I shall translate basho – can exhibit very different properties. It doesn't specify a firm, inalterable substance, but rather should be seen as a fluid concept, which can be described with regards to wholly different connections. Chiefly it is important that Nishida names the method, that is the way a scientific judgment comes about, as an example of such a locus.[9] For him the contents of a theory are not simply 'there' or 'given', rather their existence depends on a certain context, a domain of discourse. A certain manner of thinking necessarily precedes them. This manner determines as the locus as much the properties of the elements as the kind of their relationship to one another. Therefore, Nishida regards the content of a theory as immediately dependent on how the scientist conceives it. The method, or more precisely the context, in which is formulated, accrues a logical priority before the content itself. It is by way of the locus that the existence of a thing as a this or a that is determined.

Following this course of thought to its conclusion, we will discuss some examples found in the literature around Nishida's philosophy, in order to extract consequences for economic theory. For instance, philosophically, one can ask what is primarily given in a general judgment such as "red is a

---

[7] K. Nishida, *Logik des Ortes*, translated and edited by R. Elberfeld, Darmstadt 1999, 72.

[8] Ibid., 72.

[9] Ibid., 87. Also see R.J. Wargo, *The Logic of Basho and the Concept of Nothingness in the Philosophy of Nishida Kitarō*, Michigan 1972, 188. Wargo does not use the concept of method, but speaks more generally of a *domain of discourse*.

color."[10] What is it that logically precedes this sentence? It is often assumed that the subject of the sentence (the red) is immediately given and that its existence precedes every judgment. And if one believes this, than we could abstract the general property of color extrapolating from the individual colors. The general concept of color would then be that which is common as the essence of many colored objects. Nishida, however, unmasks this way of thinking as a delusion:

> "The point he (Nishida, SG) wants to make is that one does not first come into contact with specific colors and then abstract from these to form the abstract notion of color in general. In order to see a specific color, e.g., red, as a color, it is already necessary to have the notion of color in general."[11]

The general notion of the concept 'color' must firstly be on hand before a specific color ('red') is recognized as a color at all. Red is a color because the general concept of color contains the specific colors like red, green, etc. in itself. The general concept of color is thus more original, and the individual colors are merely different determinations of this concept. "Color is not merely a conceptual product of abstraction ... but it is a system of distinctions of which 'red' is a specific instance."[12] This becomes particularly clear if you pose questions that are seemingly without sense. Because what would it mean if one said, for example, red is not a color? This statement doesn't make any sense because it is, so to speak, impossible for red to move outside of the concept of color; you can't accord it an existence independent of this general concept. It is not only valid that the general concept encloses some elements in itself, but it also determines which elements or properties may not be observed. So the general concept of wine, for instance, includes concepts such as 'red' or 'white', but excludes a concept such as 'convex:'

> "So, if I say 'this wine is convex' you will not tell me that there is something about the string of terms that offends you, but that your intuition of wines of all sorts make it impossible for such a uniting of terms to be a genuine judgment. The standard is one's initial intuition, in this case, of this wine, but in general of any and all wine."[13]

---

[10] The color example can be found in K. Nishida, *Logik des Ortes*, 87.
[11] R.J. Wargo, *The Logic of Basho*, 193.
[12] R.E. Carter, *The Nothingness beyond God, An Introduction to the Philosophy of Nishida Kitarō*, St. Paul (Minn.) 1997, 28.
[13] Ibid., 27.

Clearly, in this passage, general concepts such as 'wine' or 'color' are themselves preceded by something. They are conceived in something. For Nishida, an initial intuition serves as the locus preceding every judgment or every scientific statement, giving these a determined shape or direction.

> "Basho is the given-in-intuition prior to the analysis and expression of objectification."[14]

This intuition is grounded in the experience of everyday intercourse with objects that are usually designated as 'wine' or 'color.' It can also refer to the experience of thinking in a particular theory in which the concepts are always applied in a certain manner.[15] In each case, the intuition is an original experience that not only determines the elements and their properties, but also the relationship of these elements to one another. It thus determines whether we are to regard them as 'habitual', 'regular', or 'law-like.' At first glance, this statement seems odd. Aren't laws something inherent in the nature of things? But let us again look at the example of colors. It proves logically impossible, here, to deduce the relationship of colors to one another out of their 'nature.' Instead the understanding of this relationship must arise out of the idea of the entire color system in the sense of an initial intuition. One must presuppose this (unconscious) idea in order to be able to recognize these relations at all.

> "The relationship between 'red' and 'color' is not one of degrees of abstraction, nor is one of two independently existing things or entities which we must somehow struggle to unite. Rather, they are united from the beginning, for 'red' and 'color' are both parts of, or grounded in the color-system itself. Thus, the real subject of the sentence 'red is a color' is not 'red', nor even the grammatical predicate 'color' but the system of colors itself. To have a concept of 'red' is already to have a concept of 'color', and to have a concept of color is already to have something of a system of colors. (...) Subject ('red') and predicate ('color') are not inexplicably brought together in a judgment, then, but are specific features of, and are carved out of, one and the same (whole) thing – the system of colors. They are intrinsically and inextricably related from the start. (...) The color system includes precise specifications

---

[14] Ibid., 32.
[15] In this connection Nishida distinguishes between a *Concrete Intuition* and an *Intellectual Intuition*. Both share the property of indicating a context in which these concepts are originally experienced or learned or conceived. Both are denoted as the *Initial Intuition*.

of the individual colors that make it up, and an account of the relations among the colors."[16]

When we ask how laws or functional connections exist between things, Nishida finds it problematic to answer this question with reference simply to their 'nature' or 'essence.' Rather such laws and connections, like the properties of the connected elements, are dependent upon the particular domain of discourse in which they are mentioned. To translate this statement to the realm of economics, let's briefly examine the functional connection between prices and quantities of a given commodity. It doesn't simply lie in the nature of a thing to only manifest price and quantity as its properties such as the neoclassical theory of demand postulates. Rather, the concept of demand or the idea of a demand curve precedes the determination of these properties (and with them the idea of the thing as a commodity): the concept of demand constrains the perception to the extent that price and quantity appear as the unique properties of a commodity and all other possible influencing factors are screened out.[17] It necessarily precedes these properties. But that thus a functional (or regular) relation between these properties can be postulated, the concept of demand must still presuppose something else that is not explicitly reflected by neoclassical theory itself. This is the initial intuition of the scientist, who simply presupposes a negative relationship between price and quantity, or in other words a downward sloping demand curve. You can't deduce the negative trajectory of the demand curve out of individual prices and quantities. Rather the relation is exactly the inverse. Just as you must implicitly presuppose the color system, when you say 'red', so too the negative course of the demand curve always presupposes the functional connection of prices and quantities. Speaking generally, that means the form (Gestalt) of a function must be implicitly given, before the function itself and its variables are determined. Or to speak yet more generally: what a thing appears as is dependent on the manner and way in which the scientist speaks about it.

"'To be assumed as an entity is, purely and simply, to be reckoned as a variable.' (...) [One can] speak of the similarity of the acceptance of an ontology with the acceptance of a scientific theory ...Our acceptance of an ontology is 'determined once

---

[16] R.E. Carter, *The Nothingness beyond God*, 28-29.
[17] H.W. Spiegel, *The Growth of Economic Thought*, Durham (North Carolina) 1983, 566.

we have fixed upon the overall conceptual scheme which is to accommodate science in the broadest sense.'"[18]

The initial intuition of a negatively declining demand curve is grounded very differently in economics. So it has been attempted to deduce the law of demand from another law, that of utility maximization.[19] But as Samuelson, for instance, clearly concedes, the grounding process in economics is nearly arbitrary:

> "Take a little bad psychology, add a dash of bad philosophy and ethics, and liberal quantities of bad logic, and any economist can prove that the demand curve for a commodity is negatively declining."[20]

Samuelson has no other recourse but to call upon healthy human understanding, which finds it prudent to assume the law of demand. "This law corresponds to the healthy human understanding and has actually been known since the beginning of the historical tradition – if not in this precise form."[21] In other textbooks the negative descent of the demand curve is called merely "usual."[22] "In normal cases there exists a negative relation between prices and the amount of demand of a commodity."[23] In this way the initial intuition of the scientist evades an exact justification by presenting instead an obscure tacit consensus.

As the examples of colors, wine and demand should have made clear, the domain of discourse determines what the things and their relationships among each other appear as. The latter are, in this sense, context dependent existents. As Wargo formulates this view:

> "One could then say that one's ontological commitment depends solely on the domain of discourse one is willing to use."[24]

This means nothing less than the fact that the viewpoint of the scientist precedes and determines the content (and thus the elements and their inter-

---

[18] R.J. Wargo, *The Logic of Basho*, 233. Here Wargo cites W. Quine.
[19] A. Marshall, *Principles of Economics*, 92.
[20] P.A. Samuelson, *Foundations of Economic Analysis*, Cambridge 1983, 4. See also L. Mainwaring, "Marginalism and the Margin," in: J. Creedy (ed.), *Foundations of Economic Thought*, Oxford et al. 1990, 94.
[21] P. A. Samuelson, *Volkswirtschaftslehre*, Vol. 1, 89.
[22] H.R. Varian, *Grundzüge der Mikroökonomik*, 101.
[23] W. Cezanne, *Allgemeine Volkswirtschaftslehre*, 90.
[24] R.J. Wargo, *The Logic of Basho*, 185.

connections). In other words: the content is dependent on the method. From which it is immediately evident that all statements over the 'nature' of things are valid only in the specific context of a method. They can't explain any phenomena in other contexts.

> "He (Nishida, SG) will repeatedly say that to claim that something exists is just to say it is located in a basho and that the meaning of existence changes as the basho changes."[25]

We can transpose this statement with the help of an example into the realm of economics:[26] We often begin, in economics, by designating some economic 'data,' for example prices, as (objectively) given. These should objectively represent some given property of goods. Rarely is the question raised - for whom are these data actually under control? A closer look shows, that prices are not simply given. Rather, they appear in very different ways depending upon the context in which they are being determined. Neoclassical price theory, for example, expresses no opinion about the way a retailer or consumer sees the price of peanuts or aluminum, but merely confines its opinion to how a researcher or group of researchers observes it. The theory doesn't enable us to research the price in the sense of a given, unchanging property of things, but always determines the price as this or that depending on the context. Its own method presents the context in the sense of the locus in which the things appear as 'data.'

If things appear only context-dependently as this or that, than the knowledge about these things cannot, without additional information, be transposed from one context to another. This is particularly salient when a greater or more encompassing context is selected. If one observes the influence of prices on the level of demand of umbrellas while at the same time keeping in mind the influence of the weather, you'll see that the relation of price and quantity changes in this new context of observation. Fair weather can lead to sinking demand for umbrellas even as prices themselves also fall. In this wider context we can see that the norms governing the demand curve are disturbed. Thus, the path that leads from the finding the norms in abstract connections to using them to explain more encompassing contexts, or even 'real situations,' proves to be blocked. That doesn't mean that the theories and models are flatly worthless, but only

---

[25] Ibid., 184.
[26] K. Leube, "Einige Bemerkungen zu den 'Untersuchungen über die Theorie des Preises' aus der Sicht der Österreichischen Schule der Nationalökonomie," in: K. Leube (ed.), *Die Österreichische Schule der Nationalökonomie*, Vol. 2, Wien 1995, 332.

that they prove utterly unusable when you transpose their propositions into other contexts without retaining a consciousness of their context-dependence.

> "If any of these shallower levels are taken to be complete representations of the ultimate structure in and of themselves, the explanations will prove to be utterly inadequate."[27]

But how is knowledge of more complex connections possible? A key that Nishida gives us lies in the concept of basho. Let's again examine basho, in the sense of the initial intuition, of the scientist. It is critical that the locus exhibits no properties that can be predicated of the elements that are held in it. Or in other words: a proposition that is found within a model cannot be applied to the model itself. Carter, using the example of colors and numbers, makes the meaning of this clear:

> "Of course, the system, like 'color' itself, has no color. ... The class or system-concept (color, number) does not have any specific properties of the instances of the system. Thus 'number' is no specific number, and yet it makes possible all numbers insofar as it refers to the number-system."[28]

The initial intuition cannot become the object of the scientific judgment that it grounds. It is a "higher dimensional standpoint, which cannot be reached from a particular standpoint; on the contrary, it is the basis for the generation of some determined standpoint."[29] The initial intuition is the unthought presupposition of all theoretical propositions. It is their ground, but not their object. It is the locus, which is invisible from the angle of vision of the elements that it determines. This is the sense of Nishida's formula that it is a 'place of nothingness.' This nothingness "doesn't signify that there is nothing there. On the contrary, it is the undetermined determiner."[30]

> "Basho, then, is that which is neither predicated of, nor present in, a subject, nor even the grammatical subject, but that which grounds both, and out of which both arise as specifications or determinations."[31]

---

[27] R.J. Wargo, *The Logic of Basho*, 263.
[28] R.E. Carter, *The Nothingness beyond God*, 28.
[29] Nishida, *Logik des Ortes*, 32.
[30] Ibid., 50.
[31] R.E. Carter, *The Nothingness beyond God*, 31.

Behind this statement is hidden the insight that a theory cannot make its own presuppositions its content. That doesn't mean, however, that these presuppositions cannot be exposed to reflection at all. But to do that requires a more powerful or richer cognition than what comes to be expressed within the narrow limits of the theory itself. You must change to a new domain of discourse that becomes the new locus of the previously unconceived presuppositions. In this new locus the previous presuppositions lose their property of determining elements and their relations and become themselves determined or determinable objects with defined properties. Through the change of the domain of discourse, of the locus of thought, the perspective changes. That which previously remained in the background as the unconceived presupposition determining cognition becomes an explicit object of observation in the new locus. An essential aspect of this process is successfully making the transition from abstract to concrete knowing.[32] The latter act of cognition is, according to Nishida, always already present. But it is always only operant as an unconceived presupposition as long as a science doesn't explicitly reflect its own foundation, its own locus. When this foundation becomes an object of consciousness, a deeper or more concrete knowing is revealed, that encloses in itself all abstract relations and elements. Here, in this knowing, lies the key to the knowledge of complex connections.

Our observations above allow us to derive two important, meaningful aspects arising from an explicit reflection on method. First, method represents the ground or the source of all scientific propositions. It is the science's unconceived presupposition. Therefore, scientific propositions, strictly speaking, are valid only in the context of the method; if they are put into other contexts, nothing can be claimed about their correctness. As long as we are aware of this constraint, we can actually achieve something through the use of scientific methods. But a systematic dysfunction arises when methods are, unconsciously, applied universally, and are thus transposed into connections in which another initial intuition is operant, or in other words, we are transposed to another grounding locus of thought. Only an explicit reflection on method guarantees that this systematic dysfunction will not arise. With the aid of such an explicit reflection it is possible to constantly maintain two perspectives at the same time, in which one focuses on the observation of elements (or things) and their relationships and the other concentrates on the locus.

---

[32] The concept 'concrete' is here used in the sense of 'content-rich' or 'extensive.'

Second, reflection on method holds the key to a deeper, more encompassing knowledge, one that cannot be reached through the abstract lawlikenesses that the economist investigates within his method, assembling them like building blocks. Reflection on method must abandon this frame of thought. It is necessary to make a conceptual leap to another locus of understanding that is so wide that it contains hitherto unthought presuppositions. Methodological self-reflection enables the break through to a deeper knowledge that has always already been implicitly presupposed by the original standpoint without having been made itself visible. It helps us to gain an insight into complex connections that are beyond the power of the mere composition of abstract concepts.

> "There is basically one pattern of argumentation which, when successively applied, forces a move upward from a simpler set of categories to a richer and more complex one. The point of this pattern of argumentation is not just that a more complex categorical structure develops, but further, that the richer categories are not reducible to the simpler ones. This pattern of argumentation, Nishida thinks, shows the essential dependency of the simpler categories on the more complex, i.e., the former can be abstracted from the latter, but the latter cannot be constructed from the former."[33]

Knowledge will increase in depth when the presuppositions of one's own thought are continually being re-interrogated: "One moves from the instance as verbally judged, to what such judgment necessarily implies, in increasing layers of inclusiveness."[34] For Nishida, the point is not only that content and method cannot be divorced from each other and that, just taking this into account, the standpoint of the researcher must be highlighted; but, as importantly, that the reflection on method represents the most important key to a more extensive scientific understanding of reality. It is the use of this key that will open the gate to understanding economic activity in the next chapter.

---

[33] R.J. Wargo, *The Logic of Basho*, 238.
[34] R.E. Carter, *The Nothingness beyond God*, 29.

3 The Implicit Image of the Person in Economics

Pure science, according to the conventional wisdom of objective economic method, deals merely with the "blind and ineluctable forces of nature" that operate independently of any human will.[1] In particular, neoclassical theory assumes it can either wholly ignore human agency as an explanatory object or treat it as a kind of calculable, causally-mechanical behavior. The "purification of theory occasionally even relinquishes ... the actor, in order to analyze simple thing-thing relationships."[2] It is believed that economic theory no longer requires a specific understanding of human action because the person as such has been systematically excluded, during the course of the last centuries, from what takes place in the economy. Economists only have to describe "the anonymous control of a imperturbable, systematic circle of functional states of affairs." Thus, as a rule, "the objects of modern economics are only things and relationships between things."[3] The level of abstraction has advanced so far that, generally, the person and his actions no longer even appear as objects of explanation.

As the following pages will make clear, the neoclassical theory is still a suitable starting point from which to develop an extensive understanding of economic agents. Here we can make fruitful use of an important methodical procedure that Nishida formulated in his "Logic of Place."[4] In the last chapter it became clear that Nishida discovered the key to a deeper level of knowledge in the unthought presuppositions of a theory. In the Logic of Place Nishida systematically extends this insight in order to determine anew the relation of objective apprehension and subjective apprehension, thereby showing, that every objective methodology necessarily presupposes propositions about subjective consciousness without thematizing these presuppositions themselves. Every objective methodology rests im-

---

[1] L. Walras is cited in P. Mirowski, *More Heat than Light, Economics as Social Physics, Physics as Nature's Economics*, Cambridge 1989, 220.
[2] B. Biervert, "Menschenbilder in der ökonomischen Theoriebildung, Historisch-genetische Züge," in: B. Biervert, M. Held (ed.), *Die Natur des Menschen – Zum Menschenbild der ökonomischen Theorie*, Frankfurt-Main 1991, 49.
[3] J. Wieland, *Ökonomische Organisation, Allokation und Status*, Tübingen 1993, 2.
[4] Japanese: *basho no ronri*. See the Essay, *Basho* (Ort), which Nishida wrote in 1926. (Nishida Kitarō Zenshū, Vol. 4, 208-289). Translated into German in Nishida, *Logik des Ortes*, 73-139.

plicitly on propositions about the subjective consciousness without itself making these its explanatory object. In other words: propositions about the subjective consciousness show themselves as the logical 'locus', in which any objective method is grounded, even if this locus is not recognized as its own. Borrowing from these thoughts of Nishida's, in this chapter we shall show that the neoclassical theory presupposes a field of consciousness that remains fundamentally and constantly hidden to the economist himself. Neoclassical theory thus implicitly builds on an understanding of subjective consciousness that only can be made explicit through turning to subjective methods and, again, reflecting their unthought presuppositions Yet the goal of developing an explanation of economic agents that is oriented to Nishida's Logic of Place is not simply achieved by that reflection. For Nishida, the subjective consciousness really does represent the locus of all objective apprehension, but this consciousness lies within a deeper or more extensive locus that cannot itself, from the subjective point of view, become conscious. This basho contains in itself all subjective as well as all objective styles of observation and mediates between them. It "is a subject and object embracing and unifying something, that from the outset suffuses the so-called epistemological problem of subject-object mediation."[5] With the aid of this topological thought we will develop an understanding of economic action that goes beyond all the subjective and objective interpretive statements of economic theories and at the same time makes their unthought presuppositions visible.

3.1 The Actor in Objective Economic Method

Our next task is to show the starting point for the theme of this section. Following Nishida, there exists a kind of knowledge that concerns itself only abstractly with the relation of things.[6] In economics this approximately corresponds to the kind of knowledge over the relationships of things to things, as it is formulated, for example, in the theory of demand. Moreover, according to Nishida, this kind of knowledge is clearly extremely limited, comprehending in its scope only abstract or general connections, but not the individual or special cases. Consequently it cannot explain why relationships assume specific forms. In terms of the theory of demand it becomes immediately clear what this entails, because in this theory a purely generalized connection of prices and the quantity of goods

---

[5] R. Elberfeld, *Das Verstehen der Kulturen*, 112.
[6] Nishida speaks here of knowledge of the "abstract universal." P. Mafli, *Nishida Kitarōs Denkweg*, München 1996, 150.

is formulated that is represented by an inverse relationship or by the negatively sloping demand curve. It can neither explain why this curve is presupposed, nor how the individual, specific price-quantity relation is to be ascertained. For this, we require the kind of knowledge that will give us a larger scope. And this knowledge, according to Nishida, is that of particular cases, which always serve as an implicit presupposition of the universal judgments encoded in a theory.[7] From the perspective of the theory of demand, such knowledge can be discovered in the concept of optimization that applies in the theory of utility maximization. This concept represents, for one thing, one possibility of grounding the cause of the negative decline of the demand curve. For another, with its help we can determine a specific price-quantity-relation as an actually demanded amount. The theory of utility maximization thus enables us to acquire a more extensive knowledge which, as a locus, grounds the universally formulated law of demand. Therefore it shall serve us as a departure point for the following argument: our first task is to inquire about the unthought presuppositions of the concept upon which this theory rests. In order to make them visible, we will undertake a philosophical detour through physics, since economics has expropriated the concept of optimization from the natural sciences, without explicitly reflecting on its conceptual presuppositions. Our itinerary shall demonstrate that the concept of optimization in economics necessarily follows assumptions about the consciousness as a static, unmoving field. These assumptions, which function as the unthought foundation of quantifying over actions, can only remain implicit as long as a change in time is not contemplated. But as soon as we do consider change, knowledge must deepen so as to make a change in the field of consciousness imaginable.[8] As we shall see, this makes a turn to the subjective methodology of economic action logically inescapable.

3.1.1 The Field of Consciousness as the Unthought Locus of Objective Methods

It is broadly undisputed that the core of neoclassical theory building is the concept of optimization. We find this concept not only in the theory of utility maximization, but also in the notion of profit maximization. But the presuppositions of this concept remain a place of nothingness inside which neoclassical theory is conceived without the theory being able to make those presuppositions the explicit object of its reflection. However, the

---

[7] R.E. Carter, *The Nothingness beyond God*, 33.
[8] Ibid., 35.

source of the concept can be named quite easily: it came out of physics, or more exactly the method of physics that dominated the middle of the 19th century. And yet, at least within neoclassical economics itself, there is no explicit discussion about how such an expropriation in the economic context is meaningful or under what assumptions it is justified. In particular, the essential analogies to physics have remained mostly in the dark.[9] Thus we don't have the names of the indispensable, necessary properties intrinsic to the economic domain of discourse, which guarantee the functional connection of a given optimization. And yet, this is urgently necessary, since the existence of these connections in a natural scientific context in no way gives us the right to suppose their existence in a social scientific domain of discourse. You cannot answer the question of the locus of utility maximization by gesturing towards physics. The latter certainly does give important testimony to what properties are necessary in order to think in terms of optimization. We must still require the production of evidence of economic phenomena to which these properties can be ascribed.

Many neoclassical economists either do not see the problem of the context dependence of the optimization concept at all or see it only partially. For instance, Walras is convinced that pure economic theory can be "a science which resembles the physico-mathematical sciences in every aspect."[10] The functional connections, which are the objects of research in the natural sciences, are supposed to be simply transposable into the social scientific context. Ludwig von Mises, for example, writes: "We have to research the law of social cooperation as the physicist researches the laws of mechanics."[11] However, an important condition is joined to this way of going at things: economic phenomena must be governed by the same lawfulness as natural phenomena. The validity of this condition is clearly simply assumed rather than really proven. Traditional economic theory is simply convinced, as Menger formulates it, "that the phenomena of economic life are governed according to strict laws, like those of nature."[12]

---

[9] We define the distinction between a metaphor and an analogy in the following way: "Whereas a metaphor merely suggests that the principal and subsidiary subjects have attributes in common, an analogy draws explicit parallels between them." A. Klammer, T. Leonard, "So What's an Economic Metaphor?," in: P. Mirowski (ed.), *Natural Images in Economic Thought*, Cambridge 1991, 34.

[10] L. Walras, *Elements of Pure Economics*, New York 1969, 71.

[11] L. von Mises, *Nationalökonomie, Theorie des Handelns und Wirtschaftens*, Genf 1940, 2.

[12] C. Menger, *Grundsätze der Volkswirtschaftslehre*, Wien 1871, VIII.

But to which physical phenomenon, to which natural scientific method is the induction being concretely made? Generally speaking, mechanics exercised the strongest influence on the neoclassical school: "the theory here given may be described as the mechanics of utility and self-interest"[13] and "the theory of economic science thus acquires the rigor of rational mechanics."[14] Still, mechanics circumscribes a broad domain containing very distinct methods. Thus, Newtonian physics deals with the movement of a body that once set in motion will continue to move uniformly until it is compelled to change that state by forces impressed upon it.[15] Classical mechanics, in contrast, specifies a procedure for determining the equations of motion for a mass point that is governed by certain constraints and limits. To this end, certain side conditions or conditional equations are formulated which the motion of the mass point must fulfill. The mathematical formulation of these side conditions makes it possible to loosen the Newtonian mechanical frame of reference, which strictly speaking only encompasses path coordinates in three dimensional space, and to translate the knowledge of classical mechanics to phenomena other than the spatial motion of a mass point.[16] Physical space no longer serves, here, as the guiding metaphor, but instead the metaphor of energy and of the energy- and force fields. This is the metaphor to which the founders of neoclassical theory referred in order to justify an exact copy of the mathematical structure.

> "The application of mathematics to the world of soul is countenanced by the hypothesis ...that Pleasure is the concomitant of Energy. Energy may be regarded as the central idea of Mathematical Psychics: maximum energy the object of the principle investigations in that science. (...) 'Mecanique Sociale' may one day take her place along with 'Mecanique Celeste', enthroned upon the double-sided height of one maximum principle, the supreme pinnacle of moral as of physical science. As the movements of each particle, constrained or loose, in a material cosmos are continually subordinated to one maximum sum-total of accumulated energy, so the movements of each soul whether selfishly isolated or linked sympathetically, may continually realize the maximum energy of pleasure. (...) The invisible energy of

---

[13] W.S. Jevons, *The Theory of Political Economy*, Harmondsworth 1970, 90.
[14] V. Pareto cited in P. Mirowski, *More Heat than Light*, 221.
[15] See for instance F. Scheck, *Mechanik, Von den Newtonschen Gesetzen zum deterministischen Chaos*, Berlin et al. 1994, 1.
[16] For the concept of canonical mechanics, see, for example, H. Stephani, G. Kluge, *Theoretische Mechanik, Punkt- und Kontinuumsmechanik*, Heidelberg et al. 1995, 67.

electricity is grasped by the marvelous methods of Lagrange, the invisible energy of pleasure may admit of a similar handling."[17]

Translation of the insights of classical mechanics to the economic context is far-reaching, as is made clear particularly in Irving Fischer's work. He put into a table some of the important concepts of classical mechanics juxtaposed to economic concepts. For example, energy and utility, force and marginal utility, and space and goods are all paired up.[18] Fischer was absolutely in the dark as to the commonalties of the context in which these were conceived; this mental obliquity has not essentially been shot through with light up to the present day.[19] The commonalties have always either been negligently or partially reconstructed, if they are reconstructed at all.[20] They still operate as unthought presuppositions.

In order to reflect explicitly upon the important, essential properties of physics metaphors, the locus of thought should be changed. As well as elaborating some of these properties here, we will also see after possible analogies in the economic context of utility maximization. Let's turn firstly to the physical metaphor of the field of force. This is of particular interest since Nishida cited it as an example in order to describe the way in which a basho determines and sustains elements and their relationships in itself.[21] In a field of force a moving particle encounters a force that has an effect on it only relative to the particle's position in space.[22] It is thus essentially distinct from the simple concept of space:

> "Physical objects are related to each other in space, but the relation between physical objects and space in the Newtonian sense is merely that of 'being-in.' There is no sense in saying that the relations of the objects are established and determined by this physical space."[23]

---

[17] F.Y. Edgeworth, *Mathematical Psychics, An Essay on the Application of Mathematics to the Moral Sciences*, London 1881, 9-13.
[18] I. Fisher, *Mathematical Investigations into the Theory of Value and Prices*, New Haven 1925, 85-86.
[19] This statement relates to *mainstream* economics. See. P. Mirowski, *More Heat than Light*, and P. Mirowski, *Against Mechanism, Protecting Economics from Sc*ience, New Jersey 1988. Essential aspects of my work depend on Mirowski's research.
[20] P. Mirowski, *More Heat than Light*, chapt. 5.
[21] For the metaphor of the force field see K. Nishida, *Logik des Ortes*, 80.
[22] See. *Fachlexikon ABC Physik*, Vol. 1, Thun-Frankfurt/Main 1989.
[23] R.J. Wargo, *The Logic of Basho*, 196.

Thus while space is 'open' in the sense that it supports each object's movements, the field of force determines the movements of the elements inside it. Even more importantly, the objects become determined through their positions in the field. In order to make this possible, the relations between the elements and the field must be redefined in comparison to the concept of space:

> "Merely to say that the physical objects are spatial says nothing more than objects are in space. But, if the relation of the objects and space is to be made tighter than this, if the objects are to be seen as determinations of the place in which they are, there must be a re-interpretation of the nature of objects. The substantiality of the objects is to be transferred to the field in which they lie and the objects are thus 're-duced' to energy. The objects are now seen as accumulations of energy related not in space, but in the energy field of which they are a part."[24]

Objects are only regarded as concentrations of energy. They exhibit no further outstanding properties. Their existence is solely determined by the fact that they are elements of a field of force. Or, in other words: "The substantiality of things merges into the relation to the locus in which it is found."[25] Not only the properties of elements are completely determined through the underlying energy field, but even their relationships to each other.[26] We do not observe the different concentrations of energy as independent entities which are to be subsequently related each with the other. Rather, their relationships right from the start are always determined through the underlying energy field. Accordingly, it is the field itself that mediates the unity between the different objects, the latter always being interpreted as concentrations of energy.

Nishida sees the reduction of objects to concentrations of energy and the interpretation of these concentrations as a part, or an expression of the underlying energy field as an example of basho, because the existence of an energy field must (at least implicitly) be assumed, in order to be able to determine the individual concentrations of energy in each location of the field as well as their relations to each other. And the concept of energy concentration must again be indispensably presupposed in order to reduce

---

[24] Ibid., 196.
[25] K. Nishida, *Logik des Ortes*, 80.
[26] The concept of the energy field can be used here analogously to the force field, since, as we will thematise later on, a *conservative* system is supposed as our basis. In such a system, the scalar magnitudes of energy and the vector quantities of force are merely two aspects of the same field.

all objects to states of energy. Before discussing further essential properties of the energy field as *basho*, we have to show just how the concepts of energy and of a field of force are supposed to be translated into economic terms. Normally within neoclassical theory the economic application of the field metaphor is made intuitive by way of physical phenomena. Take, for example, Samuelson, who asks his reader to imagine a magnetic field in order to gain an intuitive grasp of economic models:

> "Every student of elementary physics has dusted iron fillings on a piece of paper suspended on a permanent magnet. The little fillings become magnetized and orient themselves in a simple pattern. To the mind's eye these appear as 'lines of force' of the magnetic field."[27]

But this injunction remains empty because it doesn't express how the field metaphor in the economic context can actually be conceived, and thus what kinds of things are supposed to be represented by the iron filings, the pattern, and the lines of force in this connection. The initial intuition, here, is something else that must be explicitly represented in order to make the field metaphor in economics practically meaningful. Let's take a closer look at utility theory, seeking for possible analogies. The first thing that emerges is how the concept of physical space translates into the concept of goods or commodities in neoclassical terms, or more exactly into commodity space.[28] But we don't think of this space as emanating from the commodity itself. Rather, analogously to the field of force in physics, an invisible field underlies it, which one can call a utility field, because each point in the space of commodities is characterized solely through a specific, measurable quantity of utility. We have to recognize this by the way in which we define the so-called indifference curves as the binding points of equal utility.[29] They thus become analogous in thought to the lines of equal potential energy in a physical field. This exposes the basis for the structural identity of the concept of energy with utility, as Fisher postulated.[30] Points in commodity space, and thus bundles of commodities, are solely imagined inside of the horizon of the utility that they bring. Just as

---

[27] P.A. Samuelson, "Consumption Theory in Terms of Revealed Preference," in: J.E. Stiglitz (ed.), *The Collected Scientific Papers of Paul A. Samuelson*, Vol. I, Cambridge (Mass.) 1966, 66, footnote.

[28] I. Fisher, *Mathematical Investigations into the Theory of Value and Prices*, 85.

[29] See for example the statement: "An... indifference curve characterizes a specific utility level." W. Cezanne, *Allgemeine Volkswirtschaftslehre*, 84.

[30] This does not apply to energy in general, but only to one form of energy: potential energy. See following sections.

points of space in the energy field are thought of as energy concentrations, so, too, we understand the concept of commodities only in terms of their utility.

Yet notice: every point within a physical field represents not only an energy state, and thus a scalar magnitude, but also a direction in which the forces of the field operate. This is represented by the vector quantity of the force, which by definition shows its modulo as well as direction or tendency. This vector quantity is translated in utility theory in the concept of marginal utility.[31] This marginal utility gives us the direction of the relative position changes in commodity space, which are supported by the underlying utility field. Thus, the relations or movements between individual commodity bundles in each point of commodity space seem completely determined. Yet what determines the individual 'utility levels' and puts them in relation one with the other? Or, to put the question in other terms: when commodity space in neoclassical theory is imagined to be analogous to physical space, and utility analogous to (potential) energy, what place in this analogy is to be taken by the energy field? The concept of the field of utility certainly represents a possible answer, but it remains imprecise so long as is isn't clear how one imagines such a field. What should be emphasized here is that such a concrete reference is necessary if we are to relate economics to energetics in a meaningful way. As our previous examination of mechanics showed, an energy field in the sense of an underlying *basho* must be assumed, in order to be able to determine the different energy concentrations and position them in relation one to another. An (at least implicit) understanding of this field necessarily presupposes that of energy. Yet, within neoclassical theory, the question of how we may conceive of such a field in the economic context is seldom explicitly posed, and never correctly answered; it isn't even seen that such an analogy is not contingent.

The idea of a utility field cannot be deduced from the concept of utility, because the field in the sense of a basho is the preceding concept inside of which utility can be meaningfully conceived. Rather, an initial intuition in the sense of Nishida's 'place of absolute nothingness' must be sought. Such an intuition becomes visible if one directs one's eyes to the fact that the concepts of utility and of indifference curves are always related to the decision making processes of individuals who correlate each bundle of commodities to a specific utility and choose between different bundles in

---

[31] I. Fisher, *Mathematical Investigations into the Theory of Value and Prices*, 85.

order to maximize their utility.[32] Commodities or bundles of commodities are thus determined through individuals calculating their utility: It is "the image of mental energy suffusing a commodity space" which serves as the implicit guiding metaphor here.[33] It is a kind of consciousness field[34], which actually never emerges visibly in the utility concept, but analogously to the physical field of force, represents the locus, in which all elements and their relations are implicitly thought. Such a consciousness field is not the content or object of neoclassical theory, but an unthought presupposition that is not objectified or explicitly reflected by it:

> "The field of consciousness has a negative sense in that it is not just another phenomena of consciousness. Yet, while the field of consciousness is not just another of the phenomena of consciousness, neither is it merely the absence of phenomena. One can distinguish the field of consciousness from the various phenomena which come into being and pass away as the unchanging field in which these changes occur."[35]

The field of consciousness is the locus, in which the existence of all objects is thought. It remains a place of nothingness, however, from the viewpoint of that objective perspective in which only things and their relations among each other are described. It is, as that which underlies the relations, not a phenomena that enters into our focus, and insofar as it doesn't it is absolute nothing[36]:

> "The whole point of referring to the field of consciousness as a basho is to bring out the feature that the field is absolute nothing in respect to the elements in the field. It is not the sort of thing that could be said to exist or not exist, but, at the same time, it is precisely the field that provides the unity for the conscious phenomena. ... The field provides the defining characteristic whereby these phenomena are seen as individual elements of a certain type being related in certain ways. It provides this unity not in the sense that it is a discovered unity among previously given entities,

---

[32] In the textbooks, such an individual is usually called a consumer. See for example, H.R. Varian, *Grundzüge der Mikroökonomik*, chapt. 2-5. More abstractly, some textbooks mention the decision unit of the ‚household' as for instance in W. Cezanne, *Allgemeine Volkswirtschaftslehre*, chapt. 4.

[33] P. Mirowski, *More Heat than Light*, 218.

[34] Japanese: *ishiki no ya*. Nishida applies this concept close to this of the place to characterize consciousness, by which he leans on the metaphor of the force field in one way, but in another is making an essential distinction from it. This distinction, later on, will have a role to play. For this concept see K. Nishida, *Logik des Ortes*, 289.

[35] R.J. Wargo, *The Logic of Basho*, 200.

[36] R. Elberfeld, *Das Verstehen der Kulturen*, 111.

but it provides the unity by providing the given. It is what allows the discovery of a unity among entities."[37]

This entails that the individual herself within the objective method cannot emerge as a visible phenomena because she is always only presupposed as a field of consciousness. Don't imagine the individual as a particle that will be described within the energy field[38], but much more as an energy field that represents the invisible presupposition supporting this description:

> "The identification of a particle with an individual is incorrect. The individual in this model is only made manifest by its psychology, and his psychology is only portrayed as a field of preferences. It is the energy/utility that provides the only ontological identity of the actor in the mathematics ... The individual is to be found nowhere on the graph, just as energy cannot be conceptualized as being located at particular coordinates in a field. The energy is constitutive of the field, and is in the field, but nothing more can be said of it. It does not describe a material property. ... The somewhat spectral neoclassical economic man ...[is] a field of possibilities that can characterize an empty commodity space."[39]

The individual, who appears as the tacit foundation of economic theorizing, does not conform to the description of a commodity, nor may she be characterized by way of some specific level of utility. Also, she cannot be represented as a functional relation of variables. In this sense she exhibits the property of a *basho*, to establish or mediate unity and relation between distinct points within its confines, without thereby making itself explicitly visible. We can see, in consideration of this fact, how neoclassical theory can maintain, with a certain justice, that it describes only thing-thing relations and is in this sense an objective science. But this claim of objectivity is logically preceded by the tacit assumption of a field of consciousness that determines these things and their relations to each other as a locus, at least insofar as the core concept of optimization is concerned. The following should help us to grasp some of the most important aspects of this assumption.

The individual consciousness is the locus, in which the concepts of utility and of commodities are generated. The bundle of goods are neither given data, nor is there such a thing as a commodity space that exists independ-

---

[37] R.J. Wargo, *The Logic of Basho*, 201-202.
[38] This image is widespread in economics. See, for instance, I. Fisher, *Mathematical Investigations into the Theory of Value and Prices*, 85.
[39] P. Mirowski, *More Heat than Light*, 229.

ently of the field of consciousness. Economic constants, on the contrary, are to be construed as dependent on the human consciousness.[40] In this sense it is correct to speak of the "subjective character of the data of the social sciences."[41] But allow us to remark that the relation between commodities and human consciousness can't be described within a single domain of discourse. We must imagine them, rather, as a relation of elements and their locus, or, to put it in other words, of the determined to the determiner. As the Logic of Place furthermore indicates, human consciousness as the determining locus remains invisible from the perspective of the commodities themselves. The concept of commodities simply doesn't give us any help in predicating the 'what' of consciousness, how we are to conceive of it. Rather, consciousness is always already implicit as a given that lies in the background of all phenomena, without becoming visible itself. Here Marshall is pretty much justified in saying that one cannot measure affections of the mind directly. But he gets it upside down when he further opines that consciousness can be inferred indirectly through its effects, thus through measurable acts of decision-making within the space of commodities: "It is essential to note that the economist does not claim to measure any affection of the mind itself; but only indirectly through its effects."[42] Marshall's assessment that we are to infer from quantitatively measurable activity outputs to the consciousness of the agent is the conventional wisdom of economic theory.[43] But analogies to the field of force make it clear that neither points in space nor movements between them adequately describe the underlying field. The field determines all relations of its elements but remains itself necessarily hidden from the viewpoint of these elements. Marshall's postulated route of inference shows itself, therefore, as logically impossible.

In neoclassical theory it is often concluded that, given this logical impossibility, one cannot or need not proffer any statement whatsoever about consciousness. So, for instance, it is assumed that we can get everything necessary to derive our equilibrium or maximization theories out of the observation of the results of action, without connecting it to the concept of util-

---

[40] A.C. Pigou, *Economics of Welfare*, London 1960, 9.
[41] F.A. Hayek, *Missbrauch und Verfall der Vernunft, Ein Fragment*, Frankfurt/Main 1959, 28.
[42] A. Marshall, *Principles of Economics*, 15.
[43] See for example Jevon's statement: "It is from the quantitative effects of the feelings that we must estimate their comparative amounts." W.S. Jevons, *The Theory of Political Economy*, 83.

ity or consciousness.[44] From the viewpoint of the Logic of Place, this assumption is problematic. Because though the relation to consciousness may truly be implicit, still, consciousness always remains the context, in which the concepts of commodity, commodity space, or demand are conceived. But doesn't the Logic of Place face a dilemma then because of this insight? For on the one side, consciousness must be specified as the locus determining the commodities and their relations to each other. But on the other side, one appears to be unable to say anything about the hows and whys of its particular properties. The way out of this dilemma is to change the domain of discourse.

The field underlying the elements is actually, from the viewpoint of the elements themselves, a place of absolute nothingness; but it can become itself an object of scientific recognition in a new domain of discourse. This points to the necessity of making a conceptual leap to an act of cognition on a greater scale, one that contains that context which remained, heretofore, unthought:

> "What is important is the transition from the field as determining the elements in it, to the field as an object, in which the field itself is a particular which no longer determines entities, but merely can be said to possess characteristics."[45]

The necessary presuppositions can be reflected in a new domain of discourse. These are the presuppositions that must be assumed, in order to conceive of the elements of the field and their relations one with another in the original domain of discourse. Such an act of reflection puts neoclassical theory clearly before a problem, since it refers to the necessity to explicitly deal with human consciousness. And with that we must waive the claim to describe only the relations of things in our objective methodology, sharply separating it from all subjective methods. This is a claim that has often been fiercely defended in neoclassical theory. Nishida's Logic of Place, on the contrary, refers to the status of the division of subjective and objective science being not absolute. Rather, the objective sciences always already presuppose certain propositions about subjective consciousness:

> "So, Nishida maintains, the field or place of empirical judgments is really within the encompassing field of judgments about self-consciousness. Empiricism is actually

---

[44] For example, see V. Pareto quoted in G.M.E. Eisermann, *Vilfredo Pareto und sein „Manuale", Vademecum zu einem Klassiker der Ökonomie und Soziologie*, Düsseldorf 1992, 100.
[45] R.J. Wargo, *The Logic of Basho*, 198.

dependent on, stands within, a field of judgments about self. Since empirical judgments, as empirical judgments, ignore the being of the self, treat it as a nothing; this encompassing basho can be called the basho of relative nothingness. The self is, relative to empirical statements, treated as a nothing. Of course, from the standpoint of the basho of relative nothingness, however, the self is very much something, the very thing empiricism assumes yet ignores."[46]

It should be made clear that this doesn't mean that we can simply substitute subjective methods for objective methods. The latter is no substitute for the formal logic of objective methodologies, but its presupposition. The thing-thing-relations, thematized by neoclassical theory, are embedded in a broader or more encompassing context, which necessarily encompasses the consciousness of the economic actors. By reason of its claim to be an objective science, this further context can clearly not be explicitly thematized within neoclassical theory. Still we can elaborate the properties of the consciousness field that implicitly precedes neoclassical theory.

3.1.2 The Implicit Properties of the Field of Consciousness

Our key to understanding those properties of consciousness implicitly assumed by neoclassical economics lies in examining more closely how the theory imitates the physical metaphor of energy. As we have already shown, neoclassical economics uses this metaphor to describe economic phenomena, and in particular using the concept of energy as analogous to that of utility. But this is only meaningful insofar as the concept of the energy field underlying energy shows the same characteristics as the (implicit) concept of the field of consciousness underlying utility. Only when a locus shows the same properties as another can the elements and their relationships to each other in the former be determined in the same way as in the latter. In other words, only a formal equality of the underlying locus permits neoclassical economics to postulate the exact same mathematical relations as are found in mechanics. But this necessary pre-condition was either not recognized by neoclassical economists or treated in their surveys as superfluous. Thus, Samuelson takes as his point of departure, in his Nobel Memorial Lecture, that the functional relations in an economic system correspond to those in a physical system. Accordingly he applies mathematical formulas that describe an entropy maximizing, thermodynamic

---

[46] T.P. Kasulis, "Foreword", in: R.E. Carter, *The Nothingness beyond God*, xv. The argument in this citation is related to the natural sciences only. It is transposed here to neoclassical economics, which regards the natural sciences as its model.

system, directly to the decision-making problem confronting an economic actor and describes this as a "maximum system".[47] Yet he denotes all attempts to explicitly enumerate the analogies between the physical and economic system as nonsensical:

> "There is really nothing more pathetic than to have an economist or a retired engineer try to force analogies between the concepts of physics and the concepts of economics. How many dreary papers have I had to referee in which the author is looking for something that corresponds to entropy or to one or another form of energy. Nonsensical laws, such as the law of conservation of purchasing power, represent spurious social science imitations of the important law of the conservation of energy."[48]

Yet Samuelson himself has to implicitly proceed from such an analogy in order to speak meaningfully in the economic context of the maximum system. It always remains, in his work, an unthought presupposition.

In order to elaborate the essential properties of consciousness as they are tacitly assumed by neoclassical theory, the first requisite is to observe the concepts of marginal utility and of utility more closely. Lets start with the physical concept of unlimited degree of freedom of movement. This states that a particle in an energy field, in the absence of outer influences, moves uniformly to lower levels of potential energy. This guiding principle of mechanics is translated into the economic idea that in a commodity space movement always tends to a greater level of utility. Thus, if one traces many indifference curves in a commodity space and assumes that utility rises towards the northeastern quadrant of the diagram, every movement must infinitely follow in this direction (in the absence of further conditions). This corresponds exactly to the idea of mechanics, with the only difference being that the latter assumes a movement to energy states of lower potential.[49] This idea, in the context of economics, must be somewhat dif-

---

[47] P.A. Samuelson, "Maximum Principles in Analytical Economics," in: R.C. Merton (ed.), *The Collected Scientific Papers of Paul A. Samuelson*, Vol. III, Cambridge (Mass.) 1972, 8-9.

[48] P.A. Samuelson, "Maximum Principles in Analytical Economics," 8.

[49] This distinction leaves the graphic representation untouched. The mathematical representation is distinguished only in the second derivation between minima and maxima, so that a mathematical treatment of utility, only concentrating on the first derivation, can directly refer to the mathematics of canonical mechanics. „Calculus only distinguishes between local maxima and minima at the level of second derivatives, so most of the mathematical apparatus of first derivatives could be retained thouroughly unaltered from physics." P. Mirowski, *More Heat than Light*, 226.

ferently interpreted. After all, it implies that the consumer will always prefer a greater quantity of commodities to a smaller. Following utility theory, an increase of the quantity of commodities is automatically followed by an increase of the utility levels. This assumption is partly hidden in the neoclassical postulate that the slope of the indifference curve must be negative.[50] But it is formulated explicitly in the assumption of non-satiation.[51] It is "typically assumed, that more is better."[52] "The individual is never completely satisfied, but can, in principle, always think of an improvement through another bundle of commodities. Simplifying this, we assume a rule stating that an individual prefers to get more of all commodities."[53]

Economic theory can't countenance satiation without giving up the analogy to physics. Incorporating satiation into the theory means that a bundle of commodities could be found, by which the decision-making process of the individual should come to rest of itself, without being externally constrained. Such a resting or equilibrium point is unthinkable in physics, since in the latter every mass point is thought of as moving forward infinitely so long as it is not limited in its freedom of movement by outside forces. While this idea may work with physical bodies, its translation to the economic context implies that there is not only an unlimited space of commodities, but also an unlimited appropriation directed at a surplus of commodities. But how could one possibly explain such an unlimited appropriation? This question is not answered unambiguously in economics. Generally however one begins by saying that it implies an infinity of human needs. This becomes somewhat clearer given that the neoclassical utility theory is formulated as a "maximization of the overall satisfaction of needs."[54] Yet such an explanation remains, in itself, without content so long as the concept of need is ambiguous. In the course of further interpretation it should become clear, that the effort to obtain more and more

---

[50] See for example H.R. Varian, *Grundzüge der Mikroökonomik*, 43.
[51] K.J. Arrow and F.H. Hahn, *General Competitive Analysis*, San Francisco-Edinburgh 1971, 78. Marshall describes the phenomenon of non-satiation like this: "The total utility of a thing increases with every increase in his stock of it, but not as fast as his stock increases." *Principles of Economics*, 93.
[52] H.R. Varian, *Grundzüge der Mikroökonomik*, 42.
[53] W. Reiß, *Mikroökonomische Theorie, Historisch fundierte Einführung*, München-Wien 1996, 239.
[54] B.P. Priddat and E.K. Seifert, "Gerechtigkeit und Klugheit – Spuren aristotelischen Denkens in der modernen Ökonomie," in: B. Bernd, M. Held (ed.), *Ökonomische Theorie und Ethik*, Frankfurt/Main-New York 1987, 67.

commodities can really only be interpreted as striving to obtain an infinite amount of money.

Movement in an energy field to a lower level of potential energy is a dynamic notion. It is reduced, however, in classical mechanics to a static concept. The idea of equilibrium serves, here, as a guiding metaphor. Equilibrium describes that point in which opposing forces cancel each other out, thus bringing about a resting point. This concept, too, was translated by the neoclassicals to the economic context and elevated to an essential analogue. Accordingly, Jevons in his Theory of the Political Economy explicitly refers to the law of the lever[55], and Marshall describes supply and demand as balancing forces, which correspond to a mechanical equilibrium.[56] Let's cast a glance at the essential marks of such an equilibrium, as it is presupposed in classical mechanics. A resting place is brought about when the freedom of movement of a mass point in a physical field is constrained. A force effects a point in the field of force in that it as a vector quantity assigns direction and length (or the modulus) of movement which a mass point would achieve were it not constrained in its movement. In classical mechanics, this force is designated as impressed force, in order to put into relief its independence from all extrinsic conditions.[57] Now additional forces still have effects on this mass point, and they will exercise these effects from outside on the body of the mass point. These represent auxiliary conditions and are intuitively represented as constraining forces.[58] They exercise an extrinsic compulsion on the body that countereffects the impressing force. The body is in motion only until the constraining forces and the impressed force mutually cancel each other. If, for example, constraining forces cause a body to move along a certain path, the body will come to rest as soon as it has reached the line of least possible potential. The neoclassicals directly appropriated this form of presentation to explain their concept of utility maximization. For this, they transposed the concepts of the impressed and constraining forces to the economic context in the following manner: They interpreted the impressed force as a 'natural' striving to ever higher utility potentials, by which the force vector finds its corre-

---

[55] W.S. Jevons, *The Theory of Political Economy*, 144-47. Jevon's dedicates a whole section to the "theory of the lever."
[56] Those balancing forces "correspond rather to the mechanical equilibrium of a stone hanging on an elastic string, or a number of balls resting against one another in a basin." A. Marshall, *Principles of Economics*, 323.
[57] H. Stephani, G. Kluge, *Theoretische Mechanik*, 68.
[58] Ibid., 68.

spondence in the notion of marginal utility.[59] Thus for instance Jevons makes an equivalency between the force of gravitation and marginal utility.[60] The only movement-constraining auxiliary condition was then formulated as the budget line. In this way, the physicalistic representation of movement under auxiliary conditions received the following interpretation: selection between two commodities will follow the budget-line up to an equilibrium point corresponding to the highest possibly achievable level of utility.

But what exactly is equilibrized at such a point? A simple insight from physics says that a equilibrium of forces only exists when these forces can be measured exactly in the same fashion. One standard of measurement, as a mandatory presupposition, underlies all forces. While in mechanics this presupposition may be unproblematic, a standard measure of value in the framework of utility theory is in no way self explanatory. To begin with, however, we need to look away from the actual unity of standards of measurement and turn to the general criteria of unity and measurability. As it is so beautifully formulated by David Friedman:

> "We believe, that all of everything is numerable. My life is much more valuable than a waffle cone of ice cream exactly as a mountain is much higher than a grain of sand; but life and ice cream, just as mountain and sand, are measured with the same measure."[61]

Economic theory often simply proceeds as though the unified criteria of the standard of measurement is a property of the commodities, that can be ascribed to them next to other of their properties too. But the Logic of Place and the analogy to the (unified) field of force do show that this perception is false, or at least highly misleading. The reason is that in a field of force objects are exclusively interpreted as energy concentrations and their direction of movement as a force vector. From the view of the field the units of energy and of force are the only conceivable properties of all objects. Even though the latter might manifest different properties in other contexts, these are not to be identified in a domain of discourse that is supported by the field metaphor alone. To express this otherwise: the unified

---

[59] I. Fisher, *Mathematical Investigations into the Theory of Value and Prices*, 85. Fisher overlooks the fact that for an equilibrium of forces at least one other force must be specified.
[60] W.S. Jevons, *The Theory of Political Economy*, 146.
[61] D. Friedman, *Der ökonomische Code, Wie wirtschaftliches Denken unser Handeln bestimmt*, Frankfurt/Main 1999, 30.

standard of measurement is the horizon in which all objects are thought. It precedes them and presents the context, in which they appear as commodities. In utility theory, the unity of the standard of measurement becomes understandable by the fact that equilibrium can be specified for any point in commodity space.[62] The standard by which such an equilibrium is measured can not change from one point to another. On the contrary, its unity is what makes the concept of equilibrium intelligible in the first place. The unified standard of measurement is not something that is predicated of the objects next to other properties. Rather, it is the underlying context in which all objects are described and in which they become comparable.

To the condition of the unity of the standard of measurement in the framework of the field metaphor, we need to join that of measurability. In order to understand this condition in the economic context more precisely, we need to look at the budget line. We have already seen, that its slope represents the quantity of the constraining force which limits movement in commodity space.[63] But we haven't stated yet what unity such a 'force' is supposed to possess. The slope of the budget line describes by definition the rate of substitution of commodities: "The slope of the budget line has a nice economic interpretation. It measures the rate at which the market is willing so 'substitute' good 1 for good 2."[64] This definition clearly shows that the individual maximizing its utility presupposes the market – a social institution. (4.2.3) Here let's direct our attention not at this fact, but at a further essential presupposition. It is only meaningful to imagine the market being willing to substitute one commodity for another if a unified standard in the form of money is (implicitly) presupposed. In order to show this, let's look at a two-commodity case. An individual participating in a market exchanges commodity 1 directly for commodity 2. Out of the exchange relationship so established – for instance, 2 shirts for 3 pairs of socks – we can clearly establish the rate of substitution and thus the slope of the budget line. But this becomes harder in a three-commodity case, since here the individual can participate in three exchange markets. An unambiguous rate of substitution can be supposed to result here only if the

---

[62] See, for instance, P.A. Samuelson's statement: "By manipulating prices and income, we could cause the individual to come into equilibrium *at any (x, y) point*, at least within a given area." In: "Consumption Theory in Terms of Revealed Preference," 64.

[63] This is only valid for a *conservative* field. For the meaning of this condition in the economic context, see below.

[64] H.R. Varian, *Intermediate Microeconomics*, 23.

"transitivity of the exchange act" holds across three markets.[65] If two shirts are exchanged against three pairs of socks in one market, and in another are exchanged against four pairs of pants, then there has to be a third market in which four pairs of pants can be exchanged against three pairs of socks. Otherwise, multiple exchanges establish different rates of substitutions between two commodities, and you could not draw an unambiguous budget line. It is easy to see that this condition can be fulfilled, at most, accidentally. From this example it is clear that the neoclassicals must presuppose something totally different than the market's willingness to substitute every good for another good. The condition of the transitivity of the exchange act is always and only fulfilled when all commodities are exchanged at any given time against a single commodity. If the market is actually presupposed as the place of the determination of the rate of substitution, we can directly state: what generally takes the place of the universally distributed means of payment is money.[66] Money represents the (implicit) arithmetical unity, in which all other commodities and their ratios to each other can be expressed. By means of monetary units, the rate of substitution can without any further bother be represented as the ratio of commodity prices. Money, as Aristotle has already noticed, makes things equal. It constructs an overall equivalence.[67] This function of money as an arithmetical unity is brought up by Spinoza, when he says: "the quintessence of all things is money."[68] Money, thus, becomes a place of nothingness, in which all things are measured, while its own meaning cannot be realized through any kind of thing. At least, this holds valid within the market's sphere of transactions. And because money, like any other standard of measurement, "can only be defined, but cannot itself be measured, there

---

[65] This concept is found in K.-H. Brodbeck, *Zirkel des Wissens, Vom gesellschaftlichen Prozeß der Täuschung*, Aachen 2002, 381.

[66] J. Cartelier shows, with a similar argument, that even the neoclassical law of supply and demand can't be thought without the implicit presupposition of money. "It is", as Cartelier writes "incomplete without money, and money can only be integrated into it with some difficulty." In: *Das Geld*, Bergisch Gladbach 1996, 25. Brodbeck, too, shows with the example of Marx that commodity exchange in many economic models always presupposes money, but cannot provide the basis for it. K.-H. Brodbeck, *Zirkel des Wissens*, 375-382. From the view of the Logic of Place we can say that money is a place of nothingness, in which economic thought rests, without itself being explicitly made into an object of reflection.

[67] Aristotle, *Nikomachische Ethik*, trans. v. O. Gigon, Zürich 1952, 165. See also 4.2.2.

[68] Cited in K.-H. Brodbeck, *Die fragwürdigen Grundlagen der Ökonomie*, 213.

arise problems in finding expression for the market value of money."[69] It becomes an unthought presupposition.

At this point money is presupposed not only as the (implicit) arithmetical unity of market transactions, it also becomes the measure of individual utility. Since neoclassical economics proceeds from the assumption of an equilibrium between the price vectors of the budget line (the constraining force) and marginal utility (the impressed force), it has to follow that the same unity underlies marginal utility as the price vectors of the budget line. The marginal utility of a commodity is therefore to be determined in every point of commodity space in terms of the homogeneous standard of money per volume of commodities. Most of the first generation of neoclassical economists shrank from asserting this idea.[70] Later economists clearly formulated it. For example, Marshall says that money has a constant marginal utility.[71] But what does this mean for the concept of utility itself? The answer is revealed when we see that the neoclassical usage of 'utility' is analogous to a form of energy. Force and energy are in classical mechanics directly convertible or transformable one into the other; every continuous and integrable function of the vector quantity force can be interpreted as a form of energy. Force and energy merely describe two distinct aspects of the same field.[72] The neoclassicals normally assumed the analogy here held, and that marginal utility allowed itself to be represented as a derivative of a continuous and integrable function. This function, in turn, was interpreted as the indifference curve (thus, the line of equivalent utilities).[73] Marginal utility and utility appear thus as arithmetically transformable into one another. But this was only thinkable, if the vector quantity of marginal utility (expressed in the units of money per stock) corresponded to a clear scalar quantity, which consisted exclusively of units of money. And this means that, in fact, the concept of utility and of money must be interchangeable. "The concept of utility is structurally identical with that of money."[74] In other words: in the context of the theory of utility maximization, "money and utility are effectively ontologically identical."[75]

---

[69] H.H. Lechner, *Währungspolitik*, Berlin-New York 1988, 326.
[70] P. Mirowski, *More Heat than Light*, 241.
[71] A. Marshall, *Principles of Economics*, 842.
[72] Again, this is valid only for the conservative force field.
[73] See, for example, P.A. Samuelson, "Consumption Theory in Terms of Revealed Preference," 64.
[74] K.-H. Brodbeck, *Die fragwürdigen Grundlagen der Ökonomie*, 233.
[75] P. Mirowski, *More Heat than Light*, 231.

Thus, Money represents the unity of the measure of value. This unthought presupposition shows that the neoclassicals efforts to ground utility theory in the laws of nature and not in the everyday phenomena of money must be judged to be fruitless:

> "The overall thrust of the emulation of physics by economics was to discover the hidden fundamental natural determinants of value that lay behind the veil of everyday phenomena of money prices and incomes. Utility as a field of scalar potentials fit that pattern quite nicely, but the physics metaphor did not stop here. A potential field should have been coupled with a well-defined set of transformation algorithms into kinetic forces, because the field and the forces were just two aspects of the same ontological thing. Strictly and logically interpreted, the analogy would suggest that money and utility were the same ontological thing. (...) The whole contraption of the utility function [was] redundant, because money provided the unique and sufficient direct cardinal measure of utility in that regime. (...) If money was a sufficient and credible measure of value, then the whole project of a science-based value theory, which aimed to uncover the fundamental lawlike reality obscured by the blooming buzzing phenomenological diversity, was superfluous."[76]

The concepts of marginal utility and of utility simply conceal what experience, in the sense of a concrete intuition, underlies neoclassical maximization: the monetary process. Later, we will make clear how this can be interpreted as an essential element of economic habitualization. (3.3.2) But it is already clear, at this point, that money fulfills two essential functions. First, only the property of monetary value can be ascribed to commodities in the neoclassical domain of discourse. The utility concept, which seems to suggest the observation of a number of properties, is therefore misleading. It thus becomes clear that the concept of utility cannot be interpreted as need; a commodity isn't valued insofar as it meets a physiological need, like nourishment or sleep, but only insofar as it is either numerable in terms of money, or convertible into money. Secondly, the neoclassical assumption that higher levels of utility are always preferred to lower levels of utility can now be more pointedly formulated: it states nothing more than that more money is preferred in every case to less money. This discloses the logical substratum beneath the previously mentioned theorem of non-satiation: every greater amount of a commodity is preferred to every lesser amount only if a monetary value lies in the difference. It is therefore incorrect to interpret the theorem of non-satiation physiologically or in the horizon of the concept of need:

---

[76] Ibid., 250-251.

"Actually hardly anyone would refuse to take 1000 boxes of champagne over one box, but certainly not with the view of drinking them in some given period of time. Every commodity represents a potential monetary value and can be sold. Yet to transform this infinity... in a preference function for consumer commodities is simply a quid pro quo. Neoclassical economics reads an infinity into the need that cannot be ascribed to the need physiologically. Nobody prefers 10 tons of ice cream to 9 tons, because he wants to eat it."[77]

The meaning of money also allows us to make explicit the implicit neoclassical maxims about the consciousness of the economic actor. Most importantly, we have to recognize that utility and money become mutually identical within the field of consciousness of the economic actor himself. Only in this field are utility and money recognized as one and the same thing. Thus it hardly matters whether the economist (implicitly) accords the key role to money in his theory; it is important that the actor herself does so. What is presupposed here, is that the agent values the commodities only according to their property of being monetizable. In addition, she has to be considered a calculating and striving character. Calculating, because she values every action alternative by the standard of money. And striving, because she constantly prefers more to less money.[78] These are the necessary properties of consciousness which the neoclassical economists must implicitly presuppose when they transpose the concept of optimization into the economic context. This is the locus in which the objective methodology of utility maximization is implicitly grounded. This also means: if persons do not have a striving, calculating character, their activity cannot be described in the framework of the theory of utility maximization. The limitation of the value of this theory lies in the grounding of this unthought presupposition. It cannot be discussed explicitly within this theory itself.

It is important to remark that our argument does not signify unconditionally a critique of the unthought presuppositions of neoclassical theory with regard to consciousness. It also doesn't imply saying that persons do not actually strive for more money. Rather, our questions derive from the logical critic of the neoclassical style of reasoning, imitating the concept of optimization from mechanics without explicitly showing what conditions

---

[77] K.-H. Brodbeck, *Die fragwürdigen Grundlagen der Ökonomie*, 231.

[78] J.S. Mill describes this presupposition in regard to political economics a little simplistically: "Political economy considers mankind as occupied *solely in acquiring and consuming wealth*." In: "On the Definition of Political Economy, and on the Method of Investigation Proper to It," *Collected Works*, Vol. IV, Toronto 1967, 322.

consciousness must satisfy to make such an appropriation meaningful. Our critique is directed at the fact that these conditions are not made transparent, but continually rest as the locus of nothingness in the background of this supposedly objective methodology. This critique parallels the one Nishida directed upon the objective sciences in general. These sciences, Nishida claimed, rest their objective postulates upon assumptions about the consciousness that they ignore at the same time.[79] These assumptions guide and determine the scientist's thought without being themselves thought.[80] But such self-reflection cannot succeed without giving up the claim to be an objective science, that makes no claims about the consciousness. Rather, we have to seek a domain of discourse that is deeper or more open and so can thematize the subjective character of agency explicitly.

Yet still, an important obstacle stands in the way of this search, because it is inscribed in the conventional wisdom of neoclassical economics that one can neglect the actual, subjective character of the actor even while making implicit assumptions about it. The main argument goes that it isn't a question of approximating reality, but only of the usefulness or appropriateness of a theory. Assumptions about humans are purely "as-if constructs." One can treat humans as though they were calculating – independently of whether this is actually the case – so long as this procedure delivers useable results.[81] The problem is hidden in the term 'useable.' Within neoclassical economics, this means mostly the theory's prognostic viability.[82] A theory should not only describe an existing situation, but should also be able to predict future ones.[83] In this sense, action is supposed to be calculable. Such calculability is the overall goal of the neoclassical research program. "Economic theory, as every science, tries to make calculable its empirical subject matter in order to hold sway over it."[84] Thus, it imitates the positivistic research ideal formulated in the following way by Comte:

---

[79] K. Nishida, *Intuition and Reflection in Self Consciousness*, transl. by Y. Takeuchi et al., New York 1987, 43.

[80] T. Kasulis, "Sushi, Science and Spirituality: Modern Japanese Philosophy and Its Views of Western Science," *Philosophy East & West*, 45/2 (1995), 238.

[81] H.Vaihinger, *Die Philosophie des Als-ob, System der theoretischen, praktischen und religiösen Fiktionen der Menschheit aufgrund eines idealistischen Positivismus*, Leipzig 1920, 28 and 341.

[82] M. Friedman, "The Methodology of Positive Economics," *Essays in Positive Economics*, Chicago 1953.

[83] Ibid.

[84] A. Suchanek, "*Der ökonomische Ansatz und das Verhältnis von Mensch, Institution und Erkenntnis*," in: B. Biervert, M. Held (ed.), *Die Natur des Menschen*, 80.

"The order of nature, which in every practical case is the result of the collectivity of laws governing events, must naturally be known to us in order for us to make efficacious changes in it, or at least to assimilate and submit our behavior to it, as when, for instance, against celestial processes any human intervention is impossible (...) [This idea is encompassing:] Because technology is no longer ... exclusively geometric, mechanical or chemical, etc., but also, and in the first place, political and moral."[85]

If the assumption about the calculability of actions is justified, then the meaning of the subjective consciousness will be practically thrust into the background. Assumptions about this consciousness will be purely meaningless as-if constructs, to which one should accord no significance. In principle, one must not relativize the validity of an objective methodology to specific assumptions concerning individual consciousness. The following section shall show that this assumption is, however, not tenable. Rather, our more accurate reading unmasks it as a logical impossibility.

3.1.3 A Time and Place-Independent Field of Consciousness

Up to now we have been dealing purely with a static equilibrium, which allows for describing instantaneous states, but not movements or changes in time. For a prognosis of future action, as is striven for in neoclassical theory, we require other concepts. Here once again classical mechanics is the foundation for explaining movement as a disturbance of a state of equilibrium. In principle we conceive that such a disturbance can be provoked either by changes in the impressed force or as a change in the constraining forces. The principle of the conservation of energy states clearly, that in a closed system the sum of energies is constant; it prohibits any spontaneous self-generated movement of the system. In another formulation the same principle says that energy is neither lost nor increased but purely transformed from one form into another. A closed system can (and must) change its state only when energy is exogenously either applied or taken away. Movement proceeds solely through changes in the impact constraining forces have on the system. The latter are transformed into energy and accordingly effect an alteration of the state of the system. In other words, movement is only be imagined as causally produced by outer factors – an idea that was appropriated by the neoclassicals. In their models, for example, a movement in commodity space will be described as causally effected through a change of the budget line: an increase of income leads

---

[85] A. Comte, *Reden über den Geist des Positivismus*, Hamburg 1966, 59-61.

automatically to a new equilibrium on a higher utility level, thus becoming transformed (completely) into utility. But such an idea implies that all the preconditions which underlie movement in classical mechanics permit adequate translation into the economic context. In particular, this applies in relation to the law of the conservation of energy – a fact to which little attention has been devoted within neoclassical theory.[86]

As we have already indicated, in neoclassical theory the concept of energy is translated into that of utility. Yet this translation remains, in one crucial point, incomplete; for in mechanics many energy forms are distinguished, and the transformations between them are discussed. The indifference curves (the lines of equal utility) can only be conceived to be analogous to one of these energy forms, potential energy. We yet lack an adequate translation of kinetic energy into the economic context. As the following citation makes clear, this form of energy finds its correspondence implicitly in income:

> "If the force components (of the budget constraint, SG) are interpreted as prices, then the interpretation of the integral of forces times displacements follows directly. Displacements along the axes translate into incremental changes in the amount of the corresponding commodity. The integral $\int(F_x d_x + F_y d_y + ...)$ which in physics is interpreted as the kinetic energy or work integral, in the neoclassical context becomes total expenditure, the integral of price times incremental changes in quantity. If one were to insist that the price of each incremental quantity of a generic good be a constant ... then the integral would collapse to a simple summation Σ ($F_x \cdot x + F_y \cdot y + ...$) which, if set equal to a constant, becomes the familiar budget constraint."[87]

The unit of income – which is equivalent to the sum of all expenditures – is no other than that of utility; and thus it is nothing else than money; otherwise, we couldn't construct a meaningful analogue to the perfect convertibility of the forms of energy. Add to this consideration the aspect that the constraining forces for the neoclassicals are interpreted as price vectors, and you run into some interesting aspects with regard to movement within the space of commodities. First and foremost, neoclassical theory implicitly has to create an analogy to the mechanical principle of energy conservation, since the functional relations that it takes unstintingly from physics are only conceivable within a field for which this principle is valid. In regard to the convertibility of forms of energy into one another this means that every change in income must be transformable into a change in utility.

---

[86] P. Mirowski, *More Heat than Light*, chapt. 5.
[87] Ibid., 226-27.

An increase of income leads obligatorily to an increase of utility. We may make this picture even more concrete. Following classical mechanics, movement can't arise spontaneously, but can only be causally influenced from the outside. This law of thermodynamics disallows, so to speak, that one can get "something for nothing." This is the guiding thought that the neoclassicals carried over into their theory of action, or the choice between alternatives, and in this way projected a mechanics of behavior that agreed fundamentally with behaviorism.[88] Following the analogy to thermodynamics, this behavioral mechanics contains an "exogenous production" theory:

> "Behavior is seen as the dependent variable of outside factors working on the organism. Thus, behavior is completely defined by the environment. The organism possesses no auto-dynamism or spontaneity, but reacts to the influence of exterior forces in a deterministic manner."[89]

This idea is clearly present in the concept of the incentive by which the physical concept of constraining forces may be translated into the economic context. An incentive is an exogenous change, that influences the individual to react in determined, predictable ways. Such systematic stimulus-reactions are explicitly presupposed in neoclassical economics, as behavior is interpreted as a systematic reaction to changes of exogeneously specified restricting factors:

> "A rational individual reacts to... changes 'systematically.' This means not only that he does not react accidentally or arbitrarily, but also that his reaction doesn't follow strictly from assumed rules independently of these changes. Therefore his behavior can be systematically influenced by setting up such incentives which essentially do emerge from changes of the sphere of activities (i.e., changes of restrictions)."[90]

---

[88] D. Müller, *Beiträge der Handlungstheorie für das Verständnis des Konsumentenverhaltens*, Frankfurt/Main et al. 1983, 32.

[89] Ibid, 34. Müller refers here to authors like Watson and Pavlov (under the heading of classical conditioning) as well as Thorndike, Guthrie und Skinner (under the heading of positive feedback learning).

[90] G. Kirchgässner, *Homo oeconomicus: das ökonomische Modell individuellen Verhaltens und seine Anwendung in den Wirtschafts- und Sozialwissenschaften*, Tübingen 1991, 17-18.

Occasionally incentives are also interpreted as material constraints, although clearly without explicitly naming the analogy to physics.[91] Even in this case, movement as in classical mechanics is considered completely determined through extrinsic factors. With these material constraints it is not a question of an indeterminate form of effecting 'force' or of conducting 'energy.' Rather, they are to be imagined as wholly concrete prices and incomes, because these concepts represent the only thinkable translations of the concepts 'constraining force' and 'kinetic energy.' This means that a movement in commodity space is exclusively effected through money, which represents the only thinkable unity of 'energy' of the underlying field. In the neoclassical domain of discourse another cause of change is not imaginable.

Yet, the analogy to mechanics refers implicitly to something else: the source or the origin of the 'constraining force.' The reason being that the budget line is defined as the only auxiliary condition within the theory of utility maximization. Its determinants are thought of as implicitly defined by the market, as we have already seen. Thus, in neoclassical economics it is the market that determines the equilibrium conditions, in as much as it determines the modulus and directions of the price vectors. Through the market's price mechanism the individual's choice – or, in keeping with our physics analogy to freedom of movement, his freedom of choice – is limited. "Prices were the forces and the market was the mechanism whereby the maximum of utility was realized."[92] This is the metaphor used to think about every action within neoclassical economics.

At this point, we should elaborate an important presupposition for the calculability of social action. It rests on an essential property of the underlying field: its (relative) immutability. In order to be able to calculate a transition from one equilibrium to another, the underlying field must be invariant, because optimization under auxiliary conditions only can be calculated for so-called 'conservative' fields. This presupposition implies for example, that the properties of the field must be time independent. The static calculation of an equilibrium says nothing about how a field behaves over time; it represents a purely instantaneous snapshot. Contrary to this, the concept of movement as, for example, expressed in the physical concept of

---

[91] See, in regard to the concept of material constraints, for instance, K. Homann, F. Blome-Drees, *Wirtschafts- und Unternehmensethik*, Göttingen 1992, 108. Here, actions are regarded as completely determined through the material constraints of the (economic) system.

[92] P. Mirowski, *More Heat than Light*, 228.

work, implies a change of state over time. In order to be able to calculate such a change, it has to be measured against something that remains constant in time. In classical mechanics the underlying field is always considered such a constant. Accordingly, it is assumed to be immobile and unchangeable through time. It remains as a substance against which change can be measured. This idea of a field that is unaltered through time images the irrevocable presupposition of any form of calculation in so far as it supports itself by reference to the field metaphor. Every calculable system "must be indifferent to the passage of historical time."[93] And even more, every calculable field must remain unchanged not only across the passage of time, but must be invariant against spatial changes, too. This presupposition says that every interaction of the field and its environment must be excluded. A conservative system for example reacts in the same way independently of whether it is embedded in the physical laboratory of a German or a Japanese university. Its reactions are also independent of the order of succession by which it passes through different circumstances. Its invariance against spatial changes implies path independence.

More generally formulated, any causal principle, which explains movements or changes, implies a constancy principle: change is to be measured against something that itself remains relatively unchanged.[94] This means among other things that a conservative system exhibits no innate degree of freedom. The movement of an ice skate blade, for instance, freely varying by the direction of its track, is already something that cannot be completely calculated. Mathematically formulated, the reason for this lies in the fact that the corresponding differential equation possesses no integrating factor. The equations of classical mechanics, since they presuppose complete integrability, cannot therefore be applied to such a problem.[95] Yet it isn't as though these equations are completely meaningless, since there does exist a realm in which the knowledge of them turns out to be extremely important: the world of machines. A machine is the ideal of what is controllable and calculable. Once constructed, it always functions in the same way. It does what it was created to do, independently of space and time. There

---

[93] Ibid., 28.
[94] Concerning the constancy principle, see D. Müller, *Beiträge der Handlungstheorie für das Verständnis des Konsumentenverhaltens*, 28.
[95] H. Stephani, G. Kluge, *Theoretische Mechanik*, 84-85. Im connection with inner degrees of freedom, physics speaks of *anholonomous* conditions: „Anholonomous conditions are truly interesting, but difficult to manipulate. (ibid., 85) But this means nothing other than the fact that, given such conditions, making a calculation or prognosis is impossible.

were machines, of course, before the first discoveries of mechanics; they served the latter as paradigm.[96] But it wasn't until classical mechanics that the principle of machinery could be formulated mathematically, given the background of a conservative field. Thereafter, a calculability became possible that enabled 19th century engineering science to achieve new discoveries and progress. Even before the formulations of classical mechanics, the machine served as a cognitive model for many sciences in order to describe the objects of their research:

> "The mechanical meshing together of the cog wheel ... became a cognitive model for the collective natural and human world. More than anyone else, Descartes described 'the earth and the whole visible world as a kind of machine', but even Descartes' critic, Leibniz, said: 'What I observe is that the clockwork of the world, without requiring further improvement, goes forward.'"[97]

This thought model was brought into the social and cognitive sciences to apply to human beings. Thus, for instance, Descartes even spoke of the "machine of our body."[98] Neoclassical economics built on this metaphor and tried to calculate human actions with the aid of the mathematical formulations of the principles of machinery. The idea of humans as machines accordingly became one of their most important conceptual presuppositions. Edgeworth formulated this quite clearly:

> "The conception of Man as a pleasure machine may justify and facilitate the employment of mechanical terms and Mathematical reasoning in social science."[99]

But are humans actually to be thought of as machines? Edgeworth owed an answer to this question that he never paid, as did the whole neoclassical tradition. The equivalence of man and machine always operates as the unthought domain of discourse, in which we think and reckon without the domain itself becoming an explicit object of reflection. But our previous considerations indicate what mandatory presupposition must be given in order to imagine man as a machine: his field of consciousness must be constituted like a conservative physical field. Otherwise, the neoclassical postulate that action can be calculated and predicted, as well as the idea that actions can be steered externally through incentives, is untenable.

---

[96] K.-H. Brodbeck, *Die fragwürdigen Grundlagen der Ökonomie*, 37.
[97] Ibid., 37.
[98] R. Descartes cited in K. H. Brodbeck, *Die fragwürdigen Grundlagen der Ökonomie*, 206.
[99] F.Y. Edgeworth, *Mathematical Psychics*, 15.

Mirowski explains the condition under which the property of a conservative field of force can be adequately translated into the context of human action. The consciousness (in the sense of the utility field) must be invariant:

> "The conservation of utility is one of the least understood unobtrusive postulates in neoclassical theory. It does not mean total utility is constant before and after a trade: Obviously a major tenet of neoclassicism is that trade increases the sum of realized utility. Rather, *the conservation of the utility field is invariably posited, independent of any and all exchange activity.*"[100]

The neoclassical tradition offers a plethora of interpretative options for such a conservation principle. The mathematically formulated presuppositions found in most textbooks are not, however, particularly interesting. Simply to assume continuity and integrability, or, as Varian does, to make the convexity of preferences a precondition[101], tells us nothing about how we are to consider these conditions in the economic context. Somewhat more interesting is the assumption, one could or might proceed from stable preferences. Accordingly Gary S. Becker, for instance, recognizes that solely the assumption of stable preferences gives a firm foundation "in order to forecast reactions to different variations."[102] Graphically interpreted this statement claims that the indifference curves (the lines of equivalent utility) are presumed to be invariable and thus by appearance seem to correspond to a conservative field of force. But what does the assumption of stable preferences really mean? Nothing other than that the actor always chooses between commodity bundles in the same way. His choice is thus time and place independent. Many authors think it would suffice here to postulate preferences against restrictions (exterior incentives) as more stable.[103] This doesn't make any sense, since change can only be measured against something which relative to the changing phenomena remains unchanged itself. A relative movement of substances or phenomena to each other without supplying a further, fixed relational point cannot be represented, at least not in the frame of the field metaphor. In light of this, a

---

[100] P. Mirowski, *More Heat than Light*, 273, emphasis added.
[101] H.R. Varian, *Mikroökonomie*, München-Wien 1985, 154.
[102] G.S. Becker, *Der ökonomische Ansatz zur Erklärung menschlichen Verhaltens*, Tübingen 1982, 4 and 6.
[103] G. Kirchgässner, *Homo oeconomicus*, 26.

change of taste or of predilection has to be completely excluded.[104] But in doing so, human impulses such as error or regret are implicitly bracketed away out of sight.[105] Mirowski writes of the meaning of regret:

> "Utility is conserved throughout the exchange process. (...) The realization of utility is made independent of the processes of consumption and exchange ... If there were a theme song for this pageant of atomistic maximizing units, it would have to be, 'No Regrets.' One suspects that many neoclassical economists would, at this point, aver that these assumptions have been made implicitly made in the past; but add that this was merely one step in a larger iteration towards more realistic and/or fruitful assumptions. If so, they would miss the major argument ...: without some such prior imposed conservation rules, there would be no constrained maximization at all in neoclassical economics. For if regret ... were possible, then there would be no fixed functions and no fixed extrema which could be located by the calculus."[106]

More generally formulated, no difference ought to exist between the wish to consume a commodity and the satisfaction of this wish. Otherwise the individual would change his preferences after the act of consumption.[107] A similar rule counts for the idea that the sequential order of consuming acts has no influence on the overall level of utility. Pareto somewhat patronizingly concedes "that one does not feel the same enjoyment when one takes the first taste of soup at the beginning of the meal and the sweet at the end, as when one begins with the sweet in order to end with the soup", but misunderstands the actual problem, for consumption can never be dependent on historic time, especially not the concrete experiential history of the actor, without surrendering the analogy to the conservative field of force. Rather, it is to be construed as path and time independent. "The past is irrelevant."[108] Such a postulant also implies that the actor renounces any

---

[104] M. Farmer, "Ever since Adam Smith: The Mythical History of Individual Rationality," *Economic Analysis, Research in the History of Economic Thought and Methodology*, 9 (1992), 108.

[105] B. Biervert, J. Wieland, "Der ethische Gehalt ökonomischer Kategorien – Beispiel: Der Nutzen," in: B. Bievert, M. Held (ed.), *Ökonomische Theorie und Ethik*, Frankfurt/Main-New York 1987, 45. The authors are referring here to the presupposition of complete information.

[106] P. Miroski, *Against Mechanism*, 100.

[107] M. Dobb, *Political Economy and Capitalism, Some Essays in Economic Tradition*, London 1945, 18. Dobb refers to A. Marshall, who explicitly says that the concepts of *desire* and *satisfaction* are to be treated as identical in economic theory. A. Marshall, *Principles of Economics*, 92-93.

[108] L. Robbins, *An Essay on the Nature and Significance of Economic Science*, London 1935, 62.

ability to learn, thus any change in his level of knowledge. For "any change in the relevant knowledge of the acting person [destroys] the equilibrium between the actions undertaken ... before, and after the alteration of knowledge."[109] The valuable rule, which states that humans learn, must accordingly be excluded.[110]

Even more far reaching is the fact that the utility field must be able to be determined ex ante, in order to make it feasible to forecast over actions. This condition is often discussed using the codeword, perfect foresight: "the precondition for equilibrium is perfect foresight."[111]

> "Chief among the simplifications of reality prerequisite to the achievement of perfect competition is, as has been emphasized all along, the assumption of practical omniscience on the part of every member of the competitive system."[112]

Perfect foresight extends not only to all current action alternatives, since these relate to a momentary slice of life and so only permit a static substantiation. In a dynamic theory where the intention is to forecast actions, all future alternatives have to be grasped, too. Economists have tried to justify this claim in two different ways.[113] In one, it is assumed that the actor in a single point of time reaches all of his present and future decisions. "His role is to choose (and carry out) a consumption plan made now for the whole future, i.e. a specification of the quantities of all his inputs and outputs."[114] The dynamic problem of action in time is reduced in this way to a static substantiation and a proper equilibrium point for all action alternatives now and in the future is reached. But it remains unclear, how all decision alternatives of a total life are to be accessed in one moment at all. Among other things, doing this requires that the length of one's life is known beforehand.[115] The second way points implicitly to the analogy of a mechanical, conservative system, which remains unchanged over time. For

---

[109] K. Leube, "Einige Bemerkungen zu den 'Untersuchungen über die Theorie des Preises'," 333.

[110] D. Müller, *Beiträge der Handlungstheorie für das Verständnis des Konsumentenverhaltens*, 28.

[111] J. R. Hicks, "Gleichgewicht und Konjunktur," *Zeitschrift für Nationalökonomie*, Vol. 4 (1933), 445.

[112] F.H. Knight, *Risk, Uncertainty and Profit*, Boston 1921, 197.

[113] K.-H. Brodbeck, "Kritische Wirtschaftsethik, Skizzen zur impliziten Ethik ökonomischer Theorienbildung," in: P. Ulrich, M. Breuer (ed.), *Wirtschaftsethik im politischen Diskurs*, Würzburg 2004, 218.

[114] G. Debreau is cited in ibid., 219.

[115] Ibid., 219.

here the idea is that the individual always acts in the same way, because his field of consciousness in the course of life is presumed to remain unchangeable. Herewith we assume an "individual who neither grows old nor dies."[116] Even so, it still remains unclear at which point in time we ascertain the shape of the utility field. It would be logical to identify this with birth, thus a time point before any consumption decisions have been made. Kirchgässner clearly believes that a moment must be specified in which the "socialization process" is finished and preferences have become mostly independent from the actual possibilities of action and thus remain stable. But Kirchgässner doesn't disclose when such a point of time is supposed to occur, or how it can be determined.[117]

3.1.4 Action as Unconscious Behavior

From the previous sections, it should be clear how problematic it is to impose the condition of a space and time independent field onto consciousness. Above all, we see the reason that "the element of time [is called] the source of the greatest difficulties in economics."[118] But up to this point, the deepest ground for these difficulties has not been sufficiently illuminated. It lies in a certain idea of action. Heimann works out this idea clearly, even if he relates his analysis not to economics, but to Kant:

> "Kant argues that phenomenal changes were manifested as actions: 'action signifies the relation of the subject of causality to its effect,' and the succession of appearance is manifested as forces, for 'causality leads to the concept of action, and this in turn to concept of force.' Kant thereupon claims that this presupposes the performance of substance, stating that 'whenever there is action – and therefore activity and force – there is substance, and it is in substance alone that the seat of this fruitful source of appearance must be sought.' The manifestation of forces, that is, the phenomenal appearance of changes, presupposes an 'ultimate subject which is the substratum of everything that changes,' and this is 'the permanent, that is, substance,' for actions themselves cannot be found in a subject which itself changes."[119]

Actions are always regarded as causally effected. "As an apriori category, the principle of action is born equal to causality."[120] Another way of seeing this is, as far as the neoclassicals go, not even thinkable, since only a caus-

---

[116] K. Wicksell is cited in ibid., 219.
[117] G. Kirchgässner, *Homo oeconomicus*, 13-14.
[118] A. Marshall, *Principles of Economics*, 109.
[119] P.M. Heimann is cited in P. Mirowski, *More Heat than Light*, 44.
[120] L. von Mises, *Grundprobleme der Nationalökonomie*, Jena 1933, 13.

ally effected action can be calculated and forecast. As Heimann makes clear, the principle of causality presupposes a substance, that is itself unmoved and unchanged. Change can be measured only against something else that is itself (relatively) unchanged in time. Actions are thus always only ascribed to a subject who does not himself change. This is the presupposition on which mechanics as well as neoclassical economics is founded, but clearly with an essential difference: in the former, the presupposition is made explicit in the idea of a conservative field of force; but in the latter it remains unthought.

Can action really be ascribed to a subject who does not change herself? In the view of Nishida's philosophy, the answer has to be no, and we need to seek another locus of action. Let's look more closely at Nishida's argument. For Nishida, change backgrounded by a static actor is nothing other than abstraction, distorting the real character of the change. For in truth the agent is a moving being that changes the same as all other things. As a locus of all action he changes in time just the same as his style of action. This is the only way we can imagine an individual as an actual living being backgrounding all activities.[121] But how are we to think of such a change of the underlying place or field? The key lies in taking under consideration a change that appears to conflict with the notion of a static individual and to see in which basho the conflict can be logically grounded. This consideration relies on an essential insight of the Logic of Place.[122] Nishida speaks of an absolute contradiction, when in a specific locus two opposed statements mutually exclude each other so that the affirmation of one automatically means the negation of the other. But this contradiction is only relative, and it comes about only in a wholly specific, limited locus of thought:

> "Things that resist or conflict with one another presuppose the same underlying generic concept. For they oppose one another in the determination of the same universal concept."[123]

In another, more inclusive domain of discourse, the contradictory statements can be posited simultaneously. The domain unifies the contradictory properties in itself, without simply thereby negating the contradiction. It

---

[121] R.E. Carter, *The Nothingness beyond God*, 22.
[122] Y. Matsudo, *Die Welt als Dialektisches Allgemeines, Eine Einführung in die Spätphilosophie von Kitarō Nishida*, Heidelberg 1990, 86. See also R.J. Wargo, *The Logic of Basho*, 264 und R.E. Carter, *The Nothingness beyond God*, 112.
[123] K. Nishida, *Intellegibility and the Philosophy of Nothingness*, transl. by. R. Schinzinger, Tokyo 1958, 177.

grounds the unity or connection between the contradictory properties on a deeper level, in which they can both equally be conceived.

> "It is a dialectical logic which has the capacity to both affirm contradiction, while at the same time negating it at a deeper level by showing that 'there would be no contraction if they did not touch each other somewhere. Facing each other is already a synthesis.'"[124]

How can we grasp such a deeper level? Wargo writes here:

> "If one were strictly bound by the categories of level 's', then entity 't' would be inconceivable, for entity 't' would have to be such that it had properties which would be contradictory in terms of level 's.' Since, we do in fact conceive of 't', it must be done from the framework of some level other than 's.'"[125]

> "The appearance of the contradiction and the recognition of it as a contradiction requires the transition to a new set of categories; in other words, to a new basho which can accommodate the type of entity required to resolve the contradiction."[126]

So, contradictions in a theory must first be recognized as contradictions, and not be excluded by definition out of the total viewpoint. But, then, how do contradictions come to light in the theory of utility maximization? They always appear when actions are labeled as inconsistent. If someone, on some occasion, would rather drink wine instead of beer, and then, on some other occasion, would rather drink beer than wine, there remains nothing more to do, from the point of view of the theory of utility maximization, than to label such behavior contradictory. Such a change of preferences in this narrow conceptual framework cannot be explained. Thus, within the bounds of neoclassical theory there remains no other solution than to take consistent choice as given and lift it to an unimpeachable postulate. The standard concept of rationality, here, simply assumes that a person has a contradiction free system of preferences in relation to the possibilities consistently open to her. "Thus in the usual way, a rational person is thought to have a coherent set of preferences between the options open to him."[127] But an individual can obviously act in a contradictory manner in the utility maximizing sense. This emerges just from the fact that this possibility must be excluded by definition.

---

[124] R.E. Carter, *The Nothingness beyond God*, 112. Carter cites Nishida.
[125] R.J. Wargo, *The Logic of Basho*, 285.
[126] Ibid., 264.
[127] J. Rawls, *Eine Theorie der Gerechtigkeit*, Frankfurt/Main 1975, 165.

We are dealing here with inconsistencies in preference that are not rare, but, on the contrary, completely everyday phenomena. One happily enters a movie theater one time, and the next time one just as happily stays home to watch the TV; today, one wants to drink wine, tomorrow, one wants just as much to drink beer, etc. But how does the individual manage to unite these contradictions? What locus serves as the basis for his actions? As Nishida's Logic of Place makes clear, this can be solely conceived in terms of the self-consciousness of the actors:

> "The background of continuity must now be the self-as-consciousness-in-time which always wherever and whenever is the 'privileged' place or center from which change is marked. Action remains the factuality of experience, for all things flow, but they flow for an individual who is always the measure, wherever, whenever. Thus it is that Nishida speaks paradoxically about the self, which 'lives by dying,' for it is a continuity of discontinuity. It flows, and yet in flowing, flows not (for it is ever the privileged marker of all flowing)."[128]

This self-consciousness has, literally, the property of being conscious of its self. It can not only determine the elements in its field, but it can observe itself as it goes at these activities and can shape itself actively on this foundation. It can change itself and in so doing preserve its identity. It is possible for it to see its own dynamic development from the baby to the old woman in spite of all changes as one unity. According to the Logic of Place underlying actions is not a static substance, but a self-consciousness that consciously changes and re-shapes its self along with its perceptions. Seen like this, phenomena like learning, new knowledge, or regretting don't seem contradictory. Or more exactly: properties, that from the view of utility theory appear to be absolutely contradictory, can be held together at the same time in the self-consciousness. For the latter, it is not logically impossible to change its assessments and values and yet remain identical to itself. It can change and still remain the same. In a latter place, we will discuss this change in the sense of creativity. (3.3.4) But it is mostly important at this point that, for neoclassical economics, such creativity always appears contradictory. Neoclassical theory tries to fix the consciousness as a static substance, although in truth it is continually changing and thus causes a change in preferences.

The self-reflective property of self-consciousness grounds its dynamic character. While the neoclassicals depart from a static substance that un-

---

[128] R.E. Carter, *The Nothingness beyond God*, 23-24.

derlies all acts, they deprive the consciousness exactly of this character. They construct (implicitly) the consciousness as unconscious. Yes, the neoclassicals emphasize the consciousness of actions. So, for instance, Mises sharply distinguishes conscious behavior from such unconscious behaviors as we see in reflex processes and the tropic reactions of cells.[129] Such a consciousness, however, always refers only to knowledge of the outside world. Preferences as well as the decision field itself are, contrarily, uninterrupted. The actor is not conscious of himself. "We employ," as Jevons put it, "nearly unconscious calculations ... in all of our living circumstances."[130] And on this point he can call upon an insight derived from 19th century psychology:

> "A good deal of activity was [seen as] regulated behavior, consisting of actions that were simply automatic or instinctive performed without the attention, or the intention, or even the excitement of consciousness in the mind of the agent."[131]

The unconsciousness of one's own act guarantees that a static, unchangeable substance can be assumed as the bearer of the action or the decision, thus enabling the action to be mechanically described:

> „Wherever we are concerned with the unconscious reflections or processes in the human body, no obstacle exists to observing and investigating them 'mechanically,' that is, as caused by objectively observable outer events. This process goes on without the knowledge of the respective person and without him having the power to change it."[132]

Becker's observation that "the economic viewpoint doesn't [assume] that the decision makers are necessarily conscious of their maximizing efforts, or that they could verbalize in an informative manner grounds for the systematic pattern in their behavior or describe it in other ways,"[133] doesn't quite, in this connection, hit the target. For the economic viewpoint actually presupposes, that the individual never understands the locus of his decisions, not to speak of being able to alter it. It thus misunderstands exactly that property of the consciousness that distinguishes it from a physical field

---

[129] L. von Mises, *Nationalökonomie*, 11.
[130] W.S. Jevons, *The Theory of Political Economy*, 100.
[131] M. White, "The Moment of Richard Jennings: The Production of Jevon's Marginalist Economic Agent," in: P. Mirowski (ed.), *Natural Images in Economic Thought*, 211.
[132] F.A. Hayek, *Mißbrauch und Verfall der Vernunft, Ein Fragment*, Frankfurt/Main 1959, 29.
[133] G.S. Becker, *Der ökonomische Ansatz zur Erklärung menschlichen Verhaltens*, 6.

of force: its ability to reflect upon itself and re-shape itself: "The soul of the self can perceive itself."[134] Both the consciousness and the field of force can be thought of as loci, within which things and their relations to each other are determined. But only the first can (and must) be regarded as a *basho* that sees itself, interprets itself and determines itself. *"Basho sees itself in itself,"* Nishida writes in regard to this reflexive property of self-consciousness.[135] The neoclassical school, through its imitating from classical mechanics to sketch out an action theory, fails to do justice to this essential human property. One could even more contentiously argue that they have failed, in general, to give us a meaningful theory of human action. We can direct this argument against the neoclassicals as surely as we can against other sciences that try to reduce action to physiological, objectifiable processes:

> "To connect a 'physiological exposition' with a subsequent analysis of 'intellectual' processes was to 'tincture' psychology 'with a language of materialistic description, at once unphilosophical and repulsive.' Psychology was concerned with 'self-consciousness' (introspection), to which the very language and methods of physiological description were foreign. It was as if an artist were 'to paint his Madonna with the skin off. It is recommended neither by scientific precision, nor by illustrative good taste.' ... Since psychology required a reflecting subject, a knowing and willing self-conscious mind, it was primarily subjective and thus not a 'natural' science."[136]

3.1.5 The Logical Impossibility of Calculating Human Action

Given consciousness' property of being conscious of itself, it is clear that an objectivization or even a calculation of human action by way of an external observer is logically impossible. This conclusion shall be form the basis of a denser discussion in this section. Generally speaking, every observer must objectivize his object in some way. He must be able to say what this object is, or, at least, be able to name its properties. In order to ground a behavioral theory, the neoclassical economist must thus try to objectivize the consciousness of the actor; an attempt that stands in the center of the critique of the Logic of Place:

---

[134] K. Nishida, *Über das Gute, Eine Philosophie der Reinen Erfahrung*, transl. by P. Pörtner, Frankfurt/Main-Leipzig 2001, 113.
[135] K. Nishida is cited in R.J. Wargo, *The Logic of Basho*, 187.
[136] M. White, "The Moment of Richard Jennings," 221. White is summarizing a statement of J. Martineau.

> "The key to the issue lies in self consciousness, but the traditional method of dealing with self consciousness demands treating the self as an object and this has consistently resulted in disaster."[137]

But what is the core point of this critique? We will first cite a couple of general observations, in order to transpose them onto the neoclassical method:

> "In the Universal of Judgment (which includes all sorts of objective theories, SG), the knowing self is viewed as an object-part of the world of nature, to be known analogously to the way any object is known. 'It is essentially an ego, registering object in time.' Yet the 'I' as eye does not exhaust the 'I' as that which actually watches the 'eye' watching, and which enters into the framing and structuring of that which is seen. In short, the self, as self-activity, can never be caught via the universal of Judgment, for to turn it into an object is to lose its distinctiveness as subjectivity. To make of the *pour soi* an *en soi* is to make it what it isn't. It is self-consciousness as not conscious. But self consciousness is recursive or reflexive, and it infinitely doubles back on itself such that it always is precisely what it isn't at any moment of objectified 'freezing', so to speak."[138]

Let's assume for a moment, that the neoclassical method could produce an instantaneous snapshot of the individual consciousness and use this as the underlying foundation of the action calculus. Still, even this assumption still doesn't allow us, by reason of the self-reflexive character of self-consciousness, to say anything valid about the next moment's snapshot. It is exactly at this point that all forecasts of human action break down because it is logically impossible for the observer to calculate beforehand when and how the self-consciousness will re-fashion itself. The observer can always only know this when his proper, original forecast is contradicted by actual observation. He can identify a change always only ex post facto, but not ex ante. Calculation and forecasting are unmasked as a logical impossibility.

We can elaborate this aspect of the case even more clearly. The postulate of the calculability of action rests, basically, on the confusion between the knower and the known, or in this case of the observer and the observed. The example of the theory of 'revealed preferences' will clarify what we mean by this. This theory attempts to construct a utility field solely out of observations:

---

[137] R.J. Wargo, *The Logic of Basho*, 266.
[138] R.E. Carter, *The Nothingness beyond God*, 35.

"The individual guinea-pig, by his market behaviour, reveals his preference pattern – if there is such a consistent pattern."[139]

For such an observation, the observer and the observed must above all find themselves in the same situation. The observed completes an action (for example, some freely chosen act) and the observer observes and interprets this choice:

> "If you are observed to choose x rejecting y, you are declared to have 'revealed' a preference for x over y. Your personal utility is then defined as simply a numerical representation of this 'preference' assigning a higher utility to a 'preferred' alternative. With this set of definition you can hardly escape maximizing your own utility, except through inconsistency. (...) But if you are consistent, then no matter whether you are a single-minded egoist or a raving altruist ... you will appear to be maximizing your own utility in this enchanted world of definitions."[140]

This last sentence is decisive. Utility maximizing behavior remains limited to a world of definitions alone, which underlies the observer's judgment. It is the observer who reads into the behavior all the essential aspects of maximization.[141] This interpretation precedes the construction of the indifference curves (thus of the utility field); it is the proper locus (in the sense of an initial intuition), which structures and guides the observation. Yet this locus is not identical to the true place of action, the consciousness field of the actor. In this locus, chosen actions are interpretable in completely different ways than in the utility field, which the observer constructs. Under certain circumstances it may of course be possible to make these two fields equivalent, for instance when the observed explains, how he interprets his act. But exactly this is forbidden by the neoclassical method since it deprives itself of any communication with the observed and limits itself only to the outwardly observable. In this way nothing can be predicated about the identity of the observed utility field and the consciousness field. The assumption of the existence of a utility field that the observer constructs remains limited solely to the world of definitions in which the observer moves. It represents no locus in which the observed acts. In other words: the domain of discourse really is the locus in which the researcher

---

[139] P.A. Samuelson, "Consumption Theory in Terms of Revealed Preferences," 64.

[140] A. Sen, "Rational Fools: A Critique of the Behavioral Foundations of Economic Theory," *Philosophy & Public Affairs*, 6 (1977), 322-23.

[141] These aspects are the numerical representation as well as the idea of a 'more-is-better.'

thinks, but it is not the authentic *basho* of action, which is only conceivable as the self-consciousness of the actor.

This essential difference is not recognized in the neoclassical method. Accordingly, confusion reigns over issues such as, for example, who has to have complete foresight over all action alternatives in order that actions may count as calculable:

> "'Data' could of course only mean something 'given.' But the really all-deciding question in political economics, who disposes of them, is not therefore solved. Do we assume in the analysis that the data are ‚given' to the observer, or do we suppose, to the person whose behavior and action are to be explained through this assumption possesses this knowledge?"[142]

This question is not even posed in the neoclassical method, because the difference between the researcher's domain of discourse and self-consciousness as the locus of action isn't even seen. But it is clear, that both the observer and the observed must dispose of the same knowledge and must move in the same thought models. All action alternatives as the actor sees them must be known to the observer, and the observed actor must have, in addition, a "complete insight ... into theoretical economics"[143] so that he can act in the terms presupposed by the observing economist. We are talking about an interdependence, here, that the neoclassical method can neither recognize nor explain, because it always looks at the particular individual only. Therefore, it is unable to ground an essential presupposition of the calculability of action.

But even if such interdependence could be presupposed, calculation would always break down each time the actor's self-consciousness reshaped itself anew. For how these changes come about can't be determined in advance from any standpoint, because every standpoint always depicts an observed, and thus a past, situation. Even the actor herself can't forecast the change of her consciousness. She cannot observe her self-consciousness, because this always underlies observation without becoming itself an object of observation. Nishitani Keiji makes this clear by way of a metaphor: "the eye

---

[142] K. Leube, "Einige Bemerkungen zu den 'Untersuchungen über die Theorie des Preises'," 332.

[143] O. Morgenstern, "Vollkommene Voraussicht und wirtschaftliches Gleichgewicht," in: K. Leube (ed.), *Die Österreichische Schule der Nationalökonomie*, Vol. 2, Wien 1995, 100.

3 The Implicit Image of the Person in Economics   77

perceives everything optically, while at the same time it (as a seeing subject) does not see itself."[144]

> "The observer remains necessarily hidden in the observation. ... The subject is a subject in the act of recognition, not the recognized object. ... One observes no observer, one observes something, thus something observed. How can you distinguish an observer at all from something that is a non-observer? In order to do this, you would have to have once again observed the observer – but exactly therein lies the impossibility, since there is no possibility to denote the observer as a something, to point at it, think about it, imagine it, etc. Whatever you get out of such efforts, you always arrive only at something observed, but not the observer. A reflection of the observer on himself is thus not possible."[145]

Nishida comprehends the impossibility of a self-reflection in the following way: "A truly active subject cannot reflect, for something that reflects is no longer the active subject."[146] If one takes Nishida's precept seriously, than it must also be true that from the standpoint of an outside observer, nothing can be predicated about the self-consciousness. If the actor cannot reflect upon himself, then, too, it is impossible for the observing researcher to objectivize the self-consciousness of the actor:

> "Self consciousness cannot be accounted for without introducing new categories into our analysis, but that is just what we can't do from the perspective of the Universal of Judgment (objectified knowledge, SG). Thus, unless self-consciousness can be treated objectively, then it isn't knowledge at all. It is 'subjective', or noumenal freedom, or just nothing. The self acts, and is aware of itself, and yet it can never be the subject of a judgment! It cannot be dealt by object logic."[147]

It is the property of the actor that consists in self-reflection and self transformation, which makes it logically impossible to calculate human action in the same manner the physicist calculates the movement of physical objects. In the world of classical mechanics, the individual bit cannot reshape itself; it remains in its properties constant over time. This constancy allows the scientist to research its properties and to generalize. The internal

---

[144] K. Nishitani is cited in H. Hashi, *Die Aktualität der Philosophie, Grundriß des Denkweges der Kyoto-Schule*, Wien 1999, 50.
[145] K.-H. Brodbeck, *Zirkel des Wissens*, 243-45.
[146] K. Nishida, *Logik des Ortes*, 32.
[147] R.E. Carter, *The Nothingness beyond God*, 36.

observation of the particular is capable of agreeing with a universal law.[148] And it is this agreement that allows the formulation of the regularity and calculation of future events. But even there remains preserved the possibility of the self-determination of the individuals; it is only reduced to a minimum.[149] But the social sciences, in contrast, always have to do with individuals who change by reason of their self-consciousness. The extent of these changes may be reduced through the habitus. (3.3.3) Yet it doesn't let them, as with physical bits, border on a minimum. Because humans are not unchanging stimulus-reaction machines, the regularity of human action, if it applies, is not of the same character as the natural laws researched by classical mechanics.

> "But what equations of motion, and what laws of conservation of comparable scope do we have in economics? To ask the question is to answer it. There are none that have the definiteness and universal demonstrability of the corresponding physical laws. Our economic laws are simply empirical extrapolations of the present situation, they do not enable us to determine with certainty what, for example, the demand and supply situation will be at the next instant of time."[150]

For this reason, the method of economics must be other than that of physics.[151] And so it turns out that the neoclassical method is emulating an inappropriate model from which to hang its dream of a calculable world when it imitates from classical mechanics. As Menger was already writing in 1871:

> "The attempts so far to uncritically impose the properties of the methods of natural science onto the research project of political economics have lead to the worst conceptual mistakes in methodology and to an empty playing with extrinsic analogies between the phenomena of the political economy and those of nature."[152]

Many economists have tried to escape this insight by cutting off the appeal to physics and making the appeal, rather, to the methodological principles

---

[148] K. Nishida, "Die Welt als Dialektisches Allgemeines," übers. in: Y. Matsudo, *Eine Einführung in die Spätphilosophie von Kitarō Nishida*, 215-217. Another translation is found in K. Nishida, *Fundamental Problems of Philosophy, The World of Action and the Dialectical World*, transl. by. D.A. Dilworth, Tokyo 1970.

[149] K. Nishida, "Die Welt als Dialektisches Allgemeines," 215.

[150] H. Schultz, "The Quantitative Method with Special Reference to Economic Inquiry," *Research in the History of Economic Thought and Methodology*, 18 (2001), 352.

[151] K. Nishida, "Die Welt als Dialaktisches Allgemeines," 219.

[152] C. Menger, *Grundsätze der Volkswirtschaftslehre*, VIII.

of mathematics. Already the founding fathers of the neoclassical school, among them Jevons, Walras, Edgeworth and Pareto, identified themselves as, above all, mathematical theoreticians.[153] You could, by their lights, appropriate the mathematical equations of mechanics without claiming any kind of causal analogies to physics:

> "Let us go back to the equations which determine equilibrium. ... 'These equations do not seem new to me. I know them well, they are old friends. They are the equations of rational mechanics.' That is why pure economics is a sort of mechanics or akin to mechanics ... mechanics can be studied leaving aside the concept of forces. In reality this does not all matter much. If there is anyone who does not care to have mechanics mentioned, very well, let us disregard the similarity and let us talk directly about our equations."[154]

The mathematical turn, principally in the U.S., is observed as "the only possibility for exact research and the precise representation of actual events."[155] But what kind of meaning does economics accrue if it only supports itself on mathematics? Mathematics, according to Nishida, negates concrete perception as well as the concrete experience of the everyday and changes the particular into a sign. This sign, for instance in the form of a variable, possesses the character of being general, and can in principle stand for any concrete thing. Thus, even here, as in physics, the self-determination of the particular is reduced to a minimum. But the particular individual who is represented through a sign must not correspond to such a character in reality. The particular and the sign that represents it could very well have opposite meanings.[156] Mathematics can, of course, abstract from this. It thus divorces itself from the standpoint of seeing things concretely:

> "The new language of mathematics does not need to be made certain in relation to a an exterior reality, because it makes itself certain through its own work."[157]

Mathematics, in this sense, is irreal.[158] It only sees the sign as a universal, without assuming a real thing standing in the background. It is thus capable

---

[153] P. Mirowski, *Against Mechanism*, 12. See also T.M. Porter, Rigor and Practicality: "Rival Ideas of Quantification in Nineteenth-century Economics," in: P. Mirowski (ed.), *Natural Images in Economic Thought*, 128-170.
[154] V. Pareto is cited in P. Mirowski, *More Heat than Light*, 222.
[155] K. Leube, "Einige Bemerkungen zu den 'Untersuchungen über die Theorie des Preises'," 330.
[156] K. Nishida, "Die Welt als Dialektisches Allgemeines," 214.
[157] H. Mehrtens is cited inT.M. Porter, "Rigor and Practicality," 159.
[158] K. Nishida, "Die Welt als Dialektisches Allgemeines," 216.

of withdrawing from the real world of time and space, or flesh and blood, since it doesn't describe this world: rather, the world it postulates is its own.[159]

Herein lies an important difference with physics, which never enacts this kind of divorce. For the physical particular is not a sign, but a thing, that is concretely measurable and determinable.[160] And so for this reason, the knowledge obtained from physics is knowledge of the real world. Mathematics, here, is applied always and only as a construction principle if the self-determination of the particular individual can be actually reduced to a minimum and it can be depicted through a general sign. The accuracy or truth of such a construction remains relative to experience. Experiments can refute mathematically formulated theories. In this fact lies the whole meaning of falsification, which consistently holds the accuracy of the mathematical model to be relative to the concrete experience of the real world.

It is often stressed that in economics, the place of the concrete experiment is taken by the thought experiment. For instance, as a textbook puts it: "In a thought experiment certain operant connections and processes are played through in thought; in this way, we can abstract from a great number of possible influence factors. The outcome of such abstraction is a model. (...) Through reduction to very few variables, we simplify, or, actually, primarily enable the conceptual construction of these connections."[161] Such thought experiments remain in the mind of the scientist. It is in his head that one thing is related to another. Here, as in mathematics, we have no need to see concrete, and thus experiential, things. This is therefore distinct from experiments in physics, which at least in principle allow for their actual instantiation. In economics, we deviate so far from this standard that economists believe they can check the accuracy of the experiment through mathematics. Referring, once again, to our textbook:

> "Particularly in the economic sciences, our model will mostly be formulated mathematically in order to be certain that no error has occurred in the interpretation of some function within such a model; in this way, we can draw upon the axiomatic rules of mathematics. Mathematics is thus an aid which allows us to check the accu-

---

[159] T.M. Porter, "Rigor and Practicality," 159.
[160] K. Nishida, "Die Welt als Dialektisches Allgemeines," 215.
[161] J. Kromphardt, *Grundlagen der Makroökonomie*, München 1998, 23.

racy of our logical conclusions and keeps the thought experimenter from committing logical errors."[162]

Clearly, neoclassical method does not follow the paradigm of physics in an essential, if not decisive point, for the former misinterprets the meaning of the experience, or praxis, to which all mathematical models in the natural sciences are made relative.[163] In opposition to physics, the neoclassical school slights the experimental character of science and subordinates its own models solely to another conceptual model, the mathematical. In this way, sign is purely related to sign. This allows, certainly, for proclaiming something about the relationship of these signs in the world of (mathematical) logic, but not about the accuracy or applicability of the models in the context of concrete experience. Accordingly, we remain behind in world of pure thought. If the neoclassical method appeals like this to mathematics as its only method of checking for error, then it can, in opposition to physics, have nothing to say relevant to the existence of things in the real world. In other words: the existence of its functions, constants and variables remains singly and solely limited to its method's domain of discourse. If we let the method, thus, imitate from mathematics alone, it retires into an ivory tower, from which nothing can be said about everyday actions in the world. Here it is worth recalling the words of John Stuart Mill, who wrote:

> "Political economy, therefore, reasons from assumed premises – from premises which might be totally without foundation in fact, and which are not pretended to be universally in accordance with it. The conclusions of Political Economy, consequently, like those of geometry, are only true, as the common phrase is, in the abstract."[164]

3.2 Conceiving the Actor in Subjective Economic Methodologies

The previous section should have made clear what implicit assumptions we can expect to encounter in the objective economic methodologies: assumptions that not only represent 'as-if' constructs, but necessary presuppositions of objective statements. Thus, Mill correctly admits:

---

[162] Ibid., 23-24.
[163] T.M. Porter, "Rigor and Practicality," 157.
[164] J.S. Mill, *On the Definition of Political Economy*, 326.

"This branch of science, whether we prefer to call it social economy, speculative politics or the natural history of society, presupposes the whole science of the nature of individual mind."[165]

The subjective consciousness remains, from the objective point of view, a place of absolute nothingness, in which thinking does occur, it is true, but remains itself inaccessible to an objective analysis. It is like a field that in itself shelters and sorts out all objects, but cannot be grasped from the viewpoint of the object. Here we can say: the subjective consciousness is that locus, in which all objects are recognized as commodities, but is not itself describable through a theory of commodities. The subjective consciousness is the presupposition of such a theory, but not its result. Yet in order to be able to describe the subjective consciousness, according to Nishida's Logic of Place, a conceptual leap is unavoidable. "The impossibility of complete objectification makes the transition to another domain of discourse necessary."[166] This transition takes place by the movement from a purely objective style of observation to a new locus of thought, which Nishida describes as the locus of subjective consciousness:

> "From the vantage point of this new basho, the objects of the Universal of Judgment (of objectified knowledge, SG) are simply the contents of the field of consciousness, which now envelops them. The basho of consciousness is a deeper level of explanation, and it embraces, envelops, includes the earlier basho of the Universal of Judgment within it."[167]

These are subjective methodologies, which explicitly reflect upon the properties of this new locus. Nishida distinguishes, here, between three different explanatory dispositions, in which the knowledge of subjective consciousness is deepened step by step: 1), theories centering around reason; 2), theories centering around subjective feelings as well as desires; and 3), theories centering around the subjective will. As shall be shown, all three explanatory dispositions play important rolls in enabling our deeper understanding of economic actors. But it should also be clear that none of them in itself is able to really explain in an encompassing manner the economic actor, and therefore we must seek another locus of thought, in which the subjective style of observation can be penetrated.

---

[165] Ibid., 320.
[166] R.J. Wargo, *The Logic of Basho*, 292.
[167] R.E. Carter, *The Nothingness beyond God*, 37.

3.2.1 The Subjective Consciousness as Reason

Our first possible mode for subjectively understanding the economic actor consist in describing her with the aid of the rationality principle: her consciousness should be limited to grasping, calculating, and weighing against each other given data sets (for instance, in the form of action alternatives). Thus, the rationality principle makes explicit the implicit neoclassical idea that consciousness is not conscious of itself. For consciousness is supposed to limit itself to gaining knowledge of the outside world. The actor is not conscious of herself, but only of the alternatives between which she chooses.

> "The individual ...corresponding to his preferences values those particular choice possibilities of which he disposes, meaning he weighs the advantages and disadvantages, costs and uses of the individual alternatives against each other. Finally he decides for that possibility (or those possibilities) which corresponds most closely to his preferences and promise him the highest 'net utility.'"[168]

From the viewpoint of the Logic of Place, such a reason corresponds to an intellectual self, which solely deals with formal connections between things in time and space. "We can conceive of the self as the passive place, in which ideas arise, and which is ever at the background of objective knowing."[169] The things that neoclassical methodology casts as objectively given appear now, explicitly, as the content of subjective consciousness. The latter confines itself to passively reflecting this content. But it does not show any properties above and beyond this: it is so to speak a purely formal consciousness:

> "What were previously taken to be objects are now no more than the content of this field of consciousness. A transition of this sort, from an enfolded basho to the enfolding basho, is first seen in a purely formal way. Thus, the knowing self ... is purely a formal self; it is merely what is required to be able to speak of a self at all. It is the self whose content is spelled out in the plane of consciousness, the content of which is not the content of the knowing self, but, rather, a given noematic content (...) The content of the plane of consciousness has an essential reference to the objects of the universal of judgment (of objectified knowledge, SG). This referential character dominates the nature of consciousness at this level. (...) The content of the universal of judgment becomes the content of the field of consciousness."[170]

---

[168] G. Kirchgässner, *Homo oeconomicus*, 14.
[169] R.E. Carter, *The Nothingness beyond God*, 38.
[170] R.J. Wargo, *The Logic of Basho*, 298-99.

When the consciousness is construed as such a passive place, actions are restricted to choosing between different objects. Consequently, actions are defined for the most part in economics only as rational choice makings; they are "the result of a rational choice between alternative possibilities."[171] This corresponds to the utilitarian interpretation of action.[172] Such an idea of consciousness and action is most plainly clarified by the example of a calculating machine or a computer, for just as the computer always assesses the value of alternatives according to fixed, presumed rules, without being able to either reflect about them or even change them the least bit, the rational actor "does not have the choice, when it comes down to it, over the rules by which he makes his choice."[173] The computer, actually, corresponds the to economic ideal model of the actor. For the latter acts optimally when "he, like a ambulatory computer striding through the world, always determines with lightning-like speed the best of all given possibilities."[174] True, in the theory of bounded rationality it is granted that the normal person deviates from such an ideal, because he cannot calculate as perfectly as a computer. Yet it is implied, "that in principle the individual is in a situation... to appraise and to affix values to his action space, in order to act accordingly."[175] And so the essential aspect of ratiocinative reason (the most possibly exact calculation of all action alternatives) is preserved.

Because the calculation is purely related to objects, it remains an "exterior, and therewith mechanical business."[176] To make reflections concerning one's own proper thought processes seems impossible. If consciousness were actually exhausted in ratiocinative reason, then the actor would be unable to make reflections over the rules or the motives according to which she makes her choices. She could also give no account of the reason why she so calculated. Even more, she ought not even be conscious of the fact that she made calculations. In this way, using the reason model, even though the actor truly is explicitly recognized as a subject, her consciousness is only conceived as a field that is filled with ideas about objects. She

---

[171] O. Höffe, *Einführung in die utilitaristische Ethik: Klassische und zeitgenössische Texte*, Tübingen 1992, 10.
[172] O. Höffe, *Einführung in die utilitaristische Ethik*, 10.
[173] M. Baurmann, *Der Markt der Tugend: Recht und Moral in der liberalen Gesellschaft, Eine soziologische Untersuchung*, Tübingen 1996, 325.
[174] G. Kirchgässner, *Homo oeconomicus*, 17.
[175] Ibid., 17.
[176] G.W.F. Hegel is cited in K.-H. Brodbeck, *Die fragwürdigen Grundlagen der Ökonomie*, 225.

is an intellectual self who simply and solely constructs formal relations between objects.[177] And in this way, her consciousness occupies a truly odd position. For, on the one side, it represents the locus, in which the alternatives are both recognized and chosen. On the other side, however, we are not permitted to say that these alternatives are qualities of the consciousness. On the formal level, the consciousness doesn't even appear real, but rather appears to be a limiting concept of commodity space. A theory of choice explicitly recognizes in this way the necessity of the assumption of a consciousness field, but cannot provide a foundation for its qualities. In other words: the qualities of consciousness remain, from the point of view of the formal self, a place of nothingness, such that they are always presupposed, but never become explicitly the objects of reflection. Therefore the theory of choice cannot explain what it is that allows people to act at all.

3.2.2 The Subjective Consciousness as an Accumulation of Feelings and Desires

Because of this deficiency, which shows itself on the level of a formally determined consciousness, we must seek after a more extensive explanation of the actor. One possibility consists in explicitly defining his subjective qualities. We should describe the person in his qualities 'just as he is.' Our concern would here be to research his 'real essence', his 'nature', in the hope, "the laws of motion of human action could be discovered much as those for falling bodies and planets."[178] One makes the effort "to observe human actions and drives in the same spirit as one would take in an investigation involving lines, surfaces and bodies."[179] Accordingly, we should find a causal explanatory schema for human action. Given qualities of the consciousness should necessarily determine actions. For this, consciousness should be constructed principally as a place of feelings and desires. "To have the sense of virtue is nothing but to feel a satisfaction of a particular kind from the contemplation of a character."[180] says, for instance, David Hume.

> "Any one feeling automatically produces a definite reaction; action alternatives that are associated with negative feelings such as pain or displeasure are avoided, while

---

[177] R.E. Carter, *The Nothingness beyond God*, 37.
[178] A.O. Hirschman, *Leidenschaften und Interessen, Politische Begründung des Kapitalismus vor seinem Sieg*, Frankfurt/Main 1987, 21.
[179] Spinoza is cited in A.O. Hirschman, *Leidenschaften und Interessen*, 22.
[180] D. Hume, *A Treatise on Human Nature* (1734), Reprint Oxford 1888, 471.

positive feelings as joy or pleasure awaken desires. These desires motivate people to action. They are the main springs of human action."[181]

This metaphor of main springs, borrowed from mechanics, makes clear, that the subjective desires must be imagined as a driving wheel of action, that the individual cannot resist. Just as its gears inexorably drive the clockwork, so, too, a person reacts to his desires.

I will in a later place go into the subject of the concepts feeling and desire and their specific economic forms in greater detail. (3.3.2) At the moment, we will indicate only some general action-theoretical aspects. It is important here that the subjective qualities of the consciousness are assumed as given. "Feelings, sensations and desires are unproblematic and not criticizable: we have just this certain feeling now. A passion is an original existence."[182] This inaccessibility of desire to any form of proof is mostly grounded in utilitarianism through its relationship to reason. For, from the utilitarian point of view, the desires represent a locus, which determines or directs reason. Since the latter only deals with exterior data, it can neither recognize nor question the desires; from reason's point of view, they are a place of nothingness. "Reason is, and ought only to be the slave of the passions, and can never pretend other office than to serve and obey them."[183] MacIntyre pursues this idea of the relationship of the feelings (passions) and ratiocinative reason more precisely:

> "Reason is concerned wither with relations of ideas, as in mathematics, or with matters of fact. Neither of them can move us to act. We are moved to act not by this or by that being the case, but by the prospect of pleasure or pain from what is or will be the case. It is the passions and not the reason which are around by the prospect of pleasure and pain. Reason can inform the passions as to whether the object they seek exists and as to what the most economical and effective means for seeking it may be. But reason cannot judge or criticize the passions. It follows without paradox that 'it is not contrary to prefer the destruction of the whole world to the scratching of my finger.'"[184]

---

[181] O. Höffe, *Einführung in die utilitaristische Ethik*, 16.
[182] A. MacIntyre, *Geschichte der Ethik im Überblick, vom Zeitalter Homers bis zum 20. Jahrhundert*, Königstein/Ts. 1984, 165.
[183] D. Hume, *A Treatise on Human Nature*, 415.
[184] A. MacIntyre, *Geschichte der Ethik im Überblick*, 159-160. MacIntyre is referring here to Hume.

Out of the fact that the reason cannot question the feelings and desires, it often has followed, the latter could in no way be changed. We must see them as given qualities, as predicates or attributes of the actor.[185] They are the things that make up the person, his essence, and his nature. "The emotive content is not merely given from the outside, so to speak, but is what characterizes the self; it is what gives substance to the self."[186] Hume, along this line, speaks for instance like this: "A passion is an original existence."[187] Among other things, this leads to the idea of seeing desire as a "fundamental anthropological constant"[188] and accordingly seeing the actor as a static substance:

> "The term static is used, "because the judgments are all in terms of a given entity and its characteristics. The entity in question is not seen as creating or causing these characteristics, but only as simply possessing them. Thus ... the emotive self will simply have certain characteristics such as the ability to recognize the elements of the field of consciousness as its own."[189]

You could say, that the assumption of a static field of consciousness, which implicitly underlies the point of view of the neoclassical school, becomes explicit in utilitarian theory. The givenness of preference or indifference curves, which are postulated in neoclassical economics, corresponds to the utilitarian concept of a static actor whose essence is defined through feelings and desires. According to utilitarianism, the actor can be completely conscious of his proper essence. But he can not himself change it:

> "Emotion tends to be thought of as something that happens to us. We fall in love, or become angry, but we don't decide to fall in love, or to fell angry. We are overcome by them, in the sense of not choosing them."[190]

In this way the question of how desires and feelings are defined and changed remains cloudy. The result is a similar problem as that we encountered with the question of the calculability of actions: when we regard an actor as a substance with definite, given qualities, the change of these qualities remains inexplicable. Rather, that change always shows up as a contradiction. Notwithstanding this contradictoriness, nothing changes the fact that it is a human characteristic to change himself, and thus his quali-

---

[185] R.E. Carter, *The Nothingness beyond God*, 38.
[186] R.J. Wargo, *The Logic of Basho*, 306.
[187] D. Hume, *A Treatise on Human Nature*, 415.
[188] O. Höffe, *Einführung in die utilitaristische Ethik*, 16.
[189] R.J. Wargo, *The Logic of Basho*, 301.
[190] R.E. Carter, *The Nothingness beyond God*, 38.

ties. He unites in the course of time distinct or even conflicting qualities in himself. He is not only the slave of his desires. "Desires... don't simply emerge, they are no simple sensations. They can be modified, repressed, developed, etc. to a certain degree."[191] The person does not only relate passively to his qualities, but he defines these themselves actively.

3.2.3 The Subjective Consciousness as Will

In Nishida's Logic of Place, the quality of consciousness that consists in self-reflection and change is ascribed to the will. Concerning this, Carter writes:

> "Our observations of ourselves make it clear that we can and do reflect on the feelings that we have, and about the nature of the personality they express. We are not only passive; we are active – willfully active. 'Will' is the deepest level of ... Self Consciousness, and is manifested when we actually do determine our own nature, i.e. change it. In fact, it is only at this level that true reflexivity is apparent. We can reflect back upon our past, and ask if we want to be that way now. And in the future we can modify our selfhood. The willing, self reflective self is not limited by the past, nor by the perceptions of the present."[192]

Hirschman confirms this thought when he writes in regard to economic agents:

> "Men and women have the ability to step back from their 'revealed' wants, volitions, and preferences, to ask themselves whether they really want these wants and prefer these preferences."[193]

How is it possible, though, for the individual, acting from his own free will, to change himself, thus uniting, for instance, the quality A and not-A in himself? As long as we look at the human only 'as he is', in the sense of his given preferences, this question is unanswerable. The key to it lies, instead, in searching after the locus in which the will to change oneself can be thought.

> "The plane of consciousness only displays a set of representations. That the content of the plane of consciousness changes, and that these various dissimilar fields are

---

[191] A. MacIntyre, *Geschichte der Ethik im Überblick*, 165.
[192] R.E. Carter, *The Nothingness beyond God*, 39.
[193] Hirschman is cited in H. Stewart, "A Critique of Instrumental Reason in Economics," *Economics and Philosophy*, 11 (1995), 72.

taken to be the determination of one and the same self, demands something which supports the transition between the varied fields."[194]

In the framework of subjective economic methodologies, two theoretical figures show the way to such a locus, whereby this locus doesn't become visible as an explicit object of explanation, but serves purely as an implicit presupposition of thought. In the first case, we have the idea of the end of the act; in the second, that of habit. Let's first examine the idea of an end, or goal. Generally we can permit ourselves to say that the concept of the goal in economics plays a truly essential role, but its character remains essentially unclear. In one of the most famous definitions of economics, Robbins ascribes to the concept of ends a very important role:

"Economics is the science which studies human behavior as a relationship between ends and scarce means which have alternative uses."[195]

Robbins starts out with the fact that humans choose between different means in order to reach a wished for goal. In this way, choice making can be construed as end-directed. Thus, for the most part we begin with the fact that the chosen alternatives correspond to the function of an objectively defined means. Commodities, too, are made to correspond to a means function, as are all action alternatives.[196] Of course, the character of the choice making process itself remains cloudy. For Robbins' definition states purely that it constructs a relation between ends and means. But is the choice making in this function itself a means or an end? So far as the choice itself is interpreted as end-directed, it is obviously a means to a purpose. A person chooses, in order to reach a goal. And since in the framework of the economy every action can be imagined to be a choice making, this means nothing more than the fact that people always act in the horizon of a definite goal.[197] Mostly, in economics, our starting point is that such a goal is defined subjectively. On these grounds we often make our notions of the goal equivalent to preferences:[198] "Marginal choice theory posits the grantedness of goals as the grantedness of preferences for the acting economic subject."[199] But thereby we overlook the fact that the actor doesn't simply

---

[194] R.J. Wargo, *The Logic of Basho*, 312.
[195] L. Robbins, *An Essay on the Nature and Significance of Economic Science*, 16.
[196] This becomes clear, for example, in Kirchgässner, *Homo oeconomicus*, 15.
[197] In this connection, Stewart speaks of a presupposition of *completeness*. This says that all actions are defined instrumentally in terms of their particular goals in economic theory. H. Stewart, "A Critique of Instrumental Reason," 58.
[198] See for instance G. Kirchgässner, *Homo oeconomicus*, 18.
[199] B.P. Priddat and E.K. Seifert, "Gerechtigkeit und Klugheit," 65.

'has' goals like he has a preference for beer or chocolate, but that he redefines himself by reason of these goals. His subjective desires are themselves means in order to reach an end. The goal of an action is thus not a quality of consciousness like a feeling. For the latter is something we simply 'have', but the will to achieve a goal can allow us to feel otherwise about it.[200] As a glance at the Logic of Place makes clear, in the horizon of a goal, the agent has the possibility of affecting a critical scrutiny of current feelings and desires and their transformation.

> "The willing self is not restricted to the present fluctuating field of consciousness, for in order to be able to recognize some content as the result of its own activity, it must act in terms of goals which are not part of the present field of consciousness in the same way that, for example, sensations are. Goals direct and determine change. This change in the field of self-consciousness represents a change in the willing self, and, since this change is due to the activity of the willing self, the willing self is said to determine itself."[201]

In the confines of subjective theorizing, which sees that the act is determined and the desires given, the activity of the consciousness, erecting goals for itself, has no systematic place, for it is not a static quality of subjective consciousness, but, instead, its presupposition. It points to a locus in which the subjective character of the actor is dynamically defined, but which is not itself subjective. Perhaps this is the reason why economists frequently assume that they are neither able to say anything about the goals, nor even need to. "Economics does not deal with ends as such."[202] However, this doesn't mean that economics describes actions as being without goal or purpose. Rather, it presupposes ends as given. Actions are thus always defined in the horizon of a certain already presupposed end:

> "The criterion of economy which follows from our original definitions is the security of given ends with least means (...) Once the ends ... are given as regards the disposition of means, the terms 'economical' and uneconomical' can be used with complete intelligibility."[203]

With the aid of the Logic of Place we may specify our sense of the presupposition of the givenness of ends: ends are a place of nothingness for the economic domain of discourse, in which the subjective qualities of the

---

[200] R.E. Carter, *The Nothingness beyond God*, 39.
[201] R.J. Wargo, *The Logic of Basho*, 307.
[202] L. Robbins, *An Essay on the Nature and Significance of Economic Science*, 24.
[203] L. Robbins, "The Significance of Ecnomic Science," in: K.R. Leub (ed.), *Die Österreichische Schule der Nationalökonomie*, Vol. 2, Wien 1995, 81-82.

3 The Implicit Image of the Person in Economics 91

agent are defined, without itself becoming the object of reflection. They are a locus in which all economic action is thought. Through what process or agency this place is itself defined, however, cannot be represented in the confines of subjective theorizing.

> "The ends and purposes themselves lie beyond the action and the reason; they are for our theory ... merely data, which we cannot further analyze by means of our science. ... We can't say anything further about the goals and purposes themselves except that, to active men, they appear as goals and purposes; they themselves stand outside of our explanation."[204]

Economic action is always achieved with an eye on a set end, but the latter escapes assessment by the subjective consciousness. In this sense we can really say that the nature of ends is irrelevant.[205] It is irrelevant from the viewpoint of the subjective consciousness, which apprehends itself in these goals. The givenness of the goals refers to a locus in which the subjective consciousness is thought, but which, conversely, cannot be grasped by it. Thus, the ends become a kind of limiting concept, explaining how the subjective qualities of the consciousness are defined, but never becoming, themselves, the object of explanation. "Instrumental action requires that the act be directed to the goal and that the goal be beyond rational assessment."[206] This is the presupposition of every instrumental act. Therefore, it isn't completely correct to say, as Robbins does, that economics is neutral with regard to different ends.[207] The ends become, rather, an unthought, but nevertheless given presupposition. All action is so conceived that it is always only directed to the achievement of a defined goal. There is not, therefore, any conceivable activity that could either make the goal the object of reflection or even change it. This thought is clearly enunciated by von Mises:

> "Everything that we regard as human behavior ... is purposive rational, chooses between given possibilities in order to achieve its most passionately wished for goal. Another interpretation is not to be used by a science that will keep its eyes on the act as such, but not on the constitution of its goals."[208]

Habits possess a function similar to that of goals in economic discourse. They are also presupposed as given in order to explain economic action

---

[204] L. von Mises, *Nationalökononomie*, 15.
[205] H. Stewart, "A Critique of Instrumental Reason," 62.
[206] Ibid., 62.
[207] L. Robbins, *The Significance of Economic Science*, 83.
[208] L. von Mises, *Grundprobleme der Nationalökonomie*, 82.

without becoming themselves the objects of reflection. What is missing is an autonomous theory of habits.[209] To show this, let's begin by looking at the connection in which Mill introduces the concept of habit. First, Mill describes the relation between desire and will thusly: "will is the child of desire."[210] We want to obtain those things that arouse our desire. Will seems here to be subordinate to the desires. But Mill also mentions that this relationship can be completely reversed: we often want something, not because we desire it; rather we desire something, only because we will it. In these instances, will is no longer subordinate to desire – rather, will becomes the master of desire.[211] In this way, Mill ascribes to the will a similar function as is postulated by Nishida. The will can make subjective qualities as, for instance, the desires, the objects of reflection and therefore even change them. For Mill, habit is the locus in which all this occurs:

> "The distinction between will and desire ... is an authentic and highly important psychological fact; but the fact solely consists in this – that the will, like all other parts of our constitution, is amenable to habit, and that we may will from habit what we no longer desire for itself, or desire only because we will it. (...) Will is the child of desire, and passes out of the dominion of its parent only to come under that of habit."[212]

Here it becomes unambiguous that all subjective qualities of the consciousness can be seen as subordinate to habit. Or in other words: We can look upon habit as a locus in which all subjective qualities of the actor are sheltered. This point of view is widespread in economic theory. So, for instance, Marshall believed that "Action (is) largely ruled by habit."[213] And Becker concurs, when he says that "habitual behavior permeates most aspects of life."[214] But if habits define actions and the way they are conceived and felt, then what counts for the goals of action must also count for them. Habits precede in the order of logic the subjective qualities of the acting party and cannot, on these grounds, be determined subjectively. They constitute a place of nothingness, which determines as a limiting concept all

---

[209] This is particularly emphasized by K.-H. Brodbeck, See for example, *Erfolgsfaktor Kreativität, Die Zukunft unserer Marktwirtschaft*, Darmstadt 1996, 2.

[210] J.S. Mill, *Utilitarianism, On Liberty, and Considerations on Representative Government*, edited by H.B. Acton, London 1972, 38.

[211] Ibid, 37.

[212] Ibid., 37-38.

[213] A. Marshall, *Principles of Economics*, 20.

[214] G.S. Becker is cited in F. Reckling, *Interpretative Handlungsrationalität, Intersubjektivität als ökonomisches Problem und die Ressourcen der Hermeneutik*, Marburg 2002, 136.

subjective qualities, but cannot be conceived to be a subjective quality itself. This doesn't mean that we presuppose arbitrary habits in order to ground economic acts. Just as we have seen with goals, they must have certain qualities, even though these remain unthought. These qualities could only become explicit if we find a new domain of discourse that explains how habitual and goal-orientated action determines the subjective qualities of the actor.

Let's throw a brief glance backwards. Our topic shows a similar picture as we received at the end of our section on objective behavior theories. (3.1.5) There we saw that actions, by reason of the self-reflecting character of consciousness, could not be defined by an external observer as objectified behavior. And in the present instance, we see that action is not satisfactorily explained even in the framework of subjective methodologies. The reason is simple: even subjective methodologies try to fix the consciousness as a defined entity when they want us to think of it as a static collection of feelings and desires. "But when we think of the self as the unity of conscious phenomena what we have is the known self not the knowing self."[215] The self recognized within the framework of subjective methodologies is always only a static consciousness that as a defined thing is made into an object. So we see that even our subjective methodologies objectivize the consciousness. One can say, that the level of objectification has lessened in the transition from behavioral theories to the subjective theories. If at first we observed that behavior is defined by exterior restrictions, we now suppose that the objectifiable qualities of the individual itself causally explain action. But both description presuppose the actor as a rigid substance, whose qualities are either implicitly given or objectively definable. Nishida, in his Logic of Place, turns against both interpretations. At a minimum, he sees both conceptions as abstractions, that do not grasp the authentic qualities of the consciousness. For "what ever is to any degree objectified is not consciousness."[216] Nishida refers us to this relation: for all objects it is a rule that they are not to be apprehended as substances with rigid properties, but instead, are to be defined purely in terms of context-dependence. And we are to understand this context in essence as subjective consciousness. Objects seem to be this or that always only for or in a certain consciousness. On these grounds, an action theory must bear in mind the perspective of this consciousness. But if this perspective is sub-

---

[215] K. Nishida, "The System of Self Consciousness of the Universal," partly transl. in: R.J. Wargo, *The Logic of Basho*, 367.

[216] K. Nishida is cited in R.J. Wargo, *The Logic of Basho*, 226.

jectively defined, then the consciousness is itself objectified, and thus its qualities appear as fixed. Yet at least part of the consciousness escapes such an objectification. As dynamic flux or process, it may redefine itself within distinct contexts. If one wishes to actually illustrate such a flux, one must not only get past the belief of objective (exterior) entities, but also the conceptual apprehension of the actor as a substance. In other words: we must seek for a description of the actor beyond the subject-object split.

But how is such a description even conceivable? Let's look at the coarse features of Nishida's answer. As do so many other philosophers, Nishida begins with Descartes' 'cogito ergo sum'[217], but does not seek after an objective explanation for the 'I am.' Principally, he turns against the idea that the 'I am' is to be conceived as a static essence whose nature is defined. For in this way, those qualities of the actor himself that consist in reflecting upon himself, making his feelings and desires an object of reflection, and changing them, can't be explained. But if the actor does not show any unchanging nature, it follows immediately that actions can't be defined causally through these qualities. We can't claim that there is a backgrounding actor in the sense of a static, unchanging substance against which we can erect our explanations of changes in actions. From the point of view of the Logic of Place, the conceptual error of subjective methodologies lies in the fact that they regard the actor as primarily given, and action and perception as defined through him. For Nishida, that gets the relationship exactly backwards: "no 'I-individual' dominates his experience, but instead it is just the reverse: experience constructs our I, the particular existing self."[218] Of course, he doesn't mean that there is an experience unattached to some consciousness which in some manner gives birth to the (subjective) consciousness. Rather, Nishida is referring to two different kinds of consciousness. The one he describes as the normal consciousness, in which the I as a subject stands in opposition to an outer world, or to objects. This is the subjective consciousness. This consciousness only divides an experience, which actually represents a unity. The other is the original consciousness, which is able to apprehend this unity immediately.[219] We will

---

[217] A direct reference to Descarte is found, for example, in K. Nishida, "The System of Self Consciousness of the Universal," 376.

[218] K. Nishida is cited in H. Hashi, *Die Aktualität der Philosophie*, 30. See the concept of experience in K. Nishida, *Logik des Ortes*, 291.

[219] The distinction between the normal and the original consciousness is frequently made in Mahayana Buddhism. For an explanation, see T. Izutsu, "Die Entdinglichung und Wiederverdinglichung der 'Dinge' im Zen Buddhismus," in: Y. Nitta (ed.), *Japanische Beiträge zur Phänomenologie*, Freiburg-München 1984, 18.

later discuss more extensively the view that posits these two different dimensions of consciousness. (3.3.3) For the moment, our essential point is to indicate an important quality of the original consciousness: it is a consciousness of experience in which reality is apprehended without any involvement of the subjective consciousness.[220] Hashi writes about this consciousness of experience:

> "The normal placement of a division between subject and object has not yet emerged in the midst of intensive experience. The experiencing I communicates with the dimension of experience. Without self-consciousness, which determines its thought with claims like, for instance, 'I am', 'I think', 'I believe', 'I judge', etc., the I communicates with the experience-of-truth itself. Thus, the I is a part of the dimension of experience ... The normal structure of the predicate, 'I experience and grasp the truth', has disappeared in the midst of pure experience. There persists only the dimension of the place of experience, within which the I has fused."[221]

The original consciousness is pre-reflexive in the sense that neither the subject as a this or a that is defined nor is an action divided between a bearer of the action and an object of the action: "The action takes place of itself before any conscious thought."[222] Such a division first comes to pass in a supplementary reflection. Experience thus comes before any subjective determination; it is the locus, in which all representation of the subjective consciousness is grounded. "It must be a consciousness that encompasses [and defines] the subjective consciousness."[223]

> "The 'I' does not allow itself to be made into an object ... I think of our I as a unity of consciousness , not subjectively, but rather place specifically [*basho teki*] as the self-determination of the field of consciousness."[224]

Thus from the viewpoint of the Logic of Place, experience is not erected on the ground of subjective consciousness, but, quite the reverse, this consciousness is determined through experience. In other words, experience is the basho, in which, place specifically, that determining of the field of consciousness of which Nishida speaks comes to pass. For these reasons, in order to maintain an encompassing action theory, we must define a domain of discourse within which the locus of experience is made an explicit ob-

---

[220] See for instance K. Nishida, *Logik des Ortes*, 39.
[221] H. Hashi, *Die Aktualität der Philosophie*, 28-30.
[222] R. Deshimaru is cited in R.E. Carter, *The Nothingness beyond God*, 107.
[223] K. Nishida, *Logik des Ortes*, 41.
[224] Ibid., 63.

ject of reflection, and which further explains how in this locus the subjective (normal) view of the actor is determined.

3.3 The Actor 'Beyond' the Subject-Object Split

Just as the subjective consciousness can be described in three different ways (as the ratiocinative reason, as the collectivity of desires, and as the subjective will), so, in this section, we shall show that experience can, similarly, be divided into three different levels, and that each of these levels underlies a specific form of thinking and acting. I will name these: a), the locus of habits; b), the locus of creativity; and c), the locus of the self-conscious will. Lets look at the locus of habit first. In Nishida's Logic of Place this concept is not really explicitly applied, but he does speak of "action-directing standards or ideals," explaining them further as "the standards and the ideals which guide behavior and, as such, serve as the ground for the conception of goal-directed activity."[225]

Since Nishida's analysis of these standards or ideals is difficult to understand, I will introduce some of the fundamental theories of action in East Asian philosophy that will make the locus of habits easier to understand. Doing this, I will employ certain ideas from classical Chinese philosophy (in particular, Confucianism and Daoism), from Mahayana Buddhism, and from modern Japanese philosophy. Finally I shall try to profitably incorporate these ideas in an explanation of economic action.

3.3.1 An 'East Asian' Theory of Habits

In the center of many East Asian action theories stands the insight that a great part of our actions are not spontaneous, but instead follow the line of behavioral models that have been learned in other, past situations and then transposed or applied to new situations. People do not go at every situation with a fresh approach, but act on the basis of past experiences; in other words, we do things according to habit. The difference between actions that are habitual and spontaneous actions is emphasized also in economics. For instance, Suchanek writes:

> "The adaptability of individual people in individual situations is... limited. Often enough, it would place a supererogatory demand on the individual, one impossible to meet, to re-orient himself in each situation and make the appropriate adaptive ac-

---
[225] R.J. Wargo, *The Logic of Basho*, 312.

tion choices. Instead, his actions are mostly oriented to institutions. These play differing functional roles as systems of stereotypical and stabilizing habits, rules and sanctions. They take away the burden that comes from the compulsion to continually concentrate on the actual, present requirements of the situation. In a complex environment ... their selection effect, by way of channeling action, gains meaning. ... The 'sense' of institutions lies in the fact that they select the behaviors adapted to the circumstances and provide stabilization through imposing norms on typical situations that repeat themselves."[226]

East Asian philosophy doesn't limit itself to such a description. Rather, it concentrates on realistically explaining the process of habit building. In order to build up habits, according to an important insight in this philosophical tradition, there must be something that guides action in different contexts. There must be action instructions that the actor unconsciously follows. Such instructions, in Chinese, are called the *dao* ('guiding discourse'): "*Daos* inherently guide action."[227] The question put by classical Chinese philosophy in this connection is: how is it that we apply the *dao*, the action instructions, correctly in specific situations? The answer to this question rests on the observations of the everyday. Thus, it emphasizes the overwhelming role played by learning. Humans learn to behave in certain situations in certain ways, while they learn at the same time to give up other ways of behaving. As we will show later, this learning has a social dimension. (4.2.9) We should begin at this point to discuss the function of language for individual learning. A *dao* is an instruction for action that can be communicated between different people with the help of language. The individual learns to assimilate these instructions; he 'individualizes' them, while he lets his own thought process and his perception be guided by them. His mental habits are thus standardly defined through language. At the same time he learns to translate the communicated instructions into physical activity.

There is "an ambiguity in the notion of a *dao*. On the one hand, a dao is the actual linguistic instruction set that is transmitted from A to B. On the other hand, it is the

---

[226] A. Suchanek, *Der ökonomische Ansatz und das Verhältnis von Mensch, Institution und Erkenntnis*, 78.

[227] C. Hansen, "Qing (Emotions) in Pre-Buddhist Chinese Thought," in: J. Marks, R.T. Ames (ed.), *Emotions in Asian Thought, A Dialogue in Comparative Philosophy*, New York 1995, 187.

performance that would result from theoretically correct interpretation of that *dao* into real-time behavior. I call these 'discourse *dao*' and 'performance *dao*.'"[228]

A *dao* thus guides the thought process of the individual as well as his physical activity. This resembles the East Asian belief that actions are to be understood as being equally intellectual activity and bodily doing. For instance, this is why Nishida describes action as "acting-intuition."[229]

Let's look more closely at the function of the discourse *dao*. To elevate the universal meaning of language in this connection still doesn't tell us anything about how language actually defines perceptions. Chinese philosophy emphasizes at this point the meaning of concepts through which one learns how to distinguish things from one another:

> "The dao process was inherently a guiding process, and it proceeded by means of names and cultivated abilities to make distinctions."[230]

The connection of names (words) and the distinguished things consists in the fact that we learn with the use of the former how to see things as differentiated. To such an apprehension corresponds our way of observing the context-dependency of things. A thing does not appear as something because this is its nature or essence, but because it is so labeled within a linguistic context in opposition to other things. The East Asian theories of perception don't, then, begin by assuming an essential character of things.[231] Rather they suppose that the context in which (linguistically) a thing is differentiated from another thing precedes the things:

> "Because we differentiate, there are different things. To differentiate is more primitive than the differentiated things, and to differentiate means, really, to live. ... To recognize is a differentiating function; the distinctions made by this form of recognition is the source of all differences. There are differences because a differentiating process is given."[232]

---

[228] C. Hansen, "Qing (Emotions) in Pre-Buddhist Chinese Thought," 189-90.
[229] Japanese: *kōiteki chokkan*. See R.E. Carter, *The Nothingness beyond God*, 100 for a further explanation of this concept. I am only to discuss the function of the *Discourse Dao* here.
[230] C. Hansen, "Qing (Emotions) in Pre-Buddhist Chinese Thought," 191.
[231] See for instance, ibid., 194.
[232] K.-H. Brodbeck, *Der Spielraum der Leerheit, Buddhismus im Gespräch*, Solothurn-Düsseldorf 1995, 90.

Brodbeck illustrates this differentiating function in relation to Buddhist logic in the following way:

> "You can name a table through the word, 'table' because it is distinct from a non-table. The table is what it is (its essence) only through being differentiated from everything else. A child, learning the word 'table.'.. learns by use of this word to make a distinction. In the thousands of actions that involve tables it collects experience, meaning a memory of many situations in which such a distinction is made. Every new table is evoked through the word that calls up this chain of actions. In this way thought increasingly separates itself from actual perception; we tend to see increasingly only what we already know. All of this knowing makes us ever more expert in our dealings with tables, but inhibits the seeing of each newly perceived table in its simple phenomenality. ... To make a long story short: In us, there arises, as a more and more pressing reality, an 'essence' of the table, a rubbish heap of memories, of actions, in which tables have been included (...) It [the essence of the table -SG) is the crystallized experiential history of the differences by which the word table, spoken or thought, has played a role."[233]

Let's examine more close the function of differentiating. The concept of difference, in classical Chinese philosophy, is designated by the concept pair *shi-fei*. To designate something as *shi* (this), means to learn, at the same time what *fei* (not this, that) means.

> "The relation of a term and its opposite [can be described in the following way]: If we can apply term X to the real world, then the same discrimination ability guides our application of non-X to the world. One ability to *shi-fei* gives us two opposite names."[234]

Through a difference, there emerges simultaneously two opposite concepts, that are not separable and that mutually condition each other. Chuang Tzu writes:

> "Everything has its 'that'; everything has its 'this.' ... So I say, 'that' comes out of 'this' and 'this' depends on 'that' – which is to say that 'this' and 'that' give birth to each other."[235]

We can also put this as the following formula: opposites proceed out of a unity which lies in the differentiating activity itself. "There would be no

---

[233] K.-H. Brodbeck, *Der Spielraum der Leerheit*, 111-112.
[234] C. Hansen, "Qing (Emotions) in Pre-Buddhist Chinese Thought," 195.
[235] Chuang Tzu, *The Complete Works of Chuang Tzu*, transl. by B. Watson, New York-Leiden 1968, 39.

contradiction if they did not touch each other somewhere. Facing each other is already a synthesis."[236]

The concept pair *shi-fei* describes the faculty of descriptively differentiating things from one another. This descriptive differentiating is, however, only a part of how the perception of things functions. For, together with the differentiating you learn, according to a belief common to East Asian philosophy, to evaluate things, and so to give them certain properties. A stool is good, and a table is accordingly bad, to sit on. A *shi-fei* difference comes to pass not only in terms of description, but, equally, in terms of value.[237] How self-evident this is, for instance, in Chinese tradition, can be clearly seen by the fact that Chinese characters *shi* and *fei* don't distinguish between a description and a value. *Shi* maybe be translated by 'this', but also as well by 'correct', and *fei*, conversely, with 'not this' and 'false.'[238]

Because in the differentiating process things are named as something and at the same time properties are ascribed to them that hold positive or negative values, it is a locus, in which the objective world is thought. According to Chinese philosophy, things are always only recognized objects in the locus of differentiation. Again, difference rests on the experience accrued in dealing with things; it is the result of linguistic habits. This interpretation points to a similarity to Nishida's Logic of Place: the objective world of things is not a world that in and for itself exists. Rather, it is one that purely in a contexts shows itself as this specific world. And this context is only thinkable as a field of consciousness. It has become pretty clear that Nishida doesn't conceive of the consciousness field subjectively, but thinks of it, instead, in place specific terms. The ideas of classical Chinese philosophy show, here, how this is possible. The differentiating activity is the result of linguistic habits that can't be ascribed to a single subject, or an ego. It is very true that differentiating is an activity of the consciousness, "yet this 'consciousness" is not an individual existence form, a kind of mist in my private head."[239] Rather a social character can be ascribed to it. This becomes clear, for instance, in the example of language.

---

[236] Nishida, *Intellegibility and the Philosophy of Nothingness*, 112.
[237] D.L. Hall, R.T. Ames, *Thinking from the Han, Self Truth and Transcendence in Chinese and Western Culture*, New York 1998, 171.
[238] The double character of these symbols *shi* und *fei* is also maintained in the Japanese. The first (pronounced ZE, kore) can mean 'right', 'correct' as well as 'this.'The latter (pronounced HI) approximates to the 'un' prefix in English, negating attributes as well as descriptions.
[239] K.-H. Brodbeck, *Der Spielraum der Leerheit*, 91.

"Language ... is .. represented as an unconscious sediment of semantic effects that remains from the words that were at one time in the past actually or virtually in use. It should be noticed that the 'past' ... is not limited to the past experiences of a single individual person, for it transcends the range of what the individual person actually has experienced and reaches deeply into the collectivity of the life experience of her parents and ancestors, insofar as this has been passed down to her in the form of a native language."[240]

At first glance is seems as if the definition of the subject or of the subjective consciousness is simply being subjected to a sleight of hand. If things always exist in the locus of linguistic habits as things, how is the subjective consciousness thus defined? East Asian philosophy gives to this a very simple, but also perhaps unusual answer: the definition of the subject comes to pass in the locus of habits as well as the definition of the objective world, which it faces. Both definitions have an equal logical status. But how is this imaginable? Let's look at the answer of Mahayana Buddhism, which begins its interpretation by stipulating that "every thing only empirically exists insofar as it is an object - be it now known or at least knowable – for a knowing subject."[241] The object is not imaginable without a knowing subject. But the same thing is also conversely true: "the knowing subject, the 'consciousness' is always objectivizing consciousness. ... Consciousness is ... always a 'consciousness-of.'"[242] It is always necessary related to the differentiated objects. In the locus of the differentiating process there can never be a pure and simple consciousness. The (subjective) reason, for instance, is defined as knowledge of objects. It can't, therefore, be thought of as independent of them. But not only the reason relates itself in the locus of differentiation necessarily to the objects it recognizes. Precisely because one thing is discriminated from another, according to the conceptions of Mahayana Buddhism, does the subjective consciousness like the one thing while disliking the other. Classical Chinese philosophy explains this connection like this: every individual learns, together with the difference intrinsic to a *shi-fei* pair, also to feel in a certain way. Even feelings aren't simply given in and for themselves. They are always tied to a differentiating process. From this it can immediately be deduced that a feeling always can only arise in connection with another, opposite feeling. "A sensation that we have doesn't exist independently, but stands always,

---

[240] T. Izutsu, "Die Entdinglichung und Wiederverdinglichung der 'Dinge' im Zen Buddhismus," 29.
[241] Ibid., 16.
[242] Ibid., 16-17.

necessarily, in opposition to another."²⁴³ Mill confirms this observation: "as in truth the pleasure and pain seldom exist separately, but almost always together."²⁴⁴

This mutual dependent relationship of negative and positive feelings arises because they attach themselves to differentiated objects. Something gives us pleasure; something gives us pain. We don't simply feel pure pain or pure pleasure, but first the thought or the presence of an object makes this possible. Classical Chinese philosophy makes this thought concrete when it insists that the individual, learning a concept, simultaneously learns to feel in the face of a thing that is named by this concept: towards that, which one has learned to call *shi* (correct/good) one feels attracted. Conversely, one feels repelled by that which is named *fei* (false/bad). Subjective feelings are thus attached to specific objects, and are as dependent upon them as it is reason. In this connection, desire can also be more precisely defined. Just like subjective feelings, desire is always oriented towards objects. It is a desire-for-something. Classical Chinese philosophy thus calls desire an attitude "towards the things as named."²⁴⁵ The actor learns to discriminate between different things. Joined to this discrimination, in experience, is an evaluation, and this evaluation once again defines his attitude in the face of things. Every *shi-fei* pair brings with it an attitude of being for or against an object. It defines whether we affirm or refuse something. This thought becomes clear also in Daoism:

> "The key to mastering a dao is learning its names and being able to apply them. Learning a name consists in learning to make a socially appropriate distinction with that name and having the socially appropriate pattern of desires. Laozi focuses particularly on evaluative guiding terms. We learn evaluative distinctions (good/bad, beautiful/ugly) together, and where we draw the line between them is a matter of learning the practice of one school or group rather than another. When we learn those guiding conventions, Laozi observes, we inevitably also learn along with them that group's pattern of desire – for the beautiful and aversion to the ugly. Like the distinctions, these desires are socially conditioned. Each tradition trains us in the socially appropriate responses to things after we have named them. (...) We get those desires by learning language and names."²⁴⁶

---

²⁴³ K. Nishida, *Über das Gute*, 112.
²⁴⁴ J.S. Mill, *Utilitarianism, On Liberty, and Considerations on Representative Government*, 35-36.
²⁴⁵ C. Hansen, "Qing (Emotions) in Pre-Buddhist Chinese Thought," 202.
²⁴⁶ Ibid., 192.

If we recognize an object firstly as good, beautiful, valuable, etc., then the subjective feelings in the face of this object are positive. At the same time, the desires will guide us to obtain this object. Even Mill confirms this observation:

> "Desiring a thing and finding it pleasant, aversion to it and thinking of it as painful, are phenomena entirely inseparable, or rather two parts of the same phenomenon; in strictness of language, two different modes of naming the same psychological fact: that to think of an object as desirable ..., and to think of it as pleasant are one and the same thing; and that to desire anything, except in proportion as the idea of it is pleasant, is a physical and metaphysical impossibility."[247]

As our preceding interpretation should have made clear by now, experience – in the sense of habit – is a locus which shelters the objective as well as the subjective world and permits them to interrelatedly arise. Habit itself remains, in turn, both from the objective as well as the subjective perception, a place of nothingness. It is the given, that implicitly lies under every subjective and objective perception, without itself becoming an explicit object for reflection. From this we can conclude that the individual that is defined as a subject, cannot recognize the locus of habitualized experiences. Since her consciousness as consciousness-of is always oriented only to objects, and thus always only deals with the exterior environment, it cannot perceive the locus, in which it is itself defined. Therefore, the original unity of experience, which is split through the differentiating activity of the mind into a subjective and an objective world, remains necessarily hidden to the view of the subjective consciousness.

Up to this point, we have only explained how two concepts are differentiated from each other and how this differentiating process guides our perception of those objects designated by means of these concepts. In daily life, however, the actor isn't just using two concepts. How are we to use our explanation to talk about action in the midst of a multiplicity of concepts? East Asian philosophy responds by proceeding from a hierarchical ordering of distinctions. As the *dao* enfolds a collectivity of concept pairs, so one distinction will be superior to all other distinctions. As an ur-distinction, it becomes the locus in which, implicitly, all other distinctions are thought:

---

[247] J.S. Mill, *Utilitarianism, On Liberty, and Considerations on Representative Government*, 36.

"The relation of standards [can be explained in the following way]: A standard for practical interpretation of the entire cluster of names used in a *dao*^{guiding discourse} presupposes a prior ability to apply the set of names used in the standard. Some ur-distinction or dichotomy guides *shi-fei*^{this not-this} judgments as applied to every other term pair in the language."[248]

By way of some examples, we can more precisely define the function of the ur-distinction. In utilitarianism, for instance, the difference between pleasure and pain (Bentham) or happiness and unhappiness (Mill) is emphasized. What a super powerful position such a ur-distinction takes becomes clear, especially with Bentham:

"Nature has placed mankind under the governance of two sovereign masters, pain and pleasure. It is for them alone to point out what we ought to do, as well as to determine what we shall do. On the one hand the standard of right and wrong, on the other the chain of causes and effects, are fastened to their throne. They govern us in all we do, in all we say, in all we think: every effort we can make to throw off our subjection, will serve but to demonstrate and confirm it."[249]

According to Bentham the ur-distinction of pleasure and pain guides the perception as well as physical activity. A simple example can illuminate this: say that an actor has the two alternatives of either eating ice cream or staying at home. If her action comes to pass in the *dao* of the ur-distinction pleasure/pain, then she will judge the ice cream (unconsciously) according to how much pleasure and how much pain it will procure her. And she will put the other alternative through the same process. In this way one alternative will be judged to be a better, and the other a worse value. Towards the better alternative, desire is directed; physical activity will try to satisfy this desire. The evaluation of the action alternatives will thus happen (implicitly) in the locus of the ur-distinction of pleasure/pain. In this locus it is possible to compare in one homogeneous horizon all the concepts that are applied in a *dao*. In this way the differentiated concepts become available for comparison and preference ranking not only in regard to their opposites (A, not-A), but also in regard to all other concepts (A,B,C...) "Things then are good or evil, only in reference to pleasure or pain. That we call good, which is apt to cause or increase pleasure, or diminish pain in us."[250] The

---

[248] C. Hansen, "Qing (Emotions) in Pre-Buddhist Chinese Thought," 195.
[249] J. Bentham, *Introduction to the Principles of Morals and Legislation*, Oxford 1907, chapt. I, sect. 1.
[250] J. Locke is cited in J. Hirschberger, *Geschichte der Philosophie*, Vol. 2, Freiburg i. Br. 1980, 214.

evaluation of objects is determined like the subjective feelings and desires in the face of these objects. Whatever we name in the locus of the ur-distinction as *shi* (correct) will awaken positive feelings in us and arouse our desires.

The ur-distinction is as little simply given as all the other distinctions. It is the result of past and present experiences that the individual makes in his environmental niche. It is nothing other than a habit that is superimposed over the other processes of habituation. Within a *dao* it gives a direction and shape, in the sense of an ideal or standard, to every perception, without itself becoming an explicit object of reflection. In other words: the ur-distinction always remains a place of nothingness for all actions within a *dao*. It is in this connection that the goal-orientation of action becomes intelligible. For the goal is continually imagined to be that which we have learned to designate as *shi* in the ur-distinction. Whoever originally differentiates within a *dao* between pain and pleasure will define pleasure as the goal of his action; whoever thinks in the locus of pleasure and pain, will strive after pleasurable things. Thus, Mill can assume that "pleasure, and freedom from pain, are the only things desirable as ends; and that all desirable things ... are desirable either for the pleasure inherent in themselves, or as means to the promotion of pleasure and the prevention of pain."[251] We can also formulate this to mean that the *shi* (this, correct) of the ur-distinction determines the style and manner of desiring. The subjective consciousness can't influence this style, because it is always simply the result of these desires. The subjective consciousness can therefore question neither the goal of action nor the strivings and wishes in question. Thus we encounter MacIntyre's point here, when he writes:

> "The criticism of our desires and their rational remolding have no place in the Hobbesian system. It follows that, inevitably, our desires are for one individual object after another; and thus desires cannot include the desire for a certain kind of life, the desire that our desires should be of a certain kind."[252]

3.3.2 Economic Activity as Habit

We can now see from the previous section that the definition of the ur-distinct is, from the East Asian point of view, one of the most important

---

[251] J.S. Mill, "Utilitarismus," in: O. Höffe (ed.), *Einführung in die utilitaristische Ethik*, 86.
[252] A. MacIntyre, *Geschichte der Ethik im Überblick*, 132

keys to the explanation of habitual activity. We shall now try to show the ur-distinction in which economic action occurs. We must begin by working out a *dao* specific to economics, which I will call the *economic dao*. If we follow the arguments of the utilitarians, it seems as if the concept pairs of happiness/unhappiness, pleasure/pain are the most important ur-distinctions. Looking more closely we will show that this idea is deceptive, because these differences implicitly presume another form of difference already: the quantitative difference. This is the difference between a more and a less. For many utilitarian authors, this difference seems so self-evident that it isn't even thematized. It operates, instead, as an unthought presupposition.

Firstly, lets see what action-directing idea underlies the utilitarian concept-pair pain/pleasure, happiness/unhappiness. The first thing that strikes us is that the concept of pleasure, as well as that of pain, does not represent a homogenous concept that is immediately understandable. Rather, we distinguish different forms of pleasure.[253] In order to be able to compare these pleasures with each other, there must be some underlying standard of comparison. A standard of measurement that can be applied not only to make pleasures measurable and comparable, but also all pains. The actor should evaluate pain and pleasure with reference to the same measure and so enable us to produce one "gratification-value."[254] The common measurability of pain and pleasure is thus presupposed:

> "The subtraction and addition of degrees of gratification suggested by Bentham presupposes, of course, one common scale of measurement for pleasure and pain; without its help, degrees of gratification cannot be enumerated and without numbers they cannot be added or subtracted."[255]

This one scale of measurement is understood in utilitarianism to be numerable. "Number," as Bentham explains, "is the circumstance, which contributes, in the largest proportion, to the formation of the standard."[256] Measure and number are supposed to make it possible to grasp things as quantities and through quantitative difference construct a relation between all things. Number, understood as pure quantity, is the standard, to which all other concepts are related. This is clearly repeated by Bentham:

---

[253] J. Bentham, *Introduction to the Principles of Morals and Legislation*, chapt IV.
[254] O. Höffe, *Einführung in die utilitaristische Ethik*, 11.
[255] Ibid., 20.
[256] J. Bentham, *Introduction to the Principles of Morals and Legislation*, chapt. 1, sect. 1, footnote.

"The same process [of augmentation] is alike applicable to pleasure and pain, in whatever shape they appear: and by whatever denomination they are distinguished: to pleasure, whether it be called good (which is properly the cause or instrument of pleasure) or profit (which is distant pleasure, or the cause or instrument of, distant pleasure,) or convenience, or advantage, benefit, emolument, happiness, and so forth: to pain, whether it be called evil, (which corresponds to good) or mischief, or inconvenience, or disadvantage, or loss, or unhappiness, and so forth."[257]

But if at this point all pleasure and pain is thought in the same locus of quantity, then by this means we may surely make a claim about the actor's perception. Bentham formulates this in the form of a clear instruction: "Sum up all the values of all the pleasures on the one side, and those of all the pains on the other. The balance, if it be on the side of pleasure, will give the good tendency of the act upon the whole, with respect to the interests of that individual person; if on the side of pain, the bad tendency of it upon the whole."[258] The actor thus calculates over pleasure and pain; his perception is a calculation. "Under rational apprehension ... I understand computation. ... Rational apprehension goes back to two operations of the mind: addition and subtraction."[259] The discourse dao thus subsists in a calculus.

"He (Bentham, SG) points to four sources of pain and pleasure and eventually draws up an operative metric, the hedonistic calculus or the utility calculus, which allows all imaginable sensations of pleasure and pain, even of an heterogeneous nature, to calculate against each other and to erect a sum total of human happiness."[260]

That with the calculus we are dealing with a fundamental action-orienting idea becomes clear from the fact that utilitarianism projects a calculation process that should logically proceed any action. By it, every action alternative is evaluated by reference to the expected consequences. What people do is thus "completely evident: they deal with pleasure and pain as positive and negative quantities, that are accessible to algebraic treatment."[261] When in this way economics appears as a reckoning of pleasure and pain[262] and constructs the calculus as the dominant *discourse dao*, then

---

[257] Ibid., chapt. IV, sect. 7.
[258] Ibid., chapt. IV, sect. 4.
[259] T. Hobbes, *Vom Körper*, Hamburg 1967, 6.
[260] O. Höffe, *Einführung in die utilitaristische Ethik*, 13.
[261] B. Biervert, J. Wieland, "Der ethische Gehalt ökonomischer Kategorien," 40. The authors are referring here to Jevons.
[262] W.S. Jevons, *The Theory of Political Economy*, 44.

the ur-distinction guiding all other *shi-fei* judgments becomes immediately unambiguous. For let perception become so limited that it only comports quantities, yet it will still distinguish between more and less. This is the *shi-fei* judgment that the ur-distinction of the *economic dao* presents to us. The essential thing is that the difference more/less not only plays its role as a descriptive function, but equally, too, substantializes a value. More is always considered as a *shi* (good), while a less is understood as a *fei* (bad). In particular, this clarifies the fact that a more is understood within the *economic dao* as the single authentic goal of all action. And here we find the explicit grounds of the implicitly presupposed striving after more of the neoclassicals. For whether you call the goal of action a maximal satisfaction of need, the greatest pleasure[263], or a maximization of utility[264], it is always conceived in the locus of the 'more.' Here is the way the doctrine of action became the "theory of maximizing behavior."[265]

We already have seen that every *dao*, according to the East Asian belief, is learned in everyday life, where it is the product of past experiences, of habits. But what kind of experiential process concretely underlies the economic *dao*? When we turn back to the distinction between pleasure and pain (happiness/unhappiness), it becomes evident that its metric is not only defined quantitatively, but that, instead, its metric homogeneity is given by some economists very precisely in terms of money. So, for instance, Gossen writes that through the metric of money the "quantity of all other enjoyments" can be defined.[266] That the quantitative difference as the ur-distinction assumes a greater significance, the stronger habits are defined through interaction with money, speaks somewhat for this position. In more prudent words: money at least can be interpreted as an "example, expression or a symbol of the modern emphasis of instant quantification."[267] For it is the only thing whose quality "consists exclusively in its quantity."[268] "Neither gold nor coin in their properties and forms are important; what counts is only the number, the quantum."[269]

---

[263] O. Höffe, *Einführung in die utilitaristische Ethik*, 10-11.
[264] G. Kirchgässner, *Homo oeconomicus*, 15.
[265] K.-H. Brodbeck, *Die fragwürdigen Grundlagen der Ökonomie*, 211. Brodbeck is referring here to P.A. Samuelson.
[266] H.H. Gossen, *Entwicklung der Gesetze des menschlichen Verkehrs und der daraus fließenden Regeln für das menschliches Handeln*, Braunschweig 1854, 123.
[267] G. Simmel, *The Philosophy of Money*, transl. by T. Bottomore and D. Frisby. London 1990, 279. [My translation.-RG]
[268] Ibid., 259.
[269] K.-H. Brodbeck, *Die fragwürdigen Grundlagen der Ökonomie*, 220.

"Wherever we reduce qualitative events to quantitative relationships, there remain elements of the physical, personal, and psychological type that in themselves must be qualitatively characterized in some measure, but whose greater or lesser decides the particular outcome. One can always push these particularities so far back that yesterday's still undissolved qualitative elements are recognized, today, in terms of mass and number. But we can continue on this process indefinitely and in every given moment there will still persist a qualitative particularity of the elements with which the question of 'how much' will deal. ... only money achieves this freedom from all 'hows', this exclusive specificity of the 'how much.' Money [has] completely dissolved the corresponding ties to that which becomes through it; the pure economic value has gained a body, out of whose quantity relationships all possible authentic products derive without the necessity of having to put something other to represent its quantity. Thus, one of the great tendencies of life – the reduction of quality to quantity – finds in money its most intense and independently mobile representation."[270]

A person who has learned to interact with money can trace every thing back to one concrete, graspable, quantitative metric. Money creates the possibility of imposing an order on all things according to measure and number. It makes things comparable by their prices, independently of the (qualitative) properties they might otherwise have. Or to speak with a higher level of generality, it is the foundation of all calculating:

"Only through the development of accounting have mass and number and calculating acquired meaning for human acts and operations. All the measurements of physics and biology first obtained their meaning, in relation to action, through accounting; and only accounting makes it possible to do calculating and estimating not simply theoretically, but, instead, practically – meaning in the service of action."[271]

A still further observation is important: for the purposes of interaction with money, the solely meaningful factor is how much of it one possesses. This is the reason we can limit the differences in actuality to the difference of more and less. At least, this is valid for those interactions with money in which accumulation is the whole purpose in and for itself. But this doesn't mean that money is hoarded instead of being spent for commodities. Rather, money is spent in order to get yet more money. The exchange function of money is not used, in order to get things that you use, but in order to sell things to make a (monetary) profit. Money is applied to the pur-

---

[270] G. Simmel, *The Philosophy of Money*, 275. [My translation - R.G.]
[271] L. von Mises, *Nationalökonomie*, 219.

chase of commodities "with the goal, to gain back more money."[272] The more satisfies here not only a descriptive function, but instead also a evaluative; a surplus of money is always judged to be good. Thus the love of money can become the goal of all action:

> "Money is, in many cases, desired in and for itself; the desire to possess it is often stronger than the desire to use it, and goes on increasing when all desires which point to ends beyond it, to be compassed by it, are falling off. It may, then, be said truly, that money is desired not for the sake of an end, but as part of that end."[273]

Money becoming the goal of all action is thus "a source of that 'ratio' whose content reduces itself to the simply quantitative more."[274]. This more can be extended into infinity, just as numbers can infinitely advance. A monetary more seems always better than a less, indifferent to how much of it one possesses.

The meaning of money comes into particularly sharp focus when we look at the specific process of habituation to which the merchant is subject. For his act directs itself solely to money: "The beginning and end of his action is money."[275]

> "The merchant who sells his commodities for money, in order to make more money, is the first embodiment of this infinity as a social characteristic, or more exactly: merchants historically have been the first to apply extensively the simple thought model of 'more-is-better,' and so serve as a model for that form of rationality, that exhausts itself in a quantitative more ... Long before all forces were reduced to one force in physics, merchants calculated all commodities in the economic substance, money. ... Money becomes a thought model for everything calculable and numerable, the daybooks of the merchant become archetypes of experimental protocols, and in that sense the art of the merchant is the source of rationality."[276]

Montesquieu describes the striving of the merchant for more very perspicuously:

---

[272] K.-H. Brodbeck, *Erfolgsfaktor Kreativität*, 231.
[273] J.S. Mill, *Utilitarianism, On Liberty, and Considerations on Representative Government*, 34.
[274] K.-H. Brodbeck, *Die fragwürdigen Grundlagen der Ökonomie*, 195.
[275] Ibid., 220.
[276] Ibid., 210-213.

"One business deal leads to another: the small to the medium, the medium to the great; and the man who was so greedy to earn only a little money gets into a situation where he is not less greedy to earn a lot of money."[277]

The striving after more money originally characteristic of the merchant can become habitual for every person. Simmel speaks here of a domination that money has won over thought processes in general.[278] If action is defined through this habit, than it is no longer a question of the correct use of something,[279] but instead of "a possession, which exceeds use. He [the person - SG] evidently wants to always possess more than he can use."[280]

Even when the ur-distinction of more and less can be observed as a general thought process we have not therewith said anything about what things or concepts are defined through this *discourse dao*. For according to the East Asian belief we can only put certain concepts in relation in a *dao*. We learn at the same time that we learn the ur-distinction to what group of concepts it is to be applied. If this group is defined the circumference or extent of the *dao* become visible. The difficulty here consists in the fact that the ur-distinction always just serves as the implicit presupposition of thought and is not an object of reflection itself. Therefore it is often obscure what *shi-fei* judgments it encompasses. Yet we can still define the circumference of the *economic dao* when we focus on the question about whether the economic actor purely concentrates on the quantitative or also on the qualitative properties of objects. Bentham's utilitarianism has been reproached, for instance, with presupposing a purely quantitative orientation. It represents a hedonism that must be purely materially oriented and neglects any but bodily pleasures.[281] Opposing this viewpoint, Mill represents a utilitarianism that takes into consideration not only quantitative but even qualitative elements. In particular he includes different qualities of pleasure for instance in the realm of mental, scientific, artistic or humanitarian pleasures in his reflections. Even recent economic literature emphasizes that the economic actor is not exclusively materialist. In principle he could value all properties of an action alternative. For example, Kirchgässner sees the reason for such a turn away from the materialistic motive in the fact that the modern economic actor has a new value horizon which encompasses all

---

[277] Montesquieu is cited inA. Hirschman, *Leidenschaften und Interessen*, 64.
[278] G. Simmel, *The Philosophy of Money*, 252.
[279] B. Biervert, J. Wieland, "Der ethische Gehalt ökonomischer Kategorien," 31.
[280] A. Baruzzi, Freiheit, *Recht und Gemeinwohl, Grundfragen einer Rechtsphilosophie*, Darmstadt 1990, 3.
[281] O. Höffe, *Einführung in die utilitaristische Ethik*, 22.

values from altruism up to hedonism. "He values not only the material properties of a commodity, but also, for example, its aesthetic quality, and really in principle all properties that are bundled with a certain alternative that he can choose."[282]

At first glance it seems as if all evaluative differentiations would play the same role; distinct qualitative aspects seem to play a part near the quantitative. But this leaves completely unconsidered the question of whether being neighbors to each other actually implies a multitude of ur-distinctions or a subordination of many distinctions under one ur-distinction. In other words: it isn't clear, whether there is yet another *dao* near the *economic dao* in contemporary economic theory, or if ever more concepts and distinctions are to be subsumed under the *economic dao*. It could be argued that really the latter is the case. Already in Mill it is clear that he is thinking of the qualitative (or) mental pleasures implicitly in the ur-distinction of more or less. For he makes the induction that in a comparative evaluation the bodily pleasures will be on a lower step than the mental pleasures; people strive for the mental pleasures more strongly than for the sensual. Mill has to imply that there is a perception which interprets the kinds of pleasures quantitatively as "more or less strongly striven for"[283] just in order to make his induction work. And so it follows that Mill classifies the mental pleasures as worth calculating or calculable. On each distinction of mental pleasure and its opposite Mill superimposes a quantitative judgment. Independent of what may be ascribed to things in terms of (qualitative) properties, all of these properties could be posited in some relation to each other through the calculus. Each sort of qualitative *shi-fei* judgment is thus subsumed under the *economic dao*. So, without any ambiguity, Mill is far from the position that would let us consider another ur-distinction in place of the one that is characteristic of the *economic dao*, or even, at the very least, next to it. A similar consideration holds for contemporary economic theory: it might recognize and explicate new distinctions over and over again; but this will always occur (implicitly) within the *economic dao*, and thus in the locus in which the more or less is thought. It turns out that the *economic dao* is the exclusive imaginable locus of all perception and activity. This is especially apparent in Becker, for whom a utility calculation underlies every human activity:

> "Indeed, I have come to the position that the economic approach is a comprehensive one that is applicable to all human behavior, be it behavior involving money

---
[282] G. Kirchgässner, *Homo oeconomicus*, 16.
[283] O. Höffe, *Einführung in die utilitaristische Ethik*, 23.

prices or imputed shadow prices, repeated or infrequent decisions, large or minor decisions, emotional or mechanical ends, rich or poor persons, men or women, adults or children, adults or children, brilliant or stupid persons, patients or therapists, businessmen or politicians, teachers or students."[284]

Clearly, the assumption of the universal value of calculus as the discourse dao is found even in the way economic methodologies determine the objective and the subjective views of the individual. For here it becomes apparent that both are always only thought inside the *economic dao*. First let's take a look at objective methodologies. It has already been demonstrated with regard to neoclassical economics how all commodities are implicitly conceived in the locus of a quantitative metric. (3.1.2). We can now explain this fact, for all things are always perceived in the locus of the economic ur-distinction. The distinction of more or less precedes all things; this ur-distinction is superposed over all *shi-fei* judgments. In this way all things are recognized as commodities and as such to be evaluated and compared among each other independently of their other specific properties:

> "It would be easy to multiply examples that illustrate the growing preponderance of the category of quantity over that of quality, or more precisely, the tendency to dissolve quality into quantity, to remove the elements more and more from quality, to grant them only specific forms of motion and to interpret everything that is specifically, individually and qualitatively determined as the more or less, the bigger or smaller, the wider or narrower, the more or less frequent of those colorless elements and awarenesses that are only accessible to numerical determination ... The interest in how much ... belongs to the basis of our intellectual makeup, and is the envelope that contains the note on our interest in qualities."[285]

The objective character of things as commodity is relativized to the locus, which subsumes all distinctions under the ur-distinction of the more or less. Another view of things is practically not possible inside this locus, because all perception comes to pass in the *shi-fei* of the more or less. Shrinking perception like this can obviously not be presupposed as a universal. It remains, rather, relative to habitual interaction with money. For the property of costing money soon develops the quantitative character of things:

---

[284] G.S. Becker, *Der ökonomische Ansatz zur Erklärung menschlichen Verhaltens*, 7.
[285] G. Simmel, *The Philosophy of Money*, 273.

"The fact that an increasing number of things can be had for money, insofar as it is consistent with the fact that it has grown into the central and absolute value, entails that things now are finally only valuable when they cost money, and that our experience of their qualitative value seems to us to be only a function of the more of less of their monetary price."[286]

The property of being monetized makes it possible to neglect all other properties things may have. More precisely, while these properties may still be recognized, they will be regarded only in the horizon of getting more (money). We should once more cite a passage from Simmel, who describes this process as a destruction of all the formations:

"Money as such is the most terrible destroyer of forms. No matter what the reason is that the form of things a, b, and c cost the same price as m, their differentiation –the specific form of each of them – does not effect their fixed value at all but is submerged in the m which equally represents a, b, and c. Form is not a determining factor within economic evaluation. As soon as our interest is reduced to the money value of objects, their form – even though it may have brought about their value – becomes as irrelevant to us as it is to their weight."[287]

The crystal clarity of such form-destruction emerges before everything else in the objective methodologies of neoclassical economics. The property of being monetizable takes precedent over all things inside the *economic dao*. It is a locus of absolute nothingness, which defines the objective world of things, but without being, from an objective viewpoint, itself determinable.

Let's observe, at this point, the subjective view of the actor. Within economic methodologies the actor is construed as a field of consciousness in which commodities are, as it were, mirrored. This becomes evident in the fact that his properties are exclusively conceived in their mutual relationship to the objective world, while this relationship is (implicitly) facilitated in the locus of the *economic dao*. I would like to briefly enlarge upon this thought. It must firstly be made clear that (economic) rationality is always imagined as a consciousness-of. The individual consciousness field shelters in itself only objects that are represented in a homogenous commodity space. The consciousness is so conceived that it recognizes the things as commodities, and values them in terms of their monetary worth. In other words: its faculty of judgment is limited to a perception process which is defined by the ur-distinction of more or less. Not only does thinking occur

---

[286] G. Simmel, *The Philosophy of Money*, 279.
[287] Ibid, 272.

in this *shi-fei* judgment, but feeling does as well. Thus the consequence of the more or less is the "summoning in the subject of the most contradictory feelings, the deepest pain and the highest satisfaction, together with all the middle terms in between these poles."[288] The subject feels drawn to the commodities that promise the 'more.' The subjective desire is defined by the goal setting of the *economic dao* as it elevates its *shi* (more) judgment to a maxim. It directs itself only to those objects that promise progressively more. How very much the actor can thus be regarded to be defined through the love of money is made clear when this love is described as one of "the strongest moving forces of human life."[289] Thus, money exists not only as the unthought presupposition of the objective world of commodities, but also of the (subjective) feelings and desires. It is the implicit homogeneous measurement by which human subjective motives are valued and compared. Marshall makes this clear:

> "The motive is supplied by a definite amount of money: and it is this definite and exact money measurement of the steadiest motives in business life, which has enabled economics far to outrun every other branch of the study of man. (...) The force of a person's motives ... can be approximately measured by the sum of money, which he will just give up in order to secure a desired satisfaction; or again by the sum which is just required to induce him to undergo a certain fatigue."[290]

If a maximal need for satisfaction or a utility maximizing set of behaviors is imputed to the actor, then he is himself already defined within the *economic dao*. His existence is, thus, not simply given but should also be understood context-dependently. We can also formulate this idea like so: the homo oeconomicus so often adverted to in economic literature exists only within the *economic dao*. His rationality and will are determined - just as much as his feelings and desires - exclusively in the locus of quantitative difference. In other words, the existence of homo oeconomicus is relative to a definite context which can be characterized as a habituation process that is modeled on the ideal of the merchant. The proposition, "the new homo oeconomicus is the normal man,"[291] is only valid inside this context. It can have no claim, outside of this, to universality.

---

[288] G. Simmel, *The Philosophy of Money*, 273 (translation modified).
[289] J.S. Mill, *Utilitarianism, On Liberty, and Considerations on Representative Government*, 34. See also A. Marshall, who writes: "With careful precautions money affords good measure of the moving force of a great part of motives by which men's life are fashioned." *Principles of Economics*, 39.
[290] Ibid., 15.
[291] G.C. Homans is cited in G. Kirchgässner, *Homo oeconomicus*, 16.

3.3.3 Habit as the Unconscious Locus of Economic Activity

It is an essential property of habitual action that it is standardized. The person who is defined through habits always conducts himself in similar situations in the same or at least similar ways, because his action in the present situation is oriented to past, already lived through situations. This property of habitual action makes it possible to forecast conduct in certain situations. Mill recognized, here, an essential advantage of habits, because "both in feeling and conduct, habit is the only thing which imparts certainty."[292] If the habitual perception is defined through a calculus, then clearly we can understand why actions are not only foreseeable for others, but also are to a certain point calculable. Yet the presupposition for this factor is not only that the action be defined in the *economic dao*. Rather, this must hold for both the observed and the observer alike. That action are calculable for an observer, not only the perception of the observed, but also of the observer must be guided by calculation. In other terms: a comparable ur-distinction must underlay the *discourse dao* of the actor and the domain of discourse of the researcher. From this we can impute the fact that habits are not simply individual, but instead are general. If the *economic dao* becomes a general habit we can understand why actions appear at least circumstantially calculable. Yet to inductively make the step to thinking that all action is calculable goes too far. For, as East Asian philosophy makes clear, the predictability of actions is always limited to a certain dao. It is, so to speak, relative to the habit. Only if someone acts habitually is his action foreseeable:

> "Calculable transitions between situations are based on unchanged habits. But habits are always relative to something other: the possibility of altering the habits or to substitute others for them. (...) Because there are habits, there are also mechanical seeming structures in human action, yet these structures are always arranged in a situation that can also be voluntarily changed."[293]

But how can an action be imagined that neither submits to habits in general nor the *economic dao* in particular? This question is for the most part not generally posed in economic theory. For if it is always presupposed, that utility maximization is the exclusively given goal of action[294] or all actions

---

[292] J.S. Mill, *Utilitarianism, On Liberty, and Considerations on Representative Government*, 38.
[293] K.-H. Brodbeck, *Die fragwürdigen Grundlagen der Ökonomie*, 110.
[294] G. Kirchgässner, *Homo oeconomicus*, 15.

are defined through the utility calculus,[295] this can mean nothing other than that we are to regard the *economic dao* as a universal habit. This habit is supposed to determine all actions. Hume for instance explicitly names this presupposition, when he labels avarice as 'eternal' and 'universal.'[296]

Let's see firstly what implicit assumptions with relation to the actor are hidden behind this presupposition. As we have shown, Mill regards the will as subordinate to the habits. (3.2.3) For the human will, the habits appear as already given. They are like exogenous determinates, that cannot be put to further questioning; instead they originally determine all desires. "Wherever a desire arises, the complete cause was therefore there; in fact, the desire could not possibly not follow, meaning it follows with necessity."[297] But if something appears as the causal motive, then it cannot be changed by the human will. Menger formulated this thought when he postulated the conditions under which persons sense something as necessary as being independent of human will: "Whether and under which conditions a thing is useful to me, whether and under what conditions it is a commodity ... all this is as independent of my will just as much as a law of chemistry is from the will of the experimental chemist."[298] The economic habit of striving after more is given the status of a natural law.[299] "All the phenomena of daily life," as Gossen puts it, is explained "as the necessary consequence of the striving existing in every single person to increase the sum of his life happiness to the greatest amount."[300] The essential aspect is not to observe habits, here, as action-guiding. We have already uncovered this idea in East Asian philosophy. What is decisive is to observe habits as an outer law, to which the actor is necessarily subjected. "When they (habits interpreted as institutions – S.G.) fix human conduct on a certain course, they materialize it and subject it to outer laws."[301] In terms of Nishida's Logic of Place, this means looking at habits as the place of nothingness which defines the will while remaining itself invisible. The individual doesn't recognize the habits as a locus that it defines, but rather, conversely, lets himself be defined by them. Consciousness is passively constructed, unconscious of the actual locus of its actions. "Reason looks out

---

[295] G.S. Becker, *Der ökonomische Ansatz zur Erklärung menschlichen Verhaltens*, 4.
[296] D. Hume is cited inA.O. Hirschman, *Leidenschaften und Interessen*, 63.
[297] T. Hobbes, *Vom Körper*, 151.
[298] C. Menger, *Grundsätze der Volkswirtschaftslehre*, VIII-IX.
[299] B. Biervert, J. Wieland, "Der ethische Gehalt ökonomischer Kategorien," 37.
[300] H.H. Gossen is cited in ibid., 37-38.
[301] A. Suchanek, *Der ökonomische Ansatz und das Verhältnis von Mensch, Institution und Erkenntnis*, 78.

passively at what happens to arise out of other sources, and these sources are dark."[302] In economics, the *economic dao* – thinking in terms of more or less – becomes just such a dark source. Consciousness is completely determined by it without making it an object of consciousness. Nishida will speak here of an ideal of "truth," that the actor does not recognize as his own content.[303]

> "But while the ideal of Truth is now fully recognized as the goal of all intellectual activity, it is still a 'formal' idea, Nishida tells us. In other words, Truth itself is a formal idea from the outside, and one to which our intellectual activity ought to conform. The self does not see its own content as its own, but its focus of attention is on the ideal of Truth as an eternal standard to be achieved."[304]

For the actor it is thus, for example, impossible to recognize the goals of his action as his own goals. They appear as given and at the same time unconscious ideals that are not accessible to the reason.[305]

> "A larger portion of civilized man remains forever enslaved, in every sense of the word, in the interests of techniques. The interest on which the realization of the ultimate object depends claim their attention, and they concentrate their strength on them, so that every real purpose completely disappears from the consciousness. Indeed, they are often denied. This is encouraged by the fact that in culturally developed relations the individual is already born into a teleological system composed of many links..., the individual accepts collaboration for long established purposes, while even his individual goals are frequently seen as self evidently given by the surmounting atmosphere and gain their validity more in his actual existence and self-development rather than through a clear consciousness. All of these circumstances contribute to the fact that not only the final goals of life as such but also those within life are allowed to rise only imperfectly into the stream of consciousness and to concentrate and direct consciousness towards the practical task of the realization of means. It is surely obvious that this antedating of the final purpose takes place not in the intermediate instances of life, but rather with money."[306]

As this passage makes clear, economic theories actually describe a certain form of action sufficiently when they speak on instrumental rational action in regard to given ends. Generally we can describe such a type of action as one that occurs in the locus of a *dao* without it being made the object of the

---

[302] K.-H. Brodbeck, *Die fragwürdigen Grundlagen der Ökonomie*, 252.
[303] K. Nishida is cited in R.J. Wargo, *The Logic of Basho*, 313.
[304] R.E. Carter, *The Nothingness beyond God*, 41.
[305] H. Stewart, "A Critique of Instrumental Reason in Economics," 58.
[306] G. Simmel, *The Philosophy of Money*, 231-32.

consciousness of the actor. In East Asian philosophy such a type of action is extensively discussed in Mahayana Buddhism, which ascribes it to the habitual or normal consciousness.[307] Such a consciousness is characterized by the fact that it doesn't see through the locus of the interrelation of subjective and objective perspective chiefly because it doesn't recognize action guiding ideas as its own. Instead, it grasps itself conceptually as an ego, that identifies itself exclusively with the subjective perspective and pushes everything else into the category of objective givens in the external world. Izutsu describes this process as follows:

> "The most outstanding characteristic of the surface level of the consciousness lies in how it is polarized from the ground up into the two realms of the subject and the object. The subject-object polarization of this surface level leads naturally to identifying the consciousness in this level with the subjective realm of itself, excluding the objective realm, and grounding itself as the existential center of all personal experience as an 'ego'; thus the objective realm of the consciousness is obviously pushed into the outer world and made into an 'outer' reality that exists through itself and faces the ego. Letting the so called outer world subsist in this way means that the surface consciousness in its quality of ego takes every thing in this world as an object of knowledge. Therefore it is given that ... the consciousness under normal empirical conditions is without exception a 'consciousness-of.'"[308]

The normal consciousness identifies itself with its subjective qualities. When it observes things, they appear exterior to it and divided from it. Whatever its gaze pays attention to always appears to it as ob-jective.

> "We usually look at things, looking away from ourselves ... To look away from one's self is always to see things merely as objects, that is, as 'external' things outside of the 'internal' self. This is to confront things on the field of fundamental separation between things and the self. The field of separation or opposition between internal and external, subject and object, is the field which is called 'consciousness.'"[309]

The unity of contraries, which grounds the habitual perception, is not something the actor is conscious of. He thus denies his own, encompassing consciousness-field, while he imagines himself exclusively as his own ego. In this way it is impossible for him to recognize the locus in which his dis-

---

[307] Japanese: *zoku tai*. The symbol *zoku* can be translated as 'manners', 'usages', 'habits', and 'worldly', among other things.

[308] T. Izutsu, "Die Entdinglichung und Wiederverdinglichung der 'Dinge' im Zen Buddhismus," 19.

[309] K. Nishitani, "What is Religion?," *Philosophical Studies of Japan*, 2 (1960), 29.

tinctions, concepts and judgments are grounded. His habitual consciousness exists under a delusive influence in the sense that it regards the designated things as given, as entities. Their essence seems firm and irrevocable and disconnected through impenetrable boundaries from his own, subjective essence.

> "For [the normal human understanding – SG], the physical world in which people live is, viscerally, a firm whole composed out of an infinite volume of empirical things, by which each one of them is a real substance with multiple properties and effects. Meanwhile, these substances are outfitted with their own ontological core that is normally understood as an 'essence' operating as the unifying means for all properties and effects of substances. According to this view, each empirical thing is thus a compact, constructed ontological unit: independently, self sufficiently and immutably fixed through its own essence, about which it crystallizes and through which is differentiates itself from all others. Every essence is thus ontologically 'hardened' in the sense, that it is rigidly guarded through the boundaries of its essence against any influx of any other. ... It is easy to see, that the so constituted empirical world is finally nothing other than the product of the original subject-object opposition that arises within the collective field of the cognitive-ontological experience of human beings."[310]

Corresponding to just such a perception of the normal consciousness, action can only be understood as a something that relates to an object. All action is only "a kind of conduct directed towards objects."[311]

Japanese philosophy sees in many scientific realms a tendency to appropriate the worldview of normal consciousness and presuppose it for its research as unquestionable. "From the standpoint of its abstract logic, the world is regarded as something that has already been decided."[312] We can also formulate this insight like this: the scientific domain of discourse presupposes a discourse dao just as inattentive as the consciousness of the normal person and, thus, also remains caught in the contradiction of the objective and subjective vision. Nishitani describes this using the example of the opposition of materialism and idealism:

> "One of the contradictions manifests itself, for example, in the philosophical opposition between materialism and idealism, but, before it makes its appearance on the

---

[310] T. Izutsu, "Die Entdinglichung und Wiederverdinglichung der 'Dinge' im Zen Buddhismus," 15-17.
[311] M. Weber is cited inG. Kirchgässner, *Homo oeconomicus*, 18.
[312] K. Nishida, *Intellegibility and the Philosophy of Nothingness*, 224.

level of thought, it is already hidden in the daily mode of our thinking and being. The field which lies at the ground of our daily life, is that of the basic separation between the self and things, that is, the field of consciousness and within it Reality cannot present itself really. Reality appears only in broken fragments and in the form of tortured self-contradiction. The form of self-contradiction of Reality prevails strongly over us, especially since the emergence in modern times of the 'ego' as the self-relying subject. (....) In his (Descartes', G.) 'cogito ergo sum' is expressed the ego in its self-centered assertion of its own reality. On the other hand, however, the things in the natural world came to appear as things which have no living, intrinsic connection with the ego, as lifeless, so to speak, as the cold world of death. Even our own body, not to speak of animals, were regarded as mechanisms. Descartes equated extension with matter; and the fact that he considered it to be the 'essence' of things, meant that the natural world came to be a dead world and a mechanistic world-view came to be established. By that, it is true, the world-image of modern natural science came into being, and the way of mastering nature through the scientific techniques was able to be opened. However, it is also true, that the world simply became stuff for man as self-centered ego; and that ego with great power of controlling nature became surrounded by a cold, dead world."[313]

We can designate economics as a science that has abided in such a divide of the subjective and objective vision. For it elevates this division to one of its essential presuppositions when it rigidly differentiates between objective restrictions and subjective preferences.[314] Facing the actor, it posits a given commodity or decision space, which he cannot himself influence. "All action always comes to pass ... in a pre-existent environment."[315] The empirical things could be natural or social in nature; they always remain objective (standing-against). Immovably they stand against the individual. Thus nature, for instance, seems to exist purely as a resource, as a resistance against human action:

"The modern doctrine of value is attached to the idea of a resistant earth... 'Value (is) the measure of overcome natural resistance.' The modern national economy names this resistance scarcity. The earth, technically dominated and overcome, now generates resistance only through the merely quantitative limits of its resources: thus, it frequently puts a restraint on its renewal. The active function of the earth

---

[313] K. Nishitani, "What is Religion?," 30-31.
[314] G. Kirchgässner, *Homo oeconomicus*, 13.
[315] H.-G.Krüsselberg, "Theoriebildung im 17., 18. und 19. Jahrhundert," in: W. Korff (ed.), *Handbuch der Wirtschaftsethik*, Vol. 1, Gütersloh 1999, 388.

vanishes, being understood simply as material for human ends. As mere material, nature is limited, and this limitation counts as the economic problem."[316]

This aspect of the idea of nature in economics shall not be deepened here; but in general we can say, that alterations of natural conditions in the economy are seen through the same lens as alterations through the acts of other individuals, thus alterations of the social environment.[317] In both cases they appear as external motives, on which the ego reacts without influencing them. Fellow human beings are, just like nature, always the other, an opposing face, that is unconquerably separated from the ego through its fixed borders. In economics such an actor, who is imagined as completely separated from his environment, is exclusively described through his preferences. The latter name already given ideas, feelings and desires of an essence closed in upon itself, remaining seemingly untouched from the world of things. Economics, too, remains strictly divided between subjective and objective viewpoints even when the interdependence of both is obvious, or when contradictions emerge due to the dualistic way of seeing:

> "Any action theory which is interested in the systematically expectable and (in regards to their efficiency) analyzable consequences (effects) of action, [stands] before the problem of re-constructing the action in terms of its dependence on conditions. These conditions can be internal or external in relation to the actor. The external will be grouped together here under the concept of the incentive structure of the situation, and the internal deal with the cognitive and motivational foundations of action. ... The interdependence of these questions is undisputed, only they cannot be posed simultaneously."[318]

Economics as a science remains caught in the same *discourse dao* as the normal kind of economic thinking. The *economic dao* remains – at least for the mainstream – a place of nothingness in which all methods are conceived while it is not itself made into the object of reflection. The meaning of this for economic action theories is that they cannot possibly conceive of any other kind of action except ones that are habitual. This is why they are not able to break through the standpoint of the (economic) ego.

---

[316] K.-H. Brodbeck, *Die fragwürdigen Grundlagen der Ökonomie*, 130.
[317] G. Kirchgässner, *Homo oeconomicus*, 18.
[318] A. Suchanek, *Der ökonomische Ansatz und das Verhältnis von Mensch, Institution und Erkenntnis*, 81.

3.3.4 The Creative Actor 'Beyond' all Habits

While in economics we shape our action theory in presupposing the *economic dao* as a place of nothingness, Mahayana Buddhism in particular guards itself against postulating such a position as inaccessible to further analysis. For this means, in fact, making the actor into the slave of his habits. It means that the actor doesn't even recognize his habits, not to speak of being able to alter them. All action becomes purely unconscious; unconscious, this time, not in regard to the subjective consciousness, as is the case with neoclassical economics, but in regard to the consciousness that unifies and generates in itself the objective and subjective dimensions. In this way, the actor remains, according to the beliefs of Mahayana Buddhism, separated forever from his authentic self:

> "On the field of consciousness, in which we are separated from things and stand confronting things, we are, correspondingly, ever separated from ourselves and do not really come into contact with ourselves. (...) Ordinarily, when we confront the 'external', we fancy at the same time that we as 'internal' are in real contact with ourselves and are in our home-ground. And this 'we as internal' is what is commonly called self-consciousness. However, the self which is the 'internal' as regards the 'external' and is self-centered in its relation to the 'external', is a self that is estranged from things and shut up within itself."[319]

Mahayana Buddhism recognizes, in such separation, a fundamental illusion, without therefore denying in principle the perspective of the subjective consciousness. It "even concedes up to a certain point the reality of such a world. Yet it does add a stipulation to the effect that the empirical world, which is represented as the objective order of things, is only the phenomenal surface of reality."[320] It is purely this to the profane view of the normal consciousness, which hasn't recognized the actual locus of its actions; and thus this idea goes along with the fact that another world view is possible. We can describe the position of Mahayana Buddhism in a simplified way by saying that the consciousness is imagined to be a two-strata structure consisting of an already described normal dimension, and a "original dimension".[321] The latter dimension corresponds to the faculty of perceiving the world in another way than as the subjective consciousness

---

[319] K. Nishitani, "What is Religion?," 29-30.
[320] T. Izutsu, "Die Entdinglichung und Wiederverdinglichung der 'Dinge' im Zen Buddhismus," 18.
[321] Japanese: *shō tai*. *Shō tai* can also be translated as 'true nature' or by 'true' or 'authentic self.'

does. In Buddhism, the recognition or experience of this dimension takes a central value. Its description and logical understanding can, for instance, be considered as the essential task of that school of modern Japanese philosophy which is influenced by Zen Buddhism.

In order to explain this kind of perspective on the original consciousness, we shall look firstly at Bentham's idea that there is no going past the principle of utility:

> "Has the rectitude of this principle been ever formally contested? It should seem that it had, by those who have not known what they have been meaning. Is it susceptible of any direct proof? it should seem not: for that which is used to prove every thing else, cannot itself be proved: a chain of proofs must have their commencement somewhere. To give such proof is as impossible as it is needless. (...) When a man attempts to combat the principle of utility, it is with reasons drawn, without his being aware of it, from that very principle itself. His arguments, if they prove any thing, prove not that the principle is wrong, but that, according to the applications he supposes to be made of it, it is misapplied. Is it possible for a man to move the earth? Yes; but he must first find out another earth to stand upon."[322]

Bentham implies that perception is wholly defined through the principle of utility. If this were really so, from the Buddhist perspective Bentham is totally correct when he says that one can really never go beyond this principle in thought. For the *dao* remains for the one whose perception is defined through it a place of nothingness and can thus not become an object of reflection. So long as the *dao* is alleged, is another world perspective not actually thinkable. Yet we have often seen already that we can become conscious of such a place of nothingness from another perspective, in another locus, and thus we can discover it as "another earth," a wholly other standpoint. Yet for this to occur we have to break through the old standpoint and find a perspective that lets the principle of utility, the ur-distinction of the more or less simply be. The consciousness field must change itself in such a way that it no longer accepts this distinction as its fundamental *discourse dao*.

If we look at the economic habituation process in particular, another world view seems simple to imagine. For why should the quantitative difference be the only imaginable ur-distinction, which lies beneath all habituation processes? At the very least, from the East Asian perspective, this is not

---

[322] J. Bentham, *Introduction to the Principles of Morals and Legislation*, chapt. 1, sect 11-13.

imaginable. Rather we must proceed from a multiplicity of ur-distinctions, which are learned and applied in distinct contexts. Yet the original dimension of consciousness doesn't simply describe only another form of normal perception, but instead, a perception that breaks through all of the processes of habit. The original consciousness doesn't accept any ur-distinction as a guide for action, and so moves, so to speak, outside of all habituating processes. We will make clearer what we mean by this by turning to the discovery of novelty. It is the property of habit to apply the past to current situations. We once learned to make a distinction in a situation and apply this 'old' distinction repeatedly to 'new' ones. The normal consciousness reproduces purely old perception models without even being conscious of it. According to Nishida, this is purely something artificial, that is fixed and defined through the past; out of it can no new thing arise. "The world, as mere past, deprives us of our personal Self and our roots of life; this means: the world negates itself; and becomes uncreative."[323] The emergence of another world is made possible when we makes something new, when we creatively act:

> "As soon as something new is created, our Self is transformed from a creation to a creator. In the past it was simply something created. And now the same Self is a living dimension of poesis. When we intuit everything from the position of the past and the already created, we can say the following: the creative aspect of the here and now was a point of nothingness in the past. ... The past was in the framework of its time a given condition, self evidently. Out of this self evidence nothing creative can arise... This is exactly the negation of the birth of a new life. This negation should be transformed into an affirmation."[324]

Creativity always arises when a new way of perceiving comes about. The normal consciousness is subjective and perceives in a definite way without this way becoming the object of its own definition. Perceiving remains a place of nothingness, which defines the ego, leaving it undisturbed in the limits of its habits. The Self which creates the new can, conversely, determine the ways of its perception itself. Its creativity is directed at breaking down the barrier of normal perception. No longer is it subjectively defined within the pre-determined locus of habit, but determines its very own location itself. What this means, precisely, can be seen when we contrive our descriptions in the light of those changes that are relevant to the 'objectivity' of things:

---

[323] K. Nishida, *Intellegibility and the Philosophy of Nothingness*, 224.
[324] K. Nishida is cited in H. Hashi, *Die Aktualität der Philosophie*, 55-56.

"The first practical step to make in this direction consists in 'de-objectifying' the world and the things in it, which are fully objectified in our habitual engagements with them. This means learning to see things in their pre-objective forms of existing – which is to say, in the situation that they had before they were objectified through the cognizing activity of the surface-consciousness."[325]

Normal consciousness perceives things as rigid substances. They appear as the givens, as objectively defined. Action, correspondingly, is always only conduct dealing with objects. The perception of the original consciousness, conversely, acts as a resistance to the disappearance of the thing-identity in the moment's situation. "Preventing the latter's self-sufficient closure in itself, it [the original consciousness] plays the role of forcing open the sealed up situation."[326] It is thus a perception that gives openness. For the original consciousness the word 'as' can exceed the actual situation. If every thing objectively appeared to exist as a commodity, the 'as' now opens up the impenetrability of things; it becomes possible for things to appear as something other. There is nothing, that yet appears as a given.[327]

In Zen Buddhism, for instance, reality is referred to as a "borderless openness."[328] Each thing is 'unarticulated' in its original situation; it can always be re-defined. The original consciousness recognizes this openness of things. It names them, of course, with their names, but it recognizes no essence in them. Izutsu explains this state of affairs using the simple example of a water bottle:

> "To express ourselves concretely we should say that the water bottle is represented as realized in the unity of contradictions, not being the water bottle and yet still being the water bottle. That is only realizable when the water bottle lacks an essence, or, literally, is empty of the determining essence of being a water bottle; for it is through such an essence that it is enclosed in the walls of being-a-water-bottle and can never escape it."[329]

---

[325] T. Izutsu, "Die Entdinglichung und Wiederverdinglichung der 'Dinge' im Zen Buddhismus," 20.
[326] J. Murata, "Wahrnehmung und Lebenswelt," in: Y. Nitta (ed.) *Japanische Beiträge zur Phänomenologie*, 293.
[327] K. Nishida, *Intellegibility and the Philosophy of Nothingness*, 176.
[328] T. Izutsu, "Die Entdinglichung und Wiederverdinglichung der 'Dinge' im Zen Buddhismus," 28.
[329] Ibid., 37.

The original consciousness does not relinquish language, concepts or theories, but is not bound to these.[330] They appear to it not as irrevocable or absolute, but instead as purely possible descriptions of a borderless openness. They always remain relative to a definite context which can be cognitively and practically surpassed. The original consciousness can be described as a 'double-focus eye:' in one way, it objectifies things and fully recognizes their existence as individual realities; in another way, it sees through the lack of essence characteristic of them. "Each thing in the world is seen equally under these two mutually contradictory aspects."[331] In this way the things are 'porous' or 'liquid.' The original consciousness knows in this way the illusionistic character of the *discourse dao* that permits things to appear as firmly bounded essences.[332]

The mutual relationships of the subject and the object within a *dao* are the reason it is impossible that such knowledge can be attained from the standpoint of the subjective consciousness. For the subjective consciousness always presupposes as a consciousness-of the givenness of the things as definite objects. To put it in other terms: from the standpoint of the ego that interprets itself in opposition to an already given outer world, the outer world cannot be known in its openness. If, for example, thinking and feeling are implicitly determined in the horizon of a more or a less, the subjective consciousness will know objects exclusively as quantities. It will be only a consciousness-of commodities.

> "So long as a subject remains that has a consciousness-of things in its immediate surroundings, these stand by the force of their ontological properties as objects of knowledge ... in the face of the subject. The de-objectifying of things can never be achieved in this way, since one will simply go through the act of de-objectifying one-sidedly, through which the subject still remains untouched in its subjectivity. Rather the de-subjectification of the subject must be put in motion at the same time. The annihilation of objects must be accompanied by an annihilation of the ego. That means that the whole subject-object split of consciousness must be transcended in one blow. ... This simply gives us the realization of the ontological situation, in which every thing in the empirical world stops existing as this and that thing, as something rigidly defined through its essence. And since there is in this dimension

---

[330] G.S.P. Misra, *Development of Buddhist Ethics*, New Delhi 1984, 146.
[331] T. Izutsu, "Die Entdinglichung und Wiederverdinglichung der 'Dinge' im Zen Buddhismus," 35.
[332] R.E. Carter, "Toward a Philosophy of Zen Buddhism, Prolegomena to an Understanding of Zen Experience and Nishida's Logic of Place," *Eastern Buddhist*, 13/2 (1980), 128.

of Being nothing that subsists as this and that thing, the consciousness finds nothing fixed that it can attach itself to. If the consciousness doesn't find anything, it stops being 'consciousness-of' anything. The 'of' is eliminated and therewith the consciousness is now pure and simple."[333]

The original consciousness doesn't conduct itself passively in the face of the outer world.' It creates, instead, the situation in which it operates. The I is here an "active, creative self"[334] 'beyond' or 'antedating' all subjective and objective determinations. Hence, it is equally a self for whom the outer world is not irrevocable, or somehow standing in a hostile pose in its face. Instead, it can re-discover and re-define things and its own self. What appears to the normal consciousness as an objective, existing given decision space, appears to the original consciousness as an open situation, in which the "subject defines the object and the object the subject."[335] Or to put it more precisely: the action comes to pass before the subject and object are defined as givens. The actor thus becomes a creative element of the creative world which is shaping itself. "We are thoroughly creative, as forming factors of the creative world which forms itself."[336] In such a world "there are no such things as given data."[337] "The mere 'given' is nothing but an abstract idea."[338]

Creative action isn't untethered from all habits, but it isn't determined by them. Rather the current moment is recognized again and again as new and unique. This relatedness to the present is the reason that spontaneity is like openness an important part of creativity. "There is always an element of spontaneity, of something absolutely new in the creative process."[339] The example of artistic activity should make clear what such creativity means in East Asian philosophy:

> "It is a commonly accepted rule of artistic training that the student must first learn technique in order to transcend technique. To learn technique is to be conditioned by cumulative experience to perform certain acts in a certain way ... But to be con-

---

[333] T. Izutsu, "Die Entdinglichung und Wiederverdinglichung der 'Dinge' im Zen Buddhismus," 22-23.
[334] K. Nishida is cited in H. Hashi, *Die Aktualität der Philosophie*, 47.
[335] K. Nishida, "Die Welt als Dialektisches Allgemeines," 153.
[336] K. Nishida, *Intellegibility and the Philosophy of Nothingness*, 223.
[337] Ibid., 184.
[338] Ibid., 199.
[339] J.W.T Mason, *The Meaning of Shinto, The Primaeval Foundation of Creative Spirit in Modern Japan*, New York 1967, 75.

ditioned by these rules only opens up possibilities of response. One must overcome the danger of being determined by these rules, of becoming so attached to these conditions acquired in the past that the present is no longer creative. The transcend technique is to respond to the presence of the moment before us. (...) One is free by not being determined by the past. One is creative by being responsive to the present moment expressing itself through one's own person. (...) Though conditioned by the past, one does not let the past conceal the openness of the present."[340]

Within spontaneous action perception and physical activity converge. A balancing of the possibilities or reflection of the situation before the activity ceases and is thus no longer in the position to guide action. For to accept reflection as a guide to action means to measure the current situation against past situations. Thus, the actor orients himself on the some already finished product and delimits the openness of the situation. We can immediately conclude that creativity cannot be defined through a calculation that mediates between perception and activity. The assessment of consequences postulated by utilitarianism is foreign to creativity. Again, the example of artistic activity makes this clear:

> "Mozart sometimes became aware of an entire music piece all at once, from beginning to end. The creative intuition was complete, and the action was utterly spontaneous, joyful, and in some sense spiritual. (..) All of this is accomplished in an instant, without calculation or analysis, and without a decision which is at all separate from the Initial Intuition. The surface consciousness is not engaged, nor are its tools of deliberation and calculation involved."[341]

Creativity unfolds itself not only 'beyond' the subject-object split, but even lies 'beyond' the foundation of such a split: the interpretation antedating action, the calculation. Creativity is thus not defined by the calculus even though it can make us of the calculus. We can formulate this idea accordingly: creativity is, from the view of calculation, a place of nothingness; the former is not determined through the latter. It can, however, (freely) decide for the calculation – as for any other habit beside.

The impossibility to fully grasp creativity through reflection does not indicate that the creative actor is completely undetermined. Rather, it points to a dynamic understanding of the actor that avoids fixing him as something given, observable. The actor is always creatively re-defining herself. She is conscious of this process herself but it cannot be described through other

---

[340] T.P. Kasulis, *Zen Action / Zen Person*, Honolulu 1981, 141-142.
[341] R.E. Carter, *The Nothingness beyond God*, 106.

persons. Nishida explains this state of affairs with relation to the emotions of the creative Self:

> "It is a common idea that feeling differs from knowledge, and that its content is less clear. To this I reply that the affective feeling of a sensitive artist is not necessarily less clear to him than the special knowledge of a scientist. The alleged unclarity of feeling means nothing more than that is cannot be expressed in conceptual knowledge. It is not that consciousness in feeling is unclear, but rather that feeling is a more subtle and delicate form of consciousness than conceptual knowledge."[342]

The emotions of which Nishida is speaking here are not subjective feelings, but instead an expression of a subject-object unity, which comes to pass in the logical interval before all distinctions to which the subjective feelings can attach themselves. Nishida takes here from the East Asian idea that emotions aren't to be regarded as subjective feelings in the face of known objects, but as a creative expression of the self before all the processes of habit that are accompanied by language.[343] In this way, lived experience assumes priority before all logic and language. The experience counts as the locus of language, reflection and calculation, without itself being objectifiable. This is particularly clear when you look at the relationship of creativity and habit. Since habits are always something already created, from their viewpoint the creative self that discovers and makes novelty isn't recognized, but remains a place of nothingness. Inversely however, the creative self consciously takes habits as objects for reflection, and can affirm, alter or even negate them. The ego that endures in its habits remains on account of that always relativized to the discovery of creativity. In principle everyone can become conscious of his habits and change these spontaneously. From this we can conclude that there is an important stipulation for an action theory that presupposes a certain habit system: "There is no certain knowledge of the future in the creative present."[344] All its explanations and prognoses necessarily fail the creative self. For this self can become conscious of the *discourse dao* in which science moves. Its perception is no longer caught in a definite ur-distinction, but can break through every *shi-fei* judgment in all its dimensions, be they descriptive,

---

[342] K. Nishida, "Affective Feeling," transl. by D.A. Dilworth, V.H. Viglielmo, in: Y. Nitta, H. Tatematsu (ed.), *Analecta Husserliana 8, Japanese Phenomenology*, Dodrecht 1979.

[343] Compare the symbol 'qing' in Chinese (*JŌ*, or *nasa* in Japanese) . Hansen emphasizes that it has to do with neither an objective nor a subjective concept. See C Hansen, "Qing (Emotions) in Pre-Buddhist Chinese Thought."

[344] J.W.T. Mason, *The Meaning of Shinto*, 74.

evaluative or emotional. This breakthrough makes each objectifying act of observation logically impossible.

We are now at the point where we can give an important reason for the logical impossibility of the calculability of action. Neoclassical economics implicitly presupposes, just like utilitarianism, that action is always subordinate to the calculus; because Japanese philosophy emphasizes the creativity of the original consciousness, it unmasks the delusion resting in the neoclassical position. For it shows that the creative self doesn't accept the calculus as an action guiding idea. For such a self the 'outer world' presents itself neither as a pre-determined space of commodities or decisions, nor does it exhaust its own feelings in a simple desire for more.

3.3.5 The Freedom of the Self-Aware Will

Yet even if we grant that the creative self is not to be described from the point of view of the observer, it can be defined in another dimension of the original consciousness. This dimension can be called the self-aware will, in distinction from the ego's will (the subjective will).[345] The task of this will consists in modifying and transforming the creative self. Creativity is open and spontaneous, but the self can define how it would like to unfold this creativity. In other words, the self can strive after an unbounded openness consciously.

> "We do, however, sometimes, act with the express purpose of changing, molding the self and the necessity for accounting for this is what provides the basis for the transition to a self which is active (...) On this level, the development of the self is not something which merely happens, but is something which is actively sought. One might say that the modification and even creation of the self becomes an explicit goal on this level."[346]

The self-aware will strives in opposition to the ego's will not after a given or a definite goal. It truly orients itself to an ideal, but this ideal cannot be named. For as soon as it lets itself be named it would be defined in the context of a *shi-fei* judgment. No concrete concept can describe what the self-aware will orients itself to. Instead this will may break through any specific formulation of the good, beautiful, etc. It is free to pierce every

---

[345] Nishida speaks of a "general" (jap: *ippansha*) will, distinguishing it from the individual, subjective will.
[346] R.J. Wargo, *The Logic of Basho*, 315.

dao; it never permits itself for this reason to be forced to serve any predetermined action ideal.

> "The ideal does not have any specific content. Various suggestions may be put forth as the explications of what is good and acting so as to conform to these will modify the character of the person who does so, but none of these is a complete explication of the 'idea' of good. Indeed, it is precisely because this is the case that we find that we can review, evaluate, accept and reject these various specific formulations. The 'idea' of good has no specific content; it is the form of an idea; it is the notion that there is a standard and not a specific formulation of the standard. That this is the case, Nishida would say, is shown by the fact that conscience (*ryōshin*) makes its appearance on this level. It is the immediate apprehension of conscience in the depths of the self that the moral world including the various conceptions of standards of goodness and moral rules, is constituted."[347]

The meaning of the ideal that shows no specific content and is therefore not definable by this or that can be explained using the example of the determination of happiness. Happiness in utilitarianism is imaged to be an ideal that is striven for by human beings. At first glance we seem here to be dealing with an ideal in the above named sense. For example, Tugendhat writes that "there is no objective, universally valid rule of conduct to achieve happiness... We cannot give any substantial concept of happiness."[348] This can be interpreted to mean that happiness is not an abstract idea, but a concrete whole,[349] the latter being composed of distinct elements. As Mill says, the love of music, for example, is as possible an element of happiness as health.[350] But these elements are always objects that are recognized by the subjective consciousness as good, or beautiful, etc. – they are "desirable objects."[351] Even if we can't define happiness, still, following the ideas of utilitarianism, at the very least the elements of happiness can be defined. They are objects to which the subjective consciousness-of is attached. One supposes that "human happiness consists in a continuous advancement from one object to another, in which it seems that the

---

[347] Ibid., 316.
[348] E. Tugendhat, *Probleme der Ethik*, Stuttgart 1984, 46. Tugendhat is referring to Kant's philosophy.
[349] J.S. Mill,*Utilitarianism, On Liberty, and Considerations on Representative Government*, 35.
[350] Ibid., 35.
[351] Ibid., 34.

obtaining of the one object is only the way leading to the next."³⁵² The elements of happiness are thus objectively perceived. This is the case independently of whether they are regarded as, at one point, "worldly needs and interests" or as "hopes and yearnings."³⁵³ The determination of happiness always results in this way in a split of the subject and the object.

It might be argued that this split comes to pass (implicitly) in economics in the locus of the *economic dao*, since the elements of happiness are supposed to be "additive and calculable."³⁵⁴ We can therefore infer that happiness itself should be definable in a quantitative horizon. This is why Jevons took utility to be identical to the growth of happiness.³⁵⁵ For this point, he can call on Bentham, who equated the principle of utility with that of the greatest happiness.³⁵⁶ Happiness becomes something that can be maximized, as in Bentham's dictum, 'the greatest happiness for the greatest number.' It becomes the aim of calculating rationality. In this way it seems that "the final goal of human action, happiness, can finally be subjected to an empirical-analytical test."³⁵⁷ By starting out thinking of happiness in this way it is not so amazing if money, from being a means to happiness, has come to be itself a principal ingredient of the individual's concept of happiness.³⁵⁸

Nishida turns against just this kind of arrangement of happiness when he speaks of an ideal without a determinable substance, which is not subjected to any predetermined goal. Such an ideal cannot be determined as a (conceptual) form of desire, but instead is, inversely, the locus, in which all desires are re-questioned. The unmanageability of the ideal makes it possible to always pose the questions ever anew, who one is and how one may see his environment. It shows that no form of (conceptual) desire can ever represent the authentic good or the beautiful, or authentic happiness. Such lack of control is the presupposition for the practically free exercise of the

---

[352] A. MacIntyre, *Geschichte der Ethik im Überblick*, 132. Der Autor is referring here to Hobbes.

[353] O. Höffe, *Einführung in die utilitaristische Ethik*, 15.

[354] Vg. A. MacIntyre, *Geschichte der Ethik im Überblick*, 214. MacIntyre is referring to Bentham's philosophy.

[355] W.S. Jevons, *The Theory of Political Economy*, 106.

[356] J. Bentham, *Introduction to the Principles of Morals and Legislation*, chapt. I, sect. 1, footnote.

[357] O. Höffe, *Einführung in die utilitaristische Ethik*, 15.

[358] J.S. Mill, *Utilitarianism, On Liberty, and Considerations on Representative Government*, 34.

will. For if happiness, for instance, embodied a pre-determined standard, we could think of a locus in which the self-aware will could be objectified or conceived as something certain. One could say about this will, 'this is how it is' or 'this is how it must be' in order to achieve happiness. It would become a specific entity. But this is in exact contradiction to the presupposition of a self-conscious will that freely defines itself.

> "Even at this deepest level ..., a contradiction, or an incompleteness in the story told, becomes apparent. For to view the willing, self determining, moral self as a being (object) is to conflict with a most basic requirement of morality – free will. To view the self from the perspective of its content-plane, is to view it as determined by its ideals of truth, beauty and goodness. To give content even to goodness is already to think of the self as an object within the deterministic chains of cause and effect."[359]

Along with the idea that the self-conscious will is practically free goes the fact that it requires a locus in which it is self-determined. But this locus ought to have no defined form or specific content, since otherwise the will loses its freedom and becomes a determined entity. While most economists cannot imagine such complete lack of control, for Nishida, conversely, the actual problem with each and every action-theory is positing the actor as an object without regarding the locus in which this objectifying comes to fruition. Objectifications are ideas about the self, but they are not actually the acting self. This aspect has already been discussed in the section about the impossible calculability of action. (3.1.5) The idea of the free, self-conscious will now makes clear that no objectification can embrace the character of the act. Consequently, the last step must consist in rejecting every subject-object split as a determination of the actor.

> "What Nishida does is show that the entire distinction is greatly misconceived. ... [It] is not literally a description of the structure of reality. (...) The crucial point is, that in the state of nothingness there is no differentiation of subject and object but any reference to this in language requires some use of the subject and object distinction. In short, the distinction is ultimate in language; its use is necessary in the expression of one's reflections, but it is not ultimate in the sense of characterizing that experience apart from reflection."[360]

The true (or last) locus of the action is this, in which the actor self-determines himself site specifically without being determined by some-

---

[359] R.E. Carter, *The Nothingness beyond God*, 43.
[360] R.J. Wargo, *The Logic of Basho*, 329-335.

thing. It is the unlimited locus, in which all determinations and distinctions are grounded, but which itself cannot be grasped by any of these determination and distinctions:

> "The ultimate basho is the ground of self which sees but cannot itself be seen. It is ... an ultimate intuition, out of which and on which all distinctions are based."[361]

Because we can say nothing, in the truest sense of the word, about this locus, it is often called in the East Asian context 'emptiness' or 'nothingness':

> "Nothingness has a positive and a negative aspect. Inside the negative view, it is literally nothingness in the sense that nothing can be specified that is certain and limited in the whole extent of its field. ... Yet inside the positive view, nothingness is ontological fullness. Just because the ... reality is nothing-like and empty of all, which essentially can be fixed as this or that thing, and because it has no ontological determination, it is in the position to determine itself in complete freedom from every extraneous factor. The pre-linguistic reality that is the zero point of consciousness and being is equally the original place of consciousness and being."[362]

Nishida names the true (or last) locus of action the "absolute nothingness,"[363] because it represents a site of nothingness for every other description of the actor. This concept of absolute nothingness relates to a level of experience, in which there are no distinctions made, that is not susceptible to any conceptual definition, and to which logic cannot be applied without producing contradiction. The existence of this level of experience doesn't mean that the actor cannot be defined through habits; rather, it indicates that such definition is always only preliminary and can be changed in the locus of absolute nothingness. Because their action is grounded in absolute nothingness, humans have the ability to freely chose the ends of their actions and, by so doing, define themselves anew. This ability "is the source of life," Nishitani writes, "where life is something beyond function and utility, that is, where our usual way of life is surpassed and where our ordinary mode of being is broken through."[364]

For Nishida, the absolute nothingness represents the locus in which the actor presents himself for the first time how he really is: without a final

---

[361] R.E. Carter, *The Nothingness beyond God*, 46.
[362] T. Izutsu, "Die Entdinglichung und Wiederverdinglichung der 'Dinge' im Zen Buddhismus," 32-33.
[363] Japenese: *zettai mu*.
[364] K. Nishitani, "What is Religion?," 22.

determination. He is so to speak someone seeing who cannot himself be seen, an observer who is not observable himself. In such a "determination without anything determining"[365] Nishida discovers the final consummation of the self-consciousness.[366]

> "We herein make immediate contact with the individual for the first time. That is, through the realization of Absolute Nothingness, the individual is fully known by us in its concrete immediacy without any conceptualization. Expressed in Nishida's terms, the individual is realized as 'that which lies within' Absolute Nothingness (i.e. it rests in Absolute Nothingness, its place), and in Absolute Nothingness determines itself without being determined ... by any other thing. This self-determination of the individual as it is, is the self-determination of 'place' or Absolute Nothingness."[367]

The actor whose action is grounded in absolute nothingness does not allow himself to be theoretically described; for his existence is certainly to be understood context-dependently, yet the context itself is no longer determinable. In the locus of absolute nothingness the actor surpasses every boundary within which we seek after a specification of his nature, precisely because his action is grounded in an openness which is itself undefined. From this fact, it immediately follows that – at least from the Japanese point of view – no action theory can ever completely describe or objectify the nature of the actor; it is never finally seized as this or that. "There exists no universal standard for concretely evaluating an action:"[368]

> "There is not a single standpoint that we can use to be able to look over the whole plane of multifarious situations... Those who attempt to unambiguously render a judgment on our experience and action outside our current situation in the light of a single principle are really violently interfering in our living, built connections ... One must thus not judge actions according to a 'metaphysical principle' that transcends the momentary situation." [369]

From the viewpoint of Japanese philosophy no action theory – which includes the ones in economics – can be universally valid. In absolute noth-

---

[365] K. Nishida, *Logik des Ortes*, 50.
[366] K. Nishida, "The System of Self Consciousness of the Universal," 372.
[367] M. Abe, "The Logic of Absolute Nothingness as Expounded by Nishida Kitarō," *Eastern Buddhist*, 28/2 (1995), 173.
[368] K. Washida, "Handlung, Leib und Institution – Perspektiven einer phänomenologischen Handlungstheorie," in: Y. Nitta (ed.), *Japanische Beiträge zur Phänomenologie*, 346.
[369] Ibid., 345.

ingness, action is not to be described by means of logic and theoretical interpretation. It can only be lived and experienced without seeking after a description.[370] This way of perceiving things shows us how vain it seems to strive for a "science of human action ... according to the universally valid principles of knowledge."[371] Moreover, the relationship of science and experience assumed in economics is straightforwardly reversed. While it is valid in economic theory to say: "the science of human action is ... in all of its parts a non-empiric, but rather an apriori science; like logic and mathematics, it does not stem from experience, but rather precedes it;"[372] from the viewpoint of East Asian philosophy, living experience appears instead as the locus in which even all theoretical interpretations are grounded. "We are not made conscious that we live through thinking, but rather: because we live, we think ... We don't understand the world from a standpoint outside of the world, but instead, the thinking I, also, finds itself in the midst of the world."[373]

The meaning of absolute nothingness as the true locus of all action comes into focus when we regard the question of freedom of action. Already we have seen that Nishida conceives the will, which is grounded in the locus of absolute nothingness, as free. But what kind of freedom is he talking about? It is an essential aspect of freedom that it, too, should be regarded firstly in terms of context dependence. "What defines freedom at a specific place and time comes about through the specific limitations as much as through the characteristic ends set by this time and this place."[374] With the aid of Nishida's logic of locus we can specify this thought in the following way: every *basho* of action may be conceived as a locus, which guarantees the individual a certain freedom of action. For example, if the actor is defined, as in neoclassical economics, by analogy to a physical field, his freedom would seem to equal the freedom of movement of a physical system. In the absence of incentives or constraining forces he is free to follow his 'impressed force.' Thomas Hobbes formulated a notion of freedom which corresponds to such an objective understanding of freedom: "Liberty, or freedom, signifieth properly the absence of opposition (by opposition, I mean external impediments of motion); and may be applied no less to irrational and inanimate creatures than to rational." And Hobbes says,

---

[370] R.J. Wargo, *The Logic of Basho*, 329.
[371] L. von Mises, *Grundprobleme der Nationalökonomie*, 12.
[372] Ibid., 12.
[373] K. Nishida, *Logik des Ortes*, 60-61.
[374] A. MacIntyre, *Geschichte der Ethik im Überblick*, 189. MacIntyre is referring to Hegel's philosophy.

further on: "But when the words free and liberty are applied to anything but bodies, they are abused."[375] Such a notion of freedom lacks the subjective perspective of action. This lies in the fact that such a perspective from the objective viewpoint represents a place of nothingness and thus can not be seized hold of. It is purely a horizon in which freedom is only imagined as a movement of objects. If one goes beyond the objective standpoint and discovers the dimension of (subjective) consciousness out of this new perspective, the former elbow room which yields to things a freedom of movement appears no longer as a horizon, but as the boundary that must be overcome in order to practically gain real freedom.[376] Or to put this more generally: from the viewpoint of the object determined within it the locus represents the maximum elbow room with its boundaries as yet invisible. But if we make the locus the object of reflection, the possible freedom existing inside it seems all at once to be confined. Its horizon becomes a limit, that must be overcome in order to practically gain virtual freedom. Thus, viewed from the subjective standpoint, objectively determined freedom that only permits the movement of bodies seems restricted. Because it is possible, from the subjective viewpoint, to strive for ends, a further freedom of action stands at the subject's disposal.

As in utilitarianism it is, for instance, plain, economic freedom is one that is defined in the horizon of utility maximization and the habit of striving for more. For such a notion of freedom the *economic dao* appears as the actor's optimal elbow room. The restrictions implicit in this notion of freedom do not become, as such, objects of consciousness for those who define themselves inside this *dao*. But for the original consciousness, the economically posited ends appear as limits worth surpassing. "The rational actions presupposed by economics" no longer appear as "free and optional, but always already bound up contextually in rationality."[377] They appear as slavery and utility maximization as an obstacle for a truly self-aware action. For the original consciousness is free to define itself creatively outside of the narrow limits of economic freedom and within the locus of absolute nothingness. This place is infinitely open and in the truest sense limitless. It no longer confines the self conscious will.

---

[375] T. Hobbes, *Leviathan*, Neuwied-Berlin 1966, 163.

[376] For the concepts of horizon and boundary, see A. MacIntyre, *Geschichte der Ethik im Überblick*, 188. Again, MacIntyre is referring to Hegel's philosophy. For Nishida's concept of the boundary, see K. Nishida, *Logik des Ortes*, 32.

[377] B.P. Priddat and E.K. Seifert, "Gerechtigkeit und Klugheit," 70.

By surpassing all pre-existing standpoints, limitless freedom, grounded in absolute nothingness, can make the boundaries of every other standpoint visible. "We can talk of limits, because there is something not limited."[378] If someone now tells us that the empiricist has "precisely the job of specifying the objective conditions of the implementation of freedom, which serves freedom anew"[379], then he is misunderstanding freedom as a subjective thing, standing in the face of the objective. For if a science defines objective conditions of freedom, then in fact the freedom of the actor is constricted, and he must accept this condition as a given, without being able to creatively alter it. Conversely, the freedom of the original consciousness allows the actor to actively shape his environment, just as he is shaped by it. Here, the subjective as well as the objective vision is creatively manufactured; freedom is no longer considered a subjective freedom confronted by an objective, given world. Kaneko very clearly formulates this idea:

> "The standpoint of freedom... is not I-hood (egoism); the latter is the standpoint in which the I, standing in the midst of the world, tries to regulate other people and things in terms of his arrangements, and only in this way is the world for him. From this standpoint it might seem to be permitted, in order to gain an advantage for yourself, to sell yourself and betray others... but all these actions are renounced from the standpoint of authentic freedom, because freedom in such cases would be dealing according to the terms of selfishness. The egoistical will, which stands in the midst of the world and wants to arrange everything as its own means to advantage is nothing other than the slavish will."[380]

The freedom that grounds itself in the locus of absolute nothingness is nothing other than the person's self, his actual being as such. Both "the freedom and the self (are) for people neither freely disposable nor docile."[381] They are unmanageable and can be stopped by no specific form of freedom, as, for instance, the economic. The person himself can certainly deny both freedom and his authentic self by determining himself in the horizon of the habitus. Yet he still possesses the freedom to break out of this horizon and see himself and things in a fresh fashion. We can deprive peo-

---

[378] D. Suzuki, "What is the 'I'?," *Eastern Buddhist*, 4/1 (1971), 23.
[379] T. Rendtorff, "Selbstverständnis und Aufgabe der Ethik," in: W. Korff (ed.) *Handbuch der Wirtschaftsethik*, Vol. 1, 185.
[380] T. Kaneko, "Die Freiheit als Geschenk," *The Philosophical Studies of Japan*, 3 (1961), 134.
[381] Ibid., 134.

ple of this freedom of changing just as little as they can alienate themselves from it. For the latter would only be possible through a free act.

The dimension of (true) freedom as absolute nothingness is not accessible to language, nor to description. The freedom is rather an ideal that can never assume a specific form. It can neither be defined nor proven as a principle:

> "Finally there is occasionally the challenge to scientifically 'prove' freedom. But with that challenge, freedom as well as science is misunderstood: freedom is ... no empirical state of affairs, which may be inductively elevated to another level; and to deduce it from some higher principle would be to cancel it, if this were even possible. But there is no higher principle above it: this is what autonomy tells us."[382]

But freedom can be experienced, or lived. "That there is freedom and free action is certainly neither scientifically nor empirically provable – for that would even be contradictory – but it is an overwhelming evidence from praxis and practical experience, as much out of our personal as out of our social life."[383] Such a lived freedom is that reality, which according to Nishida's position must become the locus of all theoretical interpretation and cannot be given away to support an abstract logic:

> "It is inadmissible to operate upon reality externally in order to make it approximate to the measure of our thought."[384]

---

[382] T. Rendtorff, "Selbstverständnis und Aufgabe der Ethik," 186.
[383] Ibid., 186.
[384] K. Nishida, *Logik des Ortes*, 61.

4 The Implicit World Picture of Economics

Through a gradual process of changing the place of thought in the last chapter we made visible some of the unthought presuppositions of objective and subjective economic methodologies. In particular, we showed that habits serve as the locus which grounds both kinds of perspective and mediates between them, without either perspective being logically equipped to make habits themselves an object. The habits of calculation and of striving for more are constantly in operation in the normal life of economic actors, but remain hidden in the ground of their consciousness and therefore do not explicitly step into the spotlight. While economic theory often takes unconsciousness of habits for granted as an implicit place of thought, Nishida's Logic of Place points to a yet deeper underlying locus. This is the self-awareness of the actor who actually recognizes habits as his own and is therefore free to shape them creatively or even to break them.

Yet Nishida's philosophy is in no way exhausted by this insight. Rather, Nishida makes us realize that the thought of place cannot remain stuck at the point of the self-awareness of the individual. Because, speaking strictly, the self still remains an unthought presupposition. It seems to be the case that we can explain the world from the standpoint of the self; but the world, according to Nishida's later philosophy, is not such that it can be conceived from the self's position. Rather, the inverse is the case:

> "Self-consciousness (*jikaku*) must be understood by the individuals who face one another and reciprocally determine each other in space. A person can only be called into existence through a person. Without society, our personality does not arise."[1]

Thus, we can see a "passage from the phenomenon of the self to the phenomenon of the world"[2] in Nishida's philosophy. This doesn't mean giving up the notion of place. Rather, a further place change of thought is instantiated, the angles of sight being changed, so to speak, by 180 degrees[3]: the locus is no longer defined as the self-awareness of the self, but rather as the world.

---

[1] K. Nishida cited in R. Elberfeld, *Das Verstehen der Kulturen*, 133.
[2] Ibid., 132.
[3] Y. Matsudo, *Eine Einführung in die Spätphilosophie von Kitarō Nishida*, 64.

"In the idea of the world, the question concerning the place changes ... from a question about self-awareness to a question about the historical world. The place is no longer only conceived relative to the self, but instead as the place of the self-determining of the world."[4]

Thus we should overcome an individualistic way of seeing, which takes the presupposition of the individual for granted; instead we should explicitly expose the place of the determination of the individual. The world is, at this point, understood as a social-historical affair that "encompasses our self"[5] and defines it situationally. It counts as a living place of encounter, as a "real world"[6], in which the many exist in relationships to one another.

In this chapter we will carry through such a change of place from self-awareness to the world and use this as a productive means to understand the social-theoretical aspects of economic theories. In doing so, we will try once again to develop an alternative understanding of economic phenomena by making the mostly unthought presuppositions of mainstream economic theory explicit objects of reflection. In order to do this, the position of methodological individualism as much as the economic ideas about the market and the state shall be thoroughly analyzed. In contrast to the last chapter, such an analysis cannot follow a strict Logic of Place. For in Nishida's thought, the "phenomenon of the world ... develops only in an unsystematic fashion."[7] Therefore, each of the following sections scrutinizes one certain aspect of the economy. In addition to Nishida's idea of the world, we will draw upon other ideas from East Asian philosophy, in order to elaborate essential presuppositions of economic thought. In order to do justice to distinct theoretical currents within economics, these will often be observed separately. All together the different sections are like a kind of puzzle, in which we can discern an encompassing image of the economy as an economic world.

4.1 The Definition of the Individual in Economic Methodology

When an action-theoretical hermeneutic expressly incorporates 'society', it is usually found to be in one or the other explicatory tendencies distin-

---

[4] R. Elberfeld, *Das Verstehen der Kulturen*, 133.
[5] K. Nishida, "Die Welt als Dialektisches Allgemeines," 133.
[6] Ibid., 117.
[7] R. Elberfeld, *Das Verstehen der Kulturen*, 134.

guished in the Western tradition. In one, action is supposed to be determined through a universal term, meaning a social whole in the sense of an abstract unity of all individuals. In the other, however, the individual[8] defines her actions herself and accordingly action is only to be explained individualistically.[9] While Western theories try to find a satisfactory explanation of human action within the limits prescribed by this dichotomy between the universal, i.e. social, and the individual, or the 'private, Eastern traditions – and here, in particular, Japanese philosophy – point out the fact that the development of this line of thought leads to inconsistencies, which condemns explanations based upon them to destruction.[10] I will firstly show the place wherein this contradiction lies, according to the Japanese position, before I show it in its economically specific form.

4.1.1 The Private and Social Definition of the Individual

At first glance it seems pretty easy to imagine oneself as an individual person: as autonomous and independent from all society. The individual is not determined through his relationships with others, but instead through her own 'nature.' For this to be the case, clearly the presupposition that she has an essence, over which she has entire control, must be satisfied. An "anthropological constant"[11] must exist, which is given before any social determination. "The real individual [is] the one who defines herself," as Matsudo summarizes this position.[12] This form of the individual's self determination I will call her private determination.[13] It designates "the auton-

---

[8] I will use the concept of "individual" ['Einzelner'] instead of private individual ['Individuum'] There is a simple reason for this: in Japanese there is no notion that corresponds to the private individual in the sense of a self-determined, independent entity. I thus will use the concept individual in order to mean either one person among many (*kōjin*), or a person in a context (*ningen*) I suppose, in doing this, that I will avoid interpretetations in the above named sense. See for this particular interpretation problem, T.P. Kasulis, *Zen Action / Zen Person*, 3.
[9] This distinction that can also be called one of the individual and social principle, is already found in H. Dietzel, "Individualimus," in: L. Elster et al. (ed.), *Handwörterbuch der Staatswissenschaften*, Jena 1923, 408.
[10] See in particular K. Nishida, "Die Welt als Dialektisches Allgemeines," 116-246. See also K. Nishitani, "Vom Wesen der Begegnung," in: R. Ohashi (ed.), *Die Philosophie der Kyōto Schule, Texte und Einführungen*, Freiburg i. Br. 1990, 253-274.
[11] O. Höffe, *Einführung in die utilitaristische Ethik*, 16.
[12] Y. Matsudo, *Eine Einführung in die Spätphilosophie von Kitarō Nishida*, 72.
[13] For the concept of private determination, see K. Nishida, "Die Welt als Dialektisches Allgemeines," 126.

omy and thus the independence from others or even from the universal in general."[14] If we only regard this private determination of individuals, they appear to be actually autonomous and therefore free to make decisions without the influence of others.

Next to this private determination there is yet a further form of determination in which the individual is observed purely as a part of a universal. The individual and her action appear to be defined by means of a 'higher order.' Such an order can be variously represented, for instance as God or the State, but also – as shall yet become clear – as the market. The important thing here is chiefly that all of these orders are accorded priority before the individual. They appear to face her as what is given. Without being able to influence them, it rests with the individual only to subordinate herself to their 'system wide imperatives.'

In contrast to the thesis of private determination, the individual here may no longer define herself. Her action appears much more to be determined from the outside, or, so to speak, objectively, so that she is herself reduced to a simple function inside a predetermined occurrence. It is thus the case that "the individual is subsumed under a universal, so that his self-identity or his autonomy is sublated."[15] This form of determination can be designated as the social determination of the individual.[16] In contrast to the private determination this possesses the advantage, that it guarantees the subordination or the integration of the individuals to the whole. The individual, here, seems no longer to be independent from others or from the whole in general. Her dependence is rather an already given fact. "Since the universal is totally and completely universal, this means that it determines and encompasses the individual completely or at least completely mediates the individuals as they are among one another."[17] In this way the individual's defining of herself is absolutely denied. The individual, who is conceived in these terms, is not truly an individual. It can never surpass its definition of being part of the universal.[18]

---

[14] Y. Matsudo, *Eine Einführung in die Spätphilosophie von Kitarō Nishida*, 72. See also K. Nishida, "Selbstidentität und Kontinuität der Welt," in: R. Ohashi, (ed.) *Die Philosophie der Kyōto Schule*, 55: "That an individual is completely and totally individual means that he is completely self-determined, without any help from others."

[15] Y. Matsudo, *Eine Einführung in die Spätphilosophie von Kitarō Nishida*, 72.

[16] K. Nishida, "Die Welt als Dialektisches Allgemeines," 126.

[17] K. Nishida, "Selbstidentität und Kontinuität der Welt," 55.

[18] K. Nishida, "Die Welt als Dialektisches Allgemeines," 126.

In most social and action theories, we work either only with the private determination or only with the social one. Thus it easily escapes our notice that both determinations stand in absolute contradiction to each other. If the individual is defined as an autonomous, independent essence, then the influence of the universal is excluded. For isn't it the very sense of the notion of private determination to postulate the independence of the individual from any outer influence? Inversely, if the action of the individual is determined through a 'higher order', she cannot just as equally define herself. The absolute independence that is postulated by the thesis of private determination, is inverted into an absolute subordination to a universal principle:

> "Private and social determination stand in a mutually negative relationship in the sense that they each signify the negation of the other. ... This can be formulated with the equation, 'the affirmation of the one – equal – the negation of the other.' And this represents precisely the 'absolute contradiction' of which Nishida spoke."[19]

It is logically impossible, to apply both forms of the determination of the individual in succession, since they contradict each other and mutually exclude their corresponding statements. Just as little is it an escape from this *cul de sac* to hold only to one thesis of determination. For if one holds fast to the private determination thesis, there remains the question of how the crowd of individuals independent of each other can be coordinated into a *socius*. And in regard to the social determination thesis, there remains the question of how in general we can even speak of an individual, or, to put it another way, how she can be distinguished from other individuals, when all of her properties are determined through a given order.

4.1.2 The Contradictory Determination of the Individual

In order to show the contradiction of the private and social determination of the individual in economics we, firstly, have to understand how the individual and the universal are thought. By doing this, we give particular attention to an underlying problem that is often overlooked in economic theory, but is, in contrast, emphasized in modern Japanese philosophy. This problem consists in regarding the individual and universal as substances that exist in and for themselves, and independently of the other existents. In other words: it lies, again, grounded in the postulate of context

---

[19] Y. Matsudo, *Eine Einführung in die Spätphilosophie von Kitarō Nishida*, 86.

independence. As we will make clear, the individual and the universal cannot be equally simultaneously conceived because of this postulate. This is, as we will further show, the actual reason for the contradiction of the private and social determinations of the individual.

The Determination of the Individual as an Independent and Autonomous Entity

In economics, the postulate of context independence shows itself very clearly when we look at the individual, insofar as she is determined in the sense of the terms given by methodological individualism.[20] This can briefly be demonstrated by reference to some reoccurring patterns within economics. First is the idea that the person can be independent from all spatial and temporal connections, and so all social ones, to exist in and for herself. Her essence shall be thought as logically preceding her socialization:

> "We will use a methodological artifice which has a long history in political economic analysis: the fiction of an isolated person. This allows us to loosen the relation between person and thing from all social entanglements, so that its essential features can become visible."[21]

As a metaphor for such an isolated person, economics has generally used Defoe's Robinson Crusoe:[22] a man alone on an island with his desires and experiences, cut off from the rest of humanity – such an image still imbues the idea of the person in modern literature.[23] Such as Robinson Crusoe is surrounded only by things and uses no social contacts, in the same way every separate individual should be, in principle, likewise conceivable. This methodical starting point already exists in Hobbes, who writes, in his theory of the citizen: "We will ... assume, that men are like mushrooms that suddenly grow out of the earth without one being responsible in any manner for another."[24] The problem of the fiction of an isolated man' consists in the fact that it can only be imagined with a lot of difficulty. Or, to

---

[20] The term methodological individualism was first used by Schumpeter. See J. Schumpeter, *Das Wesen und der Hauptinhalt der theoretischen Nationalökonomie*, Leipzig 1908, 88.
[21] A. Lowe, *Politische Ökonomik*, Frankfurt/Main-Wien 1965, 21.
[22] D. Defoe, *The Life and Adventures of Robinson Crusoe, a York 'Mariner'*, Edinburgh 1838.
[23] A. MacIntyre, *Geschichte der Ethik im Überblick*, 143.
[24] T. Hobbes, *Lehre vom Menschen und vom Bürger*, Leipzig 1918, 167. [translated from German, R.G]

pose our question differently: Who is supposed to be able to observe a completely isolated person? How are we actually supposed to imagine him beyond all society, civilization, culture and birth? "We can't imagine a single individual," as Nishida pointedly remarks.[25] And Hayek at least admits that the idea of an isolated, cut off individual has "nothing to contribute to our understanding of society."[26] An alternative is seen in methodological individualism by admitting the fact that the acts of people arise in specific social contexts, only in order to again gradually abstract from those contexts. In this way the true, universally valid nature of human beings is supposed to be recognized. Such a starting point can be sketched within the political philosophy of Hobbes as follows:

> "The method of political philosophy ... corresponds to that of physics: the antecedents of a given occurrence are to be isolated. The effect of every individual of them is to be observed for itself ... The analysis that Hobbes introduced into his theory from the state of nature was derived from his knowledge of the states of his time. Yet still Hobbes claimed that this theory was valid not just for the people of his time, but for all people at every time. For the abstraction, which lead to the highest universalia, it doesn't matter from what concepts one starts out, because one is abstracting from all specificity. Hobbes supposed that his theory of the state of nature was gained in an analogous fashion: because in it all political community was abstracted, the knowledge of what political community is being abstracted is irrelevant."[27]

We encountered a similar form of abstraction in the second chapter: statements that are accrued about an object in a specific context should also be transposable to another context. For this to be true it is implicitly presupposed, that the object exists in the same way when it is put in another set of connections. This means, translated to the individual that she is supposed to display the properties that are predicated of her in a specific social context in other social connections too. She remains the same in every context, and thus is not influenced in her real or practical qualities through any social context. She appears as an independent existent who steps unchanged from one context or situation to another context or situation. Thus it should be possible to specify her "pre-political, pre-social, timeless human na-

---

[25] K. Nishida, "Die Welt als Dialektisches Allgemeines," 127.
[26] F.A. Hayek, "Wahrer und falscher Individualismus," in: Hayek, *Individualismus und wirtschaftliche Ordnung*, Zürich 1952, 15.
[27] M. Esfeld, *Mechanismus und Subjektivität in der Philosophie von Thomas Hobbes*, Stuttgart-Bad Canstatt 1995, 255-56.

ture"²⁸ just in the same fashion as in chemistry we can isolate an atom²⁹ from out of a complex nexus of effects.

One finds the thought of context independence in economic theories even in a somewhat watered down variant, which no longer abstracts from all social connections, but instead simply emphasizes the independent standing of the decisions.³⁰ In this connection we often see put into relief the fact that economic theory observes neither isolated people, nor abstracts them from their life in society. Rather, it appears to be

> "completely consistent with methodological individualism, that individuals conduct themselves in a collective differently than when they are alone. Inside a group there are not only wholly other action possibilities that open up, but through such a group the evaluation of the self finds its location decisively altered – and thus its information state."³¹

Yet there persists the bias even in this variant of methodological individualism that "one takes it as a point of departure to describe specific economic processes by reference to the action of individuals."³² The individual is certainly conjoined with the occasion to make decisions in social situations, but the decisions are made on the ground of preferences that are defined exclusively by herself. "The individual acts (only) in accordance with her own interests"³³, and can thus in respect to her preferences or interests loosen herself from any societal odds. Thus, she defines the "content and borders of her societal bonds herself.³⁴ And here again, the individual appears as an "ultimate social unity"³⁵ needing no further interrogation. Mises has very clearly formulated this thought: "The I is the unity of the

---

[28] A. MacIntyre, *Geschichte der Ethik im Überblick*, 124. MacIntyre is referring here to Hobbes.
[29] P.A. Samuelson for example talks directly of "atoms" when speaking of individuals. See his "Maximum Principles in Analytical Economics," 3. See also C. Menger, who speaks of an "Atomism" in his *Untersuchungen über die Methode der Socialwissenschaften und der Politischen Ökonomie insbesondere*, Leipzig 1883, 82.
[30] See for example G. Kirchgässner, *Homo oeconomicus*, 16.
[31] Ibid., 24.
[32] J. Schumpeter, *Das Wesen und der Hauptinhalt der theoretischen Nationalökonomie*, 90-91.
[33] G. Kirchgässner, *Homo oeconomicus*, 16.
[34] E.E. Nawroth, *Die Sozial- und Wirtschaftsphilosophie des Neoliberalismus*, Heidelberg 1961, 55.
[35] A. MacIntyre, *Geschichte der Ethik im Überblick*, 124.

acting person. It is given without question and cannot be dissolved through any thought."[36]

One essential property of such an 'I' is its independence from any kind of universal. This is how Nishitani formulates this idea: the meaning of a universal is negated for the individual when we point to the "absolute status of the individual person and his unimpregnable mastery."[37] Each person is to be recognized as absolute lord over himself.[38] He is always the one who "defines himself."[39] However, Japanese philosophy points to a fundamental problem that derives from this idea. For how can one, taking this as a starting point, ever get to the point of conceiving a community of many individuals? Certainly Milton Friedman, for instance, is untroubled enough to write, "society consists of a number of independent households, a collection of Robinson Crusoes, as it were."[40] But how can we really think of these many individuals united together? Since the essential characteristic of the individual according to methodological individualism is straightforwardly her independence from other people or the universal, it appears impossible to imagine her joined with others. "The individuality of a thing excludes its universality."[41] To say it in another way, it doesn't allow the private determination of the actor to be integrated into a *socius* or subordinate itself to one. The only escape route that allows us to conceive of a unity or a community consists in assuming a kind of 'unifying force' that mediates a unity among many individuals – such is the force of an important proposition of Japanese philosophy. "In order to be able to say that the mutually facing, independent existents relate to one another a medium must be conceived between them."[42] Nishitani sharpens this thought when he asserts that every theoretical position which claims to consider the individual as a completely independent existence recognizes something universal standing either over it or immanent within itself; that is, something lawful. "By reason of precisely this recognized lawfulness, each of these standpoints can relate individual people to one another."[43]

---

[36] L. von Mises, *Nationalökonomie*, 34.
[37] K. Nishitani, "Vom Wesen der Begegnung," 260.
[38] Ibid., 260.
[39] Y. Matsudo, *Eine Einführung in die Spätphilosophie von Kitarō Nishida*, 72.
[40] M. Friedman, *Capitalism and Freedom*, Chicago-London 1982, 13.
[41] E.E. Nawroth, *Die Sozial- und Wirtschaftsphilosophie des Neoliberalismus*, 27.
[42] K. Nishida, "Die Welt als Dialektisches Allgemeines," 127.
[43] K. Nishitani, "Vom Wesen der Begegnung," 260.

"The universal which as the Being of beings is posited against the individual, be that universal the state, the practical reason, God or whatever, mediates through its law the individuals to each other and brings them to a mediated unity. In such a 'law-full' unity, the universal rules as the Being of beings, as the identical, in brief, as substance."[44]

The Determination of the Individual as Part of the Socius

Economics does contain a notion of the socius in the sense of a 'lawful unity.' For instance, it hides behind the metaphor, coined by Adam Smith of the "invisible hand."[45] Its function is to coordinate the actions of the crowd and to mediate them to a one-ness in the sense of a harmonic order. "The famous 'invisible hand' takes care that a harmonic collective product results from egoistical individual dealings."[46] Of course, how we are exactly to take the invisible hand is disputed. At least two conceptual models can be distinguished.[47] In classical political economics the invisible hand is mostly referred to divine control. It is interpreted as "willed by god, because it is a principle of nature created by him."[48] The "eternal and unchanging laws of God"[49] hold as the "force that holds together human society."[50] "The world is a system that proceeds with mechanical necessity, God and the belief in God in deistic thinking are guarantees of the uninterrupted course of the natural system."[51] Bastiat for instance, very impressively represents this position:

> "I would like to show the harmony of the divine laws ruling human society. ... I believe that he who created the material order of the cosmos has not denied his attention to the social world order. I believe that he combined the free force and set it in harmonic movement, like the lifeless molecules. ... I believe that nothing is more

---

[44] Ibid., 262.
[45] A. Smith, *The Theory of Moral Sentiments*, Cambridge 2002, 215 as well as *The Wealth of Nations*, New York 2003, 371.
[46] K.W. Rothschild, "Theorie und Ethik in der Entwicklung ökonomischer Lehrmeinungen," in: B. Bievert, M. Held (ed.), *Ökonomische Theorie und Ethik*, 14.
[47] M. Büscher, "Gott und Markt – religionsgeschichtliche Wurzeln Adam Smiths und die 'Invisible Hand' in der säkularisierten Industriegesellschaft," in: A. Meyer-Faje, Ulrich (ed.), *Der andere Adam Smith, Beiträge zur Neubestimmung von Ökonomie als politischer Ökonomie*, Bern-Stuttgart 1991, 123-144.
[48] Ibid., 128.
[49] H.H. Gossen, *Entwicklung der Gesetze des menschlichen Verkehrs*, 3.
[50] Ibid., 4.
[51] M. Büscher, "Gott und Markt," 128.

necessary to the gradual and peaceful development of mankind than that we do not cross these tendencies and don't disturb their free motion."⁵²

Gossen wrote in a similar vein:

"When he [the creator] determines the operation of this as well as other forces, submitting them to their proper laws, he achieves exactly the same thing for the co-existence of human lives as he achieved, through gravitation and its laws, for the coexistence of his worlds. As he created by means of the latter order in his worlds, he created similarly through the former order among his people; as he put his worlds eternally and unchangingly on their tracks by means of the laws of gravity, so too through the law of the force of enjoyment he eternally and unchangingly prescribed to humans their path in their co-existence with their own kind."⁵³

In contrast to Bastiat and Gossen, modern economic literature gives us another image. For here it is no longer the hand of God, but the market or competition itself, which generates the unity of the crowd. The harmony of social life appears as a consequence of the market's laws. "The principle of Laissez-faire in advanced industrial society means: market forces and material laws (material constraints) are recognized as a condition for the harmonic development of the economy."⁵⁴ Thereby the existence of such lawfulness is mostly simply presupposed without question. "The economic starting point assumes the existence of markets," as Becker puts this position succinctly.⁵⁵ As nature is ruled by natural laws, so, too, economic action of the many is "ruled by a secret law leading to coordination and alliance."⁵⁶ This idea comes into particularly sharp focus when the market is imagined as a machine, whose mechanism integrates the many individual parts into a harmonic whole. How self-evidently this mechanical metaphor is applied in economics is evidenced for example by the following citation out of a political economics textbook:

"A system of free competition is an extremely complicated mechanism which adjusts the economic activity of millions of different people to a system of prices and markets. Without a central planning office this mechanism solves one of the most

---

⁵² C.F. Bastiat, *Harmonies Economiques*, Paris 1855, citation in German in M. Büscher, "Gott und Markt," 129.
⁵³ H.H. Gossen, *Entwicklung der Gesetze des menschlichen Verkehrs*, 3-4.
⁵⁴ M. Büscher, "Gott und Markt," 134.
⁵⁵ G.S. Becker, *Der ökonomische Ansatz zur Erklärung menschlichen Verhaltens*, 3.
⁵⁶ A. Lowe, *Politische Ökonomik*, 47.

complicated problems one can imagine, for it encompasses thousands of unknown variables and equations. No person invented this system."[57]

There is hardly one concept that characterizes economics so much as the market mechanism. It is perhaps the most important common element of different economic theories:

> "The economic mechanics are united on this fact in a deep way: Eugen von Böhm-Bawerk ... chimes in this choir of mechanics-economists just as much as Leon Walras, the father of modern equilibrium theory – the former speaking of a 'mechanics of exchange value formation', the latter of a 'mechanism of competition.' Schumpeter himself recognizes a 'mechanism of commerce' and even his 'dynamic entrepreneur' is described by him as a machine. 'Even the entrepreneur is not effecting change, but is instead the placeholder for a mechanism of transformation.' Even Keynes speaks of a 'monetary machine.' Even authors who do not place their confidence in the equilibrizing tendencies of 'economic forces' remain in their dealings with equilibrium under the spell of mechanics. 'The system,' says Myrdal about the problem of underdevelopment, 'moves itself not in the direction of some balance of forces, but instead wholly in the opposite direction.'"[58]

An important characteristic of the market in the sense of the lawful is its autonomy or independence *vis-à-vis* the individual. The market represents a universal norm, which coordinates the actions of the crowd, without however inversely, being determined by it. "For economics this is almost trivial and since Adam Smith (1776) actually self-evident: Commonly none of the individuals who are active on the market have the intention to put the market mechanism in motion as a societal coordination mechanism, and yet all contribute to doing just this, consciously or unconsciously, in accordance with or against their own intention."[59] Smith took pains to compare this idea with mechanics:

> "The wheels of the watch are all admirably adjusted to the end for which it was made, the pointing of the hour. All their various motions conspire in the nicest manner to produce this effect. If they were endowed with a desire and intention to produce it, they could not do it better. Yet we never ascribe any such desire or intention to them, but to the watch-maker, and we know that they are put into motion by a spring, which intends the effect it produces as little as they do."[60]

---

[57] P.A. Samuelson, *Volkswirtschaftslehre*, Vol. 1, 64.
[58] K.-H. Brodbeck, *Erfolgsfaktor Kreativität*, 41-42.
[59] G. Kirchgässner, *Homo oeconomicus*, 22.
[60] A. Smith, *Theory of Moral Sentiments*, 102.

4 The Implicit World Picture of Economics   153

Even if this deistic world picture that hypothesizes a creator (a watchmaker) behind the mechanics of the market has lost its influence in the course of the centuries, there does remain the belief in forces, the effects of which remain for humans such that "they can certainly weaken ...but not paralyze"[61] them. But now these are ascribed to the market itself. Smith's system of natural freedom, that moves on its own accord[62], is interpreted as the spontaneous order[63] of the marketplace. The market corresponds to "the anonymous rulings of a depersonalized communication and sanction system"[64] that follows its own laws independently of social relations and human developments, becoming therewith a presupposition of the harmonic social order. "Autonomous self interests (the self responsibility) of individuals can develop itself in the free play of forces and competition to a collective harmony - 'the results of human action, but not the execution of any human design.'"[65]

If the market is to be thought of as an entity, this implies not only its independence, but also the subordination or the submission of individuals to its law. "Human freedom is ruled by a secret, inner force: by the invisible hand of mechanical laws of nature."[66] The market represents the respected higher order of material constraint[67], to which one must submit:

> "Reality is subject to a mechanical natural causality: the world is a system of moving matter determined by mechanical means into which mankind is also enrolled. To the mechanical ontology and anthropology that conceives of the world and mankind as subjects to the mechanism of natural processes belongs the praxis of a free enterprise and market society which arises from an impersonal necessity."[68]

Synthesizing this material, we generate the following picture: on the one side economic theories emphasize the independence and autonomy of the individual, which they describe as her self-determined essence; on the other side, they recognize as a lawful state of affairs something that stands over the individual in order to explain how individuals produce a unity. A more precise observation shows that this lawful something doesn't put the

---

[61] H.H. Gossen, *Entwicklung der Gesetze des menschlichen Verkehrs*, 4.
[62] A. Smith, *The Wealth of Nations*, 582.
[63] G. Kirchgässner, *Homo oeconomicus*, 22.
[64] A. Lowe, *Politische Ökonomik*, 47.
[65] M. Büscher, "Gott und Markt," 128. Büscher is referring here to A. Ferguson.
[66] K.-H. Brodbeck, *Erfolgsfaktor Kreativität*, 41.
[67] M. Büscher, "Gott und Markt," 140.
[68] Ibid., 126-27.

many individuals, completely independent from each other, in a relationship, but instead annihilates their individuality. "As soon as the individual is subject to a universal he is relativized and loses his absoluteness ... the universal acts as a kind of obstruction to absolute individuality."[69] Through subordination to the universal the individual forfeits her autonomy and independence. She loses her meaning. The "molecules of the social system, i.e., the individuals" become insignificant instances of inertia. Pareto says of these individual molecules that he will "name them, solely for the sake of brevity, residues."[70] Once degraded to such an inertial state, we come close to postulating the complete "exclusion of individuals ... from the operational market system."[71] They are no longer a determining factor in this event. Rather their private determination in the "anonymous hegemony" of an "undisturbed, systematic circle of material, functional relationships"[72] is completely negated. Herein it becomes evident that we can't simultaneously maintain the logic of the individual and the market. If we presuppose the market, the individual defined as an autonomous, independent existence is not to be thought. But if we observe firstly the individual or a crowd of individuals independent of one another, the *socius* cannot be ascribed its own autonomous existence next to this. It can only be "posited as an aggregation of individual decisions"[73] or "as the aggregated result of the interaction of rational individual behaviors."[74]

Watsuji Tetsuro puts this problem in its general form:

> "Therefore, for human beings, we cannot first presuppose individuals, and then explain the establishment of social relationships among them. Nor can we presuppose society and from there explain the occurrence of individuals. Neither the one nor the other has 'precedence.' As soon as we find the one, it already negates the other and thus stands as that which itself has suffered from the negation of the other. For this

---

[69] K. Nishitani, cited in E. Gallu, "Sunyata, Ethics and Authentic Interconnectedness," in: T. Unno (ed.), *The Religious Philosophy of Nishitani Keiji, Encounter with Emptiness*, Berkeley 1989, 191.

[70] K.-H. Brodbeck, *Die fragwürdigen Grundlagen der Ökonomie*, 65. Brodbeck is citing V. Pareto.

[71] J. Wieland, *Ökonomische Organisation, Allokation und Status*, 55.

[72] Ibid., 2.

[73] G. Kirchgässner, *Homo Oeconomicus*, 23.

[74] K. Homann, "Sinn und Grenze der ökonomischen Methode in der Wirtschaftsethik," in: D. Aufderheide, K. Homann (ed.), *Wirtschaftsethik und Moralökonomik: Normen, soziale Ordnung und der Beitrag der Ökonomie*, Berlin 1997, 23.

reason, it is correct to hold that what is here called precedence is meant only as negation."[75]

Because it is impossible to posit the individual and the market in one thought at the same time, two contradictory modes of the individual's determination are usually applied in economic theories: if one starts with the market, one accordingly shows the individual as being determined utterly by the universal and subject to its operations. If, on the contrary, one begins by presupposing the individual as an independent existence, so it will seem as though she can completely define herself. These determinations are not to be thought simultaneously. This is the root of the contradiction of the modes of private and social determination in economics.

4.1.3 Excursus: The Irreconcilability of Individual and General Equilibrium

The degree to which the contradiction of the individual and the universal penetrates economics is shown by the example of the economic idea of equilibrium. An important postulate of economic theory announces that after the closure of all market transactions, supply and demand equal each other, and thus the market finds itself in equilibrium. This state is defined through two conditions that must be filled at the same time: the first is that an individual equilibrium must exist; each individual has to maximize her utility, taking into account the relevant restrictions (resources, budget). The implication derived from this account is that her transactions are decentralized and independently instantiated from the decisions of others. The other condition supposes all situations desired by the individuals to be cohesive. There must thus be a general equilibrium, i.e., the aggregate demand must be the same as the aggregate supply. Such a general equilibrium is very important, since, according to the views of neoclassical economists, it proves the possibility of a harmony between emulative individual interests. The general equilibrium should show that "free and egoistical individuals, who adjust their actions to each other through the market, develop a peaceful society (of free exchange), that is characterized by an optimal division of available resources."[76] This is regarded as the proof, that the 'natural' (and thus egoistical) striving of individuals in a 'natural' system of free exchange and free competition leads to a desirable social

---

[75] T. Watsuji, *Watsuji Tetsuro's Rinrigaku, Ethics in Japan*, transl. by S. Yamamoto, R.E. Carter, New York 1996, 102.
[76] J. Cartelier, *Das Geld*, 51-52.

optimum of great opulence. Economically 'good' dealing is instantly transformed into universally 'good' action.[77] One can easily imagine the political, ideological and ethical conclusions, which can be drawn from the postulated equivalence of individual interest and social harmony. However, Cartelier points with justice to the fact that this is unacceptable.[78] For whatever merit might be ascribed to individual and general equilibrium, that cannot be thought to logically exist at the same time.

In order to show this, let's take as our starting point the individual actions in a society dominated by exchange. The different individuals arbitrarily meet each other bilaterally with their current exchange commodities and only conclude a business deal with each other when it corresponds with each person's own interest. Outside of the exchange partners, this process involves nobody else. The exchange is thus in a sense voluntary, for the individuals independently can decide whether and with whom they wish to exchange. It is correct that in this way the idea of individual equilibrium is completely sustained. Each only exchanges when that exchange maximizes her own utility. However, such a market process doesn't lead necessarily to a general equilibrium. For the bilateral encounter doesn't necessarily lead to enacting all possible and advantageous transactions. The explanation lies in the fact that the needs of all exchange partners only rarely mutually match up. But when "the needs don't harmonize, it is very possible, that the merchant of grain (who demands iron) with the buyer of grain (who offers cotton) can conclude no deal. The grain market closes in spite of the momentary non satisfaction of a seller and a buyer."[79] This means nothing other than that there is no mutual balance of wishes and thus no general equilibrium is generated. Neither a unified price for a commodity nor equilibrium of supply and demand will thus exist. There is "no universal grain price, no universal cotton price, etc. Possibly, the grain price, expressed in cotton, must rise, while the grain price, expressed in iron, must fall. Will we then say that the grain demand is higher or lower than the supply? That the grain price rises or sinks?"[80] The establishment of a uniform price is not imaginable in this way. "The organization of transactions in the form of acts of exchange is not consistent with the law of supply and demand, as this is generally understood."[81] If we thus assume the individ-

---

[77] K.W. Rothschild, "Theorie und Ethik in der Entwicklung ökonomischer Lehrmeinungen," 14.
[78] J. Cartelier, *Das Geld*, 29.
[79] Ibid., 34.
[80] Ibid., 27.
[81] Ibid., 27.

ual transactions in the sense of commodity exchange as the starting point for our interpretation, it turns out we won't succeed in getting to a 'harmonic whole' in the sense of a general equilibrium. The market shows itself unable to bring about such a result.

In order to get around this problem, we can begin by trying to take the condition of general equilibrium as our starting point, as is, for instance, the common practice in axiomatic value theory. With the aid of a general equilibrium system the equally weighted prices for all commodities are specified so that an equality of aggregated demand and supply for every commodity is always found. In this way we practically succeed in formulating the condition of general equilibrium. Certainly this causes another problem to arise, for such a 'harmony' shows less than many economists believe, because strictly speaking it has nothing whatsoever to do with the market economy. This becomes clear when we observe that such a general equilibrium can also be realized in a planned economy. A "planning office would modulate the prices insofar as they depend on the centrally circulating information gathered by it, until it was certain, that the wishes of different individuals are consistent with each other (aggregated supply = aggregated demand for every commodity)"[82] In other words, the postulated balancing system contains not a single element typical to market economies. It neither proves that only a market economy can ground a 'harmonic' society. Even worse, it is impossible to delineate the process of decentralized decision making and transactions, the typical properties of the market, using the idea of general equilibrium. For individual plans are not harmonized through a mechanical "allotment calculus"[83]; rather they are replaced by it. Every individual is permitted only the carrying through of those transactions that are specified beforehand on the level of general equilibrium. From the start, no individual is allowed to realize any plan in contravention to the conditions of general equilibrium. The condition of general equilibrium thus does not generate the coordination of the crowd's individual plans. Rather, it simply negates any form of individuality. Cartelier is not wrong to speak in this connection of a concept of "the market economy with the characteristic features of a totalitarian society:"

> "The whole society is implicated in the dealing of two exchange partners, so that the concept of bilateral reciprocity doesn't make sense any more. The concept of free trade – cast in terms of the reciprocity between two individuals – is devoid of

---

[82] Ibid., 30.
[83] L. Lachmann, "Marktwirtschaft und Modellkonstruktionen," in: K.R. Leube (ed.), *Die Österreichische Schule der Nationalökonomie*, Vol. 2, 182.

any content, as soon as the condition for its fulfillment is the unambiguous agreement of all individuals. The individuals of modern business theory can only trade freely when it is strictly kept to the (pre)-determined situation at the level of the whole society. Any other dealing is forbidden, and unintelligible."[84]

Summing this up with regards to the idea of individual and general equilibrium, we can draw the following picture: if we observe the process of exchange as contingent and bilateral, we cannot deduce from this any meaningful idea of general equilibrium. If the latter is given priority, however, and determined at first by means of a system of equivalencies, the idea of decentralized trade reciprocity – the authentic characteristic of the market – loses its meaning; the individuals' plans are negated. Individual and general equilibrium thus can't logically coexist. The hope for a harmony of rival interests brought about by means of the market will thus prove itself as ungrounded. This propositions has clearly, at least in mainstream economics up to now, hardly been recognized. The root of this may lie in not recognizing the fundamental problem: the logical impossibility, to determine individual and universal independently of each other and yet think them at the same time.

4.2 The Determination of the Individual as a Context Dependent Existence (I)

In the previous section it became clear that the *socius* couldn't be understood if we begin by taking up mutually independent and isolated individuals. For in this case a universal must be assumed, that subsumes the many under it. But if this is so, we surrender the idea of independent individuals, so that we can't speak meaningfully of a community of many individuals. The individualistic conception that makes the condition of individuality absolute proves itself to be just as problematic as a mechanistic philosophy, that sees the universal as the given and thereby negates the private determination of the individual. But then, from whence shall we start with our explanation of persons and society? Firstly we shall sketch the answer that Japanese philosophy proposes to this question, in order to transpose this to economics.

---

[84] J. Cartelier, *Das Geld*, 55.

4.2.1 The Context Dependence of Individuals

To begin with a little simplification, the Japanese key to an alternative explicatory model lies in seeing the individual not as a substance, but instead as a context-dependent existence. Here society – understood as the everyday, living interplay of a multiplicity of persons – presents the context of this dependency. It is therefore regarded as constitutive for the understanding of the individual. We exactly invert the relationship of the individual and society in our explanation in comparison to methodological individualism: society does not emerge out of the combined performance of individuals, but necessarily precedes any idea about the individual. It is the locus, in which individuals are determined, their unthought presupposition, but not a product of their aggregation. Kimura formulates this insight in this way: the "between-ness"[85] of person and person represents a basho, in which all ideas about individuals are encompassed:

> "The 'betweenness of person and person' (*hito to hito to no aida*) and 'betweenness' (*aida*) do not signify merely a relationship between two individuals. The 'betweenness of person and person is the 'locus' (*basho*) functioning as the source from out of which both I and others arise."[86]

This passage mirrors the Japanese belief that the isolated, independent individual represents a pure abstraction, which forgets the society as that context in which this abstraction comes to pass. The person does not firstly become a social being through the "accident of social contact"[87], but instead the relationship is exactly the reverse: "Without surroundings the individual doesn't exist."[88] The latter is defined inside "a nexus of experiential relationships,"[89] in which the individuals always stand in a concrete, spatio-temporal relationship to each other.

This idea of the context-dependence of people requires some introductory explanations. An observation of communication or language shall serve to lift us up a step. Language can be understood as a medium, which enables different people to relate to each other. It mediates between individuals.

---

[85] Japanese: *aida*.
[86] B. Kimura cited in S. Odin, *The Social Self in Zen and American Pragmatism*, New York 1996, 70.
[87] A. MacIntyre, *Geschichte der Ethik im Überblick*, 174. MacIntyre is referring to Hobbes.
[88] K. Nishida, *Logik des Ortes*, 150.
[89] I. Kōyama, "Das Prinzip der Entsprechung und die Ortlogik," in: R. Ohashi (ed.), *Die Philosophie der Kyōto Schule*, 317.

From the Japanese point of view this state of affairs shouldn't be understood to imply that individuals equipped with language as a means to represent their momentary standpoints exist before anything else in the world. Rather language is seen as a locus in which the individual is first defined. It is the *basho*, which underlies the determination of the individual, even if this fact isn't necessarily known to the speaker. This way of regarding things can be clearly demarcated from a rather 'Western' interpretation of language:

> "There is an important distinction to be made between the way Westerners and Japanese see the function of language. Suppose we represent interpersonal communication as *aRb*, where a and b are persons and R is the linguistic medium through which they communicate. The Western view typically regards a and b as two transmitters, each emitting signals to be received and interpreted by the other. In English, for example, we speak of language as a bridge spanning the gap between I and you. The isolated a and b together create an R so that communication can take place. In Japan, however, the event is viewed quite differently: the R is primary. The R is the given out of which a and b take their shape. (...) Language is being spoken from the perspective of the R not a or b. The a and b – the I and you – only become meaningful insofar as the R, the context of the language used in a given instance, gives them meaning."[90]

In Japanese we begin with the assumption that communication represents a context in which every individual defines herself. The relationship of the communicators takes precedence over the private determination of the individual. This means that the individuals are only determined as this or that when they are thought of in concrete relationship to another:[91]

> "Japanese requires each conversant to understand his or her position vis-à-vis the other person. In most social situations, a conversation between strangers can hardly begin until there has been exchange of business cards or an introduction by an intermediary so that each party is aware of the other person's relative status. In other words, a context must exist before ... people can begin to relate formally to each other. (...) Again, in terms of the original model, a and b assume meaning only in reference to the R. Without clearly established context, people are individually distinguishable, but meaningless as persons in the full sense. (...) In Japan the context

---

[90] T. Kasulis, *Zen Action / Zen Person*, 7-8.
[91] For an extended analysis of the individual in the Japanese context, see C. Nakane, *Japanese Society*, Berkeley 1972.

is given primacy over the individual: the context defines and elaborates the individual rather than vice versa."[92]

The individual can define herself with the aid of linguistic distinctions only when she finds herself in a concrete relationship to another individual. She appears as this or that person only in social contexts. Such a conception is also suggested, for instance, by Confucianism, which "suggests that relations of self and other are intrinsic and thus constitute to self."[93] This conditions, among other things, the judgment that the determination of the individual varies according to the context in which she finds herself. She is not a given substance that moves unchanged across different contexts, but a context-dependent existence, which is always determined anew in the flow of inter-personal relationships.

> "We must restrain our Western tendency to regard Mr. A as a person going from one context to the next, from one situation to another. In the Japanese secular framework, Mr. A is only a person insofar as he is in these contexts. If we could list all relational determinations (employee, customer, son, and so on) we would not have a list of roles that Mr. A plays – we would have what Mr. A is as a person. Without these associations Mr. A would be a solitary chess piece with neither a chessboard nor a rulebook to give him function and significance. Though ontologically distinct, he would still lack distinctive meaning."[94]

We can work out more precisely this idea of the context-dependence of individuals when we compare the different concepts of the subject-object relationship as they inhere in Japanese philosophy and economic theory. At least in mainstream economics it is assumed at the outset that the relationship of the individual to things that surround her are purely individual affairs. It should be seen independent of all social involvements.[95] This assumption is the reason we suppose that we are able to investigate person-thing relationships independently of person-person relationships. Even further, the person-thing relationship is understood as constitutive for the understanding of social relationships. If one has first studied the relationship of persons to objects, then we should be able to derive from it knowledge over human coexistence. From the viewpoint of Japanese philosophy this is a delusion, or at the very least a misunderstanding. For by their lights, every person-thing relationship is preceded by a social relationship.

---

[92] T. Kasulis, *Zen Action / Zen Person*, 8.
[93] D.L. Hall, R.T. Ames, *Thinking from the Han*, 27.
[94] T. Kasulis, *Zen Action / Zen Person*, 130.
[95] See for example A. Lowe, *Politische Ökonomik*, 21.

The latter is the locus which holds the subject and object in itself and mediates between them. Of course we can abstract from this *basho*. But in this way the interpersonal relationships become merely a forgotten context, a place of nothingness, which is constitutive for the specific person-thing relationship but is not explicitly made an object of reflection.

One can clarify this notion by looking closely once more at the function of habits, the object of our previous chapter. The habits can be see as a locus in which subjective consciousness and objective things of the outer world arise together and a logical relationship between them is grounded. Surely here we are not yet saying anything about whether habits are themselves of a subjective nature. In East Asian philosophy this idea is in general denied. For habits always logically precede the subjective consciousness (the I in the subject-object relationship). They are not the affairs of a isolated person, but are learned in everyday commerce with others. For instance a child learns to conduct herself in the face of objects in a certain way when she imitates her parents, playmates or relatives:

> "For a set of instructions to guide us, we need skill at applying words in different situations. Confucius probably noticed that we acquire this skill when we emulate social superiors – parents, older siblings, teachers. We mimic their ways of pronouncing or writing names; we try to act in similar ways towards similar objects; and we copy these behavior in response to the instructions containing names of things and actions. Thus we learn to interpret a dao into action. Confucius used this basic social process as the model of practical interpretation of a dao – zhen^{rectifying} ming^{names}. Rectifying names was thus the key to successful use of a dao in a social setting – to making a dao xing^{walk}. Lacking this, he said, li^{ritual} would not work and people would lack that by which they move hand and foot."[96]

"Originally, 'to learn' meant 'to imitate.' In other words, it meant to follow another person who already had the ability to do something and learn how to do it by imitation. (..) It is transacted with other persons, but is not an isolated person's contemplation."[97] Watsuji clarifies this notion using an example: when a wall is looked at, there must be someone who exists at that same time who looks at the wall. Observer and observed give us, in this way, a picture of the subject-object relationship. Yet this relationship, according to Watsuji, can never be imagined to be independent of social relationships, even when we are talking about an observer alone in a room staring at the wall:

---

[96] C. Hansen, "Qing (Emotions) in Pre-Buddhist Chinese Thought," 187-88.
[97] T. Watsuji, *Watsuji Tetsuro's Rinrigaku*, 29.

"However, in this case if I become conscious of the wall as wall, then social consciousness has already intervened. What is called a wall is that 'form' society imprints on clay or sand as a specific tool (that is, as a part of a house). The form does not belong to the consciousness of 'I' alone, but rather exhibits a meaning common to all those who are concerned with this tool. Hence, for us to look at the wall as a wall indicates that we are conscious of a meaning that is expressive of this particular thing and indicates that we have already significantly entered the realm of common consciousness."[98]

Whosoever conceives herself as a subject positioned opposite an object can do this only in the locus of habits. But these are never individual, but always already common to the may. Subject and object are wrapped in a social context and so are mediated to each other inside it. From the East Asian point of view it is for this reason logically impossible, to think of the individual separately from this context.

"The individual is... not observed as a unit of society."[99] Rather, social relationships take precedence over it.[100] The commerce of individuals with objects can for this reason not serve as a jumping off point for the explanation of social associations. Watsuji brings together this position in the following way:

> "We do not accept the scheme of individual versus object as the starting point of scientific knowledge. Objects are found, not within individual consciousness, but rather within the consciousness of *ningen* (the betweenness of human beings, SG). (...) The subject is not something static like a mirror, whose only business is to contemplate objects, but includes within itself the connections between oneself and the other."[101]

At first glance it seems as if it cannot be decided which position is more plausible: methodological individualism, which postulates the individual as independent from all social relations, or the East Asian perspective, which regards the latter relations as constitutive for the individual. But one must prefer the latter position if we can show that in economic theory there is always an implicit social context, which as a locus determines all notions

---

[98] Ibid., 73.
[99] H. Nakamura, *Ways of Thinking of Eastern Peoples: India-China-Tibet-Japan*, Japanese National Commission for Unesco 1960, 308.
[100] K. Nishida cited in E. Weinmayr, "Denken im Übergang – Kitarō Nishida und Martin Heidegger," in: H. Buchner (ed.), *Japan und Heidegger*, Sigmaringen 1989, 49.
[101] T. Watsuji, *Watsuji Tetsuro's Rinrigaku*, 31.

of individuals and their relationship to objects, without being itself an object of reflection. We will try to do this. To make things clear from the outset, we must append a brief remark: when the mutual relationships of the many are supposed to be picked out as the locus in which the individual is determined, then we are not thereby fashioning an abstract idea of such social coexistence. Rather, the latter is to be imagined as "a living and dynamic betweenness."[102] as a "place of interactive potential, a space where community happens."[103] For Japanese philosophy is not rooted in conceiving the relationships of people in an abstract sense. Rather it is more important to this philosophy to conceptually embrace the "taking-positions-versus-one–another", the "acting-mutually-upon-one-another," or even the "mutually-determining-sides,"[104] of the many in their multiplicity and fullness, without reducing it to a simple formula or a simple law.

4.2.2 The Market as a Social Context

There is hardly another concept as significant for economics as that of the market. For "the economy itself is essentially identified with the market phenomena."[105] Certainly, there is in no sense a unanimity what we are to understand under the term 'market.' Two meaning can be distinguished: one calls the market an objective mechanism or a mechanical system. (4.1.2) But the other takes the concept of market to describe, also, a place in which commodities are traded. Here we are far from supposing a mechanism or a kind of law behind the market. Rather we are nearing already the Japanese notion of a concrete place of living relationships. The meaning of the market as a place should therefore be more precisely investigated. As a starting place, we can use at this point Jevon's definition of the market:

> "By a market I shall mean much what commercial men use it to express. Originally a market was a public place in a town where provisions and other objects were exposed for sale, but the word has been generalized, so as to mean any body of persons who are in intimate business relations and carry on extensive transactions in any commodity. A great city may contain as many markets as there are important branches of trade, and these markets may or may not be localized. The central point of a market is the public exchange – mart or auction rooms – where the traders

---

[102] T. Watsuji, *Watsuji Tetsuro's Rinrigaku*, 18.
[103] R.E. Carter, *Encounter with Enlightenment, A Study of Japanese Ethics*, New York 2001, 126.
[104] K. Nishida cited inE. Weinmayr, "Denken im Übergang," 48.
[105] E.E. Nawroth, *Die Sozial- und Wirtschaftsphilosophie des Neoliberalismus*, 293.

agree to meet and transact business. In London, the Stock Market, the Corn Market, the Coal Market, the Sugar Market and many others, are distinctly localized. .... But this distinction of locality is not necessary. The traders may be spread over a whole town, or region, or country, and yet make a market, if they are, by means of fairs, meetings, published price lists, the post office or otherwise, in close communication which each other."[106]

It is clear from this, that the market designates a space in which persons go to relate with each other. We can imagine this as concrete places in which persons (physically) encounter each other. Yet it is not the marketplace in the sense of a physical space, which is the more decided meaning. A city can possess a marketplace and yet we cannot say, that in it a market is instantiated if the place was empty of people. The concept of the market doesn't point to an abstract space, but instead to a group of people which develop among one another a system of intertwining relationships. Watsuji would speak here of a "subjective spatiality" that develops through the "betweeness of people."[107] Such a 'betweeness' can be more precisely defined in regard to the market. For following Jevon's definition, we can characterize this as an encompassing mesh of narrow business relationships and transactions: "but as they sell their own, so they buy from others, and every body here trades with every body: this it is that gives the whole manufacture so universal a circulation."[108] In economics it is normal to characterize such circulation as a net of exchange relationships. We can thus say in a preliminary way that exchange is concealed as "form and function of inter-individual life" behind the concept of the market."[109]

The meaning of exchange for economics can be read off the fact that economic theory interprets all human relationships as exchange relationships. Already in the eighteenth century Smith is presupposing that "every man thus lives by exchanging, or becomes in some measure a merchant, and the society itself grows to be what is properly a commercial society."[110] He tried in this way, as for instance Hobbes also did, to "universally autonomize the vehicle of exchange."[111] And also for most succeeding economists

---

[106] W.S. Jevons, *The Theory of Political Economy*, 132.
[107] T. Watsuji, *Watsuji Tetsuro's Rinrigaku*, chapt. 9.
[108] D. Defoe cited in J. Wieland, *Ökonomische Organisation, Allokation und Status*, 52.
[109] G. Simmel, *Philosophie des Geldes* (1920), Reprint Neu Isenburg 2001, 59.
[110] A. Smith, *The Wealth of Nations*, 23.
[111] E.K. Seifert, B.P. Priddat, "Gerechtigkeit und Klugheit," 53.

it is fundamental that society is basically nothing other than exchange-society, even if this notion often remains implicit:

> "Out of the formal principles (of economic theory - SG) is often derived an implicitly enduring notion about the interaction of the social world. We can name this as the commensurability of commodities. That is the idea, that all human interactions can be interpreted as exchange. A social world is presupposed ... in which all commodities for individuals are potentially exchangeable or commensurable."[112]

Let's take a more precise look at what is packed into the notion of exchange relationships. We can regard the exchange as a relationship between different actions in a society. In exchange the exchange partners coordinate their actions. I don't want to enter into particular elements of the function of such a coordination,[113] but purely refer to one of their essential presuppositions: the existence of a communications sphere. Already in Jevon's definition of the market it is clear that the market only exists when participants communicate with each other. Communication enables people to develop a market even when they do not physically encounter each other. The fact of language, in which persons can "constantly exchange information"[114], is an important presupposition, then. It is indifferent to a market where the participants are physically found. But they must be able to understand all the relevant data in order to achieve the same state of knowledge. For "it is only so far as this community of knowledge extends that the market extends."[115] Thus it is the communication sphere which defines a market. This is seen, for example, in the English concept 'commerce', which now denotes only economic activity, but had in the eighteenth century a broader meaning: 'to ... converse, hold communication, associate.'[116]

The economic concepts of the "perfect market" and of "perfect competition" make it unambiguous how significant is the common communication of the many, because they presuppose the existence of 'perfect information.' Every market participant must act with a perfect knowledge with re-

---

[112] F. Reckling, *Interpretative Handlungsrationalität*, 53.
[113] For a more extensive explanation, see K.-H. Brodbeck, *Erfolgsfaktor Kreativität*, in particular chapt. 12 and 14.
[114] W.S. Jevons, *The Theory of Political Economy*, 132.
[115] Ibid., 133.
[116] A. Silver, "Two Different Sorts of Commerce," in: J. Weintraub, K. Kumar (ed.), *Public and Private in Thought and Practice: Perspectives on a Grand Dichotomy*, Chicago 1997, 49.

lation to supply and demand of all traded goods, thus for instance knowing about all exchange relationships. This knowledge is not something individual, but rather must be common to all. Perfect markets demand perfect consensus over how every individual good is to be valued.[117] Hayek speaks in this connection of a process of evolving opinion:[118] Information must be so communicated as to allow all market participants to exchange every good in the same exchange relationship. The claim that "in no moment can there be two prices for the same article in the same market,"[119] heralds a further important assumption of perfect competition, which is also known as the 'law of indifference.'[120] But such a law is only imaginable when the many are able or prepared to so coordinate their actions through communication that the necessary information is brought into circulation.[121]

But does a specific form of communication underlie the market? In order to pursue the answer to this question, a conceptual obstacle must first be overcome. It is a question of the widely distributed idea in economic theory that communication arises through the bringing together of independent individuals. This corresponds to an idea of language as it has previously been presented: the independent individuals pre-exist the sphere of common communication. It is plain that, for instance, exchange is regarded as shaping society: only in exchange are persons supposed to begin to interact with one another and so found society. Such an idea can be traced back to Hobbes and his concept of the 'original contract.' For Hobbes thinks that contracts between men can be referenced as constituting factors for society. Even if this idea is represented in modern economic literature, it is still not tenable.[122] For the idea of a contract presupposes exactly that which is regarded as the result of the contract: community or communication. For the concept of the contract implies "that there is a public lan-

---

[117] W.S. Jevons, *The Theory of Political Economy*, 134.
[118] F.A. Hayek, "Der Sinn des Wettbewerbs," in: *Individualismus und wirtschaftliche Ordnung*, 139.
[119] W.S. Jevons, *The Theory of Political Economy*, 137.
[120] Ibid., 136.
[121] J. Cartelier, *Das Geld*, 33.
[122] See for example J.M. Buchanan, "The Limits of Liberty: Between Anarchy and *Leviathan*," http://www.econlib.org/library/Buchanan/buchCv7c2.html (accessed 24 July 2006): "The origins of the state can be derived from an individualistic calculus in this way, at least conceptually, as we know from the writings of Thomas Hobbes as well as from earlier and later contractarians."

guage."[123] A communication sphere must always already exist in order to make a contract work. It cannot therefore be founded by means of a contract.[124] Our common notions of the contract's details (price, kind of articles, etc.) necessarily precede the contract. A fact that also counts, in a similar way, for exchange:

> "But if the exchange of goods lies in the hands of people, it is obvious that these people have approached each other already in another social relationship, before becoming exchange partners: they speak with each other, revere common ethical beliefs (that exchange is not an act of violence, but is instead the absence of violence), they recognize each other as merchants and consumers (thus also conduct themselves cognitively in these guises towards each other), etc. All of this is presupposed by exchange, so that exchange occurs, as Aristotle knew, inside a konoinia, a society – thus the exchange act cannot form this society."[125]

If contract or exchange in economic theory is still referred to as forming society, then we are clearly arguing in a circle: The community of the crowd is supposed to be derived from individual actions, but at the same time it always already presupposes these actions. On these grounds we can reasonably object to the concept of an original contract, for it cannot be logically conceived:

> "Hobbes assigned two unreconcilable claims to the original contract: he wanted it to be the foundation of all generally recognized provisions and rules, but he also wanted it to operate as a contract. But for it to be a proper contract, such generally recognized provisions must already exist, as they could not exist, according to his doctrine, before the sealing of the social contract. The concept of an original contract fails by reason of its inner contradiction and cannot even function as a coherently constructed metaphor."[126]

At this point it is clear "that exchange doesn't generate out of itself a social order; it is, instead, embedded in such an order."[127] Coordination and

---

[123] M. Esfeld, *Mechanismus und Subjektivität in der Philosophie von Thomas Hobbes*, 248.

[124] J. Hirschberger, *Geschichte der Philosophie*, 216. Hirschberger is refering to the idea that there must always be a common morality in order for contracts to be made. "If making a contract is supposed to be possible, there must already be a morality, because otherwise the first principle of contract law, 'pacta sunt servanda,' will not be honored."

[125] K.-H. Brodbeck, *Zirkel des Wissens*, 378.

[126] A. MacIntyre, *Geschichte der Ethik im Überblick*, 130.

[127] K.-H. Brodbeck, *Erfolgsfaktor Kreativität*, 201.

communication don't arise through bilateral acts of exchange, but instead are always already its presupposition.

But how are we supposed to conceive, exactly, this presupposition? In what form must the market participants communicate with each other in order to value commodities in the same way? These questions don't have a straightforward answer. Therefore I will anticipate the outline of the answer before I ground it in reasons: it is money, above all, that is implicitly thought in economics as the "medium of communication."[128] This answer seems problematic at first because it contradicts an important postulate of mainstream economics. For the latter takes the position that money doesn't represent a necessary presupposition for the coordination of economic activities.[129] Accordingly, Wicksell, for instance, ascribes to it purely the function of a "lubricant:"

> "Under the many likenesses by means of which one seeks to present an intuitive picture of the nature and function of money, that of oil in a machine is from many viewpoints the most satisfactory. Oil is not a part of the actual machinery; it is neither the driving force nor the instrumental part of it, and in an absolutely perfect machine a minimum of lubrication would be necessary."[130]

But is money really not a necessary presupposition for the 'laws of the market'? Or to ask this another way: can we actually put a homogeneous price upon every single commodity in the market when we presuppose a situation of the pure exchange of good against good? By looking closely we can see that this can be mostly a contingent case given that many commodities are exchanged against each other. The root of the problem is that a "transitivity of exchanges" is very improbable. Brodbeck delineates what this means:

> "When in Hamburg two commodity owners trade in these terms: '20 yards of linen for 1 shirt;' and in Berlin two other commodity owner in these terms: '20 yards of linen for 10 lbs. of tea;' then that never ever means that in Munich, two exchange partners are in turn going to trade exactly '10 lbs. of tea for 1 shirt.' That would be a miracle."[131]

Random exchanges normally don't create a circular chain, so that it is impossible to determine the price of a commodity unambiguously. But if in

---

[128] J. Wieland, *Ökonomische Organisation, Allokation und Status*, 53.
[129] M. Friedman, *Capitalism and Freedom*, 14.
[130] K. Wicksell, *Vorlesungen über Nationalökonomie*, Vol. 2, Jena 1922, 4-5.
[131] K.-H. Brodbeck, *Zirkel des Wissens*, 381.

economic theory we still take as a starting point the existence of a homogeneous price, the reason for that is always that a wholly specific form of communication is implicitly assumed: that of a homogeneous metric. For satisfying the condition of the transitivity of exchange does not happen when all commodities are exchanged against each other but only when they are exchanged against a single commodity. The different bilateral actions are always consistent with each other when every market participant is prepared to communicate her supply and demand in a universally recognized currency, which is common to all participants. Now this presupposes nothing other than the "development of a symbolically generalized medium of communication." And one can correctly add: "We have known since Aristotle, that this economic medium is money."[132] For in the Nicomachean Ethics Aristotle says: "Thus every thing that can be exchanged must be comparable. Money is used to this end."[133] When there is decentralized and bilateral exchanging in the market, it is solely money that guarantees the equilibrium of supply and demand and the existence of a homogeneous price.

Individual exchanges are thus only bilateral or contingent insofar as they presuppose no immediate knowledge of other exchanges. Yet they are not completely independent of each other as is for the most part postulated in economic theory. For a common sphere of communication precedes them. Money and exchange unfailingly socialize and bind people together. It is the monetary payment relationship, which holds together society.[134] Before two individuals exchange with each other they implicitly recognize that they are comparing their goods in monetary prices. This is the "most important condition for the communication of individuals."[135] Clearly one should be prudent here and not fall into the trap of conceiving money as an entity in the sense of an object or a specific commodity, because its meaning is defined exclusively within the communication of market participants. Its value is defined in the communication process of the market, but cannot itself be measured or otherwise defined. For money can neither be expressed as a market price nor be otherwise measured.[136] It is a social reality, taking precedence over any notion of a perfect market, without itself being objectifiable. We can also formulate this to say that money repre-

---

[132] J. Wieland, *Ökonomische Organisation, Allokation und Status*, 53.
[133] Aristotle, *Nikomachische Ethik*, 165.
[134] F.A. Hayek, *Recht, Gesetzgebung und Freiheit*, Vol. 2: Die Illusion der sozialen Gerechtigkeit, Landsberg am Lech 1981, 155.
[135] J. Cartelier, *Das Geld*, 73.
[136] H.H. Lechner, *Währungspolitik*, 326.

sents a form of the living, dynamic interaction of people that represents for the economic theory of free market exchange a place of nothingness.

If money is implicitly presupposed as a medium of communication, than this no longer merely validates the universal imperative to exchange, but the imperative to sell and to buy.[137] Already Smith clearly sees that society is actually being imagined as a society of buyers:

> "But though the necessary assistance should not be afforded from such generous and disinterested motives, though among the different members of the society there should be no mutual love and affection, the society, though less happy and agreeable, will not necessarily be dissolved. Society may subsist among different men, as among different merchants, from a sense of its utility, without any mutual love or affection; and though no man in it should owe any obligation, or be bound in gratitude to any other, it may still be upheld by a mercenary exchange of good offices according to an agreed valuation."[138]

I don't want to extend our analysis of this idea of the society of buyers as the betweenness of people here. Rather, let's try to pursue the question of how far a society in which money has become the most important means of communication implicitly underlies the definition of the individual in economic theory. Is the striving for more really a natural drive, an individual quality, as it is seen by methodological individualism? Or is it a context dependent quality of those people who define themselves in a monetarily sealed society of exchange? I want to guide us by using some examples, which show why something speaks for the latter possibility.

4.2.3 The Context-Dependent Properties of the Economic Actor

As we have shown in the previous chapter, the striving after more or the infinity of needs is regarded in economic theory as an essential property of persons. But is this property actually an 'anthropological constant'? John Locke pointed out that this isn't the case. In his Second Treatise Locke deals with the question concerning the amount of property man strives for.[139] His answer makes clear that we can in no way universalize an endless striving. For there are societies, according to Locke, in which each only possesses whatever he knows how to immediately utilize, without destroying or wasting it:

---

[137] A. Silver, "Two Different Sorts of Commerce," 45.
[138] A. Smith, *Theory of Moral Sentiments*, 100.
[139] J. Locke, *Two Treatises on Government*, Cambridge 1988, chapt. 5.

"As much as any one can make use of to any advantage of life before it spoils, so much he may by his labour fix a property in. Whatever is beyond this is more than his share, and belongs to others. Nothing was made by God for man to spoil or destroy.... As much land as a man tills, plants, improves, cultivates, and can use the product of, so much is his property."[140]

This upward bound of property, Locke goes on, is immediately discernable to the understanding. Who wants to strive for yet more property when nothing immediately necessitates this striving and it therefore leads to spoiling? Locke thus holds a limitation of needs to be completely possible. However, he does not take it to be an innate characteristic of an isolated individual. Rather, it has another reason: the absence of money within a community.[141] This becomes clear especially when Locke formulates the inverted idea:

"The same rule of propriety- viz., that every man should have as much as he could make use of, would hold still in the world, without straitening anybody, since there is land enough in the world to suffice double the inhabitants, had not the invention of money, and the tacit agreement of men to put a value on it, introduced (by consent) larger possessions and a right to them."[142]

Locke regards an endless striving for more as imaginable only in a society that uses money and in which one is in agreement to exchange this against commodities. "Find out something that hath the use and value of money amongst his neighbours, you shall see the same man will begin presently to enlarge his possessions."[143] Striving for property is consequently not a given, natural property of human beings. Or to put it differently: it only appears 'natural' in a specific social context. In a society in which money isn't used, the striving can be limited; and in a society that uses money, it will eventually become unlimited. Infinite striving is thus neither a property of isolated subjects nor a habit that is found across all societal contexts. It is conceivable only in the locus of a specific form of society. Furthermore, Locke is clear that no 'objective' properties of money put their stamp on this form of society. For money gains its authentic significance, according to Locke, only through the acquiescence of many men in its

---

[140] Ibid., 290.
[141] Ibid., 230.
[142] Ibid., 293.
[143] Ibid., 301.

use.[144] This consensus is what enables persons to pile up riches in the form of money far beyond the limits of immediate use.

The path of Locke's thought is not discussed in modern economic theory. But even in the latter we see implicitly demonstrated that individual utility maximization is thought in a specific social context. We recognize this in the fact that this notion is thought only in the locus of a *discourse dao* that bears the impress of money. (3.3.2) But this *dao* is neither a property of isolated individuals, nor an individually generated habit, but instead a habit that only can be practically exercised in a specific society. For utility maximization doesn't only presuppose that an individual calculates in units of money, but also that the crowd does this as well. This is because the second-order condition of the maximization – the budget line – is not a function relating exclusively to a single individual. By definition, it designates a rate of substitution which is mediated in the communication taking place among the crowd. The budget line "measures the proportion in which the market is ready to substitute commodity 1 for commodity 2."[145] Utility maximization presupposes an equivalence between my own desire with that of another's: or, in other words, "Men value everything by comparison with what others have."[146]

The degree to which the definition of the individual is implicitly thought within the locus of free market exchange is seen in the fact that the individual for many economists simply ceases to exist as soon as she moves outside of its sphere. Schumpeter, for example, thinks that in the market process "ineffectual people are ... de facto eliminated."[147] The possibility of participation in monetary communication is elevated to a question of existence: "Solely the binary code of paying or not paying counts: whoever pays, receives, what he wants; whoever fails to pay, because he can't or won't, becomes a bystander."[148] "Paying or not paying – that is, literally, the ontological question in commerce."[149] The communication sphere in

---

[144] Ibid.
[145] H.R. Varian, *Grundzüge der Mikroökonomie*, 21.
[146] C.B. MacPherson, *The Political Theory of Possessive Individualism, Hobbes to Locke*, Oxford 1962, 34.
[147] J. Schumpeter, *Kapitalismus, Sozialismus und Demokratie*, Tübingen 1950, 123.
[148] M.Schramm, "Spielregeln gestalten sich nicht von selbst, Institutionenethik und Individualethos in Wettbewerbssytemen," in: D. Aufderheide, K. Homann (ed.), *Wirtschaftsethik und Moralökonomik*, 150.
[149] N. Luhmann, *Ökologische Kommunikation, Kann die moderne Gesellschaft sich auf ökologische Gefährdungen einstellen?*, Opladen 1990, 104.

which money functions describes a border, and only those who are on the inside of the border can be meaningfully defined: As Jevons formulates it, "any persons who are not acquainted at every moment with the prevailing ratio of exchange, or whose stocks are no available for the want of communication, must not be considered part of the market."[150] "If he can get no access [to the market], his powers are reduced to zero, and in a competitive society he ceases to exist."[151] The man who has no possession to which others can ascribe a positive value finds his economic existence annihilated. His existence is for this reason "dependent on the actions of many other, often invisible persons."[152] The possession of money is, thus, particularly important. For money alone is valued by other people with certainty, and only its possession guarantees the existence of every person. It functions as an "entry level", as the "border of the market."[153] "The market process includes and excludes. The boundary is demarcated by money. If one has money, one has the ticket to the play of the market."[154]

Our reflections on the context dependence of economic actors are not meant to be exhaustive and can be extended in the face of the plethora of pronouncements in economic textbooks. At the very least, it should be clear that it isn't in the 'nature' of the isolated individual to strive infinitely for more, but in the integration of the individual in a specific social context. The infinite striving is the expression of a socio-historical context, but not an unchanging feature of human beings. It is interesting that this statement corresponds to the idea of many political economists until well into the 19th century.[155] Bagehot thought, for example, that the motive and taste of economic actors were an outgrowth of the extension of trade. Theories that regard humans only as buyers and sellers could on this account only be true in specific contexts: in those nations, which are exclusively concerned with buying and selling.[156] Defoe had earlier formulated this idea with the phrase: "Conversing among tradesman will make him a tradesman."[157] And

---

[150] W.S. Jevons, *The Theory of Political Economy*, 133.
[151] C.B. MacPherson, *The Political Theory of Possesive Individualism*, 56.
[152] W. Eucken cited in E.E. Nawroth, *Die Sozial- und Wirtschaftsphilosophie des Neoliberalismus*, 292.
[153] K.-H. Brodbeck, *Erfolgsfaktor Kreativität*, 220.
[154] Ibid., 229.
[155] J. Persky, "Retrospectives, The Ethology of Homo Economicus," *Journal of Economic Perspectives*, 9/2 (1995), 227.
[156] W. Bagehot cited in ibid., 227.
[157] D. Defoe cited in J. Wieland, *Ökonomische Organisation, Allokation und Status*, 57.

Mill, too, limits the validity of economic laws: "In political economy .... empirical laws of human nature are tacitly assumed by English thinkers, which are calculated only for Great Britain and the United States."[158] In modern economic theories, this insight displaying the context dependence of our definition of the human agent has been widely lost. For these theories take as a starting point that "their statements are independent of any assumption regarding the organization and the course of the encounters between economic subjects."[159]

4.3 The Determination of the Economic World

One can well ask whether we have really gained any practical advantage through the ideas we have been dealing with up to now. Even if we have shown the position of an extreme individualism to be an abstraction only, it seems at first glance as if this just forces us back once again to the beginning of so many economic interpretations. For finally, it is not denied in great parts of the economic literature that the action of the individual is oriented to his fellow man and is determined by his expectation of the latter's conduct. Hayek calls it the "most foolish of all the popular errors" that individualism presupposes the existence of isolated and self-sufficient individuals, instead of beginning with people "whose whole nature and essence is defined by their life in society." According to his position, even "individualism is primarily a theory of society."[160] Why, then, have recourse to Japanese philosophy in order to show the economic actor as a context-dependent existence, which is only imaginable in a society bearing the imprimatur of the monetary relation? In order to answer this question we must expand the representation of our last section in one important aspect. It will be our business to show, exactly, how to conceive of the social context in which the individual is defined. What is Japanese philosophy really talking about when it says that the individual only exists in such a context? Aren't we finally advocating a collectivistic notion that subsumes the individual under a universal (the collective)? In the following these questions will be given a step-by-step answer.

---

[158] J.S. Mill cited in J. Persky, "Retrospectives, The Ethology of Homo Economicus," 228.
[159] J. Cartelier, *Das Geld*, 28.
[160] F.A. Hayek, "Wahrer und falscher Individualismus," 15.

4.3.1 The Economic World as a Field of Action

In Japanese philosophy the concept of 'world' is used to describe a community or society as a place of a "living and dynamic betweenness."[161] As Nishida makes clear, the world should be regarded socio-historically:

> "The world that he [Nishida – SG] thematizes is in any case no already reified, 'objective world' in the sense of the collection of all things; nor is it simply a 'subjective world' in the sense, for instance, of a quintessence of all possible experiences. In contrast to these 'abstract' interpretations of the world, for Nishida the world must be a 'real' and 'concrete' world, i.e. the world 'in which things operate spatio-temporally on each other.' ... The real, concrete world, into which we are born, think, act and at last die ... is nothing other than a social, historical world."[162]

The concept of the world can be understood under two different views. First, it can designate an "all of existence": "the Japanese word for the world, for example, is *sekai*, formed out of *se* (time – past, present and future) and *kai* (the directions: north, east, south, west, over, under) The world as *sekai* is the whole of time and space."[163] But this doesn't mean "the world is exclusively reduced to some spatial and temporal unity. The real world in which we live and act must be straightforwardly grasped in its multiplicity and complexity."[164] The whole world contains no abstract ideas of space and time, but the multitudinous styles of existence in which persons relate to each other, oppose one another and mutually determine each other. "The real world in which we act is in fact multi-layered and has many sides: deep and broad, spatial and temporal, individual and general."[165] In distinction to this embracing world interpretation is the idea of the world, as it is expressed in the Japanese word *yo*. For *yo* "denotes... rather a limited time as the generation or the epoch of a ruler."[166] Thus *yo* signifies the world in a spatially and temporally limited sense, in which people operate in a specific way. Thus, in Japanese, something called a 'world' denotes, on the one hand, a socio-historical world in the sense of a sum of all worlds, and on the other a specific world, that can be found

---

[161] T. Watsuji, *Watsuji Tetsuro's Rinrigaku*, 18.
[162] Y. Matsudo, *Eine Einführung in die Spätphilosophie von Kitarō Nishida*, 64-65. See also S. Ueda, "The Difficulty of Understanding Nishida's Philosophy," *Eastern Buddhist*, 28/2 (1995), 182.
[163] R. Ohashi, *Japan im interkulturellen Dialog*, München 1999, 93.
[164] Y. Matsudo, *Eine Einführung in die Spätphilosophie von Kitarō Nishida*, 66.
[165] Ibid., 66.
[166] R. Ohashi, *Japan im interkulturellen Dialog*, 93.

4 The Implicit World Picture of Economics 177

within this collectivity and localized as a part of it.[167] I will use the concept of world firstly in the last, limited sense, when I speak of an economic world. Then, later on, I will discuss the relationship of this economic world to other worlds. (4.9)

As a preliminary, we can explain the world concept of Japanese philosophy through a negative definition. The world shouldn't be denoted through reference to a given order or a self-determined universal:

> "For if the world is thought of as a self-determined entity completely detached from mutually determining acts, that is, as an absolute existent, then along with the givenness of this existence, reality as a whole also appears as something determined. It comes into question merely as an object of knowledge or as a dead thing, as an affair that is already past, and appears as something 'simply given.'"[168]

But on the other hand, no unity of independent individuals is designated by the term 'world' either. This negative description of the world makes clear that we have to seek a way of defining it beyond both of the usual explanations that are characteristic for economic theories. We shall not understand the world by reference to the individual, nor to the mechanical-causal order. But is there a real alternative that will let us define the world positively? MacIntyre indicates in a study of the different ideas of the individual and the social in Japan and the USA that American social scientists for the most part answer this question with a 'no,' since they regard every society, at least implicitly, as either individually or collectively oriented. The difference of individual and universal is presupposed as given in all cultural contexts.[169] In positing this it escapes them that, actually, in Japanese philosophy an alternative description of the world is projected. To make a long story short, the root of this lies in determining the world site specifically: the world is conceptualized as a locus which underlies all individual and social determination. It mediates both determinations to each other without itself being describable from the standpoint of either the universal or the individual. In this sense it is a place of nothingness, which is always presupposed, but is never explicitly made the object of reflection.

If the world must not be thought from either the individual or the universal standpoint, we have to find an alternative explanatory starting point. With

---

[167] Y. Matsudo, *Eine Einführung in die Spätphilosophie von Kitarō Nishida*, 66.
[168] E. Weinmayr, "Denken im Übergang," 49. Weinmayr is citing Nishida.
[169] A. MacIntyre, "Individual and Social Morality in Japan and the United States: Rival Conceptions of the Self," *Philosophy East and West*, 40/4 (1990), 498.

Nishida, such a viewpoint becomes clear: "the world... must be the world of act, and the act requires a domicile."[170] For Nishida, every act develops a specific world. Here, Nishida interprets the concept of act very extensively, because for him all our activities belong to this category, such as perception, thinking and expression, labor or even instinctive action.[171] A world is a "location"[172], which embraces in itself a wholly specific act and at the same time is formed through this act. "The act [is] a 'consequence of the historical, dialectical and creative world.' ... The other side of the act is what constitutes the historicity of the world itself."[173] But how are we supposed to imagine such an act? To answer this question, it is necessary firstly to make an important distinction with regard to the understanding of action between economic theory and East Asian philosophy. Let's first take the former. Simply stated, in economics we should find something that causes the action or someone on whom we can pin the responsibility for the action. Forces are to be pointed out that determine the result of the action, and these forces are ascribed to either persons or the outer world (for instance a collective). Yet the search for a specific bearer of the action proves by a closer look to be extraordinarily difficult, because we can't make an action correspond to any one person or thing alone. The problem is evident already in regard to exchange: this remains incomprehensible, if we only look at a single exchanging subject, because this itself presupposes always already the many others who also participate in exchange. The exchangers are mutually and immediately dependent one upon the other, "because the two processes [of giving and taking-SG] are simultaneously cause and effect, each of the other."[174] But we can't reduce exchange to something existing independently of the mutual relationship of the exchangers either. There is, as Simmel perspicuously shows, no third independent of the exchangers on which the act of exchange rests:

> "On the subject of exchange we often run into that conceptual obscurity in consequence of which we speak of a connection, a relationship, as it if were something outside of the elements between which it operates. Yet it means only a situation or a change within each of them, but nothing exists between them, in the sense of a spatial separateness of an object found between two others. When, in the concept of exchange, we combine both acts or changes of state that actually do come to pass, the idea lies temptingly near that besides that which has occurred in the one and the

---

[170] K. Nishida, "Die Welt als Dialektisches Allgemeines," 145.
[171] Y. Matsudo, *Eine Einführung in die Spätphilosophie von Kitarō Nishida*, 65.
[172] K. Nishida, "Die Welt als Dialektisches Allgemeines," 122.
[173] Y. Matsudo, *Eine Einführung in die Spätphilosophie von Kitarō Nishida*, 54-55.
[174] G. Simmel, *Philosophie des Geldes*, 45-46.

other contracting parties, something near to or supervening has also occurred – as though it were like the conceptual hypostatisation of the concept of kiss, which one also 'exchanges,' which also tempts one to think that the kiss is something which lies outside the pair of lips, outside of their movement and sensation."[175]

Even the exchange value of a commodity doesn't logically precede the exchange acts, since it emerges first through the "mutuality of compensation."[176] It is determined in a 'test procedure' that always already at least implicitly presupposes many exchange partners. Here we can see how hard it is to trace actions back to a specific causal agent. Following the Nishida's interpretation of action, Weinmayr formulates this insight as follows:

> "'Action' denotes the active and productive performance of a person who, while acting upon others, shapes and gives rise to reality, and so makes it visible. Yet our search for the origin or motive of this action isn't going to lead us to the origin of an autonomous subject's voluntary action, or a set of fundamental action norms. The question of the ‚who' and the ‚why' of the act proves, instead, that the acting self itself exists only in the mutual determination of all existents. Consequently it is shaped by others; it is a place of the presence of countless alien wills. 'If we speak of action, we take the individual as a starting point. But we don't act outside of the world, but find ourselves, when we act, already in the midst of the world. Our acting is a being-acted-upon.'"[177]

Action is thus – if one describes it from the viewpoint of the bearer of action – always conjointly active and passive, "constructed and constructing."[178] It is not specified unambiguously. In other words: there exists no prime mover, which can be regarded as the cause or origin of an action. It can't be unambiguously localized either in the actor or in his environment.[179] For this reason, Japanese philosophy chooses another starting point that appears to be abnormal at first glance. It starts from the action, without regarding it as being determined by an agent. Action appears in a context (a world), but nobody in this context causally brings it about. We

---

[175] Ibid., 35.
[176] Ibid., 31.
[177] E. Weinmayr, "Denken im Übergang," 51-52. Weinmayr is citing Nishida.
[178] Ibid., 52.
[179] On the concept of the *prime mover,* see T.S. Lebra, *Japanese Patterns of Behavior,* Honolulu 1976, 6. For a discussion of the term and its meaning in the Japanese context, see S. Graupe, "Japanese Modes of Business Behaviour, A Cultural Perspective on Efficiency and Accountability in the Japanese Context," *Praxis Perspektiven,* Vol. 5, Würzburg 2002, 47-54.

can speak, here, of a pure activity within a world, an action without an actor. This notion appears abnormal because the German or English language forces one, so to speak, when using a verb, always to put it together with a doer. For example: *the cup* sits on the table, *one* takes the train, *it* is raining bullets. In this way, the question of the 'who,' the do-er of the deed, immediately presses upon one. In Japanese or in ancient Chinese, on the contrary, this question appears much less relevant.[180] For these are languages in which pure activity, a deed without a do-er, can be expressed. Grammatically this means that Japanese is a language without a subject:

> "It is really an essential property that the subject in Japanese grammar, in contrast to European languages, is not unconditionally necessary. This is not simply an abbreviation on the grounds of convenience. Rather this can be interpreted to mean that the Japanese language has no subject."[181]

Likewise, in Japanese we say, for example, 'taking the train' or 'raining' without saying who carries out these actions. This doesn't mean, for instance, that we are dealing with a hidden subject, but that the 'it' isn't regarded as determining the action. Thus there exists "the possibility, simply to loosen the subject and the object and only to name the process as an occurrence – or the 'deed.'"[182] Yet more: it is clear, that the occurrence itself, thus the context of action, determines the do-er in the first place. Taking the train defines someone as the train-taker or as the traveler. And walking determines someone as the walker. Thus, the subject doesn't cause a deed, but instead it is determined or elicited through the context of action itself. Or even better: in the strict sense there exists no subject at all; it becomes purely a theme elevated out of a living unity.[183] In any case the deed or eventuating process comes first. The sentence of von Mises: "we grasp the concept of action as thinking and acting persons"[184] is thus reversed: the person, his thought and deed is understood from the standpoint of the deed. „Our own life we possess in the true sense only as actors."[185]

---

[180] See for a more extensive analysis, R. Elberfeld, *Phänomenologie der Zeit im Buddhismus, Methoden interkulturellen Philosophierens – Philosophie interkulturell*, Stuttgart 2004, 85. It is still controversial how far the following claims are valid for Japanese in general or only for old Japanese.
[181] T. Shimomura, "Mentalität und Logik der Japaner," in R. Ohashi (ed.), *Die Philosophie der Kyōto Schule*, 382.
[182] R. Elberfeld, *Phänomenologie der Zeit im Buddhismus*, 93.
[183] Ibid., 109.
[184] L. von Mises, *Grundprobleme der Nationalökonomie*, 22.
[185] K. Nishida, *Logik des Ortes*, 158.

It is possible, on the basis of this hermeneutic of action, to describe the world as the context of action without there being a subject underlying it. It is thought of as a locus that is merely pure activity without this activity corresponding to a (causal) agent. In order to work out the properties of such a world, the metaphor of the field is particularly appropriate, by which we are not talking about a conservative field, but a relativistic, i.e., a self-acting and self-determining one.[186] We've already encountered the metaphor of the field in the third chapter, where it served to describe the relationship of the objective and subjective consciousness. (3.3.1) Here, with the aid of this metaphor, we shall outline how the relationship of the individual to the economic world should be conceived. To make this point, money is conceived as a field – more precisely, a field of action – which represents the source of all possible and actual acts of the economic world.[187] So, in an exemplary fashion, money makes possible the calculative apprehension or the striving after more. It must be understood as an open space, which allows a multiplicity of actions, but at the same time, determines these like a field of force. The individual can be apprehended within such an action field as a field-being; she appears as a focus or focal point of the field. Such an interpretation of the field metaphor is of particular interest, since even in economics, at least implicitly, the concept of the field is used, in order to describe the relationship between the person and society. Our purpose, as we explain the East Asian field metaphor in a more focused way and contrast it with economic interpretations of the field, is to open up a fresh perspective which comes to pass when we use East Asian philosophy to look at the economic world.

4.3.2 The Individual in the Economic World

First, lets look at the determination of the individual in the economic world.[188] In economic theory the individual is sometimes imagined as an energy charged individual substance that can radiant and receive impulses.[189] But it remains unclear what this metaphor, taken from physics, is supposed to concretely express. For instance, what does it mean, exactly, that the individual is charged with energy? As a glance at physics shows, a

---

[186] See especially L.K. Tong, *The Art of Appropriation*: Towards a Field-Being Conception of Philosophy, Fairfield 2000. See also D.L. Hall, R.T. Ames, *Thinking from the Han*, chapt. 2 and 3.

[187] L.T. Tong, *The Art of Appropriation*, 11. The idea here is developed in its general form.

[188] We are excluding in principle, here, the fact that the world is the world of many.

[189] E.E. Nawroth, *Die Sozial- und Wirtschaftsphilosophie des Neoliberalismus*, 61.

charge of energy is only thinkable within an energy field, in which its power is dependent on the position of the energy bearer inside the field. Its power is an expression of the underlying field; it is to be seen, itself, as a context dependent existence. If this thought is transposed to the economic actor, it means we must understand him, in the same way, context-dependently. She becomes a specific function inside the field of action, thought as a specific determination of activity.[190] But what is exactly to be understood by her 'energy'? According to Daoist philosophy, this denotes the result of all activity, which is realized at any time. It is the product or output of current and past activities within the action field:

> "Facts and effects are continuously made or produced by virtue of the work or dispensation of power, that is of matter-energy. Here the term 'matter energy' is to be taken in a special sense, not to be identified with its usual signification in the physical sciences. 'Matter-energy' is an abbreviation for vibrant energy and karmic matter, the latter referring to the accumulated effects or products of past actions. The appropriation of karmic matter by vibrant energy, which consists in the creative transformation of karmic matter through karmic labor, is what defines the meaning of subjectivity."[191]

This idea can be transferred in the following way to the economic world: Money as the field of action furnishes a multitude of deeds for the individual. These must not be understood as the activity of a specific individual, but as possibilities to realize these activities in general. Money furnishes the individual with something to possess or a something more to strive after in the sense of utility maximization. But it is not to be identified with a specific striving just as the physical energy field cannot be identified with a specific charge of energy. We can even say, that possession and striving firstly describe universal forms of activity, without these being specifically carried out by someone. The individual can appropriate these forms of action. Thus for example any arbitrary person can own a specific sum of money. Its possession is a possibility for many. Only when an individual claims this sum of money, and thus appropriates it, is the sum robbed of the possibility to be possessed by others. The ownership of money thus becomes an individual activity of the individual. According to the Daoist interpretation, the individual becomes an existence in the sense of field existence only through such a privation. Just as an object in the field of energy is determined exclusively through the amount of energy that it concentrates in itself, the individual is determined through appropriating the forms of

---

[190] L.K. Tong, *The Art of Appropriation*, 14.
[191] Ibid., 9.

action of the field. "Thus the *dao* of carpentry is the Way the activity of carpentry appropriates itself, ... the *dao* of government is the Way the activity of governing appropriates itself."[192] And the individual becomes an 'energy charged individual existence' in the economic sense, when she makes money her own and lets her perceptions and acts be determined by it. Or to put this more universally: she becomes such an existence when she seizes hold of money, with the seizing hold of being understood literally. The individual seizes hold of herself when she possesses money and inversely she possesses herself, when she seizes hold of money. We consider action and the subject – the agent of action – according to an important Daoist and Buddhist saying – to always arise simultaneously. Thus the existence of the economic actor is only grounded in constant contact with money. One can also formulate this to mean that her ego consists in nothing other than an "articulated activity," in the art of appropriating the 'energy' of the field of action – money.[193] The moment the individual renounces this art, her energy is annihilated; she ceases to exist in the context of the economic world.

But the charge of energy is not the only property through which we are able to describe the individual inside a field of action. The individual still has the force to apprehend herself anew in action, and thus to alter her position in the field of action. It is this process through which the existence of the ego is sustained. "Every articulate action desires to perpetuate itself, that is, to continuously affirm itself in its own form of articulation."[194] Tong describes this striving as a "will to power." "It is the Will to Power, which generally manifests itself as the will to grasp, to hold, and to control, that renders effective the lure of definiteness."[195] Such a will to power assumes a wholly specific shape in money's field of action insofar as power is apparently unlimited here. For it lies in its nature to always progressively increase itself.[196] The force of the individual in money's field of action is thus not only directed at sustaining its own existence in the field, but also extending it. It is a striving for endless appropriation.

Without approaching any nearer the metaphor of energy and force, we can already indicate that East Asian philosophy evidently does not see the actor as an essence or a substance, but as an ongoing process. The actor is noth-

---

[192] Ibid., 5-6.
[193] Ibid., 7.
[194] Ibid., 22.
[195] Ibid., 22.
[196] T. Hobbes, *Leviathan*, Book 1, Chapter 13.

ing other than current and past activity.[197] "Our self ... is thoroughly active."[198] "There is no difference between being and doing at all in the Field-Being scheme: being is doing, and doing being. For all is activity!"[199] Hence, we can speak no more of an essence of the individual in a meaningful sense. The individual is not a stable substance; rather, she continuously changes in the course of activity. Further, the individual can't be imagined context independently, because she is always dependent as a focus on the field's context. "By definition, the focal self cannot be independent. The structure and continuity of the focal self is immanental, inhering in and continuous with its context."[200] It is the 'nature' of the individual, so to speak, to display the energy concentration and the vector of force in a field of action. She is inseparable from this field. 'In itself', i.e. abstracted from the field of action, the individual is merely a non-entity, a non-existence.[201] The properties of the individual are exclusively rooted in the relation to that field in which it finds herself. [202]

> "From the Field-Being standpoint, the world or universe is not a discrete collection of rigidly bounded 'substantial entities', but is in reality a dynamic plenum or continuum of empowered activity, an encompassing and unified field of power concrescence. Every determination in the universe is a field-topological event, a warp of power – of energy, experience and meaning – arising from a holo-reflexive articulation or complexification of the dynamic plenum in its undivided wholeness. Strictly speaking there are no things at all, conceived as intrinsically separate and independent individual substances. The differentiated beings, entities or objects which show themselves in our ordinary conscious experience are not substantial entities but are what we call field individuals, which, as worldly existents, are more or less enduring centers of empowered activity, or field-topological loci of power concrescence. Indeed, it is out of the self-definition of power concrescence as lim-

---

[197] R.T. Ames, in regards to classical Confucian thinking, brings this out particularly well in: "The Focus-Field in Classical Confucianism," in: Ames et al. (ed.), *Self as Person in Asian Theory and Practice*, New York 1994, 198.
[198] K. Nishida, *Logik des Ortes*, 242.
[199] L.K. Tong, *The Art of Appropriation*, 14.
[200] D.L. Hall and R.T. Ames, *Thinking from the Han*, 43.
[201] L.K. Tong, *The Art of Appropriation*, 21-22. Tong adds that this idea of non-essence in Buddhism is expressed in the concept of 'emptiness': "As the Buddhists would say, the so-called things are in themselves empty, devoid of self-nature."
[202] K. Nishida, *Logik des Ortes*, 80.

ited and shaped by the holo-reflexive complexification of the dynamic plenum that individuals are born in the Great Flow, in the universal process of becoming."[203]

4.3.3 The Logical Impossibility of the Determination of the Economic World

But how can we now describe the action field itself? It seems at first convenient to interpret it as a collection or aggregation of energy concentrations or as a mutual interaction of these concentrations. Such an interpretation is clearly problematic. For a field, as we can see by a glance at physics, is not to be described through the energy concentrations found in it, "because the whole field does not equal the sum of its parts."[204] It displays neither a specified energy concentrations nor an aggregation of them, nor, clearly, is it specified through their absence. The field is, rather, a locus, in which the different energy concentrations emerge, change and pass away, without that locus being knowable from the standpoint of one of these concentrations. This means, transposed to the field of action: from the actors' viewpoints, the field is a locus that is always presupposed and never objectifiable. From their viewpoint you cannot say, whether it exists or not. The field of action is not a unity, which is compounded out of given individuals, but defines the individual itself site specifically. It isn't the realization of an aggregate of individual existences, but, inversely, is just its presupposition.[205] This means, in regard to the economic world, that it truly displays a collectivity of activities, but must not be imagined as a collection of individuals:

> "The plenum is itself not a digitum, nor analyzable into a collection of digiti. (...) The world as a dynamic and fluid articulate totality of field action is not be digitized into a collection of substantial entities or assembled into a machine made up of mechanical parts, however intriguing and orderly that substantial or mechanical assembly is."[206]

If a field of action can't be understood as a collection of entities, then one might suggest that it can be apprehended as a field order. Hayek, for instance, discusses this possibility when he speaks of society as an "abstract

---

[203] L.K. Tong, *Dao and Logos: Prolegomena to a Quintessential Hermeneutics*, unpublished manuscript.
[204] P. Mirowski, *More Heat than Light*, 81.
[205] R.J. Wargo, *The Logic of Basho*, 201-202.
[206] L.K. Tong, *The Art of Appropriation*, 18-23.

collective order"[207] shaped by the "forces of spontaneous ordering."[208] What counts, here, is whether the ordering forces are seen as context independent, thus making the field order an autonomous or independent existence. In many places this is clearly the case; as when, for instance, Hayek speaks of a "bending before impersonal and anonymous social processes"[209] or even of a "superconscious mechanism."[210] A 'spontaneous order' is supposed to exist that is created by "transpersonal, self-organizing forces."[211] On can argue that a new form of the invisible hand is postulated through this idea. Thus the order's function of binding the many into a lawful unity is realized by an unconscious; a course of thought that Simmel has already described:

> "The mutual operations of the economy act in general with such a wonderful purposiveness, in such finally organized, innumerable, imbricated elements, that one has to assume a spirit of superindividual wisdom as a guide, overseeing and directing, if we don't want to fall back upon the unconscious purposiveness of the man's species life."[212]

In this way the field metaphor seems purely to lead to describing the economic world in terms of a "given whole."[213] This impression is clearly deceptive, since Hayek's statements rest on a false interpretation of the metaphor. Running under it is a conceptual error that Simmel already criticized. One infers from the fact that the conscious will of individuals is not sufficient to hold the economy's mechanism in that harmony which it shows despite all its fearful dissonances and insufficiencies, that one must assume unconscious experiences and calculations that accumulate in the historical course of the economy and regulate it.[214] But to deduce, from unconscious ideas, to the actual existence of the order, is "doubtlessly logically unjustified. The simply negative fact, that we are not conscious in these cases of any grounding idea we turn invert under our hands into a positive, that unconscious ideas are present." To treat unconscious processes as an operant

---

[207] F.A. Hayek, *Recht, Gesetzgebung und Freiheit*, Vol. 2, 159.
[208] F.A. Hayek, *Recht, Gesetzgebung und Freiheit*, Vol. 1: *Regeln und Ordnung*, München 1980, 63.
[209] F.A. Hayek, "Wahrer und falscher Individualismus," 18.
[210] F. A. Hayek, *Studies in Philosophy, Politics and Economics*, London-Henley 1967, 61.
[211] F.A. Hayek, *Recht, Gesetzgebung und Freiheit*, Vol. 1, 79.
[212] G. Simmel, *Philosophie des Geldes*, 138.
[213] F.A. Hayek, *Recht, Gesetzgebung und Freiheit*, Vol. 2, 43.
[214] G. Simmel, *Philosophie des Geldes*, 138.

cause is a distortion of the fact that "they are simply a symbol of the real course of things."[215]

But how did this idea of an unconscious process as an operant cause ever come about in the first place? We've already seen, how the individual as a context dependent existence can be determined in the action field. Looking exclusively at this specification, it seems that the field affirms the individual absolutely.[216] It gives her the possibility of appropriating field activities and accordingly perceiving herself as an individual. But the field still offers a wholly other possibility for the process of perception, which becomes clear when we remember that not only an individual, but also the many, are determined in a field of action. An action is not only private but also universal, in the sense that each person can perform it. It can thus not only be individualized, but at the same time also universalized, in that it is understood as a universal rule of action. This is the direction in which we must imagine the field order. Hayek formulates this clearly: it is the "regularity of conduct" which "determines the universal character of a self-actualizing order."[217] In the economic world this regularity of conduct has its roots in the fact that all individuals perceive themselves in the field of money, and these many perception processes are bound up with each other. "No longer does the unappeasable greed of the salesman travel restlessly up and down the world. Instead, it is caught in a network."[218] In economics, in this connection, one speaks of a circular net, for instance, or a "circle of commerce."[219] Yet by this economists do not denote an interweaving of relationships, but rather an abstract work of law. They aren't busy describing a face-to-face society, but instead an "abstract society... in which ... only abstract rules and impersonal signals define the activities."[220] In this way, we completely abstract from the individual and his specific relationships to others. The field of action is to be apprehended as a purely anonymous functional relationship. And here money takes on a renewed and particular importance because it alone can allow the assumption of such a functional relationship. For only through money can all activities be codified homogeneously in prices, so that we can assume a price mediated

---

[215] Ibid., 138.
[216] K. Nishida, "Die Welt als Dialektisches Allgemeines," 130.
[217] F.A. Hayek, *Recht, Gesetzgebung und Freiheit*, Vol. 1, 62.
[218] J. Wieland, *Ökonomische Organisation, Allokation und Status*, 48.
[219] J. Wieland, *Ökonomische Organisation, Allokation und Status*, 48.
[220] F.A. Hayek, *Recht, Gesetzgebung und Freiheit*, Vol. 3: *Die Verfassung einer Gesellschaft freier Menschen*, Landsberg am Lech 1981, 219.

functional connection.[221] Endowing the action field with such "action structuring power"[222] allows us to generalize so far that we can regard the functional relations as autonomous and the field of action as a self-subsisting reality. The latter becomes an objective thing-thing nexus, a system, that "makes itself wholly by itself."[223] "Thus the path is cleared to think about the economic order as a mechanical system,"[224] in which the entire world appears as an artificial body, as a mechanical circle of events. It becomes a machine itself, by which it is thought that it "absolutely determines ... its own self."[225]

In such a causal-mechanical interpretation of the world, the abstract universalization of the action field is driven to its ultimate expression. While the individual is absolutely affirmed, so that we look at his individual appropriation of field activities and abstract from all others, the absolute character of the field is also affirmed so that we look at field activities as irrevocable rules applying to all activities inside the field, without looking at any specific action of an individual. It is immediately apparent that the individuality of the individual is absolutely negated in the latter case. All activities appear only as expressions of universal rules, which seem to be given objectively. Even if in this way the economic world can actually be thought of as an 'imaginary machine', in which "in the imagination the different movements and operations are put together, which are executed in reality,"[226] still it actually remains only that: an imagination, an abstraction. In particular this is the case when we suppose a self sufficient existence behind such a machine. For just as no field existent is context independent, so, too, the idea of a universal order remains necessarily related to the context of the field. There exists no self-sufficient order independent from the field of action, which could specify the activities of the many causally or mechanically. Rather, the many who exist in a field of action are the logical and necessary presupposition for it being possible to represent any abstract order at all. Independent of the fact that the many determine their perceptions and actions in the action field of money, thus making this action field universal, there is no 'market mechanism', no 'material constraint.' The economic order is no entity that we could disentangle from the

---

[221] J. Wieland, *Ökonomische Organisation, Allokation und Status*, 53.
[222] Ibid., 55.
[223] A. Smith, *The Wealth of Nations*, 582.
[224] J. Wieland, *Ökonomische Organisation, Allokation und Status*, 49.
[225] K. Nishida, "Die Welt als Dialektisches Allgemeines," 140.
[226] A. Smith, *Essays on Philosophical Subjects*, transl. by W.P.D. Wightman, J.C. Bryce, Glasgow 1980, 66.

action field of money. The same rule applies to it as to the individual: 'in itself', i.e. abstracted from the field of action, it is merely a non-entity, a non-essence. Its substantiality lies exclusively grounded in its relationship to the field in which it is specified site specifically. Even it is a context dependent existence. We thus conclude that the action field can be determined neither by starting out from a field order nor starting out from an individual. From both standpoints, one can deduce neither the existence nor the non-existence of the field. The latter is always already the given, the implicit presupposition. And, again, what serves as presupposition cannot be made the target of an explanation.

4.3.4 The Economic World as a Place of Nothingness

If the world is interpreted as a field of action, it shows that it cannot be grasped from either the standpoint of the individual or the standpoint of a given order. "At the base of the world, there are neither the many nor the one."[227] The world shows itself, instead, as a "determination without a determiner, which from an absolutely superior level determines and guides what happens."[228] It is a locus, holding the individual and the universal in itself and mediating between them. We can characterize the world as follows: it is neither a collectivity of individuals nor an abstract order. It is also not to be thought as a surface of the intersections of both of these poles.[229] Rather, it determines both of these poles site specifically together.

The world manifests a place of nothingness for any explanation that posits either individuals or the universal as the point of departure. Tong clarifies this proposition with regard to the field metaphor:

> "The Field then is the universal matrix [i.e. locus – translator] conceived as the womb of all field individuals and field orders (the particulars and universals in traditional Western metaphysics), the two primary types of existence in the plenum of Field-Being. When we think of the Field as source of all possibilities and existence in articulate action, it is identified as the field potential. Since the field makes room for all particularity – all particular roles and functions – and, hence, cannot be identified with any particular roles or functions, it is the nothing that lies at the root of all things that is the 'Radical Nothing.' But the field potential, as Radical Nothing,

---

[227] K. Nishida, *Intellegibility and the Philosophy of Nothingness*, 168.
[228] K. Nishida, *Logik des Ortes*, 166.
[229] K. Nishida, *Die Welt als Dialektisches Allgemeines*, 140.

is also referred to as the 'Let-Be', the ultimate activity that is the articulate source and ground of all existence in the universe (in a specific world, SG)."[230]

The world manifests an open space, a place of possibility, which preserves the existence of all specific forms of appearance. In particular, it shelters the individual and universal equally in itself. In its "function, to position the contradictory simultaneously,"[231] the world breaks through the difference between both of these poles without dissolving it. For in it, the individual and the universal don't appear as irreconcilable opposites,[232] but instead as positively interdependent. This positive interdependence[233] can be traced back to the ability to conceive the same action form in two distinct ways. On the one hand, objectively, in the sense of order, insofar as it is seen as the 'universal character' of the many; on the other hand, as an expression of individuality or subjectivity, if it is regarded as a 'particular phenomenal form' of the individual. Both of these poles are never to be separated, since they relate originally to the same action. They are in a radical sense interdependent, i.e. in a state of mutual reference one to the other. A universal order only shows itself when indeterminate numbers of individuals are apprehended in a specific field of action and the individuals can only apprehend themselves in this field, that is, if this is recognized in the sense of a universal order. Both, order and individual refer to each other, without one of the poles being determined outside of the field. "There is nothing that we can think of or talk about which is not functional, that is, a function or determination of activity."[234]

Because the world holds the individual and universal within it and mediates between them, it can't be explained either from the viewpoint of the individual or from that of the universal. It is instead a place of nothingness, which isn't to be determined as 'something.' Because the world is a field of possible actions, it is just as little an essence as is a physical field. It is neither an aggregation of 'individual essences' nor a result of their mutual effects. Rather, it is like an open space that enables these mutual effects to happen in the first place. But the world is also not an abstract order; it is rather the locus, which logically precedes the existence of such an order.

---

[230] L.K. Tong, *The Art of Appropriation*, 11.
[231] Y. Matsudo, *Eine Einführung in die Spätphilosophie von Kitarō Nishida*, 86.
[232] L.K. Tong, *The Art of Appropriation*, 17.
[233] Y. Matsudo, *Eine Einführung in die Spätphilosophie von Kitarō Nishida*, 86.
[234] L.K. Tong, *The Art of Appropriation*, 14.

4.3.5 The Inconsistency of the Economic World

If we let ourselves think of the world as a place of nothingness, we have to recognize that it is not completely objectifiable. One sees oneself confronted with the "impossibility of an ultimate grounding of how the determination and formation of the world occurs."[235] A confrontation that for Nishida – as also for other East Asian philosophers – is unavoidable, because no center exists from which one could apprehend the world:

> "The person cannot be this center, because, even though he acts, the act does not belong exclusively to him; it is an expression of the world, from which he is derived and in which he is able to act in general. Just as little can an (abstract) universal as, for example, God, Being, the One constitute the center, which shall guide the world and bind it into a unity."[236]

In concrete terms, this means the economic world cannot be apprehended either as a market (in terms of material regularity), or as a mechanism, or as an aggregation of individuals. We cannot think of it either from the position of individuals or from that of the universal:

> "If one thinks of mankind as the formative subject of the world, meaning that the concrete givens and presence of reality all goes back to the active doings of persons, and takes these as the origin of reality – one thereby overlooks the groundedness of every person in the way all instantiated beings are determined, meaning the world as a whole. If, conversely, we look at individual persons as simply passive, a thoroughly formed instant in the continual flow of the auto-poeisis of some final, true reality, for whom only the simply passive aspect of reality remains in the process of its formation, once again we overlook how the whole of the world in truth, and finally, is only the event of the mutual determination of individuals."[237]

The world resists any rational description in the sense of a logical, unequivocal statement.[238] It can only allow itself to be described contradictorily. Nishida particularly emphasizes this contradictoriness of the world:

> "Nishida apprehends the concrete world as 'world of absolute contradictory self-identification of one and of many;' in it, the rule holds that 'the one equals the many, the many equals the one.' The world shows in this way a double face that disturbs every attempt to fix it in a glance or to sum it up in an unequivocal state-

---

[235] E. Weinmayr, "Denken im Übergang," 50.
[236] Y. Matsudo, *Eine Einführung in die Spätphilosophie von Kitarō Nishida*, 66.
[237] E. Weinmayr, "Denken im Übergang," 51.
[238] L.K. Tong, *The Art of Appropriation*, 19.

ment. The world, as the one and universal, encompasses the many individuals, mediates among them and gives in this way a place to all individuals in which they stand in relation to each other, act upon each other, mutually shape each other and so first exist as individuals. As the 'site specifical mediator' ... of completely independent, wholly discontinuous individuals facing one another, this world still doesn't have a middle, its unity and continuity is torn. Nishida called it, for this reason, 'the discontinuous-continuous mediator' or the 'place of discontinuous continuity' or a 'contradictory self-identity.'"[239]

The world "can not be objectified and shows itself essentially as an absolute negativity."[240] It cannot be seized as a given, as a "simply eternally unchanging thing."[241] Nishida thus refuses to countenance any description of the world as a coherent unity; an attitude, that also occurs in Daoism:

> "The Daoist posture of mirroring the world cannot be either dialectical or analytic, since both analysis and dialectic require a putative whole, the former in order to divide into parts, the latter in order to form the opposing parts into some synthetic whole. Neither the 'ten thousand things' nor the self that plies its way among them, may be summed to a coherent whole."[242]

The renunciation of any rational explanation of the world doesn't imply that no description is possible. Rather, in the concept of the field and the locus an alternative becomes visible, which recognizes the contradictoriness of the world as much as the mutual, site specific dependency of all existence within this world. This kind of perspective may appear unsatisfactory or even unscientific. But it represents as much for Daoism as for Japanese philosophy the only possibility of apprehending the character of the world. From its perspective, the ideas of substantive individuals and a given universal represent delusions. They are pure abstractions, which let us forget the living, socio-historical world as that context in which these abstractions come to pass. This insight leads to the refusal to countenance all rational explanations of the world as they are striven for in economics.

4.4 The Properties of the Economic World

If we refuse to describe the world as an abstract order, it is then necessary to think through the relations of individuals to one another more precisely

---

[239] E. Weinmayr, "Denken im Übergang," 50.
[240] Y. Matsudo, *Eine Einführung in die Spätphilosophie von Kitarō Nishida*, 110.
[241] K. Nishida, "Die Welt als Dialektisches Allgemeines," 144.
[242] D.L. Hall, R.T. Ames, *Thinking from the Han*, 67.

as has been done up to now. How is the world to be explained as a unity of the many, when neither a mechanism nor regularity is assumed that produces this unity? This question is of particular interest, since its answer points to a property of the world that is often brought up in Japanese philosophy: its dynamic, creative character. As shall be shown, it is this character that makes the calculability and the ability to forecast the world, as well as our domination of it, impossible.

4.4.1 The Creative, Dynamic Character of the Economic World

The thought of order rests on the ignoring of every specific determinacy of individual elements and regarding them as logically equivalent or as exchangeable. In this way, the actor is reduced to an exemplar of a specific concept class. The ordering thought abstracts from every specific situation, in which a person acts. "Where 'self' can be understood as having some univocal and hence formal definition – it reifies or entifies self as an ego or an ideal."[243] It is this abstraction – according to an important insight of East Asian philosophy – that makes it impossible to understand the authentic character of the world. This becomes clear once again with regard to the field metaphor; for a field of action does not consist of possible actions that exist in a kind of vacuum, but is empty without the concrete many moving inside it. It is a space of possible actions, true, but outside of the many actually appropriating these possibilities, this space doesn't exist. The field in itself is nothing, a pure abstraction. But it always exists as a specific field. Or to put it in other words: a specific activity is nothing without it being performed by someone. Property, for instance, is nothing if there is not an 'I' or 'Thou' that possesses it. And money as a field of action doesn't exist independently of the many who perceive, through money, a practical instrument to enact activities. Transposing this to the idea of the world, this means that the latter does not denote, in contrast to an abstract order, a "mediating something."[244] It is the case, instead, that it "has its self only in the many individuals. 'The true whole One has its self in the individuated Many.' To put it otherwise: That which makes the world as it is, is determined by the form of the world arising out of the mutual shaping events and the nexus of acts of all beings."[245] The world is always only conceivable as a specific activity, which is perceived through the many individuals in their own, particular ways. "The totality is nothing more than the full

---

[243] R.T. Ames, "The Focus-Field Self in Classical Confucianism," 208.
[244] K. Nishida, *Logik des Ortes*, 170.
[245] E. Weinmayr, "Denken im Übergang," 50. Weinmayr is citing Nishida.

range of particular foci, each focus defining itself and its own particular field."[246]

To think that every individual determines herself in the field of actions is, therefore, misleading, insofar as we represent this field as a something. Money as a field of action is not a self-subsistent or independent substance, which mediates the many among themselves. More precisely money is really a medium, but its own existence is nourished only by the fact that the many relate themselves to each other by it. Nishida would speak in this connection of a determination without a determining agent:[247]

> "But we could point to or comprehend the present just as little as the world itself; it is overall and nowhere. Since, too, the world doesn't acknowledge any single subject of its socio-historical formation, we can only describe it in such a way that it determines itself, without yet being itself the substratum of this determination. The self determination of the world... we can only denote, with Nishida, as ... 'determination without a determining agent.'"[248]

The world determines the actions of the individual, but is equally determined by them. There is in this defining process nothing that we can hold onto. It has no cause that we can causally trace back. Thus it is said, for instance in Buddhism: "Creation and the created mediate each other and have no proper essence. Creation for itself and the created for itself are never to be perceived, however earnestly one may strive to."[249] We can formulate this insight in this way: the world knows no center, around which it turns. Schäffle has clearly formulated this in terms of the economic world: "The economy ... is not ... guided by one or a few dominating centers. Every individual in the political economy makes himself a center, acting daily on his own initiative for himself and for others."[250] Everything participates in the determining event of the world without an autonomous subject existing in this event.[251]

---

[246] R.T. Ames, "The Focus-Field Self in Classical Confucianism," 207.
[247] Japanese: *genteisurumono-naki gentei*. See for example K. Nishida, *Logik des Ortes*, 155.
[248] Y. Matsudo, *Eine Einführung in die Spätphilosophie von Kitarō Nishida*, 67.
[249] Phrase from the Kegon-Sutra cited in E. Weinmayr, "Denken im Übergang,2 55-56.
[250] A. Schäffle, "Das gesellschaftliche System der menschlichen Wirthschaft, Ein Lehr- und Handbuch der Nationalökonomie," partially published in A. Kruse (ed.), *Nationalökonomie, Ausgewählte Texte zur Geschichte einer Wissenschaft*, Stuttgart 1960, 239.
[251] Y. Matsudo, *Eine Einführung in die Spätphilosophie von Kitarō Nishida*, 66.

"The world cannot be conceived by the many as a supplement of agreement and combination from an already preexisting collection of individual beings, since every individual is only in and out of the world's determining process that which it is. Yet the determining process doesn't happen as a particularization deriving from a moment of the differentiating self-determination of a previously fixed unity or of a higher generality, but as an interactive determination of uncounted individuals, which really are distinct one from another and not to be subsumed into a universal or collected as entities in a unity." [252]

The individual is thus defined in a world that is itself ungraspable. Such a process of determination, in which we settle on no first or final cause, is often described in East Asian philosophy using the metaphor of the mirror. Of course, one must be careful here, since this metaphor in the East-Asian context has another meaning than in the Western context.[253] In the first context, the mirror is not thought of as an unchanging substance, in which the many are mirrored. Rather, the mirror is thought of as an activity without a prime mover, as a 'mirroring without a mirror', so to speak. Every individual defines herself as a person when she mirrors the many others and is mirrored in others.[254] Or: every thing is "active, when it mirrors the world in itself."[255] The many mutually reflect each other, without this process having a particular beginning or end. Every part stands in a relationship of mutual dependency with an other. Nothing self-subsistent exists; nothing shows unchanging properties. There is neither a particular nor a universal that can be perceived in the sense of a substantial essence. The process of mirroring describes a kind of existence, which we can designate as "interdependent arising:"[256]

> "'Interdependent arising' ... says that no being exists for itself; only in relation to all others is it what it simply is. One of the most beautiful images illustrating this reality is the simile of the net in Indra's palace. Attached to every knot of the net there is a crystal. Since every crystal is clear for itself, that means it is empty or nothing, all the other crystals are mirrored in it, as it is also mirrored in all the other crystals. Reality is this 'inexhaustible, endless play of mirrors', a synergy in which all coheres with all."[257]

---

[252] E. Weinmayr, "Denken im Übergang," 50.
[253] D.L. Hall, R.T. Ames, *Thinking from the Han*, 51.
[254] R.E. Carter, *Encounter with Enlightenment*, 28.
[255] K. Nishida, *Logik des Ortes*, 242.
[256] Japenese: *engi*, a translation of the Buddhist term *pratityasamutpada* (sanskrit).
[257] E. Weinmayr, "Denken im Übergang," 55.

This thought can be immediately added to a wider reflection: if all and each are determined in the world's formative act, but at the same time participate in this formative act, than everything in the world is a creative act. Nobody is only created, but instead makes "himself from out of the created thing to the creator."[258] The world as well as the individual changes continually. They are dynamic, and never remain at a pre-determined endpoint:

> "The empirical I is active, exactly as the world, which makes possible the ego's pure experience, is active. The world of experience is dynamic, never remaining still. The I and the world never present themselves as categories in stasis, but (I and World) form a self moving continuum (kinesis). Basing themselves on their reciprocal action both the content of experience and the thought of the I changes. Just as the world always appears in its dynamic daily changes with another face."[259]

The individual changes herself, but doesn't thereby lose her identity. More precisely: "her identity consists rather in surrendering her identity. She is herself particularly in the loss of herself."[260] This statement firstly sounds incomprehensible, but can be easily explained. Someone in the economic world my rise from being a beggarly student to a successful employer, only in the course of years, due to competition, to stand before the ruins of his existence. This 'someone' is always going to understand herself to be still the same. Yet her existence in the economic context is always to be someone else. She is thus neither substantially the same, nor is she someone wholly other. Nishida would speak in this connection of our self as a "self-contradictory existence." [261]

> "As the abode of an 'equivalency' of the self contradictory, as absolute contradictory self-identity, no being, no Gestalt possesses enduring substance. "All things alter, fall apart, nothing is eternal.' ... 'What lives is something that dies. It is really a contradiction, but our existence consists of this contradiction.'"[262]

In every action the actor defines herself and her environment afresh. Similarly, the environment determines her. Every action marks a transition, "in which ... the arising and the passing away of reality occurs and continues. All that is finds itself not only in movement, but is itself a 'movement from

---

[258] K. Nishida, *Logik des Ortes*, 247.
[259] H. Hashi, *Die Philosophie der Aktualität*, 48.
[260] R. Ohashi, *Japan im interkulturellen Dialog*, 88.
[261] K. Nishida, "Selbstidentität und Kontinuität der Welt," 74.
[262] E. Weinmayr, "Denken im Übergang," 52. Weinmayr is citing Nishida.

a thing composed to a composer.'"²⁶³ The world itself is like a relativistic field that defines itself and changes in time. Thus the act "proves itself to be the creative element of the historical world."²⁶⁴ Within this creative doing there is, according to the East Asian belief, nothing that is not changed – not even the world itself.

> "The reality in the whole is an open and creative 'movement from shape to shape' in a radical and precipitous sense ... in which the 'world of contradictory self identity of the one and the many ... forms itself wholly and completely and endlessly without any fundamental ground."²⁶⁵

The world determines itself as an "act of formation. This formative act is creative in the sense of being a determination without a determining agent."²⁶⁶ One can also describe such a determination so that we see that the context of the act itself is found in a continuous change without any possibility to measure this change against a relatively invariant reference point outside the forming event:

> "Reality in the Japanese context cannot be linked to any transcendental point of reference. It is rather perceived as the world of appearances, which one has to accept, as it is contingent on a given place and time. Reality is therefore not structured by principles but rather by multiple, continually shifting contexts, between which it continuously flows. (...) For the Japanese, thus, the world is not something the subject can impose his logic upon. ... He perceives himself and the world as perpetually changing."²⁶⁷

4.4.2 The Logical Impossibility of the Calculation of the Economic World

From the Japanese perspective "the contexts are always moving. 'The variability of each context keeps it from being a simple variant of an invariant

---

[263] Ibid., 52. Weinmayr is citing Nishida.
[264] R. Ohashi, *Japan im interkulturellen Dialog*, 159.
[265] E. Weinmayr, Denken im Übergang, 52-53. Weinmayr is citing Nishida.
[266] K. Nishida, "Selbstidentität und Kontinuität der Welt," 61-62.
[267] S. Graupe, "Japanese Modes of Business Behaviour," 48. See also A. Berque, "Das Verhältnis der Ökonomie zu Raum und Zeit in der japanischen Kultur," in: K. Werhahn-Mees, C. von Barloewen (ed.), *Japan und der Westen*, Vol. 1, Frankfurt 1986, 24.

structural rule.'"[268] We shall briefly oppose this conception to the economic notion of equilibrium. Economics knows of a static as well as a dynamic concept of equilibrium. Lets turn, firstly, to the former concept. With a 'static equilibrium', as Mises for instance would put it, the disturbing causes effect the state of rest in such a way that this equilibrium is "always disturbed in the same way and always returns to the state of rest in the same way."[269] The economists also speak of a stable equilibrium: By a stable equilibrium inner forces bring about a return to equilibrium, in case an exterior disturbance occurs.[270] This concept of stable equilibrium is very important in economics. For it claims:

> "that an equilibrium must be stable, supposing it to have economic meaning. For otherwise one couldn't conclude that an economic system strives toward equilibrium; it would rather move into a not to be approximately defined disequilibriated state. ... Only when a stable equilibrium can be constituted is a reference point to be found towards which the economic system presumably tends."[271]

But why must "human action... tend towards this kind of equilibrium point" as for instance Mises thinks?[272] Because otherwise, a mechanical description of the economic world would prove impossible. "When no stable equilibrium as a reference point of analysis and gravitation center of the system can be constructed, then nothing can be said, literally, about its lawfulness and future developments." Is this answer, however, actually an "authentic justification of equilibrium analysis?"[273] Here, rather, the issue is all about a false conclusion. For just because a mechanical analysis can only be conducted in a meaningful manner given the existence of equilibrium states, this doesn't imply that such states exist in any manner. Finally, it is always thinkable that mechanical analysis proves itself as logically impossible, because a stable equilibrium does not ground the economic world.

But is the economic world stable or not? Some economists argue with probabilities: "How many times has the reader seen an egg standing upon

---

[268] K. Washida, "Handlung, Leib und Institution," 346. Washida is citing B. Waldenfels.
[269] L. von Mises, *Nationalökonomie*, 238.
[270] B. Felderer, Homburg, *Makroökonomik und neue Makroökonomik*, Berlin-Heidelberg et al. 1999, 13.
[271] Ibid., 13.
[272] L. von Mises, *Nationalökonomie*, 317.
[273] B. Felderer, Homburg, *Makroökonomik und neue Makroökonomik*, 14.

its end?" asks, for instance, Samuelson, in order to suggest the high probability of equilibrium in the economic world.[274] Felderer and Homburg argue in the following way:

> "Why is the equilibrium concept so fundamental for economic analysis? Now ... an equilibrated state ex definitione is temporally steady, while a disequilibriated one has only an ephemeral character. It is thus more probable, that the economy finds itself in a state of equilibrium or at least tends to it."[275]

This argument is erroneous. For out of the fact that a disequilibriated state is only ephemeral it in now way follows that the world must tend towards a state of equilibrium. In this way we approach the Japanese concept that the world doesn't find itself in one disequilibriated state (which is actually logically impossible, because this state is unsteady), but is moved so to speak from one disequilibrium to another, without at any moment arriving at a resting point. That such an advance of the world is actually more probable than a temporally steady equilibrium state points to an important difference between the social-historical world and a physical world like that of an egg's. If an egg has once reached a resting point, it only moves out of this point when it is caused to do so by something external. Only exogenous forces disturb its state of equilibrium. As soon as these forces cease to operate, the egg returns to its original position. In other words, it is impossible for the egg to move itself through its inner force out of the equilibrium state. Yet in the economic world the inner forces are of a wholly other kind. They are not blind forces, but deeds, of which Nishida says: "Our deeds must be a forming act."[276] Since persons perceive themselves in these deeds and redefine themselves, every 'order' is, so to speak, disturbed from the inside. The world is not moved from the outside, but instead is to be so imagined "that the reality determines the reality itself."[277] In the field metaphor this doesn't mean anything other than that the action field and the field-beings mutually shape and change each other. "The shaped thing shapes its shaper."[278] In this case, the action field shows an inner degree of freedom, an inner dynamic. Because there is nothing in it that remains the same, it violates the principle of constancy that gives us a necessary presupposition for the concept of equilibrium. (3.1.3) Such a violation is not an unknown phenomenon in the natural sciences – from

---

[274] P.A. Samuelson, *Foundations of Economic Analysis*, 5.
[275] B. Felderer, Homburg, *Makroökonomik und neue Makroökonomik*, 13.
[276] K. Nishida, "Die Welt als Dialektisches Allgemeines," 172.
[277] Ibid., 172.
[278] E. Weinmayr, "Denken im Übergang," 52.

which economics tries to take its ideas of stable equilibrium.[279] All the more, "competition is by its nature a dynamic process whose essential characteristics are assumed away by the assumptions underlying static analysis."[280]

Could we overcome the problems associated with the static equilibrium concept if we start with a dynamic equilibrium? This seems at first glance to be the case. For dynamic equilibrium analysis allows us to present changes to the equilibrium point. Of course, not every kind of change can be modeled. Rather, we merely describe 'steady conditions.' This means, that the rate of change remains stable. Changes in the position of equilibrium are measured against something that remains relatively constant. Typically, time is used as such a constant and it is thus presupposed that "the rate of change over the course of time is stable."[281] Brodbeck in particular makes us aware that this is a problematic idea,[282] implying "that in mechanical models the economic variables are one-to-one with a time series, and thus are connected to a clock. ... Implicitly this supposes that between 'economic bodies' and the 'clock' here is a mobile, but functionally unchangeable connection."[283] This means that all individuals have to adapt their actions to one constant advancing body, for instance the hand of a 'world clock.' For "what modern science has chosen as representative of time is a motion that some moving physical body ... discloses along its moving track."[284] But even "the fact that someone has control of a clock and orients his actions to it doesn't in any way indicate that the actions in their collective structure are synchronizable with the clock – like a falling stone or the revolution of the moon."[285] It is true that actions could be coordinated with the aid of the clock; yet this isn't typical for them. This is, for instance, shown by the fact that it is exceedingly difficult to actually synchronize actions (as for instance in the military or some sports).

---

[279] P. Mirowski, *More Heat than Light*, 90.
[280] F.A. Hayek, "Der Sinn des Wettbewerbs," 125.
[281] B. Felderer, Homburg, *Makroökonomik und neue Makroökonomik*, 12.
[282] For an extensive consideration of the temporal dimension in economics, see K.-H. Brodbeck, *Die fragwürdigen Grundlagen der Ökonomie*, chapt. 3. See also his: "Die Nivellierung der Zeit in der Ökonomie," in: J. Manemann (ed.), *Befristete Zeit, Jahrbuch der Politischen Theologie*, 3 (1999), 135-151. Also, on the treatment of time in neoclassical economics, see P. Mirowski, *More Heat than Light*, 319.
[283] K.-H. Brodbeck, *Die fragwürdigen Grundlagen der Ökonomie*, 78-79.
[284] T. Watsuji, *Watsuji Tetsuro's Rinrigaku*, 195.
[285] K.-H. Brodbeck, *Die fragwürdigen Grundlagen der Ökonomie*, 81-82.

A synchronization of actions (insofar as it exists) is created in the action field; it is not causally evoked by something like 'the time.' From the East Asian view, the root of this is that time doesn't present us with a given, relatively unchanged cause, but is itself born and extinguished within the world.[286] "There is no time apart from mutability or appearance-disappearance of things in the universe."[287] "It is interwoven with all things."[288] "It is a fact, that time is determined, when the present determines itself."[289] Time is made through actions within the field; it is itself a function of activity:

> "There is no absolute time in which the plenum occurs, nor is there an absolute space in which the plenum is contained or situated. Time and space, like everything else ..., is a function or determination of activity, a role or state or character assumed or performed by the plenum. Thus time is the plenum performing the function of temporality, and space is the plenum assuming the role of spatiality."[290]

But if time is a function of activity then it is necessarily dependent on it and cannot, hence, be stable relative to it. Cause and effect may not be clearly distinguished from one another because everything causes and is caused alike. The dynamic equilibrium theory thus struggles with a problem similar to that bedeviling the static one: it tries to make changes dependent on an independent variable. But such variables don't exist. "There is nothing outside this plenum: it has no otherness either without or within."[291] For this reason the concept of the equilibrium is denied in the East Asian context when it is used to describe the social-historical world. Such a world is neither eternally unchanging, as is urged by the static equilibrium, nor does it run smoothly in time, as the dynamic equilibrium suggests.

If no invariant principle can be actually constituted over or outside of the economic world, then this has a broader, important consequence: the development of this world cannot be traced back to any causally operant

---

[286] K. Nishida, *Logik des Ortes*, 141. See for a basic treatment of temporality in Buddhism: R. Elberfeld, *Phänomenologie der Zeit im Buddhismus*. See also: T. Watsuji, *Watsuji Tetsuro's Rinrigaku*, chapt. 10.
[287] M. Abe, "Dōgen on Buddha Nature," *Eastern Buddhist*, 4/1 (1971), 66.
[288] N. Iino, "Dogens's Zen View of Interdependence," *Philosophy East & West*, 12/1 (1962), 55.
[289] K. Nishida, *Logik des Ortes*, 141.
[290] L.K. Tong, *The Art of Appropriation*, 14.
[291] Ibid., 14.

factors; another statement, which runs counter to the way the economy is usually thought about:

> For "as any wanderer in the history of economic ideas will immediately concede, practically all economists in the 19th and many in the 20th century believed in an uncritical way that an explanation of a given historical development was sufficiently explained by reference to the conditioning or causal factors, as an increase of population or of the supply of capital."[292]

Yet more: when the existence of causal factors is denied, than this means simultaneously regarding as logically impossible both the calculability of economic processes and their predictability. For when everything is dependent on everything else in a radical sense, than nothing presents itself to us as a foundation of calculation.

Briefly, I will show, in two examples, how hard it actually is to isolate factors in the economic world that change can be measured against: first, I will take the economic concept of the 'production function;' and second, the idea of technical progress.[293] The production function is a fundamental concept of modern economic theory, its most important variant being represented by the so-called Cobb-Douglas production function. It represents the given production technology, in order to transform capital and labor supplies into output. It thus gives us how much output can be produced with a given volume of capital and labor by a given production technology. I don't want us to go into the problems of the concrete model of such a production function, but instead take on its role in simple economic growth models as for instance the Solow model.[294] In these models the production function represents the invariant element against which the growth of the economy is measured. Growth is reduced (causally) to a growth of capital stock, and thus describes a 'uniformly progressing economy.'[295] Such an economy is moved to a pre-given stationary state, which is called the steady-state level or the growth equilibrium. "Independent of the starting point the observed economy finally gets to the stationary state. The stationary state incorporates in this sense the long interval equilibrium of the economy."[296] Even if we allow that such an equilibrium can be theoretically described, it still remains unclear, how or if this point can, in actual-

---

[292] J. Schumpeter, *Beiträge zur Sozialökonomik*, Wien-Köln-Graz 1987, 183.
[293] P. Mirowski, *More Heat than Light*, chapt. 6.
[294] See for example N.G. Mankiw, *Makroökonomik*, Stuttgart 2000, 92.
[295] Ibid., chapt. 4. See also G. Cassel, *Theoretische Sozialökonomik*, Leipzig 1927, 27.
[296] Ibid., 97.

ity, ever be reached.[297] "In fact, the problem remains open to this day. We still do not have a satisfactory specification of the conditions under which the adjustment mechanisms of an economy will guide it to its general equilibrium system."[298] In other words: a future state can be abstractly calculated, but there is no evidence that the economic world actually moves to this state.[299] The central problem consists in the assumption of a constant production function implying that the production technology would remain constant over the course of the investigated period of growth. For only so can the production function remain itself the same in a world of continual changes. Especially in the case of the aggregated production function this would mean that the production technology does not change in any sector of the economy or that changes in different sectors cancel each other out. It is hard to ground the validity of such an assumption, at least if we start out from real growth processes and aren't looking at an abstract model economy, because "in reality, macroeconomic growth is still almost always accompanied by distortions of relative volumes of the individual sectors."[300] The production function is not something that we can fix within the world. Its relative stability is in no way guaranteed:

> "It is impossible to legitimately abstract away the process whereby inputs are transformed into outputs, because the conservation principles that define the stability of the technological field are absent. There is no symmetry of the process of production ... that can be represented by an output index; neither can the output index be defined prior to the economic process. Output is not virtual in the sense of being identical ex ante and ex post, and therefore the output index is not path-independent. Further, the transformation of input commodities into output commodities is not generally a one-way street. In the language of field formalism, such a process would be analogous to a relativistic field that is self-acting and self-generating. ... Such fields possess no general global conservation principles."[301]

By reason of the problems that are associated with the assumption of a constant production function, the effort has been made to present changing economic processes more realistically. To achieve this, economists claim that the production technology is conditioned through 'technological prog-

---

[297] N. Kaldor, "A Classificatory Note on the Determinateness of Equilibrium," *The Review of Ecomic Studies*, 1/2 (1934), 122-36.
[298] R. Dorfman cited in L. Lachmann, "Marktwirtschaft und Modellkonstruktionen," 192.
[299] J. Cartelier, *Das Geld*, 33.
[300] L. Lachmann, "Marktwirtschaft und Modellkonstruktionen," 184.
[301] P. Mirowski, *More Heat than Light*, 318-319.

ress' that changes over time. It can thus itself become an important "source of economic growth."[302] Technological progress is understood here as a uniform increase in the productivity of productive factors. In order to measure this increase, the Solow model identifies a unit of efficiency; technological progress can thus be interpreted as a depreciation of capital in relation to this efficiency unit. In this way it appears to be possible to calculate technological efficiency. Of course, the model still doesn't answer the question of whether or how such a unit can be meaningfully defined. This is relevant, above all, when we don't regard technical progress as an ex post fact, but rather as an ex ante fact which we can use in order to forecast economic growth. For what technical innovations will signify a progress, or in which sector an increase or decrease of efficiency is to be expected, is never fixed ex ante – rather, it is arbitrary to fix upon any unit of efficiency and claim it to be constant. We thus have no way of judging why the economy should move into the predicted state of equilibrium. Even here, the forecasting of changes of the economic world fails, since no factor can be identified that remains the same in the process of 'interdependent arising.'

In economic theories there are, naturally, other, more realistic, or at least more complex models, as both of the ones sketched above. Yet the hope to someday better calculate the economic world through the use of these models misunderstands the actual problem. The root of this has nothing to do with not computing well enough or falsely, but with the belief that the economic world could ever be objectified with the aid of mathematical formulas. It is this belief that is generally rejected in East Asian philosophy, since it misunderstands the creative, dynamic character of a world that continually re-determines itself without a determining agent. Schumpeter approaches this philosophical position when he discovers the actual characteristic of the economy in the "process of creative destruction:"

> "Capitalism, then, is by nature a form or method of economic change and not only never is but never can be stationary... [It is a process, which] revolutionizes the economic structure from within, incessantly destroying the old one, incessantly creating a new one. This process of Creative Destruction is the essential fact about capitalism. (...) Every piece of business strategy acquires its true significance only against the background of that process and within the situation created by it. It must be seen

---

[302] N.G. Mankiw, *Makroökonomik*, 122.

in its role in the perennial gale of creative destruction; it cannot be understood irrespective of it or, in fact, on the hypothesis that there is a perennial lull."[303]

Economists have tried to escape from this insight by "simply postulating the steadiness and continuation of the equilibrium of progress, which they are unable to explain."[304] "One simply acts as if the end state (a stationary state) has already been achieved. It is utopia that is analyzed, not the daily world of 'chaos.'"[305] But thus all "problems of human action in a world of unexpected changes... [are hidden] behind a smoky veil of formulas and functions."[306] They become an unimportant residue, a mere transitional step. But such a step encompasses nothing less than the complete economic reality. "In reality, everything phenomenal becomes only a transitional stage to an unreached, yet further goal," concedes von Thünen.[307] One can say it like this: the economic world always only proceeds from transitional state to transitional state, without ever reaching the calculated final state of the economists.

One can conclude from this, that the economic world – insofar as one conceives it as a really living one, and not simply as a model world – actually presents us with no static (conservative) field and on this account can be described through no mechanical law. It is a steady formative event, a creative act. More precisely, it is both at the same time: shaped and shaper. It is – as Schumpeter said – adaptive and creative response. But when the creative aspect can never "practically be understood ex ante: meaning, that it cannot be foretold through the application of rules concerning conclusions from pre-given facts," than the state of the world cannot, similarly, be forecast. "A creative response changes social and economic structures forever. In other words, it brings situations about from which there is no bridge to those situations that might have emerged in its absence."[308] A determination of the end result ex ante proves on this account to be logically impossible. The dream of calculability remains at every moment nothing more than a utopia.

---

[303] J. Schumpeter, *Kapitalismus, Sozialismus und Demokratie*, 136-138.
[304] L. Lachmann, "Marktwirtschaft und Modellkonstruktionen," 183.
[305] K.-H. Brodbeck, *Die fragwürdigen Grundlagen der Ökonomie*, 118.
[306] L. Lachmann, "Marktwirtschaft und Modellkonstruktionen," 183.
[307] Cited in K.-H. Brodbeck, *Die fragwürdigen Grundlagen der Ökonomie*, 117.
[308] J. Schumpeter, *Beiträge zur Sozialökonomik*, 183.

4.5 The Determination of the Individual as a Context Dependent Existence (II)

By now we see that the determination of the individual cannot arise out of autonomy or independence of the individual. "The individual can ... not be the absolute individual, who emerges totally without reference [to others]."[309] One can also formulate this insight in this way: the private determination is not the sole form of the determination of the individual, as methodological individualism postulates. In this section we shall show an alternative to this form of determination, without falling into the other extreme of regarding the individual as exclusively determined through a pre-given order.

4.5.1 The Determination of Individuals in East Asian Philosophy

In intercultural comparisons, it is often emphasized that people in East Asian societies are much more strongly oriented to collectives than those in the West. It is seen as, for instance, a Daoist or Confucian ideal, to subordinate one's self to the greater group. Ames and Hall, referring to this, cite two examples:

> "'Selflessness ... is one of the oldest values in China, present in various forms in Taoism and Buddhism, but especially in Confucianism. The selfless person is always willing to subordinate his own interests, or that of some small group (like a village) to which he belongs, to the interest of a larger social group.'

> 'Most Chinese view society as an organic whole or seamless web. Strands in a web must all be of certain length, diameter, and consistency, and must all be fitted together in accordance with a preordained pattern. ... The hope is that each individual will function as properly as a cog in an ever more efficient social machine.'"[310]

Clearly, it escapes social scientists that they are describing the position of the individual in society according to their own (i.e. 'Western') categories. Intercultural differences between understandings of the human are described as a variation within the categories of the social and of the individual, but not as a difference in how the categories themselves are understood. Such a way of going about things proves problematic insofar as the East Asian philosophical tradition actually does rest on an alternative un-

---

[309] K. Nishitani, "Vom Wesen der Begegnung," 263.
[310] D.L. Hall, R.T. Ames, *Thinking from the Han*, 24. The authors are citing D.J. Munro und R.R. Edwards.

derstanding of individual and society. I want to tease out the fundamental features of this understanding, here.

It is correct that, for instance, the Chinese ideas about individuals contain no clear notion of individuality. "The Western notion of the separate, distinct, individual in its various forms is anathema to the Chinese."[311] The latter aren't prepared to regard the divided up, the differentiated in and for itself, and thus in its isolation. In order to separate something, one must implicitly presuppose something whole. "What would it mean to divide something that was not first a whole or a unity of some sort? The distinction serves to reveal the original unity, as well as to mark a significant distinction within that unity."[312] But when the individual as a distinct thing always already points to its original unity, then it cannot be represented as something individual in the sense of something indivisible, isolated, or closed in upon itself. This does not at all signify that the individual is to be automatically subsumed under a whole, giving up its own character completely. Instead, she is understood as being unique within a context. "A unique individual has the character of a single and inalienable particular, such as a work of art, that might be formally comparable to other such works, but that remains, nonetheless, qualitatively unique."[313] The meaning of qualitative uniqueness can be explicated with the aid of the field metaphor. Any field existence mirrors the field in its wholly particular way. It is like a focal point, which perspectivally focuses its environment. It is not separate from the field, but still has its own proper, unchangeable character; it is not simply and arbitrarily to be exchanged with another focal point. Its uniqueness is rooted in the "place of authenticity" within the field.[314] This means, transposed to the thought of the world, that every individual defines herself in a unique way in the world. She is like an irreproducible microcosm, mirroring the world in herself and thereby being mirrored by other irreproducible microcosms.[315] In the process of mirroring, she is unique in her relationship to the others:

> "In the model of unique individual, determinacy lies in the achieved quality of one's multivalent relationships. A person becomes recognized, distinguished, or re-

---

[311] D.L. Hall, R.T. Ames, *Thinking from the Han*, 25.
[312] R.E. Carter, *Encounter with Enlightenment*, 128.
[313] D.L. Hall, R.T. Ames, *Thinking from the Han*, 25.
[314] L.K. Tong, *The Art of Appropriation*, 36. For the Chinese notion of the „unique place" see also D.L. Hall, R.T. Ames, *Thinking from the Han*, 26.
[315] M. Yusa, "The Religious Worldview of Nishida Kitarō," *Eastern Buddhist*, 20/2 (1987), 69.

nowned by virtue of communal deference to the quality of one's character. Much of the effort in understanding the traditional Confucian conception of self has to do with clarifying this distinction between autonomy and uniqueness. While the definition of self as irreducible social certainly precludes autonomous individuality, it does not rule out the second, less familiar notion of uniqueness expressed in terms of my roles and my relationships."[316]

The individual is recognized within the world as unique, but is not completely determined through this world. In other words: she is not exclusively determined through a universal, in so far as this is represented in terms of a given order. Such an order necessarily abstracts from all uniqueness because it observes an individual as a substitutable element of a group or class. It relativizes each individual in so far as all seem of the same type, or exchangeable. If the universal, however, is understood as a field of action, the social determination of the individual does not imply such exchangeability, but instead something rather like "'on the same footing', 'affinity', 'resemblance', 'analogy.'"[317] In this way we can think of a social determination of the individual that simultaneously allows for its private determination: the individual appears neither to be exclusively an exchangeable element of a machine, nor to be a completely independent substance. "I and thou are born out of the same surroundings,"[318] but aren't identical. Each is rather unique in his surroundings. This constitutes his private determination. Thus an either-or of the individual and the social determination of the individual is avoided, without wiping out the distinction between the two. They appear as two contradictory determinations equally united in the individual acting in the world. Both determinations are absolutely different from one another, but emphasize merely two aspects of an original unity. This original unity is to be understood as a locus that is neither individual nor universal. If we still want to apprehend its nature, then the way to denote it is just as the unity of opposites or, better, as a "contradictory self-identity."[319]

Watsuji in particular makes the point, that the Japanese concept '*ningen*' denotes such a contradictory self-identity and thus is clearly to be distinguished from the idea of the individual as an independent existence. The word *ningen* is composed of two different Chinese characters, of which the

---

[316] D.L. Hall, R.T. Ames, *Thinking from the Han*, 25.
[317] D.L. Hall, R.T. Ames, *Thinking from the Han*, 59.
[318] K. Nishida, *Logik des Ortes*, 145.
[319] Japanese: *mujunteki jikodōitsu*. The phrase is Nishida's. For an explanation, see K. Nishida, *Logik des Ortes*, 308.

first, NIN, can be translated as 'person', the second, GEN, as 'connection,' 'in between.' *Ningen* is used in Japanese to denote both the public on the one hand and the person, the human being, the self on the other.³²⁰ Consequently, we can't reduce the term to a social or private determination:

> "Ningen is the public and, at the same time, the individual human beings living within it. Therefore, it refers not merely to an individual 'human being' or merely to 'society.' What is recognized here is a dialectical unity of those double characteristics that are inherent in a human being. Insofar as it is a human being, ningen as an individual differs completely from society. Because it does not refer to society, it must refer to individuals alone. Hence, an individual is never communal with other individuals. Oneself and others are absolutely separate. Nevertheless, insofar as ningen also refers to the public, it is also through and through that community which exists between person and person, thus signifying society as well, and not just isolated human beings. Precisely of its not being human beings in isolation, it is ningen. Hence, oneself and the other are absolutely separated from each other but, nevertheless, become one in communal existence. Individuals are basically different from society and yet dissolve themselves into society. Ningen denotes the unity of these contradictories."³²¹

The concept *ningen* makes it clear that the actor, in the Japanese context, isn't to be understood exclusively as a social being, nor as an independent individual. "It is apparent that the concept of human person in Japan includes both the person or self as individual, and the self or person as inextricably and inescapably involved in community or group interaction. Thus, we are neither just individual, nor social beings, but both."³²² The individual's contradictory self-identity is due to the contradictory character of the world. If in the world there exists neither substantial individuals, defining themselves, nor a substantial universal to which the individual is wholly subservient, then there is no position in which the actor can be univocally determined. This doesn't mean giving up on the idea of determination, as the concept ningen makes clear. It can rather be formulated like so: the individual is neither exclusively individually nor socially determined, nor is she the junction of both determinations. She unifies both determinations site specifically in herself and mediates between them, without being fully objectifiable from the point of view of either of these determinations. The real roots of her character lie in this site specifical mediation.

---

³²⁰ T. Watsuji, *Watsuji Tetsuro's Rinrigaku*, 14.
³²¹ Ibid., 15.
³²² R.E Carter, *Encounter with Enlightenment*, 126.

4.5.2 The Economic Actor as a Contradictory Self-Identity

In the seemingly absolute contradiction of private and social determination, from the point of view of the forms of determination, there lies a deeper or more extensive determination of the individual, from which both directions of determination equally flow.

> "Judgments of logical contradiction are at best penultimate judgments, which may point us in the direction of a more comprehensive and accurate understanding of experience. A more profound understanding would reach below the surface level of contradiction and comprehend that opposites are necessarily opposites within some specified context."[323]

Can we transpose such a statement to the determination of the actor in the economic world? By which we mean, apprehending the economic actor as an contradictory self-identity, encompassing both forms of determination: private determination, as an independent, autonomous subject, and social determination, as a part of the market's mechanism. The economic actor must appear equally as absolutely self determined and as absolutely determined by something alien to it: as free from all social connections and inescapably dependent on society. The following reflection shall show us that there are some features that speak for such a position.

The determination of the actor in the sense of a private determination that is equally social must begin with his activity in the world. It observes how the many stand facing each other in the field of action, mutually reflecting one another; and how out of this process arises the directions of the individual's determination. The individual must, as Nishitani says, be understood in the encounter with others. The encounter with the 'thou' shows how each as well is determined as "Lord of the absolute", as well as "the absolutely relative."[324] I want to show this for the economic world in concentrating on one concept of action, which is important for understanding the economic world but up to now has not yet been discussed: labor, or wage labor. We shall understand this to be a pure activity, thus an action without an acting agent, as it is approached in East Asian philosophical systems, even if this contradicts the current economic perception of the labor concept.[325] Starting out with the economic world, labor can be con-

---

[323] Ibid., 127.
[324] K. Nishitani, "Vom Wesen der Begegnung," 261.
[325] See for various definitions of labor, J. Kruse, *Geschichte der Arbeit und Arbeit als Geschichte*, Münster-Hamburg-London 2003.

ceptually exploited in two different ways. In one, it designates the property of the one who performs the labor, and thus the laborer. For labor is without question the possession of whoever incorporates it with his body and hands, as Locke said.[326] As labor is carried out, the laborer perceives himself encoded in it – thinks of it as his possession. But the other way of thinking of labor is, that another can appropriate it without specifically doing it: "The turfs that my servant has cut ... become ... my Property, without assignation or consent of any body The labour that was mine, removing them out of that common state that they were in, hath fixed my Property in them."[327] Here the employer appropriates the work. Both appropriation processes, that of the laborer and that of the employer are not to be thought of as separate from each other. For the laborer is not interested in the labor (the product of labor) in itself, but expects a wage for his action. In this expectation, she is immediately pointed to the employer. Contrarily, the employer is only interested in the product of labor, but can't bring this about himself. His appropriation therefore necessarily refers to the laborer. In labor is thus expressed the mutual dependence – the laborer points to the employer, and vice versa. More precisely, there are two appropriation processes that refer to each other, without being able to reduce the labor itself to one of them. Yet it is important that labor, like all economic activities, (implicitly) is thought in the action field of money. Labor doesn't exist outside of the monetary framework, since it always refers to a wage or a gain, which the worker or the employer hopes to appropriate as property.[328] Let's leave our description of the labor concept on this rudimentary level and try to see what influence labor exerts on the economic understanding of the definition of the individual. For this task, lets use Nishitani's reflection on the relationship of the worker and the employer as a personal relationship of the I and the thou to make our observations.[329]

First, we shall observe the socio-historical transformation process, which is introduced with the growth of the labor relationship as the living form of the 'in-betweeness' of people, in order to work out the particular relationship of the I and thou that has its roots in such a relationship. The thou, which is faced by the I, is firstly always a specific human being. The I doesn't ground itself in limitation of, or difference from, an abstract oppo-

---

[326] Locke, *Two Treatises on Government*, 289.
[327] Ibid., 289.
[328] J. Cartelier, *Das Geld*, 89.
[329] K. Nishitani, "Vom Wesen der Begegnung," sowie ders., "Modernisierung und Tradition in Japan," in: K. Werhahn-Mees, C. von Barloewen (ed.), *Japan und der Westen*, Vol. 1, 183-204.

site, but in multiple, concrete relations e.g. to the father, to the family or to the community of the village. The father is not simply any father, but a specific one. Only in the relationship to this one father can the I be defined as daughter or son. The relationship of the I and father is thus particular and inalienable for the existence of the I. In particular Simmel makes us aware, that the labor concept implied such a personal relationship, before it became determined in the action field of money.[330] For in labor the servant, for instance, is bound to a single master just as the peasant to a specific piece of land. The I of the servant stands opposite to a concrete thou, which is not simply exchangeable. The same claim can be made for the artisan: "the artisans, who worked in small workshops knew their customers."[331] Artisan's labor is dependent on someone demanding something specific, for the "village shoemaker ... will not make a pair of shoes, that is not ordered."[332] "The artisan, in his product, refers to others. He finishes a product according to the ideas of those who commission him."[333] Yet more, one can even say that the existence of the artisan itself is dependent on the need of concrete customers. There is only place for him in the world, when these customers use him as, for instance, a shoemaker.[334] But if labor is related to the wage relationship, the thou no longer necessarily names a specific person. Here it – as Nishitani formulated it in another connection – "completely loses that dimension, where the I is set in the face of a thou."[335] The thou, that before designated a specific master, a specific customer, becomes exchangeable. The laborer as laborer is thus dependent on someone inducting him into a labor relationship, but this someone isn't any concrete thou. For the worker relates himself purely to a monetary wage, that can be secured to him by a number of employers:

> "Certainly the laborer is chained to the work like a farmer to the soil; only the frequency with which the monetarized economy substitutes employers, and the ample possibilities of the choice and change of the same, which secures the form of the money wage to the laborer, gives him yet a wholly new freedom inside his chains. The slave could not, thus, himself change his master, even if he was ready to take shoulder the burden of a lot of bad living conditions, - which the wage laborer can

---

[330] G. Simmel, *Philosophie des Geldes*, 314.
[331] S. de Sismondi, "Grundsätze der Politischen Ökonomie oder Der Reichtum in seinen Beziehungen zur Bevölkerung," teilw. abgedruckt in: A. Kruse (ed.), *Nationalökonomie*, 52.
[332] Ibid., 52.
[333] K.-H. Brodbeck, *Die fragwürdigen Grundlagen der Ökonomie*, 218.
[334] S. de Sismondi, "Grundsätze der Politischen Ökonomie," 52.
[335] K. Nishitani, "Modernisierung und Tradition in Japan," 190.

in any moment; thus the irrevocable dependency on the individually specified master is abolished, the way to personal freedom is opened up amongst all material restrictions."[336]

The question who exactly faces the I in a work relationship loses its significance through the relation of work to money. Positively we can say, that the labor makes the laborer free or independent from the will of specific others.[337] Here is mirrored a fundamental effect of money on the I-Thou relationship. For it makes possible relationships "out of which... all elements of an authentic individual's nature are distanced." It grounds the "substitutability of persons" in those relationships, in which the individual defines herself.[338] So, for instance, the buyer is no longer dependent on a specific seller and vice versa. The unique properties of the face to face relationship become meaningless, because "the only thing that counts is the binary code of being paid or not."[339]

> "In this classic sense, economic exchange is wholly impersonal, which seems to be precisely the ideal-type interaction embodied in ordered anarchy. Each person is treated strictly as he is, and presumably as he wants to be, in such a relationship. The fruit stand operator may beat his horse, shoot dogs, and eat rats. But none of these qualities need affect my strictly economic trade with him."[340]

If we look at the employer, the independence from a specific thou within the action field of money becomes even more clear. For the employer too can define himself in the field of labor without being dependent on specified others, thus growing independent from specific relationships. "The liberation of the laborer must, so to speak, be compensated for by the liberation of the employer, i.e. with the abolition of the benefits enjoyed by the enslaved," with liberation understood to mean, here, "the abolition of individually fixed dependency."[341] Even the I of the employer frees himself from his ties to the concrete thou of the laborer. This process is strengthened through the growth of the division of labor; a development, that Adam Smith, already, named the driving force of commercial development and wealth.[342] We shall not take up the issue of wealth here, but instead the

---

[336] G. Simmel, *Philosophie des Geldes*, 317.
[337] Ibid, 318.
[338] Ibid, 316.
[339] M. Schramm, "Spielregeln gestalten sich nicht von selbst," 150.
[340] J.M. Buchanan, *The Limits of Liberty: Between Anarchy and Leviathan*.
[341] G. Simmel, *Philosophie des Geldes*, 318.
[342] A. Smith, "Untersuchungen über das Wesen und die Ursachen des Wohlstandes," in: A. Kruse (ed.), *Nationalökonomie*, 92.

effects of the division of labor on the relationship of the laborer and the employer. Through division of labor, the extent of the action of labor is reduced, while it limits everyone's business to a simple accomplishment and this accomplishment makes up the sole business of one's life.[343] A simple activity is to be learned by each, or at least by many. On account of this, the employer becomes independent from specific specialists just as the laborer is enabled to define himself in wholly different labor relationships. In economics, this idea of the simplification of labor achieves its ultimate point in the concept of man-power and energy. In Smith we can already see that the division of labor minimizes the extent of labor so much that the laborer can be replaced by a machine.[344] Hegel gives this idea the following form:

> "The labor of the individual becomes simpler through division, the skillfulness in his abstract labor as much as his productivity thus becoming greater... Moreover, the abstraction of the producer makes the labor ever more mechanical and thus we are able in the end to dispense with the person and put the machine in his place."[345]

The division of labor makes it possible to interpret labor as a "physical-mechanical" activity.[346] Labor is re-interpreted in terms of man-power or efficiency and thus belongs to the simple 'means of production', of which one can exploit or utilize its "material and forces."[347] This depends on expressing all the phenomenal forms of labor in one unified metric. Human action as labor is reduced to amounts of energy indistinguishable from mechanical energy. We won't go into how such a formal equivalency of mechanical and labor energy is to be conceived, but instead, are strictly interested in its meaning for the relation of laborer and employer. If labor is only a simple amount of energy, than the employer is as independent from each particular laborer as she is from each particular machine. Even more, she becomes free from every concrete environment, thus for instance a particular place of manufacture. She can thus fix the content and limits of these relationships herself, in which she is determined.

Nishitani has worked out the general structure of such 'freedom.' If actions are reduced to amounts of energy, the I can therefore stand completely indifferent in the face of the thou. The thou is robbed of his particularity; it

---

[343] Ibid., 94.
[344] Ibid., 95.
[345] G.W.F. Hegel cited in K.-H. Brodbeck, *Erfolgsfaktor Kreativität*, 176-77.
[346] K.-H. Brodbeck, *Die fragwürdigen Grundlagen der Ökonomie*, 139.
[347] H. Meyer, "Produktion," in: A. Kruse (ed.), *Nationalökonomie*, 98.

becomes a matter of exchange, so that the I defines itself independently of it.

> "Since, to humans, not only all 'things', but even other people are mechanically manipulable and pliable, there is an absence, here, of any face to face resistance. That means the subject finds no material object, finds, outside of himself, no being in itself, no being, that resists him, and to which he could attach himself. Moreover, this subject position lacks any relation to another, not to speak of a relationship to a thou. Here there is simply nothing we can call a 'thou.' Everything is in the third person, is an 'it', that may even cease being an it when it is reduced to force or energy. We are dealing with a standpoint, here, which grants the I an extraordinary power, for finally there is no longer anything left that will offer it the least resistance. In a world, in which everything is reduced to force and energy, everything is fundamentally arranged so as to be free to be managed; and everything can be arbitrarily manipulated. In a certain sense, what we have here is the standpoint of a subject who has reached the peak of his development."[348]

This clarifies an important point: the autonomous or independent existence of the I isn't rooted in its isolation or its 'pre-social', 'natural' essence, but instead the I is determined in a world in which every thou has become interchangeable, transformable and substitutable. Nishitani ascribes this possibility to the age of technology and interprets the reduction of the thou to energy and force exclusively as a physical phenomenon. This interpretation only makes it possible to understand why, in labor, man and machine have become interchangeable. However, insofar as the energy metaphor is (implicitly) rooted in the concept of money, the idea of the independent I can be extended beyond this framework. For in money's field of action the individual is freed from all specific ties. Not only in labor does the thou become meaningless, but also in exchange.

> "We are extraordinarily independent of every particular element of this society, because its meaning for us has been transferred into its one-sided, performative facticity, which therefore can be produced much more easily from so and so many other and personally different people, with whom nothing ties us than the interest restlessly expressed in terms of money."[349]

Only in the economic world can we think of the form of private determination that regards the individual as independent from any specific relationship. But this doesn't mean that the individual presents us with an iso-

---

[348] K. Nishitani, "Modernisierung und Tradition in Japan," 194.
[349] G. Simmel, *Philosophie des Geldes*, 315.

lated existence. "Individual freedom isn't a pure inner constituting of an isolated subject."[350] The private determination doesn't rest on the complete absence of relationships, but instead on an anonymous interweaving of relationships. It doesn't imply the loss of ties in general, but instead only the ties that make up a peculiar, irreplaceable face to faceness.

Lets look at the social determination of the individual at this point. I want to begin this reflection by referring to Nishitani's thought. When the I, according to Nishitani, no longer faces a thou, than it becomes meaningless in itself. "The person sees and exploits everything under the viewpoint of function, thus reducing his very self to a function."[351]

> "In the same gesture [in which the subject achieves his peak-S.G.] subjectivity loses any meaning and the person is dehumanized. When there is no longer any thou offering resistance to the I, to the point where any thou simply vanishes – so, to, vanishes the position of the 'I.' The I is now just the force that governs the forces of the world. The sovereignty of humankind is nothing more than the force which leads the world of forces. It becomes a mechanical force guiding mechanical processes. If everything is transformed into an 'it' and things exist merely for control and manipulation, then subjectivity itself slips away from us, who we have fallen into the state of being mere mechanics. Under the influence of technology, the self-consciousness of the subject runs the danger of collapsing by and by."[352]

Nishitani's thought can be followed for the concept of labor. Because the individual is a determination of activity, his character becomes correspondingly lesser, when the range of his activity diminishes. Adam Smith observes this connection, when he says that the division of labor not only reduces the range of activity, but also the range of the agents themselves:

> "In the progress of the division of labour, the employment of the far greater part of those who live by labour, that is, of the great body of the people, comes to be confined to a few very simple operations; frequently to one or two. But the understandings of the greater part of men are necessarily formed by their ordinary employments. The man whose whole life is spent in performing a few simple operations, of which the effects, too, are perhaps always the same, or very nearly the same, has no occasion to exert his understanding, or to exercise his invention, in finding out expedients for removing difficulties which never occur. He naturally

---

[350] Ibid., 315.
[351] K. Nishitani, "Modernisierung und Tradition in Japan," 198.
[352] Ibid., 194-95.

loses, therefore, the habit of such exertion, and generally becomes as stupid and ignorant as it is possible for a human creature to become."[353]

With Smith we have already reached the point where labor has been loosened from an I-thou relationship. It appears only as an I-it relationship. Yet the I is not able to persist even in this I-it relationship. When the laborer defines herself in only the simplest activities, she becomes less. She is no longer defining herself in relation to a multitude of customers, or in the construction process of an artifact, but only in a single moment of craft: the pulling of a wire or the cutting of a wire or in the welding of the needle.[354] She becomes a simple function. The economic labor concept drives this reduction, sketched in the Smithian idea of the division of labor, until it reaches its most extreme form. When every factor of production is denoted only as an amount of energy, the worker himself becomes a mere labor force in the purest mechanical sense:

> "The human becomes 'a subject on the level of labor energy.' To this corresponds, on the other side of the ledger, that everything holds the character of a 'subject of labor' on an energetic level in place of that of a material object. In this way the subject and object lose their prevailing status. Both are reduced to the level of 'abstract subjects.' ... The I from the I-it relationship is abstracted on its side to assume the character of an 'it'; the materiality of the it is abstracted at the same time, reduced to simple functionality; and the it is now only a 'subject of labor.' Both of them, the I and the it, become in an abstract sense 'agent-things.' That means that the I-thou relationship becomes, through being abstracted, an it-it relationship, with the I-thou reified in an abstract manner."[355]

In this way the laborer becomes arbitrary, interchangeable, because he is no longer characterized by any quality uniquely particular to him. "The person is in the end only a unit of labor power."[356] "Yet not only the laborer, but even all people, without distinction – the capitalist, the white collar worker, the official, become subjects on the labor energy level, or, in other words, abstract subjects."[357] Thus economists are to a certain extent justified to speak of an "exclusion of independent individuals ... out of the operational market system"[358] and to assume that they have only to deal

---

[353] A. Smith, *The Wealth of Nations*, 662.
[354] I am referring here to Adam Smith's famous example of division of labor in the manufacture of pins.
[355] K. Nishitani, "Modernisierung und Tradition in Japan," 199.
[356] Ibid., 190.
[357] Ibid., 199.
[358] J. Wieland, *Ökonomische Organisation, Allokation und Status*, 55.

with thing-thing relations. "'Ecce homo.' This statement of existence becomes progressively abstracted, is no longer graspable, or rather: this original and authentic reality is lost."[359]

In the measure that this loss is strengthened, the dependency of individuals on unspecified others becomes ever greater. This too becomes transparent when we look at the division of labor. The individual becomes free of particular ties through this division, but equally her existence is determined by an indeterminate number of other people with whom she is not acquainted. She becomes dependent on an anonymous mass. "Since great capital unites in one factor not only the artisan but the factory worker, these people no longer know the people who use their products, who live perhaps hundreds of miles from them; they no longer have any intimate knowledge of their wants or of the lessening of their demand."[360]

> "Observe the accommodation of the most common artificer or day-labourer in a civilized and thriving country, and you will perceive that the number of people, of whose industry a part, though but a small part, has been employed in procuring him this accommodation, exceeds all computation. The woolen coat, for example, which covers the day-labourer, as coarse and rough as it may appear, is the produce of the joint labour of a great multitude of workmen. (...) If we examine, I say, all these things, and consider what a variety of labour is employed about each of them, we shall be sensible that, without the assistance and co-operation of many thousands, the very meanest person in a civilized country could not be provided, even according to, what we very falsely imagine, the easy and simple manner in which he is commonly accommodated."[361]

In such a net of anonymous dependencies the individual seems interchangeable. Just as he has become independent from any specific face-to-face situation, so, too, his specific existence is indifferent to any other. As with all others, he is reduced to a mere function, which always can be filled in by someone else. His uniqueness is lost; he is reduced to a product or an effect. He can be regarded on this account as a molecule in a chemical system, as a cog in the gears of a gigantic machine. The anonymous relationships in a society containing innumerable divisions of labor are objectified in opposition to him as a mechanism. The mutual dependencies appear a one "invisible, omnipresent power", which lead "millions of wills and

---

[359] K. Nishitani, "Modernisierung und Tradition in Japan," 193.
[360] S. de Sismondi, "Grundsätze der Politischen Ökonomie," 52.
[361] A. Smith, "Untersuchung über das Wesen und die Ursachen des Wohlstandes," 96-97.

commodity parts."³⁶² This force threatens and dominates the individual. It shapes him everywhere and at all times, as it shapes every other individual. These are the roots of the social determination of the individual; a determination, that is often designated as 'alienation' and is being described by Sōseki Natsume as the "pain of existence" in the modern world.³⁶³

The real ground for this pain remains clearly unrecognized, as long as one does not refer to the meaning of money. For only in money are all unique elements of human relationships alienated, so that they assume a wholly universal character. Through money it is possible, to come into contact with anybody and thus to be independent from specific others. In a society defined by division of labor it is at the same time increasingly harder, to define relationships other than in money. To the salesman, the unique character of the buyer is a matter of indifference. But the latter must sustain one universal characteristic: he must possess money. The relation to money lies at the root of all relationships and levels at the same time all other properties of buyer and seller.³⁶⁴ Even membership in a group or community is no longer based on birth, abilities or religious belief, but only on the relationship to money. "Social success and failure means making money or losing money," as Schumpeter says.³⁶⁵ When money becomes the "single unifying operation", it destroys all other forms of mutual relation:

> "When among the many interests that make for the union of a circle [of a community, SG], the one devastates all the others, naturally this one will survive all the others and finally show the only connection between the elements, whose other connections it has gnawed through. Not because of its immanent character, but simply because it has proved destructive to so many other kinds of human ties do we see money seal the connection between otherwise wholly disparate elements."³⁶⁶

When each defines herself only in monetary relationships, than these relationships themselves achieve an objective character. For 'objective' can be

---

³⁶² A. Schäffle, "Das gesellschaftliche System der menschlichen Wirthschaft," 239.
³⁶³ N. Soseki cited in T. Najita, "Die historische Entwicklung der kulturellen Identität im modernen Japan und die humanistische Herausforderung der Gegenwart," in: K. Werhahn-Mees, C. von Barloewen (ed.), *Japan und der Westen*, Vol. 3, Frankfurt 1986, 187.
³⁶⁴ G. Simmel, *Philosophie des Geldes*, 341.
³⁶⁵ J. Schumpeter, *Kapitalismus, Sozialismus und Demokratie*, 122.
³⁶⁶ G. Simmel, *Philosophie des Geldes*, 375.

defined as "that, which is the same for all."[367] It is this aspect that makes intelligible the reason why the existence of individuals in a society dominated by the division of labor actually seems subservient to a universal. "An economically oriented person, who has been produced by the monetary economic civilization prevalent in the modern world, is likely to be universalized only as a mere cog in the wheel of the economic system."[368]

Let's throw a glance backwards. Only in the economic world can the individual be regarded as independent from any specific relation. Persons could "finally shake off the dross of their ties to moeurs and habits"[369] and apprehend themselves as autonomous subjects. This is what Nishitani thought too: in modernity "in every individual there arises a consciousness for his own subject-existence."[370] Yet this development only mirrors one direction of the individual's determination in the economic world. For with the consciousness for autonomy and independence of the individual, there arises at the same time the idea of the absolute subservience of the individual to a gigantic mechanism, which he no longer shapes, but only endures. "Apart from the social determination there is ... no private determination."[371] The regularity of things and the inner-oriented, externally independent personality arise at the same time.[372] They reciprocally condition each other, while the economic world displays the locus of its mediation:

> "If the idea of personality, now, as a counterpoint and correlate to the laws of material relationships, develops in tandem with the later, then out of this connection it should be clear that a stricter modeling of the concepts of material law goes hand in hand with that of individual freedom. Thus, we see the real parallel movement of the last three centuries: on the one side natural law, the material ordering of things, the objective necessity of events emerges ever more clearly and exactly; on the other side, the emphasis on independent individuality, personal freedom, the for-itself-ness in the face of all external and natural forces becomes ever more sharp and powerful."[373]

---

[367] J. Cartelier, *Das Geld*, 46.
[368] T. Watsuji, *Watsuji Tetsuro's Rinrigaku*, 108.
[369] B.P. Priddat and E.K. Seifert, "Gerechtigkeit und Klugheit," 53. The authors are referring to T. Hobbes.
[370] K. Nishitani, "Modernisierung und Tradition in Japan," 183.
[371] K. Nishida, "Die Welt als Dialektisches Allgemeines," 169.
[372] G. Simmel, *Philosophie des Geldes*, 358.
[373] Ibid., 320.

4 The Implicit World Picture of Economics

MacPherson speaks here of a paradox of market society: individual freedom and subsumption under a universal are mutually contradictory and yet inextricably entangled with each other:

> "The market makes men free; it requires for its effective operation that all men be free and rational; yet the independent rational decisions of each man produce at every moment a configuration of forces which confronts each man compulsively. All men's choices determine, and each man's choice is determined by, the market."[374]

One can also formulate this paradox regarding the supposed opposition of individualism and collectivism like so: The more individual self-sufficiency is emphasized, the stronger becomes the idea of a universal to which the individual must submit. Both contradict each other, but are yet mutually dependent on each other. Together they form the ground in which is rooted the absolutely contradictory self-identity of the economic actor. Individualism, which is always being prized in economics as the essential achievement of modernity, is inseparable from the idea of a collectivism that compels many individuals to exist under one law. Individual freedom and submission to an anonymous crowd are two sides of one and the same coin. Thus, it isn't correct to distinguish between purely individualistic and purely collectivist oriented societies and to suppose that the degree of individualism in a society is inversely related to the degree of collectivism. The truth is that the stronger the individualism, the stronger we will find the collectivism.[375] This connection is easy to overlook, if we just look at one side and forget the living reality of the economic world as that locus that takes in both side and mediates between them. In spite of their opposition, individualism and collectivism have their roots in a similar cognitive error: the economic world is always presupposed as a place of nothingness, but is not made into an object of reflection. In this way we overlook the fact that each position implicitly presupposes at any moment the counter-position in order to ground its own standpoint. Not unjustly, Nishida writes: "Individualism and collectivism are said to be diametrically opposed to each other, but I think they coincide."[376]

We should emphasize that private and social determination in the economic world, while they are entangled from the very beginning, are still impossible to join together. The independence of the individual can never

---

[374] C.B. MacPherson, *The Political Theory of Possessive Individualism*, 106.
[375] Ibid., 256.
[376] K. Nishida cited in S. Odin, *The Social Self in Zen and American Pragmatism*, 86.

simply be assimilated into a universal, and just as little as her subordination can be interpreted as autonomy or even freedom. Both conflicting poles of action can never be reconciled with each other; yet they are still joined in the actor. The individual defines herself in her constant conflict as a "determination without a determining agent." While this form of determination in economics is mostly not recognized, MacIntyre, for instance, points out that the person is determined in modern commercial society as a divided self, and even as a self-divided self, that joins equally and contradictorily in itself private and social determination. Using this, he analyzes American society:

> "The present characteristic American self I take to be a divided self, often enough a self-divided self. ... From the individualism of the Enlightenment there derives a capacity of the self to abstract himself from the particular social role which it happens inhabit and indeed from the social order of which that role is a constitutive part, so as to reflect upon itself as an individual qua individual, rather than qua family member or member of a this or that social group ... It involves a belief that the individual is free to withdraw him- or herself from these influences and take toward them whatever attitude he or she chooses to adopt in accordance with those preferences which are truly his or hers qua individual. So there is this part of the self which views itself as beyond all social roles, capable of escaping from its past history and of making it new. (...) [On the other hand] there emerges a part of the self which wears and responds to the badges of acquisitive and competitive success, an aspect of the self dominated by the social relations of an at once bureaucratized and individualist market economy, for which society appears not as that from which I am able to abstract myself and upon which I sit in judgment, but as the source of an impersonal vocation inflicted upon me. (...) There are a remarkably large number of individuals who find within themselves ... all .. these attitudes, each partially constitutive of a divided and inconsistent self. Moreover, these attitudes when spelt out, are not merely mutually incompatible, they are incommensurable. There are available in the shared culture of modern America no standards by appeal to which these conflicts can be rationally resolved."[377]

The actor's self-consciousness is split: from the point of view of private determination it appears as a subject of consciousness; from the point of view of social determination, as an object of consciousness. It equally holds in itself "self-attachment and self-estrangement."[378]

---

[377] A. MacIntyre, "Individual and Social Morality in Japan and the United States," 491-92.
[378] M. Abe, "The Problem of Self-Centeredness as the Root-source of Human Suffering," *Japanese Religions*, 15/4 (1989), 17.

4.6 The Significance of Egoism for the Economic World

In the last section, an alternative understanding of the economic world and economic actors came into focus. We can sum up our new understanding by saying that it is grounded in thinking of the world as well as the actor site specifically: while the economic world is manifested as a locus, which holds in itself the notion of the individual and the (mechanical) order and mediates among them, the individual emerges as that something which defines itself in this world, as much in the sense of private as of social determination. World and actor thus escape any rational description; from the point of view of methodological individualism as well as the ideology of the market, both constitute a locus of nothingness that serves as a presupposition of our explanation, without itself becoming an object of reflection. In this section we shall show why, nevertheless, it will pay to examine the position of methodological individualism once again. For in one specific form this does not make the claim that the individual actually exists independently from others, as we have assumed up until now, but instead, that that is how every individual sees himself. A characterization generated by an outside observer no longer holds the center stage, but instead an assumption about the self-interpretation of the individual: the assumption, that he conceives himself in opposition to any other individual and acts exclusively in his self-interest or egoistically because of this perception. In this variant of methodological individualism, an image that people might often have of themselves is taken seriously, serving as the starting point for understanding the interactions of the many. As we shall show, East Asian philosophy also gives us a thorough discussion of this exegetical tendency. Here, individualism is traced back to a person's habitual point of view or normal consciousness. It is seen through as a form of self-perception that distinguishes fundamentally the mine and the thine, the I and the thou, without perceiving the common locus of these differences.[379] We will elaborate on this habitual point of view in the form it is given by the economic actor in 4.6.1. We will make it clear that, from this standpoint, the interactions of the many can only appear as a struggle of all against all; a struggle in which the absolute status of the individual as well as the universal order is continually threatened; one in which, finally, the world is experienced only as suffering.

---

[379] See for example A.D. Brear, "The Nature and Status of Moral Behavior in Zen Buddhist Tradition," *Philosophy East & West*, 24/4 (1974), 429.

4.6.1 The Egoism of the Normal Consciousness

"The first principle of Economics is that every agent is actuated only by self-interest."[380] It begins in general with the fact that she only follows her own interest: she fundamentally considers her own advantage; is egoistical.[381] One of the most important anthropological claims of economics can be reduced to this meager formula.[382] It isn't related exclusively to individuals per se, but instead, at least implicitly, relates to the encounters of many individuals who strive after their own interests. The egoistical actor operates in the midst of a world in which his interests oppose countless other interests. In the economic literature it is often emphasized how this claim gives us a realistic picture of human beings:[383] "The human image implied in economics is not so unrealistic."[384] Yet what does such a human image describe, exactly? Japanese philosophy gives an interesting response to this question. According to it, every form of egoism arises from an overview of reality given by the standpoint of the normal consciousness. Egoism is rooted in the habitual manner of seeing through which the individual identifies himself exclusively with his private determination. His interests appear internal or subjective to him; they belong to his inner world, which he defends or triumphs with against an outer world.

This judgment requires some explanation. In the previous chapter, it was already clear that our habitual manner of seeing things put an impediment in the way of seeing through the reciprocity of subjective and objective perspectives or inner and outer worlds in the locus of habits. (3.3.3) This exegetical tendency clearly limited itself to the interactions of people with objects; it is now supposed to be broadened to include the relations of individuals to their fellow kind. In principle this means that the individual habitually perceives himself as an inner unity, which he regards as independent from all other people and their actions. He understands himself as a free and indomitable ego in the midst of a world of mutual dependencies. In other words, the actor identifies himself exclusively with that direction of the world's determination that emphasizes his freedom and independence, perceiving himself as an 'absolute lord.' "Inner unity is nothing more than the direction of self affirmation by which we think that we define

---

[380] F.Y. Edgeworth, *Mathematical Psychics*, 16.
[381] G. Kirchgässner, *Homo oeconomicus*, 45-46.
[382] A.K. Sen, "Rational Fools," 317.
[383] See for example A. Marshall, "Handbuch der Volkswirtschaftslehre," in: A. Kruse (ed.), *Nationalökonomie*, 25.
[384] G. Kirchgässner, *Homo oeconomicus*, 47.

(ourselves) as individuals."[385] Yet such mastery is not imaginable in isolation, since the private determination doesn't exist independently of the social determination. The subjective standpoint necessarily unfolds itself as it limits and denies the social determination. The latter is experienced as a "direction of self-negation" and thus as "external."[386] The mutual dependencies in the world are seen as something exterior from the standpoint of the ego, standing in absolute opposition to it. "Because we simply stay on the standpoint of the subject-object opposition, we are thus inclined to think that the inner and the outer unity stand in a thorough opposition to each other."[387] In this way in normal perception one's fellow humans are pushed into the outer world. They appear as ob-jective, as a threat, against which one has necessarily to defend oneself. The individual finds himself in a kind of "unsympathetic isolation;"[388] the irrevocable mutual dependencies are nothing more than an evil for him, something that he must unwillingly suffer. The community in which he lives is for him an external reality that seemingly exists through itself, hostilely pitting itself against him.[389]

> "To be a self-conscious existence is for a human being to be conscious of the distinction between self and others. From the dimension of consciousness the self regards others as objects against which the self stands as subject. Out of the subject-object dichotomy thus created, consciousness grasps everything from that dichotomous point of view. Putting itself at the center of the world, the self regards all others from the outside, as existing peripheral to itself. This is the case not only in knowing, the self's cognitive activity, but also in doing, the self's volitional activity. In other words, from the dichotomous point of view the self regards others not only as objects of cognition, but also as objects of emotion and volition, that is, as objects of like and dislike, love and hate, affection and detestation. In this way, the human self becomes inextricably involved in the subject-object dichotomy and the persistent self-centeredness engendered by it."[390]

---

[385] K. Nishida, "Die Welt als Dialektisches Allgemeines," 131.
[386] Ibid.
[387] Ibid.
[388] F.Y. Edgeworth cited in A.K. Sen, "Rational Fools," 326.
[389] T. Izutsu, "Die Entdinglichung und Wiederverdinglichung der 'Dinge' im Zen Buddhismus," 19.
[390] M. Abe, "The Problem of Self-Centeredness," 16-17.

4.6.2 The Economic World as the Struggle of All against All

The standpoint of normal perception is one that is directed against others. "Feeling ourselves in tension with objectified others leads us to act in an aggressive or defensive manner to effect our will."[391] Hobbes, for instance, presupposes this manner of acting as a given. For according to him each has the "wish and will to injure."[392] Humans stand irreconcilably opposed to each other: an alliance of the forces of two men is unthinkable for Hobbes:[393]

> "And because the power of one man resisteth and hindereth the effects of the power of another, power is simply no more, but the excess of one above that of another. For equal powers opposed, destroy one another; and such their opposition is called contention."[394]

In the literature of economics, such contention is often called the 'state of nature.' The concept of nature here refers to that state in which people lived before they came together in society. Conflict is supposed to (historically) precede the society of exchange and trade, but not itself to characterize the latter. From the viewpoint of Japanese philosophy, some skepticism should be applied with regard to this assessment. For in its understanding, there is no concept of nature that can denote a "state before cultivation."[395] For Japanese philosophy, above all else, no human interaction is thinkable outside of a definite culture or community. A 'state of nature' always only exists in the world, but never beyond it.[396] Thus, even human contention must appeal to a form of encounter, as it manifests itself in the world.

Nishitani has clearly elaborated the universal structure of this form. In order to go completely through the course of his thought, we must again look at the relation of the I and thou. Insofar as the I and thou are grounded in normal perception, both remain stable as though self-evidently standing on the "irreplaceable mastery of their being."[397] Each identifies herself with herself. She will solely in her own person decide over herself. It is in this

---

[391] D.L. Hall, R.T. Ames, *Thinking from the Han*, 57.
[392] T. Hobbes, *Lehre vom Menschen und vom Bürger*, 84.
[393] C.B. MacPherson, *The Political Theory of Possessive Individualism*, 17.
[394] T. Hobbes, *The Elements of Law, Natural and Politic* (1640), I, 8,4.
[395] R. Ohashi, *Japan im interkulturellen Dialog*, 29.
[396] MacPherson for example represents this position. See *The Political Theory of Possessive Individualism*, 18.
[397] K. Nishitani, "Vom Wesen der Begegnung," 261.

4 The Implicit World Picture of Economics 227

way "that the I as well as the thou are absolute all the way through ... for both are the Absolute."[398] Yet this point of view is not the only exclusively valid one, because the standpoint of one is being represented at the same time in the other's place. From the standpoint of the I, the thou is merely a something that he faces, who is submissive to the absolute mastery of the I. And inversely, the thou tries to subordinate the I. This means that both also appear as absolutely subordinate, so long as they each remain steady in their own 'mastery of being.' "And this itself tells us that the I as well as the thou are each absolutely relative."[399] The ego acts in the world of relations, but it can't allow any relation to others without feeling the threat to its own self sufficiency and independence. The I as well as the thou strives, on these grounds, to negate or to subjugate the other. The power of the other should be purged or assimilated into one's own power.

> "The best way to gain superiority over others ... is to try to transfer the means of another person's power into oneself. (...) This relationship consists at first of trying to appropriate another's external properties. Yet the greatest triumph lies in eliminating the other as a rival, which happens when one not only appropriates the external properties but also rules the other's person, and thus takes control of his inner goods."[400]

The life of the ego is like a continual boxing match. If one is struck, this means misery; if one strikes the other, this is called happiness.[401] Each person tries to beat the other so far into submission until his mastery of being is annihilated:

> "Where the absolute acts in the world of relations, it indulges itself completely to its actions, without reserve, so that it does not leave behind any relation – meaning that the absolute captures each of the others who come against it, tears them out of themselves, and so appropriates them. As long as a self is a self sufficient, independent master and wants to be a true self, this indulgence will happen automatically. ... As long as the thou is also a master, the same indulgence will occur with him."[402]

This is the absolute standpoint presupposed by economic theory when it begins with self-interested actors. This is made clear for example by the

---

[398] Ibid., 264.
[399] Ibid.
[400] M. Esfeld, *Mechanismus und Subjektivität in der Philosophie Thomas Hobbes*, 217-18. Esfeld is referring here to Hobbes.
[401] T. Hobbes, *The Elements of Law, Natural and Politic*, I,9,21.
[402] K. Nishitani, "Vom Wesen der Begegnung," 266-67.

way altruism is treated. For "even the non-exploitative encounter with the thou is always only seen from the I."[403] I am only interested in your well-being, if I promise to make use of it for myself; I let the thou go on his way only when this makes the I feel good about itself, etc. As Amartya Sen shows, this is the only form of altruism recognized in economics. An action from which others profit, and not oneself, appears, contrarily, to be excluded.[404] Adam Smith early on already formulated this position pregnantly: "It is not from the benevolence of the butcher, the brewer, or the baker that we expect our dinner, but from their regard to their own interest."[405] Someone else will always and only serve as means to one's own self preservation, self satisfaction and self advancement.[406]

Of course, it is correct that the self-interested actor in a certain sense conducts himself neutrally against his fellows. For "in so far as he does not stand in any specific relationship to his neighbor, it doesn't concern him whether these relations are good or bad in particular. He looks neither with envy nor with *Schadenfreude* on him, but he also does not rejoice in his well being."[407] Yet such a mutually disinterested rationality is unmasked, on closer examination, as a deeper egoism. For it says that for the ego, no real facing agent exists any more. The thou is only meaningful when I can use him. "Here there is no longer any relation, no itself and no others, in short no 'person' and no 'personal relationship.'" The thou is only "that which belongs to my proper self."[408] In this way the I stands indifferently in the face of the thou. While Kirchgässner, for instance, believes he sees in this indifference a not wholly "unsympathetic" characteristic feature of economic man,[409] Nishitani recognizes, here, the authentic cause for the absolute opposition of the I and thou. For it denotes a lack of relation in the sense of an "absolute opposition, in which both are sundered from each other as absolutely indifferent, and this indifference belongs to each as part of their authentic being."[410] The standpoint of the I annihilates completely the thou, just as, from the standpoint of the thou, the I is absolutely negated.

---

[403] E.E. Nawroth, *Die Sozial- und Wirtschaftsphilosophie des Neoliberalismus*, 55.
[404] A.K. Sen, "Rational Fools," 326.
[405] A. Smith, *The Wealth of Nations*, 17.
[406] M. Esfeld, *Mechanismus und Subjektivität in der Philosophie von Thomas Hobbes*, 260.
[407] G. Kirchgässner, *Homo oeconomicus*, 46.
[408] K. Nishitani, "Vom Wesen der Begegnung," 268.
[409] G. Kirchgässner, *Homo oeconomicus*, 46.
[410] Ibid., 268.

"This state of things is a complete conflict and a complete violation of sense. It shows an absolute opposition, in which the I and the thou, as deadly enemies, never wish to coexist with each other under the same heaven in a common world. So long as both desire never to be together under the same heaven, one must kill the other. Here an Either-Or is king, namely ...swallowing or be swallowed, in which relationship each must be a wolf to the other. ... Each party's absoluteness makes it unendurable to remain in the relationship."[411]

We shall now inquire into the question of whether such a conflict can establish a stable relationship between people. To this question economists often give the answer, yes. If in the course of conflict, one side were completely negated, the relationship between both competitors would be disturbed. A stable relationship should thus in principle exist, only if "both people, who never want to coexist under the same heaven, nevertheless live with each other in complete peace."[412] But the later state can only exist if there is no weaker or stronger – thus, the competitors have, at least in some regard, to be equal. In economic literature, the attempt to ground such equality is made in various ways. An exact glance shows that clearly, this is always only presumed. It is not the result of the conflict, but rather its presupposition. I would like to explain this briefly with some examples. The equality of individuals can be interpreted as the equality of forces. As stress and counterstress in a physical system mutually hold themselves in equilibrium, so should the forces of the egos mutually cancel each other out and so ground a stable state. "The competition of self-seeking individuals against one another ensures that their self-seeking is limited."[413] But that the forces of the individuals are actually mutually canceled, an anterior equality is to be presupposed; it can thus not be the result of egoistical competition. I and thou must control the same quantity of power, before they compete against one another. That this presupposition is in no way always given in the economic world is immediately apparent: within economic competition, the destitute can stand in the face of a mighty individual, great corporations can compete against small groups, organizations against states. In none of these situations will the conflict of competitors make each equally strong. Their relations, instead, threaten constantly to collapse. At the very least, the inequalities of force in competition will rather magnify then decrease in the direction of an equilibrium. In a second argument in the economic literature, the attempt is made to ground the equality of the competitors in the fact that both conclude contracts with

---

[411] Ibid., 264.
[412] Ibid.
[413] K.-H. Brodbeck, *Erfolgsfaktor Kreativität*, 32.

each other.[414] The argument in this case goes, an equality must be present "for otherwise the contracting partners wouldn't be prepared to trade."[415] The contract appears "as merely the consequence of the equal power of the parties."[416] The last formulation is at the very least subject to misprision, because contracts can be made between people with very distinct power, for example in the case of labor relationships. It is of course correct that the contracting partners themselves in a certain sense are equal, insofar as they uphold together the arrangement. Yet this equality is no result of competition. Rather, it is a compromise between contracting parties, which can be presupposed, but yet is continually threatened. For it is rooted in the logic of "calculating opportunism" "always to reckon with violations of contractual obligation if these appear to be cost free."[417] Each will only recognize a contract as long as it serves one's calculation. A contract cannot effectively limit the power of individuals; rather, it threatens to be destroyed by it. Moreover: a contract often doesn't arise even in situations where it would be rational for the parties to cooperate with each other. The mistrust of the rivals in effect impedes the equality that might arise through the use of a contract. This makes the so called 'prisoners dilemma' clear: for two prisoners it would be advantageous to cooperate with each other in order to minimize their punishment. In spite of which, it is rational not to cooperate, due to the lack of trust each has that the other will behave cooperatively. Here the central difficulty becomes visible: there is no universal (in the sense of a contract or law), to which both competitors are subordinated equally, so that their equality is guaranteed. The equality that does exist is only a compromise, which can always collapse.[418] Given egoistical conflict, no stable relationship can grow, but instead "out of this infinite confusion and suffering comes," as Nishitani formulates it.[419]

One can take the measure of this suffering in looking at the economic world as a struggle for survival, in which each fights in the conflict of egoistic interests for his very existence. As Schumpeter put it, this struggle is like a "poker game", with its promise of riches and its threat of poverty, is whipping up everyone, again much more efficaciously than a more equal

---

[414] This idea goes back to Hobbes' theory of justice. See his *Leviathan*, book 1, chapter 14.
[415] B.P. Priddat and E.K. Seifert, "Gerechtigkeit und Klugheit," 70.
[416] G. Simmel, *Philosophie des Geldes*, 305.
[417] J. Wieland, *Ökonomische Organisation, Allokation und Status*, 47.
[418] K. Nishitani, "Vom Wesen der Begegnung," 264.
[419] Ibid.

and more 'just' system of penalties would."⁴²⁰ Here we have reached the point where it isn't only the case of the relation of the I and the thou, but an interweaving of the relationships of countless egos. It is no longer a matter of the struggle of two competitors, but the fight of all against all.⁴²¹ The I no longer faces one single thou, but uncounted other egos, which each claim absolute mastery for themselves. Before we can put the question of the stability of the social order properly, another important question is posed: how can such an absolute opposition of uncounted egos be thought in general? I will anticipate the answer before I give my reasons for it: we must (implicitly) presuppose the economic world as the locus of encounters, because only in it can each be understood in distinction from every other. It is true that "egoistical conduct doesn't first come into play in our (capitalist) epoch"⁴²² but an encounter of uncounted persons in which each struggles with each is only thinkable in the economic world.

We can easily imagine a state in which some people struggle against each other, but others ally themselves in enduring bonds and act in common. For instance, an alliance of a few sealed in order to guard themselves against the power struggle of others is just as thinkable as a common utilization of natural resources.⁴²³ But why isn't such an interaction thinkable for Hobbes and the greatest number of economists? Hobbes gives a simply answer to this: reliable trust is the one great lacking thing. More precisely: it is impossible, to distinguish the ones we can trust from the ones that will evil:

> "For though the wicked were fewer than the righteous, yet because we cannot distinguish them, there is a necessity of suspecting, heeding, anticipating, subjugating, self-defending, ever incident to the most honest, and fairest condition'd."⁴²⁴

In modern economic literature this thought is grasped without anything new being added to it. For even here we begin with the idea that a single

---

[420] J. Schumpeter, *Kapitalismus, Sozialismus und Demokratie*, 123.
[421] This idea goes back to Thomas Hobbes, *Lehre vom Menschen und vom Bürger*, 87. See C.B. MacPherson's commentary in: *The Political Theory of Possesive Individualism*, 29.
[422] G. Kirchgässner, *Homo oeconomicus*, 47.
[423] C.B. MacPherson, *The Political Theory of Possessive Individualism*, 37. See also M. Esfeld, *Mechanismus und Subjektivität in der Philosophie Thomas Hobbes*, 258.
[424] T. Hobbes cited in M. Esfeld, *Mechanismus und Subjektivität in der Philosophie Thomas Hobbes*, 258.

egoist can undermine and even destroy these decisions or unions. "A single defector can... bring about the collapse of interaction because he can force all others to preventive counter defections."[425] But to do this it must not be known which persons want to gain ever more power for themselves.[426] As Esfeld shows, we have to start from a state in which all traditional social groups are seen to be extinct. For only in this way can the individual understand himself as in opposition to each specific other. Only when each person can conceive himself as absolute master against every other person is a mutual trust unthinkable:

> "The full development of individuality in the form of self-understanding of all actors as individuals distinct one from the other presupposes that, for the individual, there is no specific life path pre-given from his birth, but instead that he creates this path himself, or at least consciously gives his consent to it. All actors can consequently develop such a self understanding only when the agrarian-artisan social structures are dissolved. ... That such a self understanding can be attributed to all actors is a specifically modern premise."[427]

To see the agrarian-artisan social structures as they dissolve means nothing other than that the economic world is at the very least implicitly put in its place. Or to put it in other words: only in the economic world is it possible for individuals to perceive themselves in distinction from every other person and on this account to no longer trust anyone. Thus only in such a world we can think of a struggle, in which each singly and equally stands in opposition to everyone else.

But can the "unsociable society" of many egos become the cause of a law bound order, as for example Kant thought?[428] The affirmation of this question gives us the core statement of economics. In particular, classical economics represents the idea that the self-interested activity of the many leads to a social order.[429] From out of egoistical actions, social harmony shall result. Some economists do concede that this idea runs counter to healthy human understanding. For example, Arrow and Hahn write:

---

[425] K. Homann, "Sinn und Grenze der ökonomischen Methode in der Wirtschaftsethik," 19.
[426] M. Esfeld, *Mechanismus und Subjektivität in der Philosophie Thomas Hobbes*, 258.
[427] Ibid., 262.
[428] I. Kant cited in P. Ulrich, "Der kritische Adam Smith – im Spannungsfeld zwischen sittlichem Gefühl und ethischer Vernunft," in: A. Meyer-Faje, Ulrich (ed.), *Der andere Adam Smith*, 174.
[429] See K.-H. Brodbeck's extensive discussion, *Erfolgsfaktor Kreativität*, 16-28.

"The immediate 'common sense' answer to the question 'What will an economy motivated by individual greed and controlled by a very large number of different agents look like?' is probably: 'There will be chaos.'"[430]

Japanese philosophy follows in the immediate wake of this assessment. As Abe Masao writes: "When each human self insists on an absolute, substantial selfhood, serious conflict will inevitably arise."[431] I want to briefly present the example of Adam Smith, in order to show why, in particular, classical economics arrived at yet another result.[432] At the center of the stage stands Smith's belief that the egoistical way of action, from which usually only disorder and the disarrangement of society come about, is in truth implanted in humans by a nature that, as in all other cases, has "intended the happiness and perfection of the species."[433] Kant presents the same idea:

> "The means nature employs to bring about the development of all its talents is their antagonism in society, in so far as this becomes, in the end, the cause of a law abiding order. By antagonism, I mean the antagonism of the unsociable society of human beings .... Persons who are as mild as the sheep they tend would hardly create any greater value out of their existence as their domesticated beasts do; they would not fill in the emptiness of creation in the light of their purpose, as rational creatures. Thanks are due, then, to nature for the irritability, for the dissatisfied, always competitive vanity, for the never to be satisfied desire for possession or even for power! ... Man wishes concord, but nature knows better what is good for the species: it wishes discord."[434]

But how does nature arrange it so that social cooperation can solely arise "from a sense of its utility, without any mutual love or affection?"[435] Numerous egos won't bear standing in relations one with another. They are, rather, watching to destroy any order that results from these relations, in so far as they can promise themselves an advantage from so doing. The relations of the ego could not thus be a cause of the order. They are, as Kant makes clear, purely a means used by nature in order to enact its own purposes. We can phrase this like so: the relations of the ego represent at most an effective cause of an order, but not its actual final cause. The latter takes

---

[430] K.J. Arrow and F.H. Hahn, *General Competitive Analysis*, vii.
[431] M. Abe, "The Problem of Self-Centeredness," 18.
[432] This argument rests on P. Ulrich, "Der kritische Adam Smith."
[433] A. Smith, *Theory of Moral Sentiments* , 123.
[434] I. Kant cited in P. Ulrich, "Der kritische Adam Smith," 174.
[435] A. Smith, *Theory of Moral Sentiments*, 100.

logical precedence over all human relationships. It unifies the many egos from the outside, making them into an order. Smith and many of his followers believed that they have found such a final cause in the wisdom of God, in the heavenly watchmaker, whose invisible hand makes it the case that "a commercial action that is 'initiated purely to strive after its own gain', so that 'profit is the highest value aimed at' in truth serves the 'good of the whole.'"[436] Each person is free in his relations with other people to follow his own interest, but all are subordinated equally to a divine law. The freedom of the individual is unbounded within the 'free play of market forces,' but it is limited by laws from without. On this account, egoism is not tamed by the struggle of all against all, but rather through an exterior force, a lawfulness that stands equally over all egos and subjects them to itself. It is this side of subordination that makes the egoistical freedom a penultimate rather than ultimate cause and which leaves all persons 'equal' to an extent that seems guaranteed by an order.[437]

Persons each relate themselves to a universal and only by the force of this relation are they interactively related. The order, then, doesn't grow out of the competition of egos, but instead comes from a wholly other source: a universal, that at the same time lies beyond or before the egoists. What exactly this universal is thought to be isn't explained by the deistic metaphor. The assumption of a divine order rests on a belief incorrigible to scientific explanation.[438] Its ways of functioning are subject neither to human control nor, completely, to human knowledge. "The natural course of things cannot be entirely controlled by the impotent endeavors of man."[439] How divine law binds up egoism and thus brings about a harmonic order remains on this account unclear. Everyday observation in itself can undermine the belief in the persistence of such an inexplicable function. A long list of the problems of the economic world points to the fact that a society of egoists, contrary to the beliefs of many economists, doesn't show us a stable order, but rather one always vulnerable to collapse.[440] Think, here, on the bitter struggles for existence of so many people, the existence of crises and depressions, and, last but not least, the obviously unresolved promise that the invisible hand will lead to an arrangement between the rich and poor.[441] "A war of all against all doesn't lead to the eternal peace between bold market

---

[436] P. Ulrich, "Der kritische Adam Smith," 178. Ulrich is citing Smith.
[437] K. Nishitani, "Vom Wesen der Begegnung," 261.
[438] P. Ulrich, "Der kritische Adam Smith," 177.
[439] A. Smith, *Theory of Moral Sentiments*, 196.
[440] F.H. Knight, *The Ethics of Competition*, London 1936, 57.
[441] For this hope, see A. Smith, *Theory of Moral Sentiments*, 215.

participants, but to monopolistic exploitation, to discrimination against minorities, to that kind of capitalism of which there is and always has been numerous examples on different places on the globe."[442] Thus we have gotten used to the eternal return of headlines using the concept of "predator capitalism" – and not unjustly.

But why is the hope for a universal law that ensures a harmonic coexistence repeatedly disappointed? Japanese philosophy gives us a simple answer: this hope itself is simply ungrounded. For the universal always just shows itself as a (mental) abstraction of our activities in the world. (4.3.3) Because it is an outcome of action, it cannot logically precede action as an ordering principle. Even a divine law may not stand wholly outside the world and from this standpoint set limits to egoism . It is not this "which wholly presses down on and exceeds individuals and cuts their roots."[443] Rather, it is itself a part of the creative world; thus creating and created equally.

How difficult it is to maintaining the position that the law stands as it were outside of the world can be seen in Smith. For he concedes that actions can factually disturb the predetermined order:

> "The perfection of police, the extension of trade and manufactures, are noble and magnificent objects. The contemplation of them pleases us, and we are interested in whatever can tend to advance them. They make part of the great system of government, and the wheels of the political machine seem to move with more harmony and ease by means of them. We take pleasure in beholding the perfection of so beautiful and grand a system, and we are uneasy till we remove any obstruction that can in the least disturb or encumber the regularity of its motions."[444]

A law has ordered all things, but this ordering can be distorted. The course of things may perhaps be planned, but the actual course can deviate from this plan. It is not the invisible hand of God, which helps the order back to its path, but human action itself. We – according to Smith – lay aside the obstacles. People shape the empowering governance, trade and manufacture, in order to guide them to the 'right' path. It is merely an arbitrary option to say that this formative act is re-defined through a higher order. Rather it is pretty plain that an order independent of human shaping may well be postulated, but not conceived without inconsistency. We find that

---

[442] K.-H. Brodbeck, *Erfolgsfaktor Kreativität*, 34-35.
[443] K. Nishitani, "Vom Wesen der Begegnung," 263.
[444] A. Smith, *Theory of Moral Sentiments*, 216.

the maxim here, that human power may lead to an order other than the divinely sanctioned one, is particularly significant. Our (egoistical) freedom may rebel against the invisible hand and creatively destroy its ordering power. It is a formative principle that cannot be limited from the outside:

> "No subordination under the universal can completely drain the freedom of the 'I' in individual persons. The freedom, that is released from the network of the universal can become, in its resistance, the freedom of the unlawful... The holiness of divine law may not hold up against human self-seeking – and the person, turning his back on God, can easily be seduced by Satan."[445]

Thus we may not count on egoistical freedom being so completely subordinate to a universal law that finally a stable order results. "The stronger ... the freedom of the individual grows, the more the unity of the law is disturbed up to the point of decay. This shows itself, for instance, in the tendency of liberalism to anarchy, which is nothing other than a intensified state of nature."[446] But this also means that the freedom of the many cannot completely come to pass. For there will always be people in such an anarchy who are relativized up to the point of losing their very existences.

4.7 The State and Its Relationship to the Market

In the last section we clarified why just pain and confusion, rather than a stable order, grows out of the coexistence of egoists. This position does go against that advocated by Adam Smith and the other political economists, who all postulate a harmony of interests. But it would be false to maintain that we are really expressing a new insight. For the inherent instability of a world, in which each perceives himself as being opposed to everybody else is also a central theme for economic theory. So for instance modern economic research shows how irrational cooperative behavior is, because it is always exposed to the danger that others will profit from it without paying a cost. Because it is to each person's advantage to act egoistically if everybody else is behaving purely cooperatively, all efforts at peaceful coexistence are regularly dashed into pieces. This is known as the problem of the free-rider.[447] But skepticism concerning the peaceful coexistence of egoists is considerably older. Thus, Hobbes already draws a very negative picture of mankind: the struggle of all against all is never overcome purely

---

[445] K. Nishitani, "Vom Wesen der Begegnung," 261.
[446] Ibid., 263.
[447] See for example G. Kirchgässner, *Homo oeconomicus*, 56.

by the force of the egoists. Without a "general power holding them all in check," people's lives are condemned to be lonely, poor, nasty, brutish, and short."[448] Without "higher level rules," no market economy is able to guarantee a total regulation of social life," as Müller-Armack formulates the idea.[449] The skepticism that East Asian philosophy brings to egoism is thus shared by many economists.

As we are going to show, in spite of commonalties between the two above mentioned kinds of thought, significant distinctions remain with regard to the question of whether the negative consequences of egoism can be effectively combated. In one part of economics, this answer to this question is, yes. Since the invisible hand of the market mechanism is impotent, the current argument goes, a substitute has to be made with the "visible hand" of an economic leader or form of governance. It is a matter of ennobling the primitive society of barter into a consciously shaped commercial order.[450] On this account, there is little doubt that the state will take on that task. The latter must compel the order, since it can't voluntarily or spontaneously emerge from egoistical activity. When all individuals are subject to its laws, their peaceful co-existence is guaranteed, in spite of or even because of their egoism. This belief on the ductility of egoism is seen by Japanese philosophy as a delusion. For according to its view, the state only represents just another form of an (abstract) universal that is posited against the individual and through its laws mediates individuals in their interactions. With the help of this argument we will show that the state, as little as the market, represents a context independent substance that from the outside can make individuals into a unity. This substance, instead, just proves itself to be one more of the economic world's universal directions, which as little as the market can effectively limit egoistical freedom. Instead, the state faces that freedom in an indissoluble opposition; an opposition, in which both poles are mutually strengthened, but equally threaten to annihilate one another. The taming of the struggle of all against all through a constraining force shows itself, by reason of this opposition, just as much an illusion as the belief in a mechanical order. What follows from this conclusion is interesting, since it makes clear that from the viewpoint of Japanese philosophy we have to give up on the idea that either the market or the state can provide an explanation for the co-existence of the many.

---

[448] Hobbes, *Leviathan*, Book 1, Chapter 13.
[449] A. Müller-Armack, "Wirtschaftslenkung und Marktwirtschaft," in: A. Kruse (ed.), *Nationalökonomie*, 279.
[450] Ibid., 275.

While the conflict between different trends in economics (particularly in macro-economics) is mostly carried out within the dichotomy between the private in the sense of markets and the public in the sense of the state, Japanese philosophy reminds us of an alternative beyond this dichotomy.

4.7.1 The State as a Context Independent Universal

"Where subordination to the universal has not been able to completely drain the freedom of the 'I' in individual persons, the excited universal will realize equality by means of totally strangling the individual's freedom," Nishitani writes.[451] This idea of being able to choke or bind egoism finds its expression in economics in the concept of the state and its law. Insofar as the destructive force of self-interest is not only tied down through the conflict of egoists in the market, it is canalized through rules that are in the last resort even put in place against the individual through coercion. The egoists are attached to "artificial chains"[452] in order to keep them from completely destroying one another. I am not going to offer a complete overview of the idea of the state in economics here, but instead merely want to draw attention to an important parallel between this thought and the concept of the market mechanism. The parallels lies in the tendency to think of the state, as well as of the market, as a universal in the sense of a context independent substance, to whose lawfulness the individual is subject even up to the point of negating his private determination.

Hobbes believed, for instance, that he recognized an 'artificial man' in the state, who is created in order to secure the freedom and self preservation of people.[453] When the multiple egoists all bow their heads to the same master, they can live in common without giving themselves over to fighting. They can act egoistically within the framework of the law, but in the face of the law they have "nothing to do but to obey."[454] For here "the norms are given and confront them with unconditional claims."[455] The laws are seen as universally valid in the sense that they are held as binding on everyone. All people are equally subject to them. In this regard, the unique-

---

[451] K. Nishitani, "Vom Wesen der Begegnung," 262.
[452] T. Hobbes, *Leviathan*, book 1, chapter 16.
[453] Ibid.
[454] I. Kant cited in J. Hirschberger, *Geschichte der Philosophie*, 199.
[455] K. Homann, "Sinn und Grenze der ökonomischen Methode in der Wirtschaftsethik," 15.

ness of people is lost; they are so to speak reduced to a cog in the state machine.[456]

Egoism is limited by the universal, binding relation of the individual to the law. The power of each single individual is limited to the extent that nobody can destroy anybody else. "Each limits his will in order that there remains a play space for freedom."[457] Through this limitation a peaceful coexistence should be guaranteed without erasing the egoistical struggle of people with each other. Egoistical freedom against one's neighbor is preserved. For "where the sovereign has prescribed no rule, the subject possesses the freedom to act according to his own lights."[458] The individual is free in his intercourse with other people, but is completely unfree in the face of the law. Her private determination is negated against the law, her autonomy and independence surrendered. The freedom to be able to proceed with her egoistical interests against her neighbor is purchased through her absolute submission to the universally valid law. Accordingly, we can think of this merely as an "individualistic freedom under the law."[459] There is a point beyond which the individual's freedom cannot go.[460]

Next to the subjection of the individual to the law, another important mark of the state is that it is thought of as context independent, just like the mechanism of the market. Especially, it is conceived as independent from any social context. "The state stands sovereign, and even absolute over its subjects."[461] It is "a centralized, unified, and omnipotent apparatus of rule which stands above the society and governs it through the enactment and administration of laws."[462] The state guarantees human interaction through its law and thus provides the basis of society. Thus the state acts as the presupposition of society and not as its product. Hobbes makes this idea unmistakably clear: humans, standing in continual struggle with each other,

---

[456] See K.-H. Brodbeck for the idea of the state as a machine. In: *Die fragwürdigen Grundlagen der Ökonomie*, 37.
[457] J. Hirschberger, *Geschichte der Philosophie*, 196. Hirschberger is referring here to T. Hobbes.
[458] T. Hobbes, *Leviathan*, 170.
[459] F. Böhm cited in E.E. Nawroth, *Die Sozial- und Wirtschaftsphilosophie des Neoliberalismus*, 95.
[460] K. Nishitani, "Vom Wesen der Begegnung," 262.
[461] J. Hirschberger, *Geschichte der Philosophie*, 196. Hirschberger is referring here to Hobbes.
[462] J. Weintraub, "The Theory und Politics of the Public/Private Distinction," in: J. Weintraub, K. Kumar (ed.), *Public and Private in Thought and Practise*, 11.

finally agree upon a covenant by which everyone submits to a sovereign. This contract provides the basis of society. Hobbes "doesn't seem to distinguish state and society in order not to make political authority dependent upon some previous existence of social life, but instead, conversely, to show it as constitutive of the latter."[463] The state is seen as a pre-given unity, to which every individual is related on the basis of his unconditioned obedience to the rules. The person faces the state in original solitude. Only through the individual's relation to the state can individuals be related to others and join a community. The subjection of the individual to the state is thought of, accordingly, as providing the basis of society. This goes along with the thought that the state itself is independent from all social conditions:

> "'For the first time the absolute individual faces the absolute state,' writes J.N. Figgis of the era following the Reformation. The state becomes a quantity separated from society. In the Middle Ages, the social and political relations constituted one unified system of connections, as with the Greeks. Now a person stands in his relationship to the state simply as a subject, and no longer as an element in a web of social relationships united through the complexities of higher and lower ranking. A person does not relate to the economic order by means of his well defined status in an interconnected whole of unions and guilds, but simply as someone having the legal power to make contracts."[464]

The state forms society when it administers the actions of individuals. In so far as it correctly formulates and enacts the rules, it can produce almost any social outcome. The invisible hand of the market is replaced by a conscious steering or guiding of the state's own visible hand. The state possesses an advantage against the market in that it can compel its desired result. The faith in a spontaneous order is replaced by the hope for the law as a matter of "compulsive exterior measures," the state as an "exterior institution,"[465] which through the monopoly of coercion can, in the last instance, require obedience to its orders.[466]

---

[463] A. MacIntyre, *Geschichte der Ethik im Überblick*, 128.
[464] Ibid., 119.
[465] J. Hirschberger, *Geschichte der Philosophie*, 352. Hirschberger is referring here to Kant.
[466] R. Zintl, "Wirtschaft im Spannungsfeld von Staat und Gesellschaft," in: W. Korff, *Handbuch der Wirtschaftsethik*, Vol. 1, 781.

4.7.2 The Interdependence of the State and Individual Calculation

But why can the individual do nothing other than obey the laws? Why can economists presuppose a validation of state laws that approaches that of natural laws and guarantees, likewise, a calculability and regularity of conduct? The idea of coercion is important here. We obey the rules because "they are enforced by the sanction of the sovereign."[467] Yet this coercion must obviously be of a totally other kind than, for instance, the gravity that applies to the apple when it falls from the tree. For while the apple cannot defend itself against the power of natural law, the validity of the laws of the state remain relative to the free will of individuals. A man can reject any law, even if he must pay for this rejection with his death. If a person has no fear of death, then he isn't going to be moved when he is threatened with death, as Lao Tzu, for instance, objected to the idea that one could totally determine actions through coercion.[468] Watsuji emphasizes that actions are free in principle relative to the laws of the state. The concept of compulsion, according to Watsuji, already carries inside it the possibility of rebellion. Unless individuals are able to revolt against society, there is no possibility of coercion.[469] One can shape the laws in such a way that such revolt is improbable; but it cannot be totally excluded.

But what makes obedience to the law at the very least plausible? According to Watsuji, it is an interior coercion that permits persons to follow the law. "Coercion, even though being coercion from the outside, nonetheless, is self-coercion arising out of the individual's fundamental source."[470] Such a self-coercion is implicitly thought of in economics when a specific desire is presupposed as given and thus for the individual, opaque. This idea, too, leads us back to Hobbes, since he saw the obedience to the law as universally valid, "because our desires are of a kind such that we prefer to obey the sovereign in order to escape death by the hands of some other person."[471] The individual considers whether following a rule offers him advantages or not. People want to subjugate themselves to the law "insofar as they all have advantages from it."[472] Or to say it the other way around:

---

[467] A. MacIntyre, *Geschichte der Ethik im Überblick*, 128. MacIntyre is referring here to Hobbes.
[468] Lao Tsu, *Tao Te Ching*, transl. by G. Feng, J. English, chapter 74.
[469] T. Watsuji, *Watsuji Tetsuro's Rinrigaku*, 112.
[470] Ibid., 117.
[471] A. MacIntyre, *Geschichte der Ethik im Überblick*, 128.
[472] K. Homann, "Sinn und Grenze der ökonomischen Methode in der Wirtschaftsethik," 16.

"Fear before the immediately unpleasant consequences of transgressing the law must serve as a sufficient motive to discontinue transgressing the law. Therefore, the law must be combined with a punishment for cases in which it is offended that is so constituted that it is a greater harm to the doer than the short term use that he would have gained through the unpunished transgression of the law."[473]

Any trespassing on the law, even when this presents an obvious harm, is supposed to be impossible. The free will to decide against the outcome of a benefit-harm analysis is negated, because the later (implicitly) is regarded as inevitably causing action. To Hobbes, the value preference seems to be a sufficient ground for unconditional obedience. This likewise applies to those economists who have followed the Hobbesian concept of the calculus of advantage, but have extended the concept of preference much further than the preservation of one's life. What is now preferred seems "whatever the individual may understand by 'advantages.'"[474] The Hobbesian benefit-harm analysis, in which the fear of death stands in the foreground, is translated into a universal pleasure/pain calculus. For example, Bentham makes it clear that solely the superfluity of pleasure is what forces us to obey: "In order to make us obey the rules, the single necessary motive for the social life is the pleasure that one gains as a consequence of obeying, or the pain resulting from disobeying."[475] According to Mill, our task is to make "the person desire virtue – by making him think of it in a pleasurable light, or of its absence in a painful one."[476] Obedience to the rules is thus only thought of in the horizon of shi-fei (right/wrong) judgments of more or less. (3.3.2) A calculus lies implicitly at the base of unconditioned obedience, which accepts this horizon as given and defines itself in the action field of money. Homann for instance speaks of incentives, which are supposed to make it the case that the rules are reliably followed out. The rules are binding, for they are automatically obeyed because of the incentives attached to them.[477] The concept of incentive or stimulus suggests that people react to rules in the terms of a deterministic stimulus-response mechanism and are not free to act otherwise. Action seems as causally

---

[473] M. Esfeld, *Mechanismus und Subjektivität in der Philosophie Thomas Hobbes*, 330. See for example T. Hobbes, *Lehre vom Menschen und vom Bürger*, 139.
[474] K. Homann, "Sinn und Grenze der ökonomischen Methode in der Wirtschaftsethik," 16.
[475] A. MacIntyre, *Geschichte der Ethik im Überblick*, 216.
[476] J.S. Mill, *Utilitarianism, On Liberty, and Considerations on Representative Government*, 37.
[477] K. Homann, "Sinn und Grenze der ökonomischen Methode in der Wirtschaftsethik," 14.

4 The Implicit World Picture of Economics   243

conditioned through stimuli. This can only be assumed if the manifoldness of human habits "can be conceptually neutralized through the stimulus response machinery of homo oeconomicus."[478] The rules apply as universally binding because their obedience is supposedly guaranteed as soon as their advantageous aspect is seen from the viewpoint of individual utility maximization. As soon as rules withstand the "homo-oeconomicus test" – meaning that they seem advantageous from the point of view of this calculating machine - their obedience is considered certain. As soon as laws are constituted that are "homo-oeconomicus-resistant", "they are in position to play the desired role."[479]

In this conception of obeying the rules one easily overlooks the fact that the validity of the law is (implicitly) limited, because it only counts for economic man. It not only recognizes the factualness of the homo oeconomicus, but also makes him its presupposition. This implicit reference to homo oeconomicus in the law is found in some models of game theory, in which the effect of alternative rule systems only can be weighed by the expected payouts. Here, too, utility maximization proves the implicit presupposition for the postulated value of 'game rules.' Also, a similar thing applies to Becker's thesis, which is supposed to explain the effectiveness of institutional rule systems. For Becker, obedience to the rules often only counts as assured when the players can expect a positive utility.[480] For him, a strategy that keeps criminals from their act is effective only when the costs of the punishment are higher than the utility that emerges from the acts.[481]

What we see here is that the state's laws aren't conceived independently of the individual, but instead are related to him implicitly. For their validity presupposes the individual's calculus. Not only the standpoint of normal perception and thus of egoism is thus recognized as a fact, here, as it is emphasized in economics; the undomesticated individualism that unfolds in the struggle of all against all is rather presupposed. In economic terms, the ones who obey the law are coincident with those who perceive themselves to be in opposition to everyone else and calculate individually on in-

---

[478] J. Wieland, *Ökonomische Organisation, Allokation und Status*, 57.
[479] K. Homann, "Sinn und Grenze der ökonomischen Methode in der Wirtschaftsethik," 21.
[480] G.S. Becker, "Menschliches Dasein aus ökonomischer Sicht," in: K.-D. Grüske (ed.), *Die Nobelpreisträger der ökonomischen Wissenschaft*, Vol. 3, Düsseldorf 1994, 210.
[481] G.S. Becker, *Der ökonomische Ansatz zur Erklärung menschlichen Verhaltens*, 47.

centives. The "untrammeled striving for advantage" is not only the "core of all morality", as Homann formulates it,[482] but even the presupposition for the existence of the state as lawgiver. The state should not be thought of as an independent order any more than the market is, for these reasons. Conversely, we cannot think of the economic actor without the state, as the following reflection suggests: The individual can only exist in the economic world when the power of the state guards his egoistical desires and striving from the egoism of others. Even those economists who pay little heed to the role of the state recognize that the economic actor is dependent on the enforcement of the property laws by the state. "His actions are dependent on a safeguard. The abstract property law must be made valid; and it is only valid if the claims lying within it are seen to be guarded by an exterior authority."[483]

The state and the economic actor stand in a reciprocal relation that cannot be loosened by either side. This relation can be more precisely explained if we observe both sides as possible directions of determination in the economic world. This is most easily seen by looking at the changes that come with the introduction of the money economy. (4.5.2) By way of these, the individual holds the possibility of escaping at any time the rights and duties weighing on him regarding specific other persons, as for instance the family or a tribe. The possibility of practicing coercion upon him is thus lesser. Conversely, the individual can no longer be sure that specific persons or groups will preserve his rights. Rather, he is stepping into a monetary field of action that puts him in relation with an unknown number of unknown people who he himself cannot coerce into abiding the rules. Only a universal law can guard him from their arbitrary acts. But this is only possible if the forms of activity within the economic world are abstractly safeguarded, independent of who performs them. The more independent the forms of activity become from specific groups, the stronger must be the universal enforcement of the laws. "The increase of universalization and the strengthening of coercion cannot be separated from one another."[484] The individuals can only become free from all obligations to specific other people if they equally bow to the coercion of the universal law. They subject themselves to the universally valid rules in order to be able to perceive themselves in opposition to any specific other person. This may sound

---

[482] K. Homann, "Sinn und Grenze der ökonomischen Methode in der Wirtschaftsethik," 37.
[483] K.-H. Brodbeck, *Die fragwürdigen Grundlagen der Ökonomie*, 222.
[484] T. Watsuji, *Watsuji Tetsuro's Rinrigaku*, 108.

paradoxical, but the subjection of all to the universal law of the state actually strengthens the feeling of individual freedom. For this subjection liberates the individual from all specific obligations to any specific other person. State authority and the individual (freed from all specific bonds) are reciprocally dependent on each other, as the following reflection of Simmel's makes clear:

> "The technically refined character of legal concepts is firstly constructed as the correlate of that abstract individualism that goes hand in hand with the money economy. Prior to the time that Roman law was adopted in Germany – at the same time that the money economy was also adopted – German law had the concept neither of representation in legal affairs, nor the concept of the juristic person, nor of property as an object of individual will but only as a representative of rights and obligations. A legal system that operates with such concepts is no longer possible once the individual has been separated from his fusion with the particular conditions of possession, social position, and of the material contents of existence and has become completely free and self-reliant, and yet has become conceptually divorced from all specific existential tendencies that belong to the money economy."[485]

This implies that the state and the economic actor are mutually conditioned within the monetary field of action. In this way, "the recovery of the notion of sovereignty [happens] to complement the notion of the atomistic liberal individual."[486] Both are mutually interrelated in the economic world; they can only be thought of in tandem. The individual in itself doesn't exist. In his striving for power and riches, he is immediately dependent on the safeguarding by the state. "Individualism ... does not exclude but on the contrary demands the supremacy of the state over the individual."[487] And also – the state 'in itself', i.e. as a self-sufficient, independent entity is "nothing more than a mere legal construction."[488] We can make an analogy here to the relation of the individual to the market mechanism: Individual and universal mutually condition and strengthen one another. The stronger the individual conceives herself as an individual personality, the more irrevocably becomes the thought of a super-powerful, universal coercive authority, mediating the interactions of the many. And vice versa: the more powerful the universal law becomes, the stronger becomes the individual's sense of herself as an individual personality, since it makes it possible for her to

---

[485] Simmel, *Philosophy of Money*, 334.
[486] J. Weintraub, "The Theory and Politics of the Public/Private Distinction," 13.
[487] C.B. MacPherson, *The Political Theory of Possessive Individualism*, 256. MacPherson is referring here to Locke.
[488] T. Watsuji, *Watsuji Tetsuro's Rinrigaku*, 25.

untie herself from every specific relation. Both standpoints, methodological individualism and the state, overlook this mutual dependency. They neglect the economic world as that locus out of which emerges both directions of determination at the same time. This world can thus not unfold from merely one of the standpoints. It subsists, rather, as a place of nothingness. This reflection points to the fact that neither the law of the state nor the mechanism of the market can be regarded as constitutive for the economic world. The economic world is presupposed by the concept of both the market and the state, rather than resulting from them.

4.7.3 The Inherent Contradiction of the State's Coercive Authority

But if we shouldn't think of the state as an independent magnitude, can its laws still enforce a harmonious co-existence of egoists? Can the state practically stabilize a system of institutional rules and normatively apply them? Japanese philosophy makes us see a problem that is tied in with this idea. The problem lies in "the inherent contradiction nestled within the universal."[489] In order for everyone to be subject to the same law, there must necessarily be a conflict between them, they must be dominated by the struggle of all against all. The normal perception of the economic world is presupposed here, in which each sees himself opposed to everybody else. The law presupposes fear of other people's striving for power. One subjects oneself, for this reason only, to the power of the sovereign, as Hobbes makes clear, because it guarantees protection against other people's power. But this guarantee would be quite superfluous if the power of other people presented no threat, for instance because one trusted them. The Hobbesian logic also excludes the possibility that some may not fear other's power and may make an alliance with it. For this threatens the universality of the law and thus the universal order erected by the state. Yet not only are we supposed to presuppose fear of others, but also the striving for individual advantage. For state power rests only the fact that every person is acting according to their own calculus. Only the striving for individual betterment guarantees the enactment of an incentive-compatible set of laws. But if, on the contrary, the individual's cost-benefit calculation is broken in two, this notion of planification and governance must be given up.

The effectiveness of the law rests on each thinking of himself as free and independent from all others, just as he sees his fellow humans as free and

---

[489] E. Gallu, "Sunyata, Ethics, and Authentic Interconnectedness," 192.

independent.[490] "One's self-awareness and autonomy are affirmed by recognizing the autonomy of the other."[491] At first, such recognition seems positive. But it rests on our normal perception and thus on the fundamental separation of the I and the thou, the ego and the other. It "creates a stance of opposition whereby one consciously distinguishes between the two and thus we find manifest a spirit of division rather than connectedness."[492] Or to speak more clearly: the notion of state authority presupposes the natural state of the struggle of all against all. The state uses egoism to create order.

The contradiction in the universal validity of the laws lies in the state presupposing an egoism, on the one side, that it is at the same time threatened by, on the other. As long as we look at the state as being independent from the economic world, this threat doesn't even swim into view. Its laws seem to be able to lead egoism without itself being influenced by egoism. Japanese philosophy looks at this idea as a delusion. For it, every universal is not only creative, but at the same time created; it is shaped by the activities of the many just as much as it shapes them. (4.4.1) The following reflections show that something speaks for such an idea: State law not only governs egoism in the world of economics, it is also formed from this same egoism. Egoism is not only an instrument of the state, in order to compel an order. Rather, the laws of the state threaten to become themselves a means to express egoistical interests. The lawgiver, for instance, can misuse her power for her own ends and harm others.[493] We can illustrate this danger in an example given by Baruzzi: Commercial egoism often enough determines in modern society what the law in general is supposed to mean. The interests of business, for instance, become a fact that is not formed by the law, but instead forms the laws:

> "The law can grasp and normativize that which in commerce, technology and science corresponds to our human sense of right. But this is rarely the case. Looking at decisions regarding fraud in commerce, we have to concede that the state of the law's decisions corresponds only to the views of the commercial class. Literally. It is said that only that can be subjected to legal norms, which does not endanger the 'functioning of business.' We could cite a pile of similar formulations. The law is

---

[490] J. Hirschberger, *Geschichte der Philosophie*, 216.
[491] E. Gallu, "Sunyata, Ethics, and Authentic Interconnectedness," 190. Gallu is referring here to Kant.
[492] Ibid. Gallu is here referring to Nishitani.
[493] T. Hobbes, *Lehre vom Menschen und vom Bürger*, 143.

hardly a gadfly... We must admit, that technology and commerce actually determine the law, and not vice versa."[494]

Often, the law cannot set bounds to egoism, but is itself put into the service of the individual striving for riches. The state cannot represent, for this reason, an autonomous guiding power. Rather, its elbowroom for action is formed by the conflict of egos. In the global competition of interests we can sharpen this formula still more, for here every national code of law threatens to become simply an object of individual calculation. It is reduced, for instance, in the global competition for business locations to a mere cost factor, appears only as a variable in the calculation of the entrepreneur. The discussion about the competitiveness of states shows how very much the state and its law itself has become a 'creator that is equally created.' Thus, the code of law cannot form a stable basis from which the state could forecast or manipulate egoistic actions. We can apply essentially the same argument here that we mounted against the calculability of the economic world before. (4.4.2) In particular, the state cannot prognosticate how the egoists will react to its code of laws. Only one thing is certain, and that is that they will find ways either to get around the laws or break them if this promises them some advantage. Egoism creatively reacts to every law and thus is always bringing about consequences that the legislator has not suspected. In this way the given order is continually threatened with turbulence and the intended order is never achieved.

Our previous reflections show, that the state doesn't possess the resources to absorb egoism. Rather, both sides mutually condition each other. The order of the state is continually threatened with turbulence by egoism; but it cannot wholly stifle egoism, because it presupposes the striving for individual advantage. The state is equally endangered by and dependent on egoism. This contradiction is the reason that it is an illusion to believe that the state can really dominate egoism and guide the struggle of all against all along stable pathways. This conclusion ought not to be taken to mean that all of the state's regulations should be undone. Nor should Japanese philosophy be interpreted as going in this direction.[495] But it does sink

---

[494] A. Baruzzi, *Freiheit, Recht und Gemeinwohl*, 205-206. Baruzzi refers to Maus for further examples of legislation being influenced by economic interests. I. Maus, "Verrechtlichung, Entrechtlichung und der Funktionswandel von Institutionen," in: G. Göhler (ed.), *Grundfragen der Theorie politischer Institutionen*, Opladen 1987, 188-203.

[495] Gallu, for example, refers to Nishitani's philosophy in this connection. See: "Sunyata, Ethics, and Authentic Interconnectedness," 191.

those hopes that are invested in the state's guidance and planning. "Even the authority of the state's laws cannot make perfectly white sheep out of 'wolves,'" Nishitani reflects. Egoism and the state stubbornly wrestle with each other and thus mutually strengthen each other, without the state finally being able to win the upper hand. "The more rules and regulations, the more thieves and robbers," as Lao Tzu said.[496] This contradiction can't be resolved without risking a collapse of human interaction. For if egoistical freedom wins the upper hand, the struggle of all against all would be unchained; but if, on the contrary, the state gains absolute might, freedom would be totally strangled and the coexistence of all would be subject to arbitrary dictates of the few. If we want to avoid both of these extremes and still maintain a firm notion of egoism and the universal order, we necessarily oscillate between "totalitarianism and anarchy ... Totalitarianism carries in itself the possibility of immediately changing into anarchy and vice versa. And the tendencies to one or the other are all tangled up between and within both poles."[497]

The tendency to such entanglement conditions the fact that egoism is, one the one hand, often admired, while there equally arises the loud cry for the state to stamp it out, on the other. Both attitudes are united in the normal perception in a contradictory fashion. They wrestle with each other in the economic world and do more to mutually strengthen each other than they could do to extinguish each other. This is how MacIntyre describes this struggle with regard to American society:

> "Unacknowledged incoherence is the hallmark of this contemporary developing American self, a self whose public voice oscillates between phases not merely of toleration, but of admiration of ruthlessly self-serving behavior and phases of high moral dudgeon and indignation at exactly the same behavior, a self which remarkably often no longer sees incoherence in the promises of its political leaders as a disabling fault. And this is perhaps unsurprising in a moral culture in which radically individualist modes of thought and action are both systematically practiced and praised and yet also systematically put into question, and in which both the practice and praise on the one hand and the systematic questioning on the other are functional prerequisites for a social and economic system in which the self-interested

---

[496] Lao Tsu, *Tao Te Ching*, chapter 57. See also chapter 30: "Whenever you advise a ruler in the way of Tao, counsel him not to use force to conquer the universe. For this would only cause resistance."

[497] K. Nishitani, "Vom Wesen der Begegnung," 263. Nishitani adds: "We understand totalitarianism and anarchy not simply as political types, but also as categories that apply in general to the phenonomenological regions of human interaction."

acquisitiveness of the marketplace needs to be complemented by the kind of cooperativeness that keeps markets in being, and in which the destructive self-expression of those individuals whose overriding priority is their own personal growth and satisfaction is contained, and the wounds deriving from it are healed, by loyalties to just those institutional forms whose disciplines and constraints are in another guise barriers to what is taken to be creative self-expression."[498]

Japanese philosophy takes up a skeptical position here vis-à-vis such a contradictory self-perception, as much as it also does against the idea of a state that is supposed to bring about the universal rules of behavior by force. This observation may surprise some, because it is often taken as a given that in East Asian societies only individualism is little valued and the state or the collective is looked upon favorably. Yet this impression is deceptive, in so far as the state and collective are conceived of as self-sufficient, exterior powers to which unique human relations are sacrificed in favor of universal rules of conduct. A state, as Watsuji, for instance, believes, which leaves no elbow room for differentiated, situatively conditioned, spontaneous encounters, merely represents "a defective form of solidarity." For "any form of living solidarity here only becomes visible as an abstraction of its authentic qualities, and the communal character becomes a narrow, unified system, that no longer recognizes distinctions between light and shadow. Every form of solidarity here can only find its expression in a law, and responsibility and duty can only be enacted through coercion."[499] The problem, Nishitani adds, lies in the idea of a universal which, in the way persons encounter it, promoted through unyielding rules of conduct, stifles the space for the uniquely varied encounters of persons among themselves, for spontaneous responsibility and sympathy:

> "The universal is problematic for Nishitani, ... for ... our absoluteness in the sense of sheer uniqueness or suchness is lost to an interchangeability – an homogenized equality that dilutes our authentic autonomy. ... Nishitani seems to suggest ... that whether equality is the product of a totalitarian enforcement or democratic doctrine, such equality, in either case, rules out individual uniqueness in favor of a conforming mediocrity. ... Whether God or political ideology, Nishitani cautions against the ancillary relationship between self and universal saying that '...where interhuman relationships are subordinate to such universals with the result that equality and freedom accompany one another in their completeness, no authentic encounter be-

---

[498] A. MacIntyre, "Individual and Social Morality in Japan and the United States," 492-93.
[499] T. Watsuji, *Watsuji Tetsuro's Rinrigaku*, 25.

tween human beings is possible ... The original character of man's encounter with man is hidden by laws, be they civil, moral or divine.'"[500]

"Ritual is the husk of faith and loyalty, the beginning of confusion," as Lao Tzu stated long ago,[501] rejecting the idea of guidance through the state's laws. A rejection that is shared by many classical Chinese philosophers, as Hall and Ames reveal:

> "It is a rejection of the disingenuous in its most obvious and common form, where one's authentic expression is subordinated to and disciplined by abstract regulations. Government so defined distracts the rulers from their natural inclinations through unhealthy attachments to wealth and fortune, and prevents the flourishing of the ruled through oppressive, dehumanizing laws and regulations."[502]

It isn't the concrete content or verbiage of the laws that is problematic from the viewpoint of East Asian philosophy. Upham affirms that the Japanese idea of right and law rejects abstract rules as the measure for social action, not because of the content of a specific rule, but instead because the abstract nature of these rules as well as their formal and rational enactment are abominable in themselves.[503] East Asian philosophy centers on the insight that "almost all of the actual rights and duties that the sociopolitical order promotes are sustained by extralegal institutions and practices, and are enforced by social pressure rather than punishments."[504] A solidarity that is limited to obedience to the law cannot long endure. It becomes a dead matter, because it is not filled with any concrete connectedness to life.[505] And more than this: the state's law subverts precisely that cooperative and communal human activity that its enactment immediately relies upon:

> "In fact, reliance upon the application of law, far from being a means of realizing human dignity, is fundamentally dehumanizing, impoverishing as it does, the possibilities of mutual accommodation, and compromising our particular responsibility to define what would be appropriate conduct."[506]

---

[500] E. Gallu, "Sunyata, Ethics and Authentic Interconnectedness," 191.
[501] Lao Tsu, *Tao Te Ching*, chapter 38.
[502] D.L. Hall, R.T. Ames, *Thinking from the Han*, 173-74.
[503] F. Upham, *Law and Social Change in Postwar Japan*, Cambridge (Mass.) 1987, 207-208.
[504] D.L. Hall, R.T. Ames, *Thinking from the Han*, 284.
[505] T. Watsuji, *Watsuji Tetsuro's Rinrigaku*, 25.
[506] D.L. Hall, R.T. Ames, *Thinking from the Han*, 284.

4.7.4 The Conflict of the Market and the State

The skepticism of East Asian philosophy regarding any kind of universal that promotes binding people to rules of action hides a further interesting aspect: that of the relationship of the market and the state or of the private and the public sector. While it is usual in economics to rely either on the invisible hand of the market or on the visible hand of the state, Watsuji in particular makes us notice that both ideas of order cannot be separated from each other. These are merely two directions of abstraction of the same economic world, in which they reciprocally condition each other.

The distinction of public and private is one of the Western thought's 'great dichotomies.' While this dichotomy is variously filled with wholly different contents, it is usual described in economics with the help of the opposition between the market and the state or the state's law.[507] Behind this opposition is hidden a very old conflict, which has lead to bitter intensity as much in economic theory as in political economics. The conflict turns on the question whether it is the state or the market that safeguards the social order. A question, to which the classical economists have already given both possible answers:

> "Locke and Adam Smith on the one hand, Hobbes and Bentham on the other, might be taken as the most distinguished representatives of the two poles...: the side that leans toward a 'natural' harmonization of selfish interests, whose grand theoretical achievement is the theory of the market; and the more technocratic, social-engineering side, which posits the need for a coercive agency standing above society (epitomized by Hobbes's Leviathan) that maintains order by manipulating the structure of rewards and punishments within which individuals pursue their 'rational' interests. ... The 'invisible hand' of the market and ... the 'visible hand' of administrative regulations recur as the two key solutions."[508]

I don't wish to dwell on the conflict of both of these solutions within economics, but instead point to one of their commonalties: "Both sides are operating within a common universe of discourse, drawing different conclusions from the same premises."[509] One such premise lies hidden in the fact that both sides implicitly presuppose the economic world as a given. For both sides base their reflections on the monetary field of action. A further

---

[507] J. Weintraub, "The Theory and Politics of the Public/Private Distinction", 1. Weintraub borrwos the term "grand dichotomy" from N. Bobbio.
[508] Ibid., 9.
[509] Ibid., 8.

premise consists in the fact that the economic world is considered as being ruled by a universal law. The proponents of the market side think that the quasi-natural regularity of a spontaneous order will transform action into a mechanically calculable process. The proponents of the state, on the contrary, believe in a consciously shaped order, that assures, through the compatibility of incentives, the certainty of expectation in regard to activities.[510] In both cases, we are asked to think of a universal absolutely over or beyond human interaction that can causally make a social order. In this way, the conflict has to logically happen. For if something is causally responsible for a result, then there can't be a second cause next to it. Thus, for instance, when the market is recognized as a quasi-natural mechanism that rules over the market, a second ruling principle can't exist next to it. Its absoluteness endures no further absolute near it. Just as the idea of mechanism doesn't allow for any absolutely independent individuals, but negates them, so, too, it also doesn't endure a further, self-sufficient universal near it. It is small wonder then, when the market's disciples seek to destroy the arguments of the state's – and vice versa. The problem lies in the notion of conceiving the market or the state as entities and wanting to identify them, as such. If one accordingly forgets the context in which both equally exist, they absolutely contradict one another.

But how can our thought do equal justice to the market and the state? Relations in the economic world can be distinguished between those that are voluntary and those that are coerced. Trade and exchange are to be named as the primary voluntary relations, or more basically the exchange of commodities and information. The individuals freely coordinate their activities (at least formally), because they promise themselves an advantage by doing so. Since the existence of one agent doesn't endanger the existence of another agent, a common existence seems possible. The 'unity' of the many arises, consequently, in a peaceful fashion. It is this property of relations that is generalized in the theory of the market into a social ordering principle. As Friedman writes:

> "Exchange can ... bring out co-ordination without coercion. A working model of society organized through voluntary exchange is a free private enterprise exchange economy – what we have been calling competitive capitalism."[511]

---

[510] On the difference between spontaneous and consciously designed order, Hayek is particularly emphatic. F.A. Hayek, *Recht, Gesetzgebung und Freiheit*, Vol. 1, 58.
[511] M. Friedman, *Capitalism and Freedom*, 13.

But the interests of the many can be fundamentally opposed, so that egoistical activities fail to form the basis for a unity, but instead simply destroy it. Only compulsion may hinder this, as the example of the free rider makes clear: The free rider seeks to profit from the community of others without making any contribution himself. If the community endures in spite of this conduct, one must force the free rider to pay some compensation. Here, it isn't the voluntary nature of the interaction, but instead the (consciously practiced) compulsion that makes possible stable, reciprocal social relations. This is the aspect that is generalized when the advocates of the state try to guarantee the social order by means of rewards and punishments.

Thus, while both sides emphasize an important aspect of social coexistence, they overlook the fact that no position can be absolutely postulated:

> "By giving heed to society as an objective fact, we can discern that these two aspects (i.e. coercion and fusion) are respectively emphasized in a one-sided way. Insofar as each of these aspects reflects an aspect of society, then these arguments cannot be said to be in error. But both of them err in their endeavor to explain society by appealing to only one aspect. Society must be understood to have these two aspects. That is to say, the communalizing and interfusing aspect of association among individuals at once indicates the existence of coercion as well."[512]

Voluntary relations presuppose the state's protection within the economic world. Freely chosen contracts for instance are safeguarded through state law against fraud. This protection is not a replacement for the voluntary signing of contracts; rather, both rely on each other mutually. Thus, the rule applies: the more general are the rules of action of freely chosen social co-existence, the more general become, too, the state's code of sanctions. For instance, voluntarily undertaken labor relationships in which no notice is given to the unique properties of the contracting parties are to be guarded by labor law that fixes universally all rights and obligations arising out of these relationships and compels their maintenance, if necessary, with state authority. Market and state condition each other here reciprocally in the claim to outline generally valid rules of action and carry them out. One commits two conceptual errors if one believes that either the market or the state, operating as an absolute universal, could exclusively define the reciprocal social formations of the many: first, this overlooks that these social formations cannot be objectified as an abstract social order that negates the private determination of the actors. (4.3.4) Second, this forgets that these

---

[512] T. Watsuji, *Watsuji Tetsuro's Rinrigaku*, 114.

social formations are equally voluntary and coerced and thus not reducible to only one of these aspects. Both errors arise because the economic world, as that context in which the market is based as well as the state, becomes a locus of nothingness. If we were to become conscious of this place, contrary to the above positions, we would recognize that market and state in spite of their oppositions are interrelated. Their opposition is a construct that never can be resolved in favor of one side, but instead is one we must continually bear with in the economic world. It is neither methodologically to be explained through a one sided emphasis on the state or the market, nor can it be organized in actuality by means of a political economy that either exclusively rests upon the arms of the coercive power of the state or upon the unconscious, invisible power of the market mechanism.

4.7.5 Ordoliberalism: A Unity of Market and State

The reciprocal dependency of the market and state upon each other is not completely overlooked in economics. Thus, ordoliberalism or the social market economy strives "to develop a framework of political economic measures that are ordered in their collective intent to support the survival of a functioning market economy." [513] To that end, we need as our basis a synthesis of state and market that "renounces conflicting forms of control in the market economy.... The union is ... possible insofar as it uses a framework for allocating control that is directed, as a total system and in every individual measure, in supporting the survival, and even the growth of the market economy."[514] The market is here identified as an order which suggests a comparison to a self-regulating mechanism.[515] The market is autonomous in regard to its function.[516] But such autonomy doesn't exist with regard to its ends. These are given, instead, through an outer frame:

> "If we conceive of the market economy as a machine producing variable calculations and signals, then it can equally be said, if we agree upon this formal definition of its nature, that this machine does not itself define the goal of the economy, but receives it as a datum. Whether we simply assume the volume of demand given through the market's distribution of income or change it through an income distributional switching mechanism is, for the calculating machine, a matter of indif-

---

[513] A. Müller-Armack, "Wirtschaftslenkung und Marktwirtschaft," 276.
[514] Ibid.
[515] Ibid., 278.
[516] See for example J. Wieland, *Ökonomische Organisation, Allokation und Status*, 54.

ference. Seen from this point of view, it is a formal process, which can function in the most different social frames."[517]

Here, the market represents no "total regulation of social life"[518] because it doesn't determine the goal of the economy. Rather, such a total order is now conceived as the coordinated play of the market and the state. The state specifies the goal of the economy; the market helps to automatically apply it. While the market so to speak works as a giant calculator, in which maximizing utility or profit causally determines activities, the state manipulates the conditions serving this machine so that in the end we receive the state's wished for results. MacPherson intuitively describes how we can imagine this:

> "What the state does thereby is to alter some of the terms of the equations each man makes when he is calculating his most profitable course of action. But this need not affect the mainspring of the system, which is that men do calculate their most profitable course and do employ their labour, skill, and resources as that calculation dictates. Some of the data for their calculations is changed, but prices are still set by competition between the calculators. The prices are different from what they would be in a less controlled system, but as long as prices still move in response to the decisions of the individual competitors and the prices still elicit the production of goods and determine their allocation, it remains a market system. The state may, so to speak, move the hurdles in advantage of some kinds of competitors, or may change the handicaps, without discouraging racing."[519]

Economic calculation, the 'mechanics' of economic activity, is instrumentalized by the state, which applies chiefly to social goal setting. The social state can shape the consequences of market activity in a more socially conciliatory fashion without disturbing the mechanism. It can for instance through its law produce better outcome positions for the weaker or give stronger inducements not to wholly crush the existence of the weak. Competition is not thereby erased; it is merely manipulated from the outside. In economics the metaphor of the game is used to describe the logic of such an economic system.[520] The moves of the game symbolize the actions that are strictly based upon economic calculation. Each individual player struggles for the best possible position, in order to gain power and the prospect

---

[517] A. Müller-Armack, "Wirtschaftslenkung und Marktwirtschaft," 279.
[518] Ibid.
[519] C.B. MacPherson, *The Political Theory of Possesive Individualism*, 58.
[520] See for example K. Homann and F. Blome-Drees, *Wirtschafts- und Unternehmensethik*, 21.

of profit. The laws are interpreted, contrarily, as general game rules to which all players are subject. They describe the strictly laid down action framework in which the game of the struggle of all against all comes to pass. Negative consequences of the game are not combated through a change of the game's moves, but exclusively through changes of the game's rules. To speak more clearly: it is as though humans were stepping on a gigantic board game among various framing conditions to compete with each other until the optimum total performance is achieved.

Even this coordinated play of the market and the state implies a universal, that combines the many into a harmonious or stable order from, so to speak, the outside. An order is presupposed that is pre-given for the economic world. This is created neither through some manifestation of divine power nor through a quasi natural mechanism. Rather, it is a product of the human will to shape it. The wheels of the market machine are not aligned by a creator into a harmonious structure, but by a social engineer, who welds it, repairs it and if necessary revamps it.

> "A consciously shaped market economy is not a complete automaton. If we wish to retain this image, which is never without its dangers, we can compare it to half automatons requiring service and control. Like an automobile motor, in itself a functioning mechanism that nevertheless requires a series of commands coming from outside in order to fulfill its end, market exchange must also depend on a circle of safeguarding and troubleshooting manipulations tailored to the peculiarities of its function. It requires certain measures to start the market exchange, corresponding to the function of bringing oxygen to the fuel mix; it requires a constant guarding of the competitive function, the regulation of its total path, which is the equivalent of lubrication and the use of the gas and the brake pedals; it requires structural regulations that correspond to the car's steering mechanism; and last but not least, the market economy, in spite of its thorough rationality, shows certain errors in construction that require periodic repair, and in part even certain constructive overhauls."[521]

Even in ordoliberalism we presuppose an independent power, which gives us the shape and goal of the economy. One could say that "although the old God dies, an old sin lives: God's erstwhile children often try to take his place. The independent existence (the aseity) traditionally ascribed to an omnipotent personal being called God can be vainly arrogated by human

---

[521] A. Müller-Armack, Wirtschaftslenkung und Marktwirtschaft, 280.

beings themselves."⁵²² But can such an independent existence really be conceived? This question is aimed at a blind spot in economic theory, which I will briefly show in some examples. For instance, in Smith, the invisible hand of God serves as the presupposition for the idea of social harmony, but equally marks "the border of all scientific intelligibility."⁵²³ It lies beyond any explanation, because it lies outside of what is humanly conceivable. For the effect of the invisible hand is "in reality ... the wisdom of God,"⁵²⁴ on account of which no rational account of it is accessible to us. (4.6.2) It can be merely believed.⁵²⁵ A similar difficulty shows itself in relation to the assumption of a worldly ruler in the form of a sovereign or state, since how are we going to prove that a benign and omniscient ruler really exists, imposing upon the struggle of egoists a social order in the interests of all? According to Hobbes, states have the right to do that which leads to their own benefit.⁵²⁶ This does not thereby say that this right actually promises benefit to those who must submit to the law:

> The sovereign "can as monarch or majority of a union proceed with violence against individual citizens or against a minority. Since by such an action its rule is not unconditionally weakened (but instead, perhaps even strengthened), Hobbes cannot condemn it generally as irrational. ... The oppression of a minority does not unconditionally provoke rebellion that endangers the rule of the sovereign. It can, on the contrary, lead to a tighter union of the majority. Furthermore, the sovereign can also preempt a rebellion by playing mighty citizens off one against the other, liquidating them one after the other, and building a strong army or secret police which he pleases through the reward of privileges. The purging of all doctrine that could shape a rebellion Hobbes himself recommends. Hobbes' philosophy of state contains neither a legal nor pragmatic guarantee that the sovereign will fulfill his functions in the interest of the survival and welfare of all citizens."⁵²⁷

Since the ruler stands over the people and is not bound by contract to them, we can apply the maxim that there is nothing else for them to do than to obey his commands.⁵²⁸ Against this, Kant objects: "This proposition is hor-

---

⁵²² S.H. Stenson, Beyond Science and Technology to Absolute Emptiness, in: T. Unno (ed.), *The Religious Philosophy of Nishitani Keiji*, 122-23.
⁵²³ P. Ulrich, Der kritische Adam Smith, 177.
⁵²⁴ A. Smith, *Theory of Moral Sentiments*, 102.
⁵²⁵ See P. Ulrich's discussion, Der kritische Adam Smith, 176.
⁵²⁶ T. Hobbes, *Leviathan*, 166.
⁵²⁷ M. Esfeld, *Mechanismus und Subjektivität in der Philosophie Thomas Hobbes*, 344-45.
⁵²⁸ J. Hirschberger, Die *Geschichte der Philosophie*, 199.

rible on general principles." Yet even for him there remains nothing more to do than to invoke as a belief that the existence of the ruler is yet for the good of all. The servant who wishes not to be obstreperous "should at least be able to assume, that his master wishes to do him no injury."[529]

Naturally, one cannot reproach ordo-liberalism with the Smithian or Hobbesian faith. But the fundamental problem remains. For the question is still not answered as to who, exactly, defines the rules of competition. Of course people should democratically decide over the rules of their common existence; an idea that goes all the way back to Locke. But it remains unclear how we are supposed to think about this. This isn't to say that the thought of democracy in itself is untenable. But from the standpoint of a theory that presupposes the normal perception as given, it remains unintelligible. For presupposing the egoistical calculation of individuals makes the necessary cooperation to shape the laws inexplicable. This already applies to participation in democratic elections, because there are no incentives for such an activity; its marginal utility is not positive. Participation in elections "is not explainable out of a selfish individual calculus."[530] In addition: egoistical calculation can "explain the relative stability of authoritarian and totalitarian regimes, but not their overthrow and even, and before all else, the emergence and flourishing of democracies."[531] The reproach "the homo oeconomicus is fundamentally unable to generate something like morality or moral rules"[532] is thus completely justified. If here, for instance, Homann argues the contrary position: "I have never observed that morality is brought about by the homo oeconomicus; but by 'humans,' who possess control over precisely the abundant spectrum of motives that are brought against me,"[533], then he actually only affirms the fundamental problem. For he himself cannot give us a picture of the human being who can theoretically conceive of such 'abundant spectrum of motives.' As long as we are fixated upon egoism as our unique theoretical explication, the assumption that those people not being motivated by egoism could agree upon a 'generally desirable rule' remains unproven. It has no real content and can be believed, in the best case, like we are to believe in the omnipotence of God or the benevolence of the sovereign ruler.

---

[529] I. Kant cited in J. Hirschberger, Die *Geschichte der Philosophie*, 199.
[530] G. Kirchgässner, *Homo oeconomicus*, 57.
[531] F. Reckling, *Interpretative Handlungsrationalität*, 156.
[532] K. Homann, Sinn und Grenze der ökonomischen Methode in der Wirtschaftsethik, 21.
[533] Ibid., 21.

From the point of view of Japanese philosophy, it isn't a question of discovering another or better idea of an absolutely independent ruler. Instead, the faith that something from outside could come to govern egoism is in principle seen through as an illusion. The hope of limiting the struggle of egoists through an exterior force or to be able to shape it into something that is for the good of all is regarded in itself as a delusion. Nishitani very clearly stated this: The infinite terror of a world of egos cannot simply be thrust aside in "the renunciation of the opposing sides being imposed by something from outside."[534] Every effort aiming at releasing the suffering of people, which lies in the daily reality of their absolute opposition, through reference to a pre-given universal, "seems like trying to scratch your feet through the soles of your shoes."[535]

4.7.6 Excursus: The Standpoint of the Social Scientist

I want to close this section with a few thoughts about the standpoint of the social scientist. In the East Asian denial of the idea of a universal that absolutely rules the many there is a hint not only of a critique of the explanatory schema of economic methodology, but also of the self-understanding of the economist. Many economists want to explain the world in order to help it realizing its potential. They are concerned to produce an "explanation aimed at social shaping."[536] Thus there emerges in many cases the impression that the economist is an omniscient social engineer, who cannot only see through to the mechanisms of the economic machine, but also promote himself as builder and director of this machine. It seems as though the economist stood as if he were outside the world and watched its development from this position. The economy acts like a "game, for which the political economist develops the rules."[537] Now whether the economist wants to set aside all obstacles that hinder the perfect motion of the state machine's wheels, or wants to enact a regulatory system desired by all sides, he always seems to come from outside to be able to shape the economic world.

Clearly, the economist's status is hard to explain without losing oneself in contradictions. I want to sketch out this problem with the help of a ques-

---

[534] K. Nishitani, Vom Wesen der Begegnung, 259.
[535] Ibid., 260.
[536] K. Homann, Sinn und Grenze der ökonomischen Methode in der Wirtschaftsethik, 23.
[537] A. Kyrer, Neue Politische Ökonomie 2005, München-Wien 2001, 7.

tion: does the economist's image of homo oeconomicus, presupposing the egoistical standpoint of normal perception, encompass the economist himself? If we affirm this question we must concede that the economist acts in a self-interested and egoistical manner. But if this is the case, why trust him any more than any other of the egoists? Why should one rely on his knowledge and leave it to him to undertake the shaping of the economic world? But if we say that the economist is not stuck in the normal perception, another problem results. For in this case the economist can't explain his own standpoint, because his theory doesn't outline any other than the normal perception. The social scientist – as a real, existing person – finds himself outside of his own theoretical structure. Here we are confronted with an "unbridgeable divide between the philosopher (social scientist – SG) and his own system; an aporia seems to exist here in so far as the idea itself as the result of cognitive activity cannot encompass the cognitive activity itself."[538] While "science ... seems to regard its own scientific standpoint as a position of unquestionable truth,"[539] this divide represents for Nishida a central problem that makes the scientific statement simply untrustworthy.[540] This means, applied to economics, that the attitude of many economists (who presuppose as given the struggle of all against all, but don't explicitly position themselves in this struggle) gives us a reason to take a very cautious attitude in confronting their theoretical and political economic knowledge.

For East Asian philosophy there does not exist a meta level of wisdom above the world that can fully explain the latter: "There is no view from nowhere, no external perspective, no decontextualized vantage point. We are all in the soup."[541] Thus, there isn't any final science that could advise one as to the correct intermixing of these forms of order.[542] Therefore, East Asian philosophy gives up the claim to universally valid explanations. At the same time it demands that each science be able to explain its own standpoint. "The philosopher must be integrated into his own system."[543]

---

[538] Y. Matsudo, *Eine Einführung in die Spätphilosophie von Kitarō Nishida*, 52. Matsudo is not refering her to economics, but to Hegel in particular, and Western philosophy in general.
[539] S.H. Stenson, Beyond Science and Technology to Absolute Emptiness, 114.
[540] For an explanation of Nishida's position, see Y. Matsudo, *Eine Einführung in die Spätphilosophie von Kitarō Nishida*, 52.
[541] R.T. Ames, D.L. Hall, Dao de Jing, A Philosophical Translation, New York 2003, 18.
[542] D.L. Hall, R.T. Ames, *Thinking from the Han*, 186.
[543] Y. Matsudo, *Eine Einführung in die Spätphilosophie von Kitarō Nishida*, 52.

The social scientist must become part of the world that she describes. She always operates in the midst of the world.[544] She is never simply only an outside observer, but instead she is a 'created creator.' She cannot claim for herself the status of observing the world, or intervening as a guide upon the events of its shaping, from some place outside the reciprocal dependence of all things. So if the economic world is really a struggle of all against all in the eyes of the economist, she cannot exempt herself from this struggle. But if, on the other hand, she takes another viewpoint beyond this perception, she thereby shows that the world is more open and broader than her theories allow for. In other words: she shows through her own activity that the universal claim of her theory is not tenable.

4.8 A World 'Beyond' Egoism

Japanese philosophy doesn't point to any alternative to the market and the state in the sense of another abstract universal because it holds the very idea of that universal in itself to be illusory. The world creates and is equally created; this dynamic and incalculable process of shaping is not finally determined through anything. (4.4.1) In spite of this evaluation of the case, Japanese philosophy, too, holds the idea of harmonious co-existence to be central. This clearly implies no stable order as in economics. It expresses, rather, a very concrete desire of human beings: the absence of suffering. Suffering arises through the normal perception, in which each person sees the other as being irreconcilably opposite. We receive the impression of the mutual dependence of all things as an external coercion, as a foreign authority, against which we have to defend our egos. The subjective defensive reactions as much as the persistent disappointment that in spite of those reactions, we have still become the objects of alien power, is what permits all suffering to arise, as Buddhism in particular intones: "Infinite confusion and infinite suffering"[545] is the result of the habit of the ego to perceive itself as absolute lord:

> "The 'human as wolf' and the struggle, which has split today's world into two halves, reveals itself, when it is questioned on a fundamental level, as rooted in the attachment of the I, where on the basis of the I's ipseity we distinguish between it and the other."[546]

---

[544] Ibid., 51.
[545] K. Nishitani, Vom Wesen der Begegnung, 264.
[546] Ibid., 271.

4 The Implicit World Picture of Economics 263

The key to overcoming suffering doesn't consist in dominating the attachment to the I through extrinsic laws. Thus, for instance, Zen Buddhism tells us: even for a Buddha it is impossible, to enforce the harmonious interaction of egos from the outside.[547] Prescriptions and laws are merely more or less successful attempts to merely manipulate the egos in such a way that a feeling of solidarity re-emerges.[548] Here, a kind of superego is constructed, which programs egoistical self-interest to follow the common good.[549] Japanese philosophy doesn't concern itself with trying to get egoism and the common good to reconcile with each other in this way, but instead aims at overcoming the egoistic standpoint itself, and thus cracking the attachment to the ego in a radical sense. Thus the basis of self interest is eliminated because the ego itself is negated.[550] This makes possible a harmony of spontaneous, creative and voluntary actions; a harmony that makes any coercion and law simply superfluous.

4.8.1 The Normal and the Original Consciousness

In economic methodology, it is commonly denied that there is a standpoint in which egoism might be seen as something that can be overcome. On account of this, we must firstly present an important distinction between the characteristic observational modes of economics and Japanese philosophy, in order to make the Japanese starting point easier to understand. In economic theory the factual possibility of non-egoistical action is only seldom denied.[551] Yet egoistical action is mostly presupposed as the socially given and discussed as the unique form of action. It should suffice for us to deal with the "lower elements of human nature," and thus exclusively with the "economic calculus."[552] This position commonly grounds itself upon the thought that such calculus represents the "probable" or "typical" conduct. It is merely a matter of "exhibiting the essential points of human behavior and to be realistic in terms of this understanding, and not describe human

---

[547] See for example Lin-chi's saying, "Do not seek for the Buddha outwardly." M. Abe discusses this in *Zen and Comparative Studies*, edited by S. Heine, Honolulu 1997, 74.
[548] R.E. Carter, *Encounter with Enlightenment*, 22.
[549] D. Loy, *Nonduality, A Study in Comparative Philosophy*, New York 1988, 130-131.
[550] Ibid., 130-131.
[551] So for example G.S. Becker, who starts with the idea of the universal validity of self-interested or utility maximizing behavior. See: *Der ökonomische Ansatz zur Erklärung menschlichen Verhaltens*, aaO.
[552] F.Y. Edgeworth, *Mathematical Psychics*, 52-53.

conduct in all of its facets."[553] This reasoning corresponds to a methodological procedure that is preferred in many economic explanations, for which it is often only a question of giving a sum over the pattern of behaviors or average results.[554] Thus it isn't odd that economic action theory only deals with the 'morally average person.'[555]

The Japanese philosopher Yuasa Yasuo specifically criticizes this emphasis on the average.[556] For Yuasa, we can fundamentally distinguish the 'Western' and 'traditionally Eastern' social scientific procedures that investigate human action as follows: in Western social sciences the point of departure is always normal human circumstances; it therefore observes an unspecified, multiple quantity of cases. It is easy, in this way, to formulate empirical laws that apply in general or at least, roughly, on average. Clearly we have to avoid dealing with extraordinary cases. The latter are either wholly ignored or observed as outriders that are cancelled out by the average. East Asian sciences proceed in exactly the inverse fashion. They don't aim at the average state of affairs, but instead observe persons who, after a long phase of practice, have developed extraordinary abilities. Their theories cannot, thus, claim general validity, but have the advantage of being able to describe specific modes of thought and action that would otherwise remain inexplicable. Modes of thought and action that may be used as "ideals or potential states that promise some possibility for all people."[557] Eastern modes of thought emphasize this possibility not because they are interested abstractly in a 'superman', but because they would like to point out to every person a path of self-transformation. They are concerned to show how each can shape and develop her action herself, without being bound to a supposedly unchangeable average:

> "Human dispositions and capacities vary from person to person ... It is impossible to make them equal by means of political power. What is important is rather to find a way of enhancement appropriate to each person's capacity and disposition. The fundamental principle is the same in regard to issues such as bodily capacity, health and growth of personality (or mind). In each one cannot enhance one's endowed

---

[553] G. Kirchgässner, *Homo oeconomicus*, 62.
[554] K. Homann, Sinn und Grenze der ökonomischen Methode in der Wirtschaftsethik, 26.
[555] G. Kirchgässner cited in F. Reckling, *Interpretative Handlungsrationalität*, 152.
[556] Y. Yuasa, The Body, Self-Cultivation and Ki-Energy, transl. by S. Nagatomo, M.S. Hull, New York 1993, 61. Yuasa is principally aiming his criticism at Western medicine.
[557] Ibid., 62-63.

potential capacity unless one makes an effort. It cannot be left up to medical doctors. In this respect, the Eastern elitist view of human being does not take the essence of human nature simply as given, but takes it as an unknown which needs to be practically investigated."[558]

In economic theories we exclusively describe factually predominant behavior and explain it through the supposedly unchangeable law of self interest or utility maximization. An action that doesn't fit this paradigm is either diminished or completely ignored. Non-egoistical action remains for this reason an unexplained phenomenon. When East Asian philosophy makes this seemingly inexplicable phenomenon an object of its explanations, it shows how perception and action can change and thus break through the supposed law of egoistical action. In this way we see the contours of an alternative action that is, of course, not 'lawful,' but represents a possible alternative for all persons. One that can be reached through "the growth of the personality and the transformation of human nature."[559] Of course, Japanese philosophy doesn't just concentrate on explaining the extraordinary. Rather it expressly recognizes the usual human point of view. But it also, equally emphasizes that this point of view is not the only conceivable one and outlines an explicit theory of breaking through it. Here we encounter, following Buddhism, a distinction that has already been discussed in the third chapter: the distinction between the normal and the original consciousness. (3.3.3) While we are going to elaborate a further important distinction between both of these modes of consciousness, it should become clear how it is possible to break through normal perception.

One important insight of Buddhism is that the perception of the normal consciousness rests on the illusion that one is a self sufficient and independent existence, although one, in fact, lives in the midst of a world of interdependencies. This illusion isn't a purely cognitive phenomenon; instead, it is an a action guiding idea that represents the root cause of all suffering:

> "According to the teaching of the Buddha, the idea of self is an imaginary, false belief, which has no corresponding reality, and it produces harmful thoughts of 'me' and 'mine,' selfish desire, craving, attachment, hatred, ill-will, conceit, pride, egoism, and other defilements, impurities and problems. It is the source of all the trou-

---

[558] Ibid., 63.
[559] Ibid., 65.

bles in the world, from personal conflicts to wars between nations. In short, to this false view can be traced all the evil in the world."[560]

In the usual perception, a person thinks of herself as independent and self-sufficient, although she in fact lives in a world in which everything is interrelated. She can only do this in when she defends herself against other persons. This "dualistic state of consciousness emphasizes separation from the world, and it is this sense of separation that is itself the root cause of both evil and suffering."[561]

> "Rather than speaking of 'evil', the Buddhist speaks of 'suffering.' Suffering is the result of ignorance, and ignorance is the result of delusion, namely, the sense of separation, individualization without a sense of the whole of things. The result is one's alienation from the world and from the cosmos, and eventually from other people as well, and finally from oneself. Evil is separation, willful aggression, selfish separation, painful isolation. 'Someone who manipulates the world merely for his own advantage increasingly dualizes himself from it. Those who live in this way cannot help expecting the same from others, leading to a life, based on the fear and the need to control situations.'"[562]

The illusion of a self sufficient, independent ego rests on ignorance. It became clear in the last chapter, that the habitual interrelationship of subjective perception and objective things represents a place of nothingness for the normal consciousness. The latter apprehends itself subjectively within the web of habits as an entity, but doesn't see these habits as its own, that can be creatively shaped or changed. Here we can consider a similar ignorance: The many apprehend themselves in the world as self sufficient egos and close themselves off to each other. Each person expels each other person into that seemingly objective outer world, which threatens his own proper interiority. In this process the multitude doesn't realize that the same world lies at the root of all of them. In this world, they are always already mutually related to each other even before they perceive themselves as egos. They are blind to the fact that they apprehend themselves within a field of action that is common to all. The world remains a locus of nothingness, and, thus, is not understood as a mutual shaping process, in which one actively participates. It remains entirely unconscious, hidden in a fog of unknowing.[563] We can also say that the world remains an unconscious

---

[560] W. Rahula cited in M. Abe Masao, Zen and Comparative Studies, 149.
[561] R.E. Carter, *Encounter with Enlightenment*, 27.
[562] Ibid., 29-30. Carter is citing R. Loy.
[563] Sankrit: *avidya*. K. Nishitani, Vom Wesen der Begegnung, 271.

presupposition of the ego. Or more precisely: it remains hidden in the unconscious part of the consciousness. By reason of this fact, the normal consciousness exhibits a characteristic double structure.[564] It encompasses the subjective consciousness (I or ego consciousness), which the individual is conscious of. In terms of our field metaphor, this consciousness captures the standpoint of a field entity from whose point of view the field is invisible. The field is an element of consciousness as the presupposition of subjective consciousness, but remains itself unconscious. So called human 'self-consciousness' encompasses an ego consciousness, that is conscious, and a part that always remains unconscious. "'Self' is the total personality which, though always present, cannot be fully known. (...) (Self as the total personality consists of the consciousness as 'I' or 'ego,' which is known to itself, and the unconscious, which remains unknown."[565]

> "The consciousness calls itself 'I', while the 'self' is not 'I' at all. The self is the whole, because the personality – you as the whole – consists of the 'conscious' and the 'unconscious.' That is the whole or the 'self.' But 'I' know only the consciousness. The 'unconscious' remains unknown to me."[566]

The double structure of the consciousness is at least implicitly used in economic theories as a heuristic model. The habitual utility maximizer simply reacts to prices and stimuli from the market without being able to give the reasons why he acts like that. Also, he cannot know the interdependencies in which his I-consciousness is entangled. His actions follow, instead, social rules, that he doesn't himself even know. Hayek has described such an unconscious rule orientation. The consciousness, according to Hayek, does not create rules, but instead follows these unconsciously. It can't put them into words, but is only able to follow them in practice.[567] According to Hayek there are two attributes of rules that lead human action and make it appear intelligent:"

> "The first of these attributes, which most rules of conduct possess primordially, is that they are followed in practice without being known to the actor in an articulate (verbalized or explicit) form. It reveals itself in the regularity of action that can be explicitly described, but this regularity of action is not due to the actor being able to

---

[564] M. Abe, Zen and Comparative Studies, 149. See also: Y. Yuasa, The Body, Toward an Eastern Body-Mind Theory, 60. Yuasa speaks here of a „dual layered consciousness".
[565] M. Abe, Zen and Comparative Studies, 153.
[566] C.G. Jung cited in M. Abe, Zen and Comparative Studies, 153.
[567] F.A. Hayek, Recht, Ordnung und Freiheit, Vol. 1, 34.

represent it in this manner. The second is that such rules are followed over the long term because they confer a real superior strength to those groups in which they are practiced; and not, because this effect is recognized by those who have deduced it. Although such rules finally are generally accepted, because the results of following them leads to certain consequences, they are not followed with the intention of bringing about these consequences – consequences, which the actor need not know."[568]

Hayek reduces economic action to unconscious habits ('rule governed activity'). Thus we are not concerned with individual habits, but instead social ones: all people follow universal rules of conduct of which nobody is conscious. They learn the rules "from one another... even though neither those which give the example nor those that learn from it are able to fully be conscious of the existence of rules that they still strictly adhere to."[569] Rules determine the perception without itself being an object of perception. A conscious perception of the action determining rules is thus impossible – not to speak of an active shaping of these rules.

Hayek grounds the pregiveness of social rules for the consciousness in their proven success. Rules exist "because actions in agreement with them are proven to be more successful than those of competing individuals or groups."[570] Hayek thus develops a kind of evolutionary theory that is supposed to secure the binding of the individuals to the rule; a position that Becker further develops, in regard to utility maximizing behavior. One can interpret Becker as saying that this behavior is no longer to be attributed to the actors themselves, but instead to social mechanisms that inalterably operate behind the actor's back.[571] These mechanisms are supposed to arise through evolution and be pre-given to the individuals.[572] They appear as unquestionable facts. They determine how the individual thinks, feels and acts; they determine his will, without him being conscious of it. In this way we seem to have found a functional explanation for utility maximizing action. Social structures, interpreted as unconscious rules of action, are supposed to causally condition actions. Thus "all actions and even those that are understood as disinterested and non-purposive, and thus freed from the

---

[568] Ibid., Vol. 1, 35.
[569] Ibid., 35-36.
[570] Ibid., Vol. 1, 34.
[571] F. Reckling, *Interpretative Handlungsrationalität*, 137.
[572] G.S Becker cited in ibid.

economy, [are to be understood] as economic actions built upon the maximization of material and symbolic profit."[573]

Against this kind of functionalized explanation, depending on evolutionary/biological functions, objections have been raised even within economics, which often lead to rejecting the entire explanation.[574] In Japanese philosophy, we see indications of a middle way between such a complete rejection, on the one side, and an uncritical acceptance, on the other. The structure of normal consciousness that consists of a conscious and an unconscious part is not completely denied, but it is not regarded, also, as universally applicable. This is clear in the Buddhist distinction between the normal and the original consciousness. Buddhism agrees with economics that the normal consciousness doesn't conceptualize social habits, because it always perceives itself in the web of them only subjectively, as an ego. The habits remain unconscious, although being part of the self.[575] This lack can be eliminated when the person 'awakens' to the original consciousness and thus achieves a complete insight into his authentic self. He breaks through the barriers of normal perception when he recognizes social habits, which were, before, only given, unconscious presuppositions of his thought and conduct, as his own. It is in this sense that, for instance, in Zen it is said that "the self is to be clearly known."[576] Through this breakthrough the person achieves a form of freedom that seems to be impossible from the standpoint of normal perception. For the self, which knows the social rules of action as his own, is no longer defined through them, but, on the contrary, can define those rules himself. The social rules of action become, in this way, something created, something that is consciously shaped. Buddhism would agree with Hayek that the rules are not "a permanent or unchanging part of 'human nature,' but are only constant "as long as they are not articulated in words and thus not discussed or consciously put to the proof." [577] But Hayek always clearly presupposes, in spite of this confession, only the normal consciousness. Thus the consequences of such a testing remains to he himself, the observing social scientist, inexplicable. Or more exactly: the unconscious social rules of action are unknown both to the analyst and to the analyzed subjects.[578] Against this, Buddhism opens a way to human beings to overcome this unknowing, by razing all

---

[573] P. Bourdieu cited in ibid.
[574] See for a survey of these objections, ibid.
[575] I. Kōyama, "Das Prinzip der Entsprechung und die Ortlogik," 332.
[576] M. Abe, *Zen and Comparative Studies*, 153.
[577] F.A. Hayek, *Recht, Ordnung und Freiheit*, Vol. 1, 36.
[578] M. Abe, *Zen and Comparative Studies*, 157.

conceptual barriers that have held humans chained in unknowing and blindness.[579] This way must be unusual. But even if it is only tread by a few, it is in no way irrational. Or to put it better: it leads to a locus that lies previous to all rational reflection and cannot be known from the point of view of a theory that presupposes as given the 'average man':

> "The esteeming of the individual fact rather than the universal principle is not mere irrationalism or mysticism, for it does not altogether exclude the rational: it penetrates the depth of a fact by breaking through the rational framework. It is beyond both relative rationality and relative factualness, beyond both rationalism and irrationalism."[580]

Arrested in the normal consciousness, persons don't even know about their own proper, deeper knowledge. Thus Buddhism rejects the trend to elevate the normal consciousness to the status of an unquestionable methodological principle. It tries rather to illuminate the fog of egoism,[581] and to break through the unknowingness in which human existence lies.[582]

4.8.2 Harmonic Human Engagement

We shall now discuss the meaning of the original consciousness for human relations. In the third chapter the standpoint of original consciousness is already analyzed in the light of the overcoming of the subject-object split. (3.3.4) There we showed that the original consciousness 'liquefies' the subject as well as the object. It looks through the interdependencies of both in the locus of habits and thus knows their non-substantiality or emptiness. Here it is free to see and shape itself and things anew. We are now going to treat the idea of this 'liquefaction' on a deeper level, and translate it into the area of human encounters.

The break through to original consciousness rests on the insight that the I as an independent, self sufficient existence represents nothing more than an illusion. It is not a something, but instead a more or less continual process in a world of interdependencies. In order to pre-empt any eventual misunderstandings: we are not casting any doubt, here, on the practical meaning of the concept of the I. But behind it hides a real, independent essence just as little as it hides behind other concepts. The I doesn't exist in and for it-

---

[579] E. Gallu, "Sunyata, Ethics and Interconnectedness," 194.
[580] M. Abe, "The Japanese View of Truth," *Japanese Religions*, 14/3 (1986), 2.
[581] S.H. Stenson, "Beyond Science and Technology to Absolute Emptiness," 132.
[582] M. Abe, *Zen and Comparative Studies*, 199.

self, but is a process that is dependent on other processes that are similarly designated with concepts. Tong describes clearly what is meant here, as he relates this to the concept of the field:

> "The denial of things and entities in our ordinary experience may seem at first incomprehensible and extravagant. But what is being denied here must be properly understood. There are of course thing-like or entity-like phenomena like apples, trees and machines, animal bodies, and so on in our everyday experience of the world and ourselves. They present themselves as enduring individuals that sojourn for a while in the world of appearance. The point is that these thing-like phenomena are not themselves things, that is, not the way we ordinarily attribute to them, and certainly not the way substantialist philosophers would make them to be. What the Field-Being thinker denies in the commonsense or prevailing cognition of things is not the phenomena themselves, not even their thing-like or entity-like appearances as such, but the conceptual constructions of rigid identity we habitually attribute to them. What is being denied here ... is not the phenomena themselves but the conceptual attribution to these phenomena. To be more exact, what Field-Being denies is the existence and reality of substantial entities, things or beings that are supposed to be in themselves complete wholes – inert, separate, self-contained, and independent, each endowed with a rigid identity."[583]

"Conventionally, objects exists; really, they are empty."[584] This insight means, when we transpose it to the human domain, that the "self is not an absolute but a relative entity. As soon as one talks about self one already presupposes the existence of the other. There can be no self apart from the other, and vice versa. Self and the other are entirely interdependent and relational."[585] The person is an activity, a process, which only exists insofar as he is related to other processes. Who knows this no longer perceives himself closed off from and in opposition to others, but within a net of interdependencies. He no longer sees his interrelations with others as a threat to his ego, but instead unfolds within these relationships.

Our first evaluation of the standpoint of original consciousness is clearly to be regarded with some caution, since it tends to evoke misunderstandings. Thus, we are not to assume that the I, on the basis of its radical de-

---

[583] L.K. Tong, *The Art of Appropriation*, 18.
[584] M. Abe, *Zen and Comparative Studies*, 51.
[585] Ibid., 210. See also D.L. Hall, R.T. Ames, *Thinking from the Han*, 27.

subjectivation, becomes purely the "'scourge' of the Other."[586] For not only is the subject de-subjectified, but also the object (the Thou) is equally de-objectified. Just as the I is seen through as a process holding in itself and presupposing the thou, so, too, the thou loses its absoluteness, which threatens the I or makes it a 'scourge.' In this way, every sort of subordination and superiority is overcome.[587]

> "Once we awaken to our own no-selfhood, we also awaken to the no-selfhood of everything and everyone in the universe. In other words, we awaken to the fact, that, just like ourselves, nothing in the universe has any fixed, substantial selfhood, even while maintaining relative selfhood. So, on the relative level, all have our own distinctive selfhood; yet, on the absolute level, we have no fixed, substantial selfhood but, rather, equality and solidarity in terms of the realization of no-self. Accordingly, from an absolute standpoint, we can say that, because of the absence of substantial selfhood, I am not I, and you are not you; thereby, I am you and you are me. We are different relatively but equal absolutely, interfusing with one another, even while retaining our distinct identity."[588]

We shouldn't take this interfusing to mean that firstly two entities exist independently of each other, which then are put into a relation. It lies, rather, before every (rational) distinction or separation of the I and thou, subject and object, inner and outer reality. "The field of true human existence opens up beyond inner and outer."[589] The encounter of the I and the thou doesn't follow from the accidental union of two egos, but is the locus out of which both are generated on the same ontological level. At this point "the attachment to self as subject is extinguished; hence, others as object are also dissolved."[590] Both are so liquefied that they reciprocally influence each other without interfering with each other. They are no longer masters of the absolute, so that they no longer each have to aspire to master the other.

---

[586] This idea occasionally is represented in economic ethics in order to describe unegoistical activity. See M. Schramm, "Spielregeln gestalten sich nicht von selbst," 154.

[587] C.-J.E. Robinson, "The Conflict of Science and Religion in Dynamic Sunyata," in: T. Unno (ed.), *The Religious Philosophy of Nishitani Keiji*, 112.

[588] M. Abe, *Zen and Comparative Studies*, 210-11. For a similar interpretation, see K. Nishia, *Logik des Ortes*, 197 and K. Nishitani, "Vom Wesen der Begegnung," 268.

[589] Nishitani cited in S.H. Stenson, "Beyond Science and Technology to Absolute Emptiness," 127.

[590] E. Gallu, Sunyata, "Ethics and Authentic Interconnectedness," 195.

4 The Implicit World Picture of Economics

This liquefied form of existence, which is designated as non-self in Buddhism, distinguishes itself not only from egoism, but from altruism as well. The egoist knows himself as an absolute, immutable essence and is consequently busy trying to maintain the existence of this essence. To this end, he absolutely subordinates the other. The non-self overcomes this position because it is no longer fixed around a hard ego-core, which must be defended against other people. Egoism is transformed into a love "which must be the emptying and the negation of the ego orbiting around itself."[591] Such a love is not simply altruistic. At least not in the sense that the non-self negates itself and submits to the (egoistic) demands of the other. The relation to the other is not simply a duty to the non-self, or a service that is prescribed to him.[592] It lives, instead, inside its own existence. The non-self realizes itself "spontaneously and value-free" within relations to others."[593] Buddhism speaks of a "'simultaneous attainment' of self and others;"[594] an idea that is similarly spoken of in Confucianism:

> "We must remember that Confucian distinctions such as 'self/other' are mutually entailing and interdependent correlatives, and are not dualistic in the sense of representing some underlying ontological disparity (...) 'Oneself' is always a 'becoming other', and an 'other' is always 'becoming oneself' (...) Such a model construes the relatedness of individuals to social groupings in such a manner as to enrich and intensify the self-actualizing potential of the individuals."[595]

A further possible misperception consists in taking the 'simultaneous attainment' of self and others as a leveling of all distinctions, as sheer conformity. The harmony innate to this attainment is not "absolute equality, for this would negate their individuality."[596] Rather, "'oneself' and the 'other' are, as we say, not-one and not-two."[597] Not-two because the original consciousness doesn't distinguish two self-subsistent essences. And not-one, because persons are still not melted into one undistinguishable unity. Individual uniqueness lies, rather, in its encounter with the other, based in its unique place in the world, as classical Chinese philosophy makes clear:

---

[591] K. Mutō cited in S. Odin, *The Social Self in Zen and American Pragmatism*, 117.
[592] E. Gallu, "Sunyata, Ethics and Authentic Interconnectedness," 195.
[593] K. Nishida, *Logik des Ortes*, 201.
[594] Japenese: *dōjijōdo*. M. Abe, *Zen and Comparative Studies*, 73.
[595] D.L. Hall, R.T. Ames, *Thinking from the Han*, 27.
[596] C.-J.E. Robinson, "The Conflict of Science and Religion in Dynamic Sunyata," 112.
[597] K. Nishitani, "Vom Wesen der Begegnung," 269.

"The Chinese believed, by and large, in a unique personal existence, no doubt fortified by the concept of a structure of kinship ascendants and descendants, stretching indefinitely forward into the future, in which the individual occupied his unique place.' This Chinese conception of unique place stands in contrast to the autonomous individuality that attends the isolation of the soul from other souls and from the illusory world of sensual perception. The uniqueness of the Chinese person is immanent and embedded within a ceaseless process of social, cultural and natural changes. (...) The function then, of disciplining *ji* (self, SG) ... is to take up the appropriate place ... for oneself in relationship to other persons in community."[598]

The non-self can actively shape its unique time and place in the world because it is conscious of its manifold relations to others. He doesn't blindly follow the rules of action, but instead fulfills these in a unique, and creative way. For it, the world is not an unconscious locus of nothingness, in which it apprehends itself in absolute opposition to other people, but is like a game, the rules and features of which it can shape in cooperation with other people. In this game, absolute opposition is transformed into absolute harmony.[599] Such a harmony doesn't rest on blind subjection to a law or mechanism. It also doesn't imply the union of autonomous individuals or an aggregation of individual happiness. On the contrary: it breaks through all these ideas of the normal consciousness. Far beyond obedience to the law and autonomy, it signifies an equal balance of community and uniqueness. The etymological root of the concept 'harmony' in Japanese and Chinese, which lies in the art of cooking, makes this clear:[600]

"Harmony is the art of combining and blending two more foodstuffs so they come together with mutual benefit and enhancement without losing their separate and particular identities, and yet with the effect of constituting a frictionless whole. An important characteristic of this harmony is the endurance of the particular ingredients and the cosmetic nature of the harmony. It is an order that emerges out of the collaboration of intrinsically related details to embellish the contribution of each one. (...) Important is ... the respect for each of the 'self-awakening' ... ingredients

---

[598] D.L. Hall, R.T. Ames, *Thinking from the Han*, 26-27. Die Autoren zitieren hier M. Elvin.
[599] K. Nishitani, "Vom Wesen der Begegnung," 269.
[600] I am referring here to das chinesische Character für 'harmony', that is pronounced as *WA* or *he* in Japanese.

and the need to find a proper balance by acknowledging the parity that obtains among them."[601]

Since the insight in this form of harmony lies beyond that which can be known to the normal consciousness, it cannot be described from the view of a theory that presupposes this normal consciousness. The harmony we are speaking of exists beyond a logic that postulates humans firstly as separate entities one from the other in order to contingently assemble them through a mechanism or law into a unity. More precisely: it is a state in which humans don't seem absolutely divided from each other. Its logic is thus neither that of the market, resting on contracts between self-utilizing individuals, nor of a state, that subjugates humans out of fear of each other. It can't be labeled 'private' or 'public' in the economic sense. It is like what Weintraub writes about the concept of the public realm:

> "The 'public' realm is above all a realm of participatory self-determination, deliberation, and conscious cooperation among equals, the logic of which is distinct from both civil society and the administrative state. (...) Attempts to use the public/private distinction as a dichotomous model to capture the overall pattern of social life in a society ... are always likely to be inherently misleading, because the procrustean dualism of their categories will tend to blank out important phenomena."[602]

It is equally true that the perception of the original consciousness is not going to be explained through a theory that presupposes the individualistic calculus. For this consciousness doesn't exert control over preferences independent of the outer world. Rather, preferences arise in the conscious interactions of the many, so that the postulate of their independence cannot be sustained. Besides, the original consciousness is in no way calculating. Rather, "actions spring naturally as expressions of who one really is, without calculation, for no reason, for no gain, as expressions of our suchness."[603]

---

[601] D.L. Hall, R.T. Ames, *Thinking from the Han*, 181. Of course, this doesn't mean to refer to some kind of cosmic cook, who adds ingredients for the benefit of all. Order here emerges only through the co-actions of the many.

[602] J. Weintraub, The Theory and Politics of the Public/Private Distinction, 14-15. Weintraub defines *civil society* as: „a world of self-interested individuals, competition, impersonality, and contractual relationships – centered on the market." Ibid.., 13.

[603] R.E. Carter, *Encounter with Enlightenment*, 30-31.

"One's actions and reactions toward the world are ... imbued with genuineness and compassion; they are free of self-centeredness and are truly other-regarding, not through rational choice, but via an inherent unifying force of life."[604]

In contrast to rational preferences, the actions of the non-self are spontaneous. The latter accepts no decision space as given, but is continually reshaping it relative to situations. Such spontaneity implies – as Confucianism makes clear – no complete independence of all social habits, but rather a creative shaping of these habits. What is decisive is the meaning of rituals.[605] Rituals describe a specific relation between people (father-son, wife-husband, etc.). They are in this sense habits of human practices that survive in a society over space and time. But thus they represent no fixed or irrevocable modes of actions that must blindly be followed. They are rather vague rules of thumb over the ways humans should interact. They are in every situation to be authentically filled by individuals with life:

> "For the Confucian, the achievement of true selfhood 'is measurable in terms of quality of the relationships that one is able to effect. It is 'ritualizing', taken in its broadest sense, that enables persons to assume roles which define their appropriate relationships with others.' Ritualized sociality serves as ground of shared values and meaning, and allows one to effectively interact with others, and through such activity to further enhance the well being of the social whole of which one is an esteemed part. Yet such ritualized practice must be 'personalized' by the agent, and expressed in ways that are unique to him or her, appropriate as to time and place, and transparently expressive of the feelings and concerns of the agent."[606]

Ritualized action demands, in opposition to simple rule obedience, acting creatively and spontaneously, "in the midst of the demands and the relentless habits of the everyday."[607] From this, we can deduce no strict laws and no calculations that are independent of time and space. Ritual, for these reasons, can't guarantee law-abiding conduct. It guarantees rather the uniqueness of individuals in a specific world. "Ethical activity arises spontaneously as a manifestation of who we have become, and not as a result of the memorization of externally imposed rules, or some sort of casuistic calculation."[608] It follows that ritualized action can be neither calcu-

---

[604] E. Gallu, Sunyata, Ethics and Authentic Interconnectedness, 193.
[605] Chinese *li*.
[606] R.E. Carter, *Encounter with Enlightenment*, 71-72. Carter is citing Hall und Ames.
[607] Ibid., 72.
[608] Ibid., 155.

4 The Implicit World Picture of Economics 277

lated nor forecast. At most, from the standpoint of theory, which implicitly presupposes the normal consciousness, it can be negated:

> "There is a domain of living experience which is conscious of its own authentic self. But it remains incomprehensible for those people who only continue within normal reality. Such a living experience can, just because it is living, not be proven by reference to the question of its existence or non-existence. Those who move about in the field of everyday reality most commonly observe its non-existence."[609]

The human interaction that is based in original consciousness is a locus of nothingness for habitual action. The locus is, in fact, the implicit presupposition of the latter. Harmonious interaction is not simply an alternative to egoistical action, existing next to this, but is rather its foundation. Watsuji in particular makes us see this point, when he discusses the role of trust in society:[610]

> "Incidentally, ... all human relations involve trust to some extent. It is not correct ... that the Gesellschaft-oriented relationship is originally based on distrust. It is certain that it lacks the trust relationship peculiar to Gemeinschaft. But a trust relationship peculiar to Gesellschaft exists. Otherwise, no business relations could arise. Therefore, we are allowed to insist that, in any human relationship whatsoever, makoto (integrity, truthfulness, SG) takes place in accordance with each of them."[611]

Watsuji observes that economic action presupposes a trust that from the view of normal perception cannot be conceived. Trust in the honor of others is the presupposition of (individualistic) utility maximization, but isn't its product. For by the valuing of preference alternatives one must be able to rely on the statements of other people. If one is tricked, for instance, over the properties of an exchange commodity, the necessary level of assurance supporting expectation of utility maximization is not preserved.[612] Besides, trust is based in many situations neither on short term nor long term calculus, but instead follows spontaneously. It arises though immediate insight into interdependencies without making distinctions between I and thou, mine and thine. It arises in a locus which logically precedes every dualistic perception of the I and the other, individual and social interests. Watsuji goes a step further when he points out that even an action

---

[609] I. Kōyama, "Das Prinzip der Entsprechung und die Ortlogik," 330.
[610] T. Watsuji, *Watsuji Tetsuro's Rinrigaku*, chapt. 13. In order to elaborate upon the meaning of trust and reliability in a society, Watsuji begins his analysis by considering the meaning of the Japanese term *makoto*.
[611] Ibid., 276.
[612] H.H. Gossen, *Entwicklung des menschlichen Verkehrs*, 129.

that is straightforwardly based on exploiting the trust of others presupposes an original trust. How, for instance, would a free rider profit from the common action of others if an initial trust relationship isn't presupposed? "It is always at some place and on some occasion in the complex and inexhaustible interconnections of acts that truthfulness does not occur ... However countless these places and occasions may be, they cannot arise except that truthfulness nevertheless takes place at bottom."[613] Economics might explain how an original trust relationship is disturbed through egoistical action; but it can't motive why this relationship exists in the first place. The latter remains an implicit presupposition, which "contradicts every current economic theory," but at the same time – as new empirical research shows – is yet practiced in economic co-existence. For in experiments concerning economic action the participants conduct themselves completely contrarily to current doctrine. "The persons are prepared to trust even where it is risky. And they reciprocate trust even if it costs money."[614] Thus, "trust ... counts as a chief driver of economic success."[615] It is the locus of egoistical action, its presupposition, but not its result.

Such trust, in the Japanese view, cannot be explained by rule governed behavior or a biological mechanism.[616] Rather, exactly the reverse is argued: trust in the sense of a conscious, spontaneous action is regarded as the presupposition for there being both rules and changes of rules. Japanese philosophy seeks after no functional explanation making the insight of original consciousness superfluous, but instead emphasizes the necessity of an active and spontaneous shaping of human co-existence. Rules and laws are "tentative steps"[617] for it, which must be creatively tested and spontaneously filled with life. The shaping of rules is thus neither left to the logic of evolution nor applied as "the consequence of the operation of social powers that are as inevitable as natural laws."[618] It is also not ascribed to any 'individual morality' or an 'ethos of individuality.' Rather Japanese phi-

---

[613] T. Watsuji, *Watsuji Tetsuro's Rinrigaku*, 281.//
[614] R. Stadler, "Mit Sicherheit ein gutes Gefühl," *Süddeutsche Magazin* vom 9. Juli 2004, 6. Stadler is referring K. McCabe, Professor of Economics at George Mason University in Virginia, USA.
[615] Ibid., 5. Stadler is relying on the work of Paul Zak und Stephen Knack.
[616] McGabe tries to do just this. For he supposes, behind trust, the working of some biological mechanism. a "drive that lies outside our conscious control." Cited in R. Stadler, ibid., 6-7.
[617] R.E. Carter, *Encounter with Enlightenment*, 192.
[618] A. Giddens cited in F. Reckling, *Interpretative Handlungsrationalität*, 141. Giddens is making a critical point against functional explanations in economics.

losophy emphasizes that no standpoint can motivate the shaping of human interaction if it presupposes the normal perception. This view is confirmed by at least some research: persistent social habits or institutions can be explained, in part, through the calculations of normal perception, but the latter can't explain the dynamic process of change and situational formations. Thus, for instance, the arising and protection of democracies, the establishment of new social orderings and the overthrow of systems are neither explained by egoistical calculation nor forecast through economic models.[619] And a simple glance at the everyday should be enough to show that action cannot be exclusively guided through incentives. "The regulatory thickness of modern democratic society, with their inducements and sanctions, represents the exceptions rather than the rule when compared to the multiplicity of human interactions."[620] Simply the fact, that we neither live in a totalitarian state nor are totally regulated by deeply ingrained habits and yet co-exist, proves that our interactions aren't exclusively grounded in normal perception, as is presupposed by methodological individualism but instead in a spontaneity and creativity that doesn't presuppose rules, but creatively shapes them.

4.8.3 Spontaneously Mindful Actions and the Meaning of Rules

Japanese philosophy doesn't try to give us a rational explanation of the rules of living together; it also doesn't label them as irrational either. Rather it points to the rules as the locus of lived experience beyond rationality and irrationality. As such a locus, the rules aren't completely objectifiable, but instead represent, conversely, the presupposition of all objective observation. The missing objectivity doesn't mean that the rules of commonly shared lives are unconscious to the actors, but purely that their rationality can't be grasped by any outside observer. While for instance Hayek begins with the assumption that rules are not conscious objects of actors, Japanese philosophy intentionally argues exactly the opposite:[621] in the original consciousness are the rules (in the sense of rituals) known to the actors. They are thus not simply strictly adhered to, but instead are spontaneously and creatively shaped. No ossified lawfulness underlies ac-

---

[619] F. Reckling, *Interpretative Handlungsrationalität*, 158 as well as his bibliographical references.
[620] Ibid., 156.
[621] F.A. Hayek, *Recht, Gesetzgebung und Freiheit*, Vol. 1, 35. Hayek starts from assuming that the rules of behavior can be "explicitly described" but that actors are unable themselves to "conceive them in this manner."

tion; it is for an external observer describable ex post facto at most, but not causally explicable. There glimmers here an alternative understanding of action beyond both alternatives that are discussed in economics. For one thing, Japanese philosophy rejects "that we as individuals must bow to forces and obey principles that we cannot hope to understand, while still progress and even the survival of civilization depends on them."[622] For another, it also denies the idea of conscious control and governance of the total sum of activities in the claim "that the conscious individual reason can grasp all purposes and knowledge of 'society' or 'humanity.'"[623] It is concerned neither to find proofs of spontaneous, unconscious action, nor those of conscious, plan governed action. Rather it emphasizes the meaning of spontaneous, while at the same time conscious action.

Since such an understanding of action is unusual from the viewpoint of economics, I briefly want to comparatively oppose it to the economic view of action by which I aim particularly at the differentiated meaning of rules. Often economics demands a firm and unconditioned obedience to the rules of action, independently of whether obedience is to be thought of as a moral duty or a 'natural law' of human action. As an example we can introduce Smith here, who sees in hardnecked obedience to rules a praiseworthy property:

> "The man who ... adheres with the most obstinate steadfastness to the general rules themselves, is the most commendable, and the most to be depended upon. Though the end of the rules of justice be, to hinder us from hurting our neighbour, it may frequently be a crime to violate them, though we could pretend, with some pretext of reason, that this particular violation could do no hurt. A man often becomes a villain the moment he begins, even in his own heart, to chicane in this manner."[624]

The relationship of strict punctiliousness and spontaneous action is of particular meaning here; a relationship, that is elaborated clearly in economic ethics in regard to the question whether spontaneous aid has a meaning or whether we should adhere strictly to the rules in the face of emergency situations of need. Homann makes unmistakably clear that the latter has to be the case. Spontaneous help is for him a "mortal help," spontaneous sympathy for one's neighbor is unethical: "The conduct of a Saint Martin will only sharpen the poverty problem in developing countries and would

---

[622] F. A. Hayek, *Mißbrauch und Verfall der Vernunft*, 127.
[623] Ibid., 127.
[624] A. Smith, *Theory of Moral Sentiments*, 204.

be in that respect unethical, perhaps even a crime."[625] Spontaneous help for the poorest of the poor must be suppressed since it is inefficient: "We must not yield to the intention, in the face of hungry children of the poorest of the poor, to give unedited 'spontaneous' help, because such conduct not only doesn't solve the problem but makes it worse."[626] The other is best helped when one continues to adhere strictly to firm rules of action that are pre-given from some external agent (for instance, the state). More: Help is mostly to be left to the proper institutions, which can handle it efficiently. Spontaneous help should not be allowed to contravene the universal rules of action. In exceptional cases it may be called for when such action rules don't (yet) exist. One ought then "in the end, in actual cases of catastrophe cases perhaps allow for spontaneous help."[627] It is purely a stopgap if no incentive system exists that guides aid legally through payment and punishment. Only as long as the "sanctioning would cause prohibitively high costs ... as long as we can complain of gaps in the social order, of inadequate sanctioning mechanism or even of their complete failures, might individual morality intervene in case of totally undesirable social situations as a stopgap."[628] Of course, only "in order to [initiate] the development of a appropriate formation of the framing rules."[629]

Japanese philosophy rejects this interpretation of aid. In its view, aid isn't something that comes from some impersonal, outside agency, so that a person passively relates to it. Rather, aid counts as compassion in the sense of an active deed that is shaped out of the original constitution of one's own self. It is a situational action that is neither calculated nor subject to universal rules of action. Hisamatsu makes this position clear when he discusses the significance of mercy:

> "Compassion ... cannot be mercy in its authentic mode of existence that is transmitted to us from somewhere else. It is thus not a simply passively received thing from beyond. It must be totally realized from our own selves: not working on us as something given by the totally other, but an active deed coming out of ourselves. ... In Buddhism compassion... deriving from the other is not something absolute, against which we have to remain passive until the end, but instead an aid that can awaken us to our own most authentic being. It is thus not something in which we

---

[625] K. Homann, *Anreize und Moral, Gesellschaftstheorie – Ethik – Anwendungen*, Münster 2003, 21.
[626] Ibid.l, 20.
[627] Ibid., 21.
[628] M. Schramm, "Spielregeln gestalten sich nicht von selbst," 160-61.
[629] Ibid., 161.

ought to persevere in any way. In short, to become totally active in compassion and not simply remain passive in it, that is the originally essential Buddhist mode of existence."[630]

We don't help when we first look to the law and then turn to our fellow men. The law is never the final value that defines our action with regard to our neighbor.[631] It cannot as the totally other regulate us externally in the relation between persons, but instead must be re-interpreted and shaped in every situation. It is itself a created thing, and thus shouldn't be assumed to be universal in its given shape. Laws and rules are purely gross rules of thumb; not substitutes for spontaneous action, but instead only orientation points, and for this reason not to be simply blindly obeyed.

According to Japanese belief, rules of action should not be a kind of exterior coercion. They must instead become a spontaneous, natural expression of the individual in the world.[632] Suzuki Daisetsu uses the example of Zen to show what this means:

> "Where coercion reigns, man is a convict, not a free being. He no longer lives as he should, he suffers under the tyranny of relationships; he feels chained and loses his independence. The business of Zen is to preserve human liveliness and inherent freedom and before all else, the wholeness of his personality. In other words, Zen wants life to be lived from the inside. Not bound to rules, but instead with each person creating his rules."[633]

We must not interpret rule following in this instance subjectively, standing in the face of an objective rule. Rules (in the sense of rituals) are rather understood site specifically. They are the loci in which actions are determined, without themselves becoming objectively determinable. They are like an open space in which a multiplicity of actions are protected and at the same time are shaped and developed through these actions themselves. While the normal consciousness divides this space and apprehends itself as a subjective ego subject to an objective rule, the original consciousness understands itself as a creator-cum-creation, actively shaping and being shaped by the rule.

---

[630] S. Hisamatsu, Philosophie des Erwachens, Satori und Atheismus, Zürich-München 1990, 98-99.
[631] Ibid., 62.
[632] R.E. Carter, Encounter with Enlightenment, 176.
[633] D.T. Suzuki, Die große Befreiung, Einführung in den Zen Buddhismus, Frankfurt/Main 1980, 64.

The site specific character of rules emphasizes the necessity of spontaneous action. "An ethical theory shouldn't be legalistic, reduced to a stiff program of rules and regulations. It must instead be context-dependent and flexible."[634] Not regarding the world as something ruled by universal law is the decisive motivation for such an attitude. Since the world continually changes, there cannot be an ultimate standpoint that could tell a person how compassion or other actions directed to one's fellow humans have to be regarded in every situation. Even if following the rules might be appropriate for the 'average' person, it isn't thus guaranteed that one will act in a situationally correct manner. Even more: the suppression of spontaneous action in support of fixed rules of action destroys the ability to act uniquely and immediately in a situation:

> "A 'heartfelt' gesture is also a 'mindful' and a spontaneous act. It arises naturally and spontaneously from the depths of one's self, from deeper than one's surface will; it is not mere acting but an authentic expression of one's whole person as 'knower', 'feeler,' and 'willer.' Such acts are not acts of calculation, not because they are mindless – for indeed they are allegedly mind-full – but because calculation implies being at an objective remove from the situation. Acts of calculation are more like running down the list of debits and credits on a cluttered sheet in order to decipher what would be best in this case. Calculation can result in ignoring or setting aside of one's feelings and one's sense of how to act in this circumstance here and now. Instead an abstract principle or law is applied to an instance that is rarely ever exactly like what the law envisioned or what is set out in the manual as a test case."[635]

There is a danger that a stiff obedience to the rules will be transformed into a means to a selfish purpose and is demanded even if it fails in its original purpose to secure peaceful co-existence with one's fellow humans. It can thus be instrumentalized through the egoistical will of a few. If all people submit blindly to the rules and don't know them as a locus, they themselves shape, than they will neither see through such instrumentalization nor resist it actively out of spontaneous sympathy. Besides, automatic obedience to the rules supports the normal human viewpoint and lets people persist in their own egos. Thus, it threats to aggrandize the suffering and errors of people, and thus the disharmony among them, instead of purging it. "Justice, when carried to its final conclusion, often results in punishment, conflict, revenge, and even war, whereas wisdom entails rapproche-

---

[634] D.A. Fox, "Zen and Ethics," 39.
[635] R.E. Carter, *Encounter with Enlightenment*, 21.

ment, conciliation, harmony, and peace."[636] For this reason, Japanese philosophy emphasizes the need to break through calculation and unconscious obedience to rules and becoming conscious of the locus in which rules are shaped. Even "those forms of attachment which absolutize the divine or the holy as something substantial, self-existing, eternal, and unchangeable must be overcome."[637]

In this overcoming demanded by Japanese philosophy there seems to lie a problem, of course. For if the laws of action themselves become the object of conscious reflection and thus become a creator-cum-created changing its shape from moment to moment, than the results of action can neither be governed nor planned. The world seems damned to sink into a chaos in which no action can be judged against an objective, universal measure. "But why shouldn't one wish to bring order out of chaos?"[638] The wish is self-evident if chaos is negatively interpreted as a suffering state. When one combines, as Hobbes did, the concept of chaos with the suffering of the religious wars,[639] then the wish for certain knowledge and firm laws ruling human actions is completely justified. Here, of course, egoism is implicitly always presupposed, dividing people and casting them into pain and confusion. Against this vision, East Asian philosophy in general uncouples the concept of chaos from the suffering state of humankind. It rather designates a state of the world that is free from striving to apprehend something or someone as a self-subsisting existence. Chaos is thus free of all suffering, which arises from being stuck on the ego and the law. It simply designates the 'being so' of the world as a noncoherent sum of all orders. It is the indeterminate element that guarantees novelty and uniqueness.[640] The world shows itself to be chaotic in the sense that it

> "actually exists as a shifting set of ways of being, a myriad set of overlapping worlds, a chaos of thises and thats, a multifarious congeries of orders. Chaos, *hundun*, understood as the totality of all orders, names the way of things."[641]

East Asian philosophy doesn't put a negative value on such chaos. What is negative, on the other hand, is the delusion that one can press this chaos into a specific, unmoving order through an unconditioned obedience to

---

[636] M. Abe, *Zen and Comparative Studies*, 214.
[637] Ibid., 199.
[638] D.L. Hall, R.T. Ames, *Thinking from the Han*, 66.
[639] J. Wieland, *Ökonomische Organisation, Allokation und Status*, 49.
[640] D.L. Hall, R.T. Ames, *Thinking from the Han*, 66.
[641] Ibid., 71.

rules. The problem is not seen in the continual change in a world of interdependencies, but in the effort to form this change and manipulate it for one's own ideals. It is rooted in the normal consciousness to want to stop by force the world's transformations. At this point it becomes clear that the planification and governability of action and the world is neither considered necessary nor worth striving for. Instead, it is regarded as the root course of suffering itself.

In particular, Japanese philosophy doesn't look for rules or laws that order the world. When it emphasizes the meaning of original consciousness, it describes, instead, a state in which these become superfluous. Naturally this doesn't mean that rules or laws are fundamentally rejected. For finally even Japanese philosophy recognizes how many people are arrested in a state of normal consciousness, and would injure or annihilate themselves and others in the absence of laws. But even in such conflict cases social sanctions and informal orthodoxies that are contextually assimilated to situations and variables are preferred to universal laws. This position is exhibited, too, in Japanese social life. For here it is not the task of the state "to enforce faceless laws in faceless ways."[642] Rather it is to be noted that the rules of human interaction even in modern Japan lack any relation to an abstract, external measurement of action:

> "Law was not seen as representing some higher or transcendent vision; accordingly it did not acquire any institutional and symbolic autonomy. The main role of law was the upholding of the contexts and bases of social life and the restoration of whatever social harmony might have been destroyed by contention, conflict or criminal behavior. Law was embedded, both institutionally and symbolically, in the basic premises of the community or nation, or of the numerous social contexts of different sectors of Japanese society. It exhibited ... the major characteristics of ... [an] 'authority without power.' It is this basic conception of law that seems to have persisted, despite all the great changes in the organization of law that have taken place, especially in the modern period."[643]

In economics the laws apply as irreplaceable guarantees of a peaceful life, while unconditional obedience to them is often elevated to a (moral) duty. Because egoism is merely oppressed, but not repealed, with the destruction of laws the struggle of all against all threatens to break out anew. Contrarily, Japanese philosophy views the laws as rules of thumb to be tested and

---

[642] R.E. Carter, *Encounter with Enlightenment*, 186.
[643] S.N. Eisenstadt, *Japanese Civilization, A Comparative View*, Chicago-London 1996, 126-27.

taught in human interaction, and needing at least from time to time to be consciously revised. Finally, they are nothing more than aids to the original knowledge, supposed to help people break through the normal way of seeing in order for them to turn to their neighbors in spontaneous and creative ways, out of insight. Rules and laws should help people break out of the hard shells of their egos, like a hen helps a chick free itself from its eggshell:

> "It is just like the old verse says: 'to push from the inside and to peck at it from the outside at the same time.' (*sotsutaka-dōji*). The meaning of the pushing is that the chick from inside the egg picks and destroys, while the meaning of the pecking is that the hen pecks at this same egg from the outside. Then suddenly the egg breaks due to the two's simultaneous cooperation. (...) The hen doesn't create the whole being of the chick by pecking at the egg, nor does the chick melt into the hen, when it breaks through the shell. The chick as such steps out with its own, wholly self-subsistent being, when it destroys the shell from the inside. Thus there is in the chick an original being of the self, so that the hen is only a help in the process of the bringing forth the chick's being as such ... That being which broke the shell and stepped out represents the authentic and original. Once it has presented itself, it acts completely free from its whole being. Nothing more remains that would let us say that it is dependent on or belongs to the hen. It therefore acts completely free from its whole being, according to its own law."[644]

If the help of the law is successful, both the ego and the (exterior) law jointly disappear: "'With one blow, the frozen metrification of truth and equality is broken and the icy covering... is melted.' This signifies the overcoming of the dependency on the I and ... the law."[645] Action is no longer determined through law; instead, it is creative like the movements of a dancer, who perfectly controls the individual steps without being bound by them. Laws are thus not inevitable over the long term; rather, they should help people to achieve a state in which they are superfluous.

> "If one has had the nondual experience of interconnectedness, then one spontaneously and effortlessly flows with the whole of things of which he or she is now fixedly conscious. (...) One can simply live and act in accordance with things such that one respects them as being of the same worth and of the same stuff as one's own self, and one's own beloved, and one's own family, and it might never arise therefore, that you would wish to harm or destroy another. It is no longer a matter of refraining from harming others, for there is no reason not to be inclined to maintain

---

[644] S. Hisamatsu, *Philosophie des Erwachens*, 96-97.
[645] K. Nishitani, "Vom Wesen der Begegnung," 272.

the whole. No law is needed to protect others, for one is others, and to become willful about it by trying to get clear about when and when not to do something will only destroy this original spontaneity and lead to a contrived series of regulations which will never be detailed enough to handle all possible circumstances and situations in a constantly changing world such as ours."[646]

Perhaps Japanese philosophy represents a completely unrealistic position when it regards laws as dispensable. Its positive image of the human, emphasizing the human capacity for insight, may seem naive. One may reply, against this reproach, that people are not to be regarded as actually free from egoistical desires. We are operating purely in the realm of the 'if/then' rule:[647] If a person breaks through his egoistical desires, and through calculation, then peaceful human co-existence is possible. This is a possibility that can be practically experienced and lived by every person in the here and now. Against this, the capacity to plan and govern egoistic action represents purely an abstract, theoretical solution for Japanese philosophy, which never, even not in the far future, will lead to social peacefulness. It is on account of this basic illusion that we always only end up in new disappointments and suffering as long as we hold onto it and won't let it go.

4.9 The Relation of the Economic World to Other Worlds

Even if we point to conscious while at the same time spontaneous action as an alternative to egoism and rule-governed behavior, this alternative still remains problematic in one respect. For isn't it strictly true that only in small groups can we have conscious and at the same time spontaneous activity, but not in the global, networked world in which humans who don't know one another are nevertheless dependent one on another? In economic theory the possibility of non-egoistic action is by all means noted, as for instance when strong emotional ties exist between actors, for example, within a family.[648] But in the face of the giant network of anonymous dependencies, such face-to-face relations seem meaningless.

Against this, East Asian philosophy does traditionally emphasize the meaning of small groups or communities for the harmonious social life. In

---

[646] R.E. Carter, *Encounter with Enlightenment*, 30.
[647] K.-H. Brodbeck, *Buddhistische Wirtschaftsethik*, 128.
[648] G. Kirchgässner, *Homo oeconomicus*, 64.

them we can see the possibility to be conscious of mutual relations and to uniquely shape them. For instance, in Daoism it is clear that the simple life of a small province is an recognized ideal:

> "A small province has fewer people. Although there are machines that can work ten to one hundred times quicker than a human, they aren't used... Although they have arms and weapons, they never show them... They are happy with their routines. Although they live in sight of their neighbors, hearing crowing cocks and barking dogs from the other side of the way, they live in peace as they grow old and die." [649]

In Buddhism, too, the value of the spontaneous and creative action of persons endows a specifically small community, as we can see for instance from the title of the first Buddhist economic ethics book, "Small is beautiful."[650] Yet, in modern society is a return to such small communities at all possible? At this point we may well wholly doubt it. For the global dependencies that have arisen through the economy and technology of the last centuries are not simple to undo. Even if one can remember life in a particular community, an important question remains unanswered: How are many communities supposed to live together?

This question points to an important aspect of our project that should be represented in as much as we come to a close. The previous reflections are supposed to make the encounter of persons within the economic world more understandable. Yet the question remains, how are we to think of the cooperation of many different worlds; and, what role should be ascribed to the economic world in this web of activities. This has a simple cause: so far, we have presupposed the economic world as given. It serves as the context in which individuals as well as their mutual encounters are determined. The context, in which this world itself is thought, is not explicitly made an object of reflection; it remains an unthought presupposition. Looking close we see that with this presupposition we are basically concerned with an abstraction. It is insinuated that the economic world is given in and for itself, while actually "the individual cultures or worlds are not to be understood as substantially given entities, but are instead essentially defined by the encountering and discussion among them as individual cultures and individual worlds."[651] One world faces many others and only through this encounter does it determine itself. No world, not even the eco-

---

[649] Lao Tsu, *Tao Te Ching*, chapter 80.
[650] E.F. Schumacher, *Small is Beautiful, Study of Economics as if People Mattered*, London 1993.
[651] R. Elberfeld, *Das Verstehen der Kulturen*, 279.

nomic one, can be understood as isolated, but instead only as dependent on to other worlds. Each world only exists in the event of interdependencies between many worlds; an event that Nishida describes with the concept of the 'worldly world' or 'worldly worlds.'[652]

We are not going to be concerned with analyzing the specifics of the determining process of the economic world in such a worldly world, but shall merely elaborate the methodological standpoint that makes such an analysis possible. In this way we want to point at a starting point for a truly and explicitly intercultural economic theory, in which the economic world itself is thought of in site specific terms, and its relation to other worlds can become an object of reflection. In this moment we can interpret in completely different ways the concept of the 'worldly world.' For one thing it is conceivable to look at a society as a worldly world, in which worlds differentiate among each other and at the same time are related to each other. Here, for instance, depending on a system theoretical view of society, the relation of the economic world to the moral or political one can be discussed. But it is also conceivable to look at an economic world as a society in itself, standing in relation to other societies, and thus, to other worlds. Economic theories claim to sketch out, partially, an encompassing theory of society: every single society should be defined in the monetary action field and thereby become conceptually available as an economic world. There are many conceivable economic worlds that mark the domain of state influence and separate themselves up one from the other. With the concept of worldly worlds we can thus grasp the relations of many states. Beyond this view, we can also understand the economic world as a culture that in a worldly world enters into relation with other cultures. The worldly world becomes a concept, which "on the one hand makes evident the aspect of globalization, and on the other, puts the individual, particular world in a worldly or global nexus."[653]

4.9.1 The Conflict of Many Worlds

We should firstly work out what problems in the Japanese context exist in thinking a real worldly world, in which many worlds exist with completely equal legitimacy. These problems show themselves in the fact that human co-existence often appears to be peaceful only in one world, while the contact of many worlds is seen as a conflict. In the last section it is already

---

[652] Japenese: *sekaiteki sekai*. Ibid., 206.
[653] Ibid., 208.

plain that rituals of a specific world are overwhelmingly given positive value in Japanese philosophy. They open a free space in which the individual himself and his relation to others can be creatively shaped. Here the pre-supposition is that people are conscious of rituals.

> "Positively ... it (the specificity of rituals, SG) is the ... the foundation for culture, which arises through a process of education among the members of a society. In this sense, the unreflected immediacy of the specific society is transfigured into a conscious and mutual mediation among individuals."[654]

Consciously shaped rituals enable us to deliver ourselves from conflicts within a world peacefully and break through the position of individual egoism. But they also hide a marked danger insofar as only a few people can define themselves within them. They apply, so to speak, only for a "willed community"[655], that may be harmonious within, but whose relationship to other communities does not have to be at all peaceful. A willed community shows itself in its interior through the "voluntary cooperation of the totality."[656] Yet at the same time it threatens to limit the individual's elbow room for action in so far as it prohibits him from freely taking part in other worlds. Inside such a community, we often find a determined form of co-existence posited absolutely; one becomes blind to other worlds and thus unable, to meet outsiders creatively and spontaneously. These just appear to be foreigners for whom the ritual of peaceful co-existence doesn't apply. In this way, the willed community becomes a "closed society"[657] limiting the freedom of the individual and apprehending itself "in contrast to the totality of humanity on the one hand and particular individuals on the other."[658]

> "Negatively ... the specificity of the social-cultural substratum is said to limit the individual, breaking the will to moral action in the name of ideals coming outside of the ethnic group. Its totality is nonrational, opposing all who oppose it with the aim

---

[654] J.W. Heisig, "Tanabe's Logic of the Specific and the Critique of the Global Village," *Eastern Buddhist*, 28/2 (1995), 209.
[655] W. Weintraub uses this phrase. See: "The Theory and Politics of the Public/Private Distinction," 13.
[656] H. Tanabe, "Versuch, die Bedeutung der Spezies zu klären," in: R. Ohashi (ed.), *Die Philosophie der Kyōto Schule*, 189.
[657] J.W. Heisig, "Tanabe's Logic of the Specific," 207.
[658] H. Tanabe cited in ibid., 209.

of mediating it through rational reflection, presenting itself as superior precisely because it is immediate and unreflected reality."[659]

One can perhaps say that the insight of original consciousness is only blazed half way because it relates itself to social co-existence in a particular world. It only sees through a specific form of human co-existence while remaining unconscious to the unmeasurable multiplicity of further forms. The tendency to "herd thinking, collective superstition, and simply sloppy thinking" is only partly overcome and in relationship to other worlds "the irrevocable inhumanity of simple blind obedience to habits of thought" takes over.[660] Egoism lives in this way on a kind of collective plane. One's own world is apprehended as an ego that is to be defended against other worlds.

Japanese philosophy has been correctly criticized because it has not warned enough about the danger of such a 'collective egoism,' or has even actively promoted it. This criticism is particularly trenchant against those philosophers who acted during WWII. Thus, even for Nishida himself a bellicose conflict of worlds in this epoch seemed unavoidable: there must be "conflict and friction between societies: war is the father of all things."[661] And also against Watsuji the reproach has been raised that Japanese nationalism was strengthened through his belief that the Japanese world must necessarily be defended against other, primarily Western worlds.[662] It is clearly incorrect to label Watsuji's ethics as a "totalitarian state ethics,"[663] for Watsuji was concerned with finding an alternative to the absolute submission of the ego to the universal law of the state.[664] Rather, the problem is rooted in thinking that this alternative is purely for a culturally, as well as temporally and spatially confined world and wanting this world to be guarded, if necessary with violence, from the influence of other worlds. Watsuji thus developed his thought in the contradiction of defending non-egoistical action inside a world (in particular, the Japanese one) with the help of egoistical, aggressive action against other worlds. Even if the extent to which Watsuji supported the actual military authority

---

[659] Ibid., 209.
[660] Ibid., 210.
[661] K. Nishida cited in R. Elberfeld, *Das Verstehen der Kulturen*, 224.
[662] R.E. Carter, "Interpretative Essay: Strands of Influence," in: T. Watsuji, *Watsuji Tetsuro's Rinrigaku*, 352.
[663] G.K. Piovesana, *Recent Japanese Philosophical Thought 1862-1996, A Survey*, Richmond 1997, 148.
[664] See also T. Watsuji, *Watsuji Tetsuro's Rinrigaku*, footnote 63, 365.

of Japan in the Second World War is controversial, he must at the very least, along with other Japanese philosophers, be subject to the reproach of having given to little reflection to the problem of 'collective egoism.' It would be clearly precipitous to condemn all of Japanese philosophy in this way. For it has grounded a standpoint which breaks through egoism in its collectivity and thus also the egoism of worlds.

4.9.2 The Idea of One Common World

While, in spite of all problems, East Asian philosophy emphasizes small communities, economic theory, in contrast, casts a generally skeptical glance at these communities. They are supposed to threaten large societies in which countless persons are interdependent one upon the other:

> "The small society, as the original human environment, remains infinitely desirable. It is true, that people are empowered by it. But ... every attempt to lend the same character to a large society as a small society is utopian and leads to tyranny. If we concede this, we must recognize, that the less we strive for the mutual trust of the common good on the model of the small closed society, the more social relations are expanded and multiplied. The small society model can lead us into error only."[665]

In the center of economic reflection does not stand the idea of a worldly world in which persons live in different societies and yet in common, but the thought of a single, unified world, in which all persons are connected to each other. Humanity has to develop itself into such a shape that all people subject themselves to a universally valid order, as for instance this passage from Hayek makes clear:

> "The great transformation out of which arose an increasingly unintelligible social order for the preservation of which all human beings had to submit themselves to learned rules ... was the transition from the face to face society or at least from groups, whose members are known to each other, to the open abstract society that is no longer held together through common concrete goals, but instead simply through obedience to the same abstract rules."[666]

Such subjection implies relinquishing the plurality of the rules of co-existence, since it demands the dissolution of all specific rules. The spon-

---

[665] B. de Jouvenel cited in F.A. Hayek, *Recht, Gesetzgebung und Freiheit*, Vol. 2, 231-32.
[666] F.A. Hayek, *Recht, Gesetzgebung und Freiheit*, Vol. 3, 221-22.

taneous and conscious interaction that can only be practiced in small groups has to yield to the "principle of equal treatment of all persons."[667] It cannot subsist next to this principle, because the latter is absolutely binding. People must not feel themselves obligated any more to a particular society as to a foreign one. "To obey the stretching out of obligations, or specific rules of just conduct applied to greater circles and finally to all people, must lead to the weakening of obligation to other members of the same small group."[668] This not only applies to the enforceable duties, but also for the spontaneous, situative instances of help:

> "Altruistic conduct supporting a known friend may be very desirable in a small group, but it doesn't have to be in the open society and could even be harmful. ... It may seem paradoxical at first glance that the progress of morality should lead to a reduction of specific duties to other people. Nevertheless, each person who believes that equality of treatment of all people is more important than special aid motivated by visible suffering, must desire such a reduction."[669]

The global interaction of persons is supposed to be possible only when universally valid rule-governed behavior is mandated and specific rules of action only valid for a particular community are negated. Transposed to the idea of the world this means seeing the economic world as the only thinkable field of action in which all people define themselves independently of space, time, ancestry and culture. A multiplicity of words is thus negated; the worldly world becomes a single, uniform world.

But is there an actual chance for peace in such a world, as Hayek thought?[670] This seems at first glance to be the case, because the many worlds are negated and thus conflict between them seems impossible. Yet this appearance is deceiving. A uniform world in which all people determine themselves is purely a hypothetical state; it has neither existed in the past nor present. Conflict between worlds can perhaps end at some time, if one world gains dominance over all others. But until then the worlds will face each other irreconcilably and reciprocally try to subjugate each other. For the world of small groups may in fact represent a form of "primitive" human society, but it doesn't of its own free will allow itself to be negated by "civilization."[671] It can only be defeated in combat; an insight, that is

---

[667] Ibid., 127.
[668] Ibid., 126.
[669] Ibid., 127.
[670] Ibid.
[671] F.A. Hayek uses this formulation in *Recht, Gesetzgebung und Freiheit*, Vol. 3, 219.

brought unmistakably to expression in economic theory. Thus, for instance, Friedman opines that differences in fundamental value systems are differences "about which one can finally only fight."[672] And Robbins considers the matter like this:

> "If we disagree about ends it is a case of thy blood or mine – or live and let live, according to the importance of the difference, or the relative strength of our opponents."[673]

There exists no excuse for the hope that the transition from a face to face to an abstract society could be harmonious. "Naturally, it hasn't always been a peaceful process," Hayek concedes.[674]

Yet the combat of worlds doesn't exclusively characterize the transition phase. It is an illusion to believe that peaceful human co-existence could ever be yielded in a uniform world. For a closer look shows that the existence of such a world cannot be thought. There is no 'world law' that all humans can equally submit to but instead different laws, for instance of different states. The egoistical struggle that one seeks to suppress within states through incentives and laws continues unabated between states. The problem of unbound egoism, as is already clear in Hobbes, simply gets bounced to another level: If we can control the individual striving for power in a state to a certain degree, states themselves are nevertheless free to unfold their powers against each other. For they possess a freedom that "is the same as any man hath ... when there is no law."[675] Therefore, a war reigns among states as it does under "masterless men." They "live in the state of continual warfare, on the edge of a battle. With armed borders and cannons directed at adjacent neighbors."[676] Every state stands in a fight with every other state. The struggle of all against all, which on the individual level has been bound in through state laws, continues as the struggle of states.

> And thus, the "state is nothing other than the concentrated power of collective egoism. For the state, the state of nature is always the rule, only the state calls it sovereignty. For this sovereign state, the state of the war of all against all continues. And this war is eternal; for the phrase that is applicable to the relation of states among

---

[672] M. Friedman, "The Methodology of Positive Economics," 5.
[673] L. Robbins, *An Essay on the Nature and Significance of Economic Science*, 150.
[674] F.A. Hayek, *Recht, Gesetzgebung und Freiheit*, Vol. 3, 257, footnote.
[675] T. Hobbes, *Leviathan*, 166.
[676] Ibid.

each other is: homo homini lupus. (...) The words 'law' and 'state' just veil this fundamental circumstance – of course only for the ones who don't go along jump into line at the sound of a rule of speech. The contract theory is not so harmless as it looks. It means an interpretation of the sense and essence of the state that presupposes and recognizes the wild individualism of cupiditas naturalis. After it is forbidden in petto, for individuals, it is allowed again for community and the state. It is even organized at large. Now the state or its majority must act according to what they want and have the capability of doing. The collective person must direct and arrange everything the way it pleases him. Man is again the measure of all things."[677]

The danger here is clearly that the states are apprehended as egos that achieve their desires against one another. The egoism is not, here, that of the individual, but of a state that apprehends itself as a unity and separates itself off from other states. Thus it enkindles a struggle of worlds, as they seek to destroy each other to achieve absolute mastery and submission, while at the same time each one of them, being absolutely relative, fears the power of and envies the others. Every state strives after its interests in this struggle against other states or only cooperates with other states if this is in its own best interest.

The assumption that many states can be forced to fall under one code of law shows itself as deceptive. One bumps up here against the same problem of the ruler as in the case of individual egoism: (4.7.5) The domination of such a law cannot be substantiated as long as one presupposes the egoism of the state as a given. Can we actually trust the self-interested calculus of the state to always correspond to subjection to the common law? Or are we going to assume a benign world dictator, who will shape the laws for the good of all? It is easier to assume that the mightier states will try to shape the common law to their will and advantage, as Abe makes clear in this passage:

> "Once set in motion nothing is able to check the machinations of sovereign states. Sovereign states neither know nor practice the principle of self-negation, because they take as their basic position self-affirmation and self-assertion which, during crisis, predisposes them to neglect, or even willfully destroy, the position of humankind. Reflected here is the fact of the sovereign states essentially self-centered nature. International organizations resulting from compromises and agreements made between sovereign states may to a certain degree be effective when it comes to resolving international conflicts and promoting cooperation. But as long as they

---

[677] J. Hirschberger, *Geschichte der Philosophie*, 197-98.

presuppose the sovereignty of the nation-states, due to the self-centered nature of sovereign states, basically international organizations can neither check national egoism and self-centeredness nor can they totally eliminate war. Instead, although such organizations are able to exert some control over smaller nations, there is imminent danger that organizations such as these may be transformed into magnificent edifices of hypocrisy wherein the arrogance of larger nations, the possessors of great military power, cannot help but to be tacitly recognized."[678]

We see here the difficulty of discovering one unique code of law for all people.

4.9.3 The Idea of the 'Worldly World'

Even Chinese philosophy partly "puts its faith in the 'great society.'"[679] Thus, the Mohists favor the "unification of society, essentially thought of as the unification of opinions and measures."[680] They sought for rules of action that would be the same for all times, situations and communities.[681] These would have to be followed with "pitiless strictness." In this way, the Mohists wanted to institute formal relationships at the expense of informal contacts.[682] While we can discern a certain agreement with economic theories here, as we might expect to see, the Mohist position is subject to some criticism within Chinese philosophy itself. Accordingly, Daoism in particular designates it as vain to search for immutable rules, which, according to Lao Tsu, for instance, have not ever existed and will not ever exist.[683] Because every rule is dependent on all other things and is part of a formative process, it constantly changes. Rules are not simply given to us a priori, but are re-created in every situation. Thus their shape necessarily changes from place to place and time to time.

But if a plurality of rules and thus of worlds is unavoidable, then isn't it also inevitable to argue from the standpoint of one world and valorize it above any other? Isn't it illusory to suppose that there is a methodological standpoint, which recognizes the equal right of every world? Especially in the postwar period, Japanese philosophers responded to that question with

---

[678] M. Abe, "The Problem of Self-Centeredness," 19.
[679] Mo Ti, *Von der Liebe des Himmels zu den Menschen*, edited and transl. by H. Schmidt-Glintzer, München 1992, 24.
[680] Ibid., 17.
[681] C. Hansen, "Qing (Emotions) in Pre-Buddhist Chinese Thought," 191.
[682] Mo Ti, *Von der Liebe des Himmels zu den Menschen*, 18.
[683] C. Hansen, "Qing (Emotions) in Pre-Buddhist Chinese Thought," 191.

4 The Implicit World Picture of Economics

a 'no,' all the while showing that there is a path that could be thought of as the harmonious co-existence of worlds in spite of, or even because of each world's uniqueness and difference. Herein, the insight of the original consciousness is diffused. It is no longer the case that only the interdependencies of humans in a particular world are recognized, but instead, the interdependencies of different worlds: the different worlds are just as 'empty' of an independent or self sufficient essence as any individual. Even they are what they are only in relation to other worlds:

> There isn't a „given culture or world a priori, out of which or into which everything is shaped, but instead there arises the one world in which we live only through the auto-poesis of many worlds, while the many worlds are really only shaped relative to the one world. The one world is also at the same time many worlds, and the many worlds are at the same time the one world."[684]

Every world participates as a non-self in the development of the worldly world. It is "constitutively related to other worlds."[685] Its supposed absolute dominance, enduring no other world beside it, is purely a delusion; an illusionary clinging that allows the worlds to act aggressively against each other. When the original consciousness consciously sees through this clinging, the aggression can be given up. Not only the harmonious interaction of humans in one world becomes thereby thinkable, but even the peaceful, tolerant co-existence of many worlds. In this manner a point of departure becomes visible. We can now analyze the relations of the economic world with other worlds without absolutizing any one of them: this is the site specific determination of all worlds in a worldly world. The worldly world is here described as the locus in which the mutual shaping process of many worlds comes to pass. It is itself neither identified with any particular world nor represents some aggregation of different worlds. To each particular world the locus is a place of nothingness. It is like an open space in which every world is uniquely shaped in its own way, but which is itself completely indeterminate. The worldly world is the presupposition of all worlds, but identified with none of them: meaning that "any specific type of culture cannot directly represent the universality of humankind."[686] No particular world can serve as the model or ideal for other worlds.

---

[684] R. Elberfeld, *Das Verstehen der Kulturen*, 208-09.
[685] Ibid., 209.
[686] M. Ozaki, *Individuum, Society, Humankind, The Triadic Logic of Species according to Hajime Tanabe*, Leiden-Boston-Köln 2001, 14.

"One ought not absolutize one's own culture against other cultures; rather, the level of worldliness increases the more open a culture proves itself against other cultures, by which it continues shaping its own tradition creatively."[687]

This applies, for one, to every small community. Hayek is justified in saying that one cannot demand that "rules apply to all fellow men which have been designed for the members of a tribe."[688] But it applies also to the economic world. While the economic world threatens to negate other worlds, thereby destroying the openness of their interdependent molding, the worldly world will be thought of as a ludic space in which alien ideas live, or can remain, spatially on the same level:"[689]

> "The 'ludic space' in which all alien ideas can exist at the same time has neither a fixed form nor fixed content – i.e., the ludic space cannot have these properties. Just for this reason, the ludic space can absorb different forms or contents. Indifferent to whatever form it has, it can not be limited through this form. ... In philosophical terms, this is called the 'absolute nothingness' or 'the locus.' This is absolutely not an objective subject."[690]

The distinction between the worldly world and the particular world can be interpreted with the help of the concept, 'place of relative nothingness' and 'place of absolute nothingness': A particular world is from the subjective view of the individual, who defines herself in it, a locus of nothingness; it can neither be apprehended nor described. Yet this doesn't mean that it cannot be conceived. For in the locus of the worldly world, that world distinguishes itself from other worlds and can on account of this be recognized relative to them. It represents in this sense a place of relative nothingness. The worldly world against this preserves every world in its uniqueness in distinction from all other worlds, but it can no longer itself be distinguished from something else. It remains, rather, completely indeterminate. It is thus a place of absolute nothingness, which cannot be apprehended through any comparison or description. This doesn't mean that the worldly world is nothingness in the nihilistic sense. It is rather the undefinable source of the infinite multiplicity of worlds.[691]

---

[687] R. Elberfeld, *Das Verstehen der Kulturen*, 209.
[688] F.A. Hayek, *Recht, Gesetzgebung und Freiheit*, Vol. 2, 127.
[689] T. Shimomura, "Mentalität und Logik der Japaner," 380. The concept of "ludic space" translates the Japanese phrase *kukan*.
[690] Ibid., 383-84.
[691] M. Abe gives an explanation why nothingness isn't to be interepreted in the nihilistic sense in his article, "Nishitani's Challenge to Western Philosophy and Theology," in: T. Unno (ed.), *The Religious Philosophy of Nishitani Keiji*, 22.

From the standpoint of the worldly world, every world can be understood as a unique process, which stands in more or less interdependence to all other worlds. The idea that a world can exist independently from all others is seen through as a delusion. A state for instance is no self-enclosed system of administration and individuals, but is irrevocably bound up with other states. Also, "nations are constituted by their interrelations."[692] As long as we apprehend every world as an ego, these relations seem to be an external threat. When every world is constituted in terms of its own absolute mastery, each will automatically fear the other worlds and want to subjugate them. In the worldly world, by contrast, a place of encounter emerges in which the worlds logically relate to each other before they are apprehended in absolute opposition. Here, difference doesn't seem to be a threat to self identity, but instead an expression of the community of the worldly world, which takes logical precedence before all differences and separations. Here, a true world culture is imaginable, which "will be formed only by various cultures preserving their own respective viewpoints, but simultaneously developing themselves through global mediation."[693]

In one important point, such mediation is distinct from human co-existence in a particular world. For since this comes to pass in the locus of absolute nothingness, we cannot presuppose, here, any rule nor ritual. It is, instead, a practice of tolerance towards the alien and unknown, which creatively occurs in every situation without being governed by any particular rules. It enables not so much a conscious shaping of the rules of co-existence as a "fluid sociability among strangers and near-strangers:"

> It is like "'a sphere of broad and largely unplanned encounter', of fluid sociability among strangers and near-strangers. The 'wealth' of the 'public life' to which it contributes lies, not in self-determination or collective action, but in the multistranded liveliness and spontaneity arising from the ongoing intercourse of the heterogeneous individuals and groups that can maintain a civilized coexistence."[694]

---

[692] J.C. Maraldo, "The Problem of World Culture," *Eastern Buddhist*, 28/2 (1995), 194. Maraldo is talking about nations.
[693] K. Nishida cited in ibid., S, 194.
[694] J. Weintraub, "The Theory and Politics of the Public/Private Distinction," 17-18, footnote. Weintraub is citing R. Scruton.

The worldly world is like "a place where people who do not know each other can meet and enjoy each other's company."[695] In it, it is true, the exact knowledge of strangers is not possible, but the self-negation of one's own momentary world is possible. "True encounter with other cultures must be by way of self-negation. ... The activity of self-negation creates an intercultural space in which encounter can take place and in which one's own culture is relativized."[696] In it lies the opportunity to relativize the economic world itself and define it – even theoretically – site specifically in the worldly world.

4.9.4 The Freedom of the Individual in the Worldly World

In closing, I would like to point out that such a site-specific determination of the economic world not only offers a chance of thinking through the relation of this world to other worlds, but also gives a new conception of freedom. From the standpoint of the worldly world it is clear that the individual is free to cross over any particular world conceptually and practically. He is neither consciously nor unconsciously imprisoned in a particular world, but can move freely between worlds and creatively define himself in this movement. Such creative determination is enigmatic as long as humans are regarded as begin determined by a particular world. Humans are continuously and spontaneously transforming themselves in the worldly world without being bound by some particular set of rules to one particular world. This still remains a riddle if the person is constructed as a 'multiple self', or as a kind of aggregation of all the social roles he plays,[697] since it is still unclear how the self unifies in itself the many roles. "The individual as the subject of logical propositions should only be entailed as the sum of all possible social or private determinations (in the sense of properties) while his actual identity still remains unknown,"[698] as Matsuda formulates this problem. The plurality of the person is actually "not communicable as a unity" as long as we want to determine this unity as something.[699] The 'unity' of a person is not a substance, nor is it a process with its roots in the place of relative nothingness of a particular world. It is rather an open process that molds itself freely in the place of absolute nothingness. Since this absolute nothingness is specified by no fixed con-

---

[695] P. Ariès cited in ibid., 17-18.
[696] J.C. Maraldo, "The Problem of World Culture," 191.
[697] J. Wieland, *Ökonomische Organisation, Allokation und Status*, 58.
[698] Y. Matsudo, *Eine Einführung in die Spätphilosophie von Kitarō Nishida*, 72.
[699] J. Wieland, *Ökonomische Organisation, Allokation und Status*, 58.

tent or given form, the person, too, is not finally definable. He is not an aggregate of social functions, but instead molds his own self in a plurality of worlds, in which he affirms every social determination but can also break through it. "The openness of the self is guaranteed by the indefinite reservoir of potential perspectives offered by familial, social, cultural, and natural environs."[700]

The human freedom to untie the bonds of obligation to particular persons is often emphasized in economics. Humans can negate every 'small society.' Even if this aspect of freedom is, indeed, important, it also, often enough, becomes the condition of a new form of unfreedom in so far as it is coordinate with subordination or subjectivation to a universal law which is "necessary to preserve freedom."[701] This 'discipline of freedom', as Hayek labels it,[702] cuts human freedom in half and makes it relative to something. In a worldly world, in contrast, there appears a freedom that is not limited by any form and that can transcend any universal law. Nishida makes this point unmistakable:

> "Our I doesn't exist separated from the concrete realm of spatio-temporal reality; it must be thoroughly determined by its environment, for we find ourselves living in history. Our I is not only in this sense a determined thing, but it must also totally surpass this determination. In this regard one can call it reasonable, being lead by a universal law, in that it is actively separated from the spatio-temporal determinants. But it surpasses not simply these spatial and temporal determinants – rather, the I even surpasses the law, and hence is irrational in this sense. This is the way we can think of the free, personal I."[703]

Freedom breaks through every universal law, even those of the economic world. "It is thus even possible to renounce the economic world and even to put up resistance against it."[704] It can make this world an object for conscious reflection; it can creatively mold it; or it can even break through it.

We don't understand such freedom in the individualistic sense. Freedom is, at most, thought of in economics in terms of the normal consciousness. It is largely egoistic, set going against other people, and seems permanently threatened by others. Freedom of this type can only mean a freedom from

---

[700] D.L. Hall, R.T. Ames, *Thinking from the Han*, 43.
[701] M. Friedman, *Capitalism and Freedom*, 2.
[702] F.A. Hayek, *Recht, Gesetzgebung und Freiheit*, Vol. 3, 226.
[703] K. Nishida, *Logik des Ortes*, 191.
[704] C.B. MacPherson, *Political Theory of Possessive Individualism*, 86.

others. To be free means "not to be threatened by or bound to external factors."[705] But by reason of the irrevocable interdependencies of all individuals, such freedom will never be developed. Individualistic freedom can truly be great "if the dependence of individuals is devoid of any personal aspect."[706] The external coercion that restrains this freedom is not, however, perfectly overcome but merely transformed into the domination of a universal law. Interdependencies represent a kind of insurmountable barrier thrust in the path to freedom, as long as this concept is interpreted individualistically.

For these reasons, Japanese philosophy calls this form of freedom illusive. There is no freedom from relations, but instead purely a freedom *to* relations: a freedom that molds the worldly world creatively with others, without being bound to a particular law. "We have the possibility to say 'No' as well as 'Yes' to anything, that is, the possibility to be free from any restraint."[707] Therefore, freedom is not subject to any law; it is undetermined. So, too, it can't be restrained through the economic world, but is rather its actual presupposition:

> "Our unique human freedom ... [is] radically creative. It is the wellspring of all meaning, the opening from which issues every manner of interpretation, including those of science and technology which are themselves mere examples of creative freedom's endless innovative utterance."[708]

---

[705] A. MacIntyre, *Geschichte der Ethik*, 189. MacIntyre is referring here to Hobbes und Hume.
[706] J. Cartelier, *Das Geld*, 109.
[707] T. Shimomura, "On the Varieties of Philosophical Thinking," *The Philosophical Studies of Japan*, Vol. 6, Tokyo 1963, 3.
[708] S.H. Stenson, "Beyond Science and Technology to Absolute Emptiness," 126.

5 Conclusion

In the course of this work, making a pilgrimage through Japanese thought, we have discovered a path that allows us to deepen our knowledge of economic actors and the economic world through a reflection on the unthought of presuppositions of economic theory. The process of going deeper has been achieved through steps: every level of explanation seeks after a way of knowing that is implicitly presupposed on this level, but is not made the object of reflection. This knowledge, as becomes clear with the help of Nishida's locus-centered logic, cannot become conscious within the limits set by its own explanatory level. Rather, we have to take a conceptual leap to a new level, from which our knowledge can encompass both the knowledge of the previous level and also its unthought presuppositions. This knowledge is necessarily wider than the previous level's, as we can see with the metaphor of space: every economic theory can be imagined as a thought space showing the necessary borders inside which it is thought. These boundaries of thought cannot be overstepped as long as we move inside the space. We must rather find a portal to a new thought space, which encloses within itself the narrower space and makes its borders visible and explicable from the outside. This new space automatically guarantees thought a more open ludic space: chiefly, it liberates us to see things that couldn't be seen inside the narrower thought-space. We can continue along this path of thought: we recapitulate with every new, open ludic space of thought the experience of seeing the boundaries and searching them for a new portal to lead us to a yet wider space. By and by we learn not to let ourselves be trapped within any particular thought space, but to move freely and creatively in different spaces and consciously perceive their boundaries. In this way, we can discover economics as a complete thought structure, or construct. The last step on this journey of discovery consists in seeking the portal that gives us the paths out of this construct into the open field of thought; a field from which many other thought structures are visible and the structure of economics only appears as one possibility in the open ludic space of thought.

The ingress point to the path of thought indicated in this work represents one vision of objective economic theory. This theory explicitly deals with the analysis of things and their relations only. It describes an objective world vision in which things are always known as commodities. As the example of utility maximization makes plain, this world vision implicitly presupposes a subjective consciousness that is conceived as a physical field. In this way, the substantiality of commodities is dematerialized. Their properties and inter-relations are context dependently determined within consciousness. The character of the consciousness itself cannot be objectively explained. The knowledge of the actors, on account of this, can only be deepened if one turns to subjective economic theory. Here, the actor first appears as a kind of limiting concept within the theory of rational choice. It is actually recognized that all preference alternatives are alternatives for a particular consciousness only, but nothing is postulated about this consciousness itself. In utilitarian theory knowledge is deepened in this direction in so far as the emotion and desires are explicitly discussed as properties of consciousness. But the theory can't explain changes in these properties; the actor appears purely as a static existence. Through an explicit observation of the subjective will, we can overcome this static observational framework, explaining how to understand consciousness' property of self-transformation. In economics, this will is implicitly determined in the locus of given goals and habits. If these habits are explicitly made the object of reflection, they exhibit themselves as a locus that encompasses within itself both the subjective and objective way of seeing. In the economic habit of always only calculating within the distinction between more or less are subordinated all other judgments. The more is made the exclusive goal of all action, and determines the subjective consciousness of the economic actor: her infinite striving, her subjective feelings and desires as well as her calculative reason. Besides which, the objective world vision is determined within the same locus: all things appear as commodities that are to be valued exclusively in terms of money. This habit remains an unconceived place for economic theory, inside which the actor unconsciously apprehends himself. But creative and spontaneous acts show that humans are not simply and exclusively determined by unconscious habits. They can actively transform and mold these habits themselves. Here we see emerge the open ludic space of human freedom, in which the boundaries of economic habits are pierced.

Our logical motivation for claiming the existence of this freedom is insufficiently explained so long as the very way we look at single persons and their relations to others remains implicit. Therefore, in this work I have tried to effect a 'turn in thought' from the observation of 'economic man' to the observation of the economic model of the world. Doing this makes it clear how the economic determination of the individual as an autonomous and independent essence, as much as the idea of the market in terms of a mechanism or a machine, are logically preceded by knowledge of the economic world as our activity context. We can conceive of the economic world as pure activity, presupposing neither the individual nor the universal as the bearer of action, but instead being itself the determining locus, logically precedent to both. It presents itself as a dynamic formative process in which multitudes of individuals are mutually determined and in which each is at the same time a shaper and an existence shaped. We will not find either a level of observation or of governance that could objectively determine this shaping act, or lead it to a particular goal. It can really not objectively be conceived as a substance, but only as a context-dependent existence. This does not mean, however, that the economic world remains utterly undetermined. The latter defines itself in the context of the worldly world, in the continual process of separating itself and distinguishing itself from other worlds. While I have taken the standpoint of the worldly world as the foundation of the analysis in this book, some properties of the economic world could also be made visible by comparison with other historical and cultural worlds; in this way, we could also contemplate alternatives to it. In this way the meaning of exchange, of the division of labor, and of money can be judged in its relation to the economic world, and alternatives to the economist's idea of egoism and rule-governed behavior can be spotlighted.

At this point, I wish to point out five results that we have discovered in the course of walking the path of thought we have sketched in this book – firstly, formulated as theses, and then supported by some of the important claims I have made in the course of this work.

1) Every economic explanation rests on knowledge that is completely presupposed within the explanation, but that is never explicitly made the object of reflection. This deeper, more encompassing knowledge cannot, in fact, be illuminated with the aid of the scientific instruments of economics.

This conclusion is made particularly clear in the example of the theory of utility maximization, which presents the application of the concept of optimization, stemming from physics. Utility maximization explicitly looks at commodities and their relations alone. But the optimization idea makes it inalterably the case that the commodities are grounded in the field that determines their properties and inter-relations. For the neoclassical point of view, this field remains an unthought presupposition that cannot become the explicit object of reflection. It is a place of nothingness, which contains in itself all objective determinations, but is not itself objectively determinable: it is the subjective consciousness of the economic actor. Such a consciousness must necessarily manifest particular properties – as, for instance, an infinite striving for more – so that we can apply the formal-mechanical tools of optimization. But these properties themselves cannot be explained in the framework of objective theory, making it necessary to postulate a deeper knowledge, that determines and encompasses the subjective viewpoint of the actor.

Our first thesis can also be supported through an important social scientific aspect, since the economic world cannot be fully described either in terms of methodological individualism, which regards the individual as the primary economic factor, nor from the viewpoint of a theory that presupposes the market as our one given universal. It is the unthought presupposition of these theories, but not the result of them. Again, this insight becomes clearer when we apply it to the field metaphor: one interprets the economic world as a field of action in such a way that individuals are determined through apprehending themselves within this field. They privatize their field activities and in this way define themselves as existences within the field. Logically, the economic world implicitly precedes all ideas about the economic actors, but cannot, inversely, be constructed from the viewpoint of the individual. Besides which, the economic world can also not be understood from the viewpoint of the universal, since this universal appears purely as an abstract direction of this world. It is implicitly determined in those cases when the action field is generalized in the direction of universal rules of conduct and all individualistic determination processes are ignored. The economic world is the unthought locus of this generalization; it logically precedes any idea of a causal-mechanical order, but cannot, inversely, be understood in terms of this order.

2) Oftentimes, methodologies in economic theories are in absolute contradiction one to the other. In the sense that one assumption signifies the negation of the other, this establishes a structure of negative relations. While such relations in economic theory are postulated as unsurpassable, we can find, with the help of Nishida's philosophy, a way to a more open place of thought, in which both positions can be intermediated. This open space doesn't cancel out the contradiction into a higher dialectical unity; but it enables us to posit the contradictory positions simultaneously and thus establish a relationship between them. Thus, it represents a thought alternative beyond the contradiction.

In economic theory, the contrast of subjective and objective methodology is regarded as insurmountable. Action is seen as either an objectively observable conduct or as guided by subjective determinants. Both methodologies seem to contradict each other absolutely. If one is affirmed, the other is automatically negated. Yet in the nexus of habits we can point to a locus that encompasses both points of view and mediates between them: the economic habits of calculation and of striving for more substantiate site specifically the subjective properties of the economic actor such as her calculating reason, her endless desire and her subjective will. They also establish an objective view in which all things appear as commodities and are determined in terms of the monetary value of their qualities. Subjective and objective points of view thus are established on equal terms in the locus of habits; they are mutually implicated one in the other. The subjective consciousness appears as a consciousness-of commodities, while the commodities are site specifically determined in the subjective consciousness.

Moreover, in the economic world we discover a locus in which the opposition of the individual and the universal (which is seemingly unbridgeable within economics) that mediates these two poles and enfolds them in itself. The economic world as the context of activities is the locus in which the individual can apprehend himself as liberated from all particular relations. In this way it preserves the idea of the individual as an independent and autonomous existence. At the same time it preserves, also, the idea of a legal order, given a priori, to which all individuals are subordinate to the same degree. The economic world proves itself, thus, as a dynamic, creative process, in which both of these contradictory ideas fight with each other. It is a determiner without a determinant. This hegemony, too, points to the fact that neither the market nor the state can represent such a superordinate level. Both show themselves purely as two contradictory abstract directions supervening on the same economic world: in the idea of the market, the idea of the freely chosen rules of conduct is generalized to the point that the impression of a spontaneous order emerges, while in the notion of the state are so generalized, through incentives and punishments, the coercive rules of conduct that the impression is awakened of a highly molded and planned social order. In this way, the economic world appears as a locus that unites in itself even the contradiction of the market and the state, or of public and private, without itself being ruled by one of these poles.

3) An important postulate of the social sciences states that we can transpose the outcomes of a research project, which observed a limited piece of reality, to other contexts too, so that, in this sense, they should be universalizable. Abstract research should thus give us a key to a larger understanding of the world. This postulate proves to be untenable, for the under-

standing of complex contexts demands a knowledge that is implicitly presupposed, on an abstract level, but that can't be explicitly represented. The limits of every single abstract thought space are bars, so to speak, to the viewpoint – they must be broken through in order to achieve a more precise image of reality. On account of this, we claim that abstract statements cannot be universalized – they are applicable only within a particular context.

Of particular significance here is the postulate that actions as well as economic processes must be calculable. The foundation for these calculations are supposed to be formal mathematical relationships as they are formulated in abstract models that take under their purview only little slices of reality. Yet these relations are applicable only in contexts which are somehow static. They presuppose that something relative to the forecasted path is inalterable. In objective methodologies that want to calculate action as a conduct, the consciousness of the actors is implicitly presupposed as an immobile field. But if this assumption is dropped, calculability is proven to be logically impossible. In our inverted deduction this means that many everyday phenomena like learning, regret or a change of preferences can't be explained with the aid of objective methods, not to speak of being forecast. For this presupposes a knowledge over why the consciousness of the actor in time and space changes; a knowledge, that cannot be generated by the implicit assumption of a static consciousness field in neoclassical economics. A similar observation also applies to the forecasting of growth and development by means of economic models. The latter always implicitly chose a variable as the immutable reference point in order to measure this movement. But it is logically impossible to describe a world with their aid, in which everything is interdependent and nothing holds as an independent constant ex ante. The abstract principle of calculability, which counts in a static model world, can thus tell us nothing over the real, dynamic processes of the economic world.

4) The standpoint of the normal consciousness is implicitly presupposed as unquestionable in economic theory. The most important characteristic of such a consciousness is that it is fundamentally polarized between the domains of the subject and the object, firstly, and thus, secondly, is identified exclusively with the subjective domain. The objective domain, in contrast, is expelled into the exterior world, where it stands hostile and threatening against the subjective domain. In this manner, the opposition of subject and object, mine and thine, I and the other is fixed in cement; egoism, which is the expression of the normal consciousness, is accepted as a given. We cannot gain insight into the economic world as a place of dynamic, mutual molding and shaping by adhering to this standpoint: for the inherent meaning of the standpoint is that we are blind to the possibility of being conscious inside it, and creatively molding it.

Since the actor, in economics, is always only identified with the subjective consciousness, it seems impossible, that the actor will recognize his habits as his own. They appear as given, unconscious ideals. The actor perceives himself subjectively within these ideals and is thus completely determined through them without being, in turn able to determine them. For this reason, habits seem to be neither shapeable or alterable. They are an impenetrable place of nothingness for economics. It follows that the economic world is looked upon as an objective one that unalterably faces the individual. A real interaction cannot be imagined because each element, from the point of view of the subjective consciousness, is identified exclusively with itself; the subjective consciousness perceives itself in opposition to others. This opposition achieves its apotheosis in the economic world because in that world everyone differentiates herself from all others and co-existence appears as the struggle of all against all. The self-interested action of egoism becomes a seemingly unquestionable fact. Among other things, this leads to the fact that phenomena like trust, or the conscious, common shaping of co-existence has to be presupposed, but cannot be explained.

5) Because the foundations of economic thought serve as the presuppositions of political economics, they cannot be transcended within political economics. A standpoint that, contrarily, does not silently accept these limits but makes them the explicit object of its reflection can be discovered with the help of Japanese philosophy. The key, here, is the idea of an open ludic space of thought that encompasses all habits of thinking without itself being determined through these habits. This space, in Japanese philosophy, is called the place of absolute nothingness. This nothingness isn't determined through economic thought, but is, rather, itself the open space that makes this thought – next to other thoughts – possible. It is a locus in which the economic thought structures base themselves.

The Buddhist notion of the original consciousness gives us the key to an open ludic space of thought. This describes an original domain of experience in which the separation of subject and object, I and the Other has not yet emerged. In this realm of experience habits can be consciously shaped and even changed. In this way we can imagine an actor that follows neither the utilitarian calculus nor some endless striving for more, but is instead spontaneous and creative. This actor points to human freedom, determined through absolute nothing. Contrary to the economic concept of freedom, such freedom can't be defined as either subjective or objective. Its basis is not the locus of economic habit, but is the deeper, or more extensive locus in which economic habits are defined. In order to be able to image such freedom, economic thought forms can no longer serve as the presuppositions of thought. They must, instead, be broken through, in order that they become, themselves, objects of thought.

The original consciousness' freedom doesn't just surmount habits. It is also a domain of experience that takes away the basis for the standpoint of egoism, and consequently the struggle of all against all. In this domain, egoism is no longer bound by coercion and obedience or ruled by some external higher power. Rather, the possibility of harmonious social interaction shaped creatively and spontaneously beyond this struggle comes into view. Such harmony, as Nishida's idea of the worldly world shows us, doesn't only represent an alternative to human egoism inside a world, but also to the egoism of the worlds themselves. Here we clearly ought not to presuppose the givenness of the rules of conduct of a specific world – even the economic one. Rather, a worldly world is recognizable from the fact that it is infinitely open and broad and enfolds in itself all particular rules without being specified by them. Such a world makes it possible to conceive not only tolerance with regard to other worlds, but opens in the same gesture an important ludic space in which the economic world can become the object of reflection. Since the worldly world defines itself as absolute nothingness, it secures a space for the kind of thinking in which the economic world doesn't play the role of presupposition, but is, instead, just a result.

The path to the unthought place of economic thought directs us into an open space that cannot be completely apprehended. It leaps every limitation which economics implicitly sets on thought. It finally indicates the fact that an inversion occurs in this path of thought: while in economics we are always looking for more abstract, more formal-mathematical models to describe reality, our new path of thought wants to show that this reality is simply a creative fullness that is located in the standpoint of our everydayness. Economics, and in particular neoclassical economics, is always trying to distance itself from this standpoint. It wants to substitute a supposedly more certain, abstract knowledge about this experience for the experience itself. Thus, the economic world comes before the consciousness as a dead thing, petrified and inalterable. A path of thought oriented by the precepts of modern Japanese philosophy dissolves this hard shell in step-wise increments and shows that the economic world is not already decided and defined. In this way, we see the task of social science to exactly specify and control this world unhesitatingly vanish before our eyes. Another task arises – that of representing the economic world as an open, creative process, which we are shaping as well as we are shaped by it. Our concern should be to not fix the economic world as a dead object of our analysis, manipulable at our will, but instead, fleeing the ivory tower of abstract theories, planting ourselves in the standpoint of everyday life. And thus the thorough understanding of our everyday life, our earnest interactions with the here and now, becomes the authentic task of economic thinking.

6 Bibliography

Abe, M., "Dōgen on Buddha Nature," *Eastern Buddhist*, 4/1 (1971), 28-71

–, "The Japanese View of Truth," *Japanese Religions*, 14/3 (1986), 2-5

–, "The Problem of Self-Centeredness as the Root-source of Human Suffering," *Japanese Religions*, 15/4 (1989), 15-25

–, "Nishitani's Challenge to Western Philosophy and Theology," in: T. Unno (ed.), *The Religious Philosophy of Nishitani Keiji, Encounter with Emptiness*, California 1989, 13-45

–, "The Logic of Absolute Nothingness as Expounded by Nishida Kitarō," *Eastern Buddhist*, 28/2 (1995), 167-74

–, *Zen and Comparative Studies*, transl. by S. Heine, Honolulu 1997

Ames, R.T., "The Focus-Field in Classical Confucianism," in: R.T. Ames et al. (ed.), *Self as Person in Asian Theory and Practice*, New York 1994, 187-234

Ames, R.T. and D.L. Hall, *Dao de Jing, A Philosophical Translation*, New York 2003

Aristotle, *Nikomachische Ethik*, transl. by O. Gigon, Zürich 1952

Arrow, K.J., F.H. Hahn, *General Competitive Analysis*, San Francisco-Edinburgh 1971

Baruzzi, A., *Freiheit, Recht and Gemeinwohl, Grundfragen einer Rechtsphilosophie*, Darmstadt 1990

Bastiat, C.F., *Harmonies Economiques*, Paris 1855

Baurmann, M., *Der Markt der Tugend: Recht und Moral in der liberalen Gesellschaft, Eine soziologische Untersuchung*, Tübingen 1996

Becker, G.S., *Der ökonomische Ansatz zur Erklärung menschlichen Verhaltens*, Tübingen 1982

–, "Menschliches Dasein aus ökonomischer Sicht," in: K.-D. Grüske (ed.), *Die Nobelpreisträger der ökonomischen Wissenschaft*, Vol. 3, Düsseldorf 1994, 206-236

Bentham, J., *Introduction to the Principles of Morals and Legislation*, Oxford 1907

Berque, A., "Das Verhältnis der Ökonomie zu Raum und Zeit in der japanischen Kultur," in: K. Werhahn-Mees, C. von Barloewen (ed.), *Japan und der Westen*, Vol. 1, Frankfurt 1986, 21-38

Biervert, B., "Menschenbilder in der ökonomischen Theoriebildung. Historisch-genetische Züge," in: B. Biervert, M. Held (ed.), *Die Natur des Menschen – Zum Menschenbild der ökonomischen Theorie*, Frankfurt/Main 1991, 42-55

Biervert, B. and J. Wieland, "Der ethische Gehalt ökonomischer Kategorien – Beispiel: Der Nutzen," in: B. Bievert, M. Held (ed.), *Ökonomische Theorie und Ethik*, Frankfurt/Main-New York 1987, 23-50

Brear, A.D., "The Nature and Status of Moral Behavior in Zen Buddhist Tradition," *Philosophy East & West*, 24/4 (1974), 429-41

Brodbeck, K.-H., *Der Spielraum der Leerheit, Buddhismus im Gespräch*, Solothurn-Düsseldorf 1995

–, *Erfolgsfaktor Kreativität, Die Zukunft unserer Marktwirtschaft*, Darmstadt 1996

–, "Die Nivellierung der Zeit in der Ökonomie," in: J. Manemann (ed.), *Befristete Zeit, Jahrbuch der Politischen Theologie*, 3 (1999), 135-151

–, *Die fragwürdigen Grundlagen der Ökonomie, Eine philosophische Kritik der modernen Wirtschaftswissenschaften*, Darmstadt 2000

–, *Zirkel des Wissens, Vom gesellschaftlichen Prozeß der Täuschung*, Aachen 2002

–, "Kritische Wirtschaftsethik, Skizzen zur impliziten Ethik ökonomischer Theorienbildung," in: P. Ulrich, M. Breuer (ed.), *Wirtschaftsethik im politischen Diskurs*, Würzburg 2004, 211-225

Buchanan, J.M., *The Limits of Liberty: Between Anarchy and Leviathan*, http://www.econlib.org/library/Buchanan/buchCv7c2.html (accessed 24 July 2006)

Büscher, M., "Gott und Markt – religionsgeschichtliche Wurzeln Adam Smiths und die 'Invisible Hand' in der säkularisierten Industriegesellschaft," in: A. Meyer-Faje, P. Ulrich (ed.), *Der andere Adam Smith, Beiträge zur Neubestimmung von Ökonomie als politischer Ökonomie*, Bern-Stuttgart 1991, 123-144

Cartelier, J., *Das Geld*, Bergisch Gladbach 1996

Carter, R.E., "Toward a Philosophy of Zen Buddhism, Prolegomena to an Understanding of Zen Experience and Nishida's Logic of Place," *Eastern Buddhist*, 13/2 (1980), 127-130

–, "Interpretative Essay: Strands of Influence," in: T. Watsuji, *Watsuji Tetsuro's Rinrigaku*, New York 1996, 325-354

–, *The Nothingness beyond God, An Introduction to the Philosophy of Nishida Kitarō*, St. Paul (Minn.) 1997

–, *Encounter with Enlightenment, A Study of Japanese Ethics*, New York 2001

Cassel, G., *Theoretische Sozialökonomik*, Leipzig 1927

Cezanne, W., *Allgemeine Volkswirtschaftslehre*, München-Wien 2002

Chuang Tzu, *The Complete Works of Chuang Tzu*, transl. by B. Watson, New York-Leiden 1968

Comte, A., *Reden über den Geist des Positivismus*, Hamburg 1966

Defoe, D., *The Life and Adventures of Robinson Crusoe, a York 'Mariner'*, Edinburgh 1838

Dietzel, H., "Individualimus," in: L. Elster et al. (ed.), *Handwörterbuch der Staatswissenschaften*, Jena 1923

Dobb, M., *Political Economy and Capitalism, Some Essays in Economic Tradition*, London 1945

Edgeworth, F.Y., *Mathematical Psychics, An Essay on the Application of Mathematics to the Moral Sciences*, London 1881

Eisenstadt, N., *Japanese Civilization, A Comparative View*, Chicago-London 1996

Eisermann, G.M.E., *Vilfredo Pareto und sein „Manuale", Vademecum zu einem Klassiker der Ökonomie und Soziologie*, Düsseldorf 1992

Elberfeld, R., *Kitarō Nishida (1870-1945), Das Verstehen der Kulturen, Moderne japanische Philosophie und die Frage nach der Interkulturalität*, Amsterdam-Atlanta 1999

—, *Phänomenologie der Zeit im Buddhismus, Methoden interkulturellen Philosophierens – Philosophie interkulturell*, Stuttgart 2004

Esfeld, M., *Mechanismus und Subjektivität in der Philosophie von Thomas Hobbes*, Stuttgart-Bad Canstatt 1995

Fachlexikon ABC Physik, Vol. 1, Thun-Frankfurt/Main 1989

Farmer, M., "Ever since Adam Smith: The Mythical History of Individual Rationality in Economic Analysis," *Research in the History of Economic Thought and Methodology*, 9 (1992), 105-127

Felderer, B., Homburg, *Makroökonomik und neue Makroökonomik*, Berlin-Heidelberg et al. 1999

Fisher, I, *Mathematical Investigations into the Theory of Value and Prices*, New Haven, 1925

Fox, D.A., "Zen and Ethics, Dōgen's Synthesis," *Philosophy East & West*, 21/1 (1971), 33-41

Friedman, D., *Der ökonomische Code, Wie wirtschaftliches Denken unser Handeln bestimmt*, Frankfurt/Main 1999

Friedman, M., *Essays in Positive Economics*, Chicago 1953, 3-43.

—, *Capitalism and Freedom*, Chicago-London 1982

Gallu, E., "Sunyata, Ethics and Authentic Interconnectedness," in: T. Unno (ed.), *The Religious Philosophy of Nishitani Keiji, Encounter with Emptiness*, Berkeley 1989, 188-200

Gossen, H.H., *Entwicklung der Gesetze des menschlichen Verkehrs und der daraus fließenden Regeln für menschliches Handeln*, Braunschweig 1854

Graupe, S., "Japanese Modes of Business Behaviour, A Cultural Perspective on Efficiency and Accountability in the Japanese Context," *Praxis Perspektiven*, Vol. 5, Würzburg 2002, 47-54

Hall, D.L. and R.T. Ames, *Thinking from the Han, Self, Truth and Transcendence in Chinese and Western Culture*, New York 1998

Hammond, J.D., "An Interview with Milton Friedman on Methodology," *Research in the History of Economic Thought and Methodology*, 10 (1992), 91-118

Hansen, C., "Qing (Emotions) in Pre-Buddhist Chinese Thought," in: J. Marks, R.T. Ames (ed.), *Emotions in Asian Thought, A Dialogue in Comparative Philosophy*, New York 1995, 181-203

Hashi, H., *Die Aktualität der Philosophie, Grundriß des Denkweges der Kyoto-Schule*, Wien 1999

Hayek, F.A., *Wahrer und falscher Individualismus*, in: Ders., *Individualismus und wirtschaftliche Ordnung*, Zürich 1952, 9-48

–, *Individualismus und wirtschaftliche Ordnung*, Zürich 1952, 122-140

–, *Missbrauch und Verfall der Vernunft, Ein Fragment*, Frankfurt/Main 1959

–, *Studies in Philosophy, Politics and Economics*, London-Henley 1967

–, *Recht, Gesetzgebung und Freiheit*, Vol. 1: *Regeln und Ordnung*, München 1980

–, *Recht, Gesetzgebung und Freiheit*, Vol. 2: *Die Illusion der sozialen Gerechtigkeit*, Landsberg am Lech 1981

–, *Recht, Gesetzgebung und Freiheit*, Vol. 3: *Die Verfassung einer Gesellschaft freier Menschen*, Landsberg am Lech 1981

Heisig, J.W., "Tanabe's Logic of the Specific and the Critique of the Global Village," *Eastern Buddhist*, 28/2 (1995), 198-224

Hicks, J.R., "Gleichgewicht und Konjunktur," *Zeitschrift für Nationalökonomie*, Vol. 4 (1933), 441-455

Hirschberger, J., *Geschichte der Philosophie*, Vol. 2, Freiburg i. Br. 1980

Hirschman, A.O., *Leidenschaften und Interessen, Politische Begründung des Kapitalismus vor seinem Sieg*, Frankfurt/Main 1987

Hisamatsu, S., *Philosophie des Erwachens, Satori und Atheismus*, Zürich-München 1990

Hobbes, T., *The Elements of Law, Natural and Politic* (1640)

–, *Lehre vom Menschen und vom Bürger*, Leipzig 1918

–, *Leviathan*, Neuwied-Berlin 1966

–, *Vom Körper*, Hamburg 1967

Höffe, O., *Einführung in die utilitaristische Ethik: Klassische und zeitgenössische Texte*, Tübingen 1992

Homann, K., "Sinn und Grenze der ökonomischen Methode in der Wirtschaftsethik," in: D. Aufderheide, K. Homann (ed.), *Wirtschaftsethik und Moralökonomik: Normen, soziale Ordnung und der Beitrag der Ökonomie*, Berlin 1997, 11-42

–, *Anreize und Moral, Gesellschaftstheorie – Ethik – Anwendungen*, Münster 2003

Homann, K. and F. Blome-Drees, *Wirtschafts- und Unternehmensethik*, Göttingen 1992

Hume, D., *A Treatise on Human Nature* (1734), Reprint Oxford 1888

Iino, N., "Dogens's Zen View of Interdependence," *Philosophy East & West*, 12/1 (1962), 51-57

Izutsu, T., "Die Entdinglichung und Wiederverdinglichung der 'Dinge' im Zen-Buddhismus," in: Y. Nitta (ed.), *Japanische Beiträge zur Phänomenologie*, Freiburg-München 1984, 13-40

Jevons, W.S., *The Theory of Political Economy*, Harmondsworth 1970

Jullien, F., *Der Umweg über China: ein Ortswechsel des Denkens*, Berlin 2002

Kaldor, N., "A Classificatory Note on the Determinateness of Equilibrium," *The Review of Ecomic Studies*, 1/2 (1934), 122-36

Kaneko, T., "Die Freiheit als Geschenk," *The Philosophical Studies of Japan*, 3 (1961), 121-149

Kasulis, T.P., *Zen Action / Zen Person*, Honolulu 1981

–, "Sushi, Science and Spirituality: Modern Japanese Philosophy and Its Views of Western Science," *Philosophy East & West*, 45/2 (1995), 227-48

Kirchgässner, G., *Homo oeconomicus: das ökonomische Modell individuellen Verhaltens und seine Anwendung in den Wirtschafts- und Sozialwissenschaften*, Tübingen 1991

Klammer, A., T. Leonard, "So What's an Economic Metaphor?," in: P. Mirowski (ed.), *Natural Images in Economic Thought*, Cambridge 1991, 20-51

Knight, F.H., *Risk, Uncertainty and Profit*, Boston 1921

–, *The Ethics of Competition*, London 1936

Kōyama, I., "Das Prinzip der Entsprechung und die Ortlogik," in: R. Ohashi (ed.), *Die Philosophie der Kyōto Schule*, Freiburg i Br. 1990, 306-348

Kromphardt, J., *Grundlagen der Makroökonomie*, München 1998

Kruse, J., *Geschichte der Arbeit und Arbeit als Geschichte*, Münster-Hamburg-London 2003

Krüsselberg, H.-G., "Theoriebildung im 17., 18. und 19. Jahrhundert," in: W. Korff (ed.), *Handbuch der Wirtschaftsethik*, Vol. 1, Gütersloh 1999, 375-461

Kyrer, A., *Neue Politische Ökonomie*, München-Wien 2001

Lachmann, L., "Marktwirtschaft und Modellkonstruktionen," in: K.R. Leube (ed.), *Die österreichische Schule der Nationalökonomie*, Vol. 2, Wien 1995, 177-193

Lao Tsu, *Tao Te Ching*, transl. by G. Feng, J. English, Haldenwang 1981

Latka, T., *Topisches Sozialsystem, Die Einführung der japanischen Lehre vom Ort in die Systemtheorie und deren Konsequenzen für eine Theorie sozialer Systeme*, Heidelberg 2003

Lebra, T.S., *Japanese Patterns of Behavior*, Honolulu 1976

Lechner, H.H., *Währungspolitik*, Berlin-New York 1988

Leube, K., "Einige Bemerkungen zu den 'Untersuchungen über die Theorie des Preises' aus der Sicht der Österreichischen Schule der Nationalökonomie," in: *Die österreichische Schule der Nationalökonomie*, Vol. 2, Wien 1995, 325-335

Locke, J., *Two Treatises on Government*, Cambridge 1988

Lowe, A., *Politische Ökonomik*, Frankfurt/Main-Wien 1965

Loy, D., *Nonduality, A Study in Comparative Philosophy*, New York 1988

Luhmann, N., *Ökologische Kommunikation, Kann die moderne Gesellschaft sich auf ökologische Gefährdungen einstellen?*, Opladen 1990

MacIntyre, A., *Geschichte der Ethik im Überblick, vom Zeitalter Homers bis zum 20. Jahrhundert*, Königstein/Ts. 1984

–, "Individual and Social Morality in Japan and the United States: Rival Conceptions of the Self," *Philosophy East & West*, 40/4 (1990), 489-497

Macpherson, C.B., *The Political Theory of Possessive Individualism, Hobbes to Locke*, Oxford 1962

Mafli, P., *Nishida Kitarōs Denkweg*, München 1996

Mainwaring, L., "Marginalism and the Margin," in: J. Creedy (ed.), *Foundations of Economic Thought*, Oxford et al. 1990, 87-123

Mankiw, N.G., *Makroökonomik*, Stuttgart 2000

Maraldo, J.C., "The Problem of World Culture", *Eastern Buddhist*, 28/2 (1995), 183-197

Marshall, A., "Handbuch der Volkswirtschaftslehre,"in: A. Kruse (ed.), *Nationalökonomie, Ausgewählte Texte zur Geschichte einer Wissenschaft*, Stuttgart 1960, 22-30

–, *Principles of Economics* (1920), Reprint London 1961

Maus, I., "Verrechtlichung, Entrechtlichung und der Funktionswandel von Institutionen," in: G. Göhler (ed.), *Grundfragen der Theorie politischer Institutionen*, Opladen 1987, 188-203

Mason, J.W.T., *The Meaning of Shinto, The Primaeval Foundation of Creative Spirit in Modern Japan*, New York 1967

Matsudo, Y., *Die Welt als Dialektisches Allgemeines, Eine Einführung in die Spätphilosophie von Kitarō Nishida*, Heidelberg 1990

Menger, C., *Grundsätze der Volkswirtschaftslehre*, Wien 1871

–, *Untersuchungen über die Methode der Socialwissenschaften und der Politischen Ökonomie insbesondere*, Leipzig 1883

Mente, B. de, *Japanese Manners & Ethics in Business*, Tokyo 1960

Meyer, H., "Produktion," in: A. Kruse (ed.), *Nationalökonomie, Ausgewählte Texte zur Geschichte einer Wissenschaft*, Stuttgart 1960, 98-102

Mill, J.S., *Utilitarianism, On Liberty, and Considerations on Representative Government*, edited by H.B. Acton, London 1972

–, "On the Definition of Political Economy, and on the Method of Investigation Proper to It," in: *Collected Works*, Vol. IV, Toronto 1967, 309-339

–, "Utilitarismus," in: O. Höffe (ed.), *Einführung in die utilitaristische Ethik, Klassische und zeitgenössische Texte*, Tübingen 1992, 84-97

Mirowski, P., *More Heat than Light, Economics as Social Physics, Physics as Nature's Economics*, Cambridge 1989

–, *Against Mechanism, Protecting Economics from Science*, New Jersey 1988

Mises, L. von, *Grundprobleme der Nationalökonomie*, Jena 1933

–, *Nationalökonomie, Theorie des Handelns und Wirtschaftens*, Genf 1940

Misra, G.S.P., *Development of Buddhist Ethics*, New Delhi 1984

Morgenstern, O., "Vollkommene Voraussicht und wirtschaftliches Gleichgewicht," in: K. Leube (ed.), *Die österreichische Schule der Nationalökonomie*, Vol. 2, Wien 1995, 96-115

Mo Ti, *Von der Liebe des Himmels zu den Menschen*, edited and transl. by H. Schmidt-Glintzer, München 1992

Müller, D., *Beiträge der Handlungstheorie für das Verständnis des Konsumentenverhaltens*, Frankfurt/Main et al. 1983

Müller-Armack, A., "Wirtschaftslenkung und Marktwirtschaft," in: A. Kruse (ed.), *Nationalökonomie, Ausgewählte Texte zur Geschichte einer Wissenschaft*, Stuttgart 1960, 275-284

Murata, J., "Wahrnehmung und Lebenswelt," in: Y. Nitta (ed.) *Japanische Beiträge zur Phänomenologie*, Freiburg-München 1984, 273-218

Najita, T., "Die historische Entwicklung der kulturellen Identität im modernen Japan und die humanistische Herausforderung der Gegenwart," in: K. Werhahn-Mees, C. von Baerloewen (ed.), *Japan und der Westen*, Vol. 3, Frankfurt 1986, 176-191

Nakamura, H., *Ways of Thinking of Eastern Peoples: India-China-Tibet-Japan*, Japanese National Commission for Unesco 1960

Nakane, C., *Japanese Society*, Berkeley 1972

Nawroth, E.E., *Die Sozial- und Wirtschaftsphilosophie des Neoliberalismus*, Heidelberg 1961

Nishida, K., *Nishida Kitarō zenshū*, Tokyo 1987 (Nishida's collected works in Japanese)

–, *Intellegibility and the Philosophy of Nothingness*, transl. by R. Schinzinger, Tokyo 1958

–, *Fundamental Problems of Philosophy, The World of Action and the Dialectical World*, transl. by D.A. Dilworth, Tokyo 1970

–, "The System of Self Consciousness of the Universal," transl. in: R.J. Wargo, *The Logic of Basho and the Concept of Nothingness in the Philosophy of Nishida Kitarō*, Michigan 1972, 363-422

–, "Affective Feeling," transl. by D.A. Dilworth, V.H. Viglielmo, in: Y. Nitta, H. Tatematsu (ed.), *Analecta Husserliana 8, Japanese Phenomenology*, Dodrecht 1979

–, *Intuition and Reflection in Self-Consciousness*, transl. by Y. Takeuchi et al., New York 1987

–, "Die Welt als Dialektisches Allgemeines," transl. in: Y. Matsudo, *Eine Einführung in die Spätphilosophie von Kitarō Nishida*, Heidelberg 1990, 116-246

–, "Selbstidentität und Kontinuität der Welt," in R. Ohashi, (ed.) *Die Philosophie der Kyōto Schule, Texte und Einführungen*, Freiburg i. Br. 1990, 54-118

–, *Logik des Ortes*, edited and transl. by R. Elberfeld, Darmstadt 1999

–, *Über das Gute, Eine Philosophie der Reinen Erfahrung*, transl. by P. Pörtner, Frankfurt/Main-Leipzig 2001

Nishitani, K., "What is Religion?," *Philosophical Studies of Japan*, 2 (1960), 21-64

–, "Modernisierung und Tradition in Japan," in: K. Werhahn-Mees, C. von Barloewen (ed.), *Japan und der Westen*, Vol. 1, Frankfurt/Main 1986, 183-204

–, "Vom Wesen der Begegnung," in: R. Ohashi (ed.) *Die Philosophie der Kyōto Schule, Texte und Einführungen*, Freiburg i. Br. 1990, 253-274

Nonaka, I. and Takeuchi, H., *The Knowledge-Creating Company, How Japenese Companies Create the Dynamics of Innovation*, New York 1995

Nonaka, I., Toyama R. and Konno, N., "Emergence of 'Ba', A Conceptual Framework for the Continuous and Self-transcending Process of Knowledge Creation," in: Nonaka, I. and Nishiguchi, T. (ed.), *Knowledge Emergence, Social, Technical and Evolutionary Dimensions of Knowledge Creation*, New York 2001, 13-28

Odin, S., *The Social Self in Zen and American Pragmatism*, New York 1996

Ohashi, R., *Japan im interkulturellen Dialog*, München 1999

Ohse, D., *Mathematik für Wirtschaftswissenschaftler*, Vol. 1: *Analysis*, München 1993

Ozaki, M., *Individuum, Society, Humankind, The Triadic Logic of Species according to Hajime Tanabe*, Leiden-Boston-Köln 2001

Persky, J., "Retrospectives, The Ethology of Homo Economicus," *Journal of Economic Perspectives*, 9/2 (1995), 221-231

Pigou, A.C., *Economics of Welfare*, London 1960

Piovesana, G.K., *Recent Japanese Philosophical Thought 1862-1996*, A Survey, Richmond 1997

Porter, T.M., "Rigor and Practicality: Rival Ideas of Quantification in Nineteenth-century Economics," in: P. Mirowski (ed.), *Natural Images in Economic Thought*, Cambridge 1991, 128-170

Priddat, B.P., E.K. Seifert, "Gerechtigkeit und Klugheit – Spuren aristotelischen Denkens in der modernen Ökonomie," in: B. Bernd, M. Held (ed.), *Ökonomische Theorie und Ethik*, Frankfurt/Main-New York 1987, 51-77

Rawls, J., *Eine Theorie der Gerechtigkeit*, Frankfurt/Main 1975

Reckling, F., *Interpretative Handlungsrationalität, Intersubjektivität als ökonomisches Problem und die Ressourcen der Hermeneutik*, Marburg 2002

Reiß, W., *Mikroökonomische Theorie, Historisch fundierte Einführung*, München-Wien 1996

Rendtorff, T., "Selbstverständnis und Aufgabe der Ethik," in: W. Korff (ed.), *Handbuch der Wirtschaftsethik*, Vol. 1, Gütersloh 1999, 152-207

Robbins, L., *An Essay on the Nature and Significance of Economic Science*, London 1935

–, "The Significance of Ecnomic Science," in: K.R. Leube (ed.), *Die österreichische Schule der Nationalökonomie*, Vol. 2, Wien 1995, 75-91

Robinson, C.-J.E., "The Conflict of Science and Religion in Dynamic Sunyata," in: T. Unno (ed.), *The Religious Philosophy of Nishitani Keiji, Encounter with Emptiness*, Berkeley 1989, 101-113.

Rothschild, K.W., "Theorie und Ethik in der Entwicklung ökonomischer Lehrmeinungen," in: B. Bievert, M. Held (ed.), *Ökonomische Theorie und Ethik*, Frankfurt/Main-New York 1987, 11-22

Samuelson, P.A., "Consumption Theory in Terms of Revealed Preference," in: J.E. Stiglitz (ed.), *The Collected Scientific Papers of Paul A. Samuelson*, Vol. I, Cambridge (Mass.) 1966, 64-74

–, "Maximum Principles in Analytical Economics," in: R.C. Merton (ed.), *The Collected Scientific Papers of Paul A. Samuelson*, Vol. III, Cambridge (Mass.) 1972, 2-17

–, *Volkswirtschaftslehre*, Vol. 1, Köln 1973

–, *Foundations of Economic Analysis*, Cambridge 1983

Schäffle, A., "Das gesellschaftliche System der menschlichen Wirthschaft, Ein Lehr- und Handbuch der Nationalökonomie," in: A. Kruse (ed.), *Nationalökonomie, Ausgewählte Texte zur Geschichte einer Wissenschaft*, Stuttgart 1960, 238-245

Scheck, F., *Mechanik, Von den Newtonschen Gesetzen zum deterministischen Chaos*, Berlin et al. 1994

Shimizu, H., "Ba-Principle: New Logic for the Real-Time Emergence of Information," *Holonics*, 5/1 (1995), 67-79

–, "Die ordnende Kraft des 'Ba' im traditionellen Japan," in: C. Maar et al. (ed.), *Die Technik auf dem Weg zur Seele*, Reinbek bei Hamburg 1996

Shimomura, T., "On the Varieties of Philosophical Thinking," *The Philosophical Studies of Japan*, Vol. 6, Toyko 1963, 1-21

–, "Mentalität und Logik der Japaner," in R. Ohashi (ed.), *Die Philosophie der Kyōto Schule, Texte und Einführungen*, Freiburg i Br. 1990, 369-385

Schramm, M., "Spielregeln gestalten sich nicht von selbst, Institutionenethik und Individualethos in Wettbewerbssystemen," in: D. Aufderheide, K. Homann (ed.), *Wirtschaftsethik und Moralökonomik: Normen, soziale Ordnung und der Beitrag der Ökonomie*, Berlin 1997, 147-176

Schultz, H., "The Quantitative Method with Special Reference to Economic Inquiry," *Research in the History of Economic Thought and Methodology*, 18 (2001), 343-355

Schumacher, E.F., *Small is Beautiful, Study of Economics as if People Mattered*, London 1993

Schumpeter, J., *Das Wesen und der Hauptinhalt der theoretischen Nationalökonomie*, Leipzig 1908

−, *Kapitalismus, Sozialismus und Demokratie*, Tübingen 1950

−, *Beiträge zur Sozialökonomik*, Wien-Köln-Graz 1987

Seibt, J., "Individuen als Prozesse: Zur ontologischen Revision des Substanz-Paradigmas," *Logos, Zeitschrift für systematische Philosophie*, 2/4 (1995), 352-384

Sen, A.K., "Rational Fools: A Critique of the Behavioral Foundations of Economic Theory," *Philosophy & Public Affairs*, 6 (1977), 317-44

Siebert, H., *Einführung in die Volkswirtschaftslehre*, Stuttgart et al. 2000

Silver, A., "Two Different Sorts of Commerce," in: J. Weintraub, K. Kumar (ed.), *Public and Private in Thought and Practice: Perspectives on a Grand Dichotomy*, Chicago 1997

Simmel, G., *The Philosophy of Money*, transl. by T. Bottomore and D. Frisby. London 1990

Simmel, G., *Die Philosophie des Geldes* (1920), Reprint Neu Isenburg 2001

Sismondi, D. de, "Grundsätze der Politischen Ökonomie oder der Reichtum in seinen Beziehungen zur Bevölkerung," in: A. Kruse (ed.), *Nationalökonomie, Ausgewählte Texte zur Geschichte einer Wissenschaft*, Stuttgart 1960, 51-56

Smith, A., "Untersuchung über das Wesen und die Ursachen des Wohlstandes," in: A. Kruse (ed.), *Nationalökonomie, Ausgewählte Texte zur Geschichte einer Wissenschaft*, Stuttgart 1960, 92-97

−, *The Wealth of Nations*, New York 2003

−, *Essays on Philosophical Subjects*, edited by W. P. D. Wightman, J. C. Bryce, Glasgow 1980

−, *Theory of Moral Sentiments*, Cambridge 2002

Spiegel, H.W., *The Growth of Economic Thought*, Durham (North Carolina) 1983

Stadler, R., "Mit Sicherheit ein gutes Gefühl," *Süddeutsche Magazin* (9 July 2004), 4-7

Stenson, H., "Beyond Science and Technology to Absolute Emptiness," in: T. Unno (ed.), *The Religious Philosophy of Nishitani Keiji, Encounter with Emptiness*, Berkeley 1989, 114-142

Stephani, H., G. Kluge, *Theoretische Mechanik, Punkt- und Kontinuumsmechanik*, Heidelberg et al. 1995

Stewart, H., "A Critique of Instrumental Reason in Economics," *Economics and Philosophy*, 11 (1995), 57-83

Suchanek, A., "Der ökonomische Ansatz und das Verhältnis von Mensch, Institution und Erkenntnis," in: B. Biervert, M. Held (ed.), *Die Natur des Menschen – Zum Menschenbild der ökonomischen Theorie*, Frankfurt/Main 1991, 76-93

Suzuki, D.T., "What is the 'I'?," *Eastern Buddhist*, 4/1 (1971), 13-27

–, *Die große Befreiung, Einführung in den Zen Buddhismus*, Frankfurt/Main 1980

Tanabe, H., "Versuch, die Bedeutung der Spezies zu klären," in: R. Ohashi (ed.), *Die Philosophie der Kyoto Schule, Texte und Einführungen*, Freiburg i. Br. 1990, 145-195

Tong, L.K., *The Art of Appropriation: Towards a Field-Being Conception of Philosophy*, Fairfield 2000

–, Dao and Logos, Prolegomena to a Quintessential Hermeneutics, unpublished manuscript

Tugendhat, E., *Probleme der Ethik*, Stuttgart 1984

Ueda, S., "The Difficulty of Understanding Nishida's Philosophy," *Eastern Buddhist*, 28/2 (1995), 175-182

Ulrich, P., "Der kritische Adam Smith – im Spannungsfeld zwischen sittlichem Gefühl und ethischer Vernunft," in: A. Meyer-Faje, P. Ulrich (ed.), *Der andere Adam Smith, Beiträge zur Neubestimmung von Ökonomie als politischer Ökonomie*, Bern-Stuttgart 1991, 145-190

Upham, F., *Law and Social Change in Postwar Japan*, Cambridge (Mass.) 1987

Vaihinger, H., *Die Philosophie des Als-ob, System der theoretischen, praktischen und religiösen Fiktionen der Menschheit aufgrund eines idealistischen Positivismus*, Leipzig 1920

Varian, H.R., *Mikroökonomie*, München-Wien 1985

–, *Grundzüge der Mikroökonomik*, München-Wien 2001

–, *Intermediate Microeconomics*, Berkeley 2002

Walras, L., *Elements of Pure Economics*, New York 1969

–, *Mathematische Theorie der Preisbestimmung der wirthschaftlichen Güter, Vier Denkschriften* (1881), Reprint Stuttgart 1972

Wargo, R.J., *The Logic of Basho and the Concept of Nothingness in the Philosophy of Nishida Kitarō*, Michigan 1972

Washida, K., "Handlung, Leib und Institution – Perspektiven einer phänomenologischen Handlungstheorie," in: Y. Nitta (ed.), *Japanische Beiträge zur Phänomenologie*, Freiburg-München 1984, 319-349

Watsuji, T., *Watsuji Tetsuro's Rinrigaku, Ethics in Japan*, transl. by S. Yamamoto, R.E. Carter, New York 1996

Weinmayr, E., "Denken im Übergang – Kitarō Nishida und Martin Heidegger," in: H. Buchner (ed.), *Japan und Heidegger*, Sigmaringen 1989, 39-61

Weintraub, J., "The Theory und Politics of the Public/Private Distinction," in: J. Weintraub, K. Kumar (ed.), *Public and Private in Thought and Practice, Perspectives on a Grand Dichotomy*, Chicago-London 1997, 1-42

White, M., "The Moment of Richard Jennings: The Production of Jevon's Marginalist Economic Agent," in: P. Mirowski (ed.), *Natural Images in Economic Thought*, Cambridge 1991, 197-230

Wicksell, K., *Vorlesungen über Nationalökonomie*, Vol. 2, Jena 1922

Wieland, J., *Ökonomische Organisation, Allokation und Status*, Tübingen 1993

Yuasa, Y., *The Body, Toward an Eastern Body-Mind Theory*, transl. by S. Nagatomo, T.P. Kasulis, New York 1987

–, *The Body, Self-Cultivation and Ki-Energy*, transl. by S. Nagatomo, M.S. Hull, New York 1993

Yusa, M., "The Religious Worldview of Nishida Kitarō," *Eastern Buddhist*, 20/2 (1987), 63-76

Zintl, R., "Wirtschaft im Spannungsfeld von Staat und Gesellschaft," in: W. Korff (ed.), *Handbuch der Wirtschaftsethik*, Vol. 1, Gütersloh 1999, 781-803